JEWISH antiques

FROM MENORAHS TO SELTZER BOTTLES

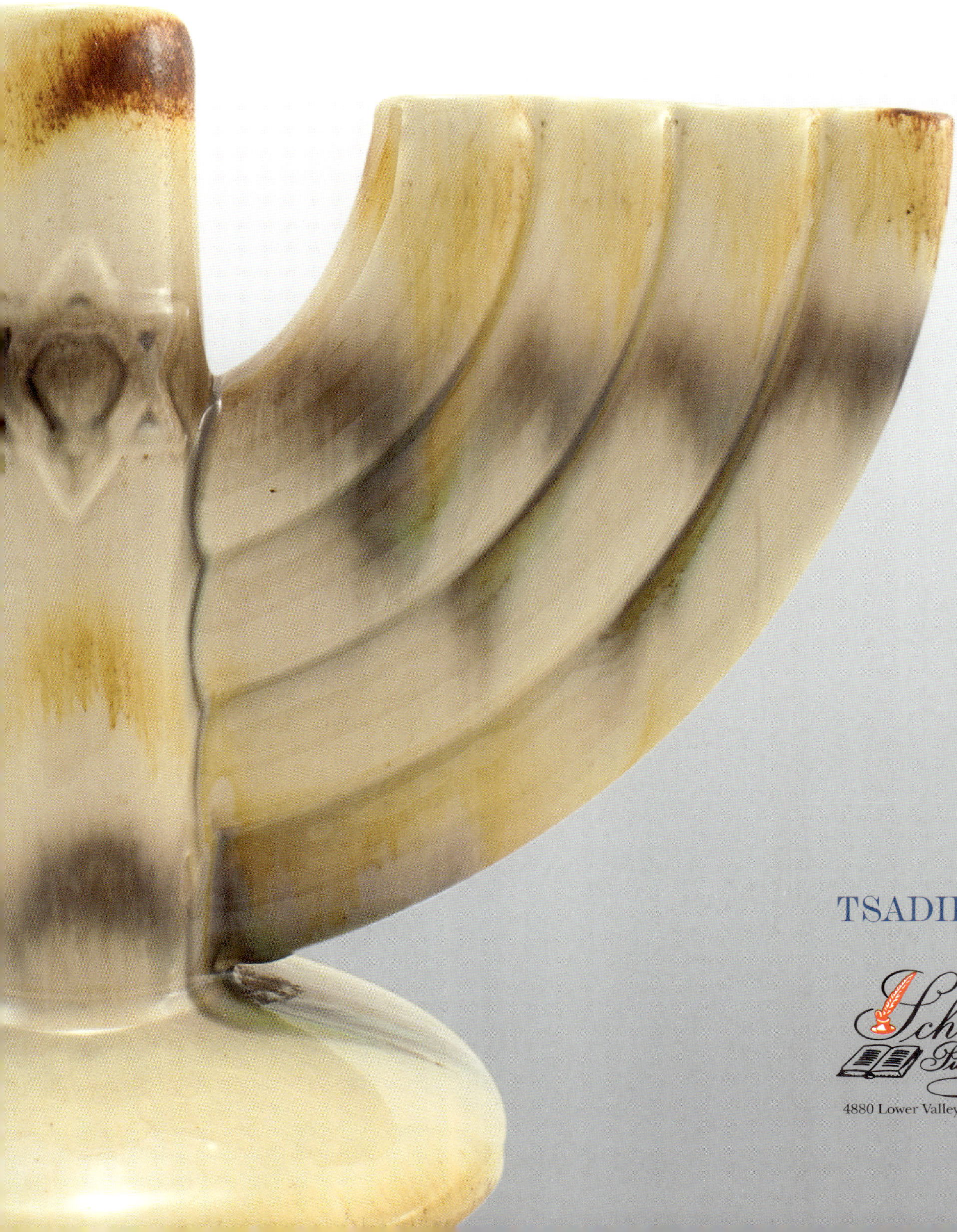

TSADIK KAPLAN

Schiffer Publishing Ltd
4880 Lower Valley Road • Atglen, PA 19310

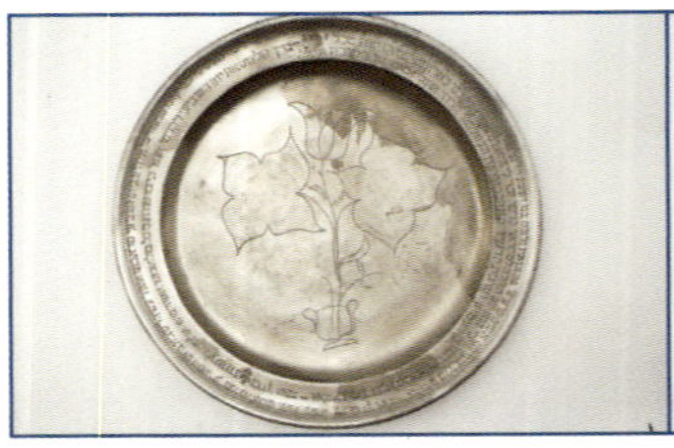 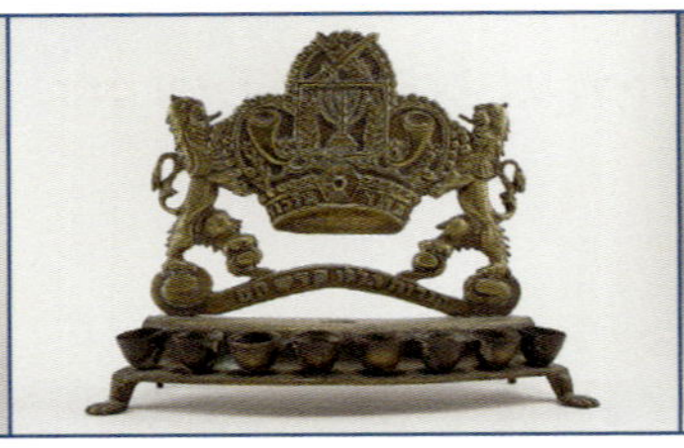 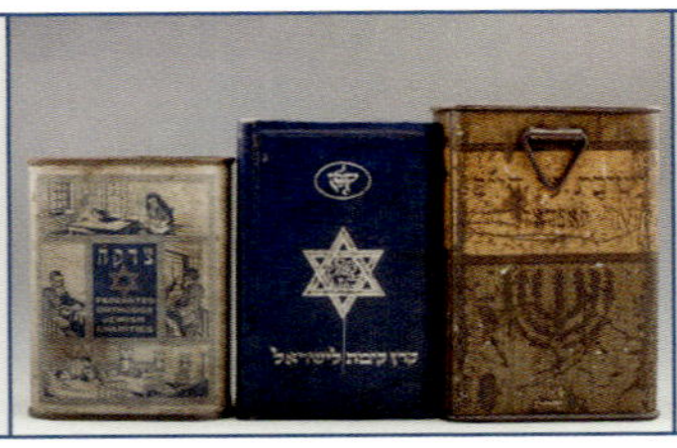 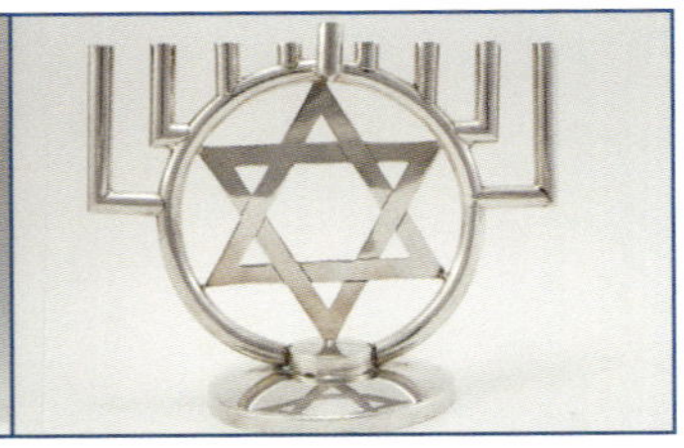

Library of Congress Control Number: 2014942680

Designed by Danielle D. Farmer
Type set in Avenir Lt Std/Divine Bt

ISBN: 978-0-7643-4650-7
Printed in The United States of America

Published by Schiffer Publishing, Ltd.
4880 Lower Valley Road
Atglen, PA 19310
Phone: (610) 593-1777; Fax: (610) 593-2002
E-mail: Info@schifferbooks.com

For my father who always believed in me.

ACKNOWLEDGMENTS

I would like to thank these people for their generous contributions to this book: My brother Urijah, who spent countless hours photographing the objects depicted. My multi-talented graphic designers, Jillian Kornsweig and Jacob Snir. Cissy Grossman, who wrote the foreward (among her many achievements, Ms. Grossman was formerly the assistant curator at The Jewish Museum of New York). Lastly my mother, as it was her idea for me to write a book on my collection, and she, along with my late father, gave me unending support in every way imaginable.

CONTENTS

FOREWORD

Tsadik Kaplan collects what he loves. He loves the richness of Jewish folk images. He discerns the meaning and metaphor in obscure images. He loves the erudition of the Hebrew phrase that decorates and enlivens the object. He appreciates the artist who created an inscription that not only explains the use of the object but also further develops the meaning of the text. He connects with that artist, and he connects with the text.

The breadth and depth of the collection is amazing. Objects used in sacred settings of prayer and ritual and those used in a joyful parade or on the Passover table are all in his field of appreciation.

Tsadik enjoys the quest and discovery of new objects to add to his collection. His Chanukah lamps are in many unusual and exciting forms and materials. He finds pleasure in the rare and beautiful, like the engraved wooden box that houses a circumcision knife. The lowliest of objects, like the handmade beaded and embroidered covers for tephillin boxes, also receive his share of exploration and explanation. He calls a homemade Polish Torah Ark Curtain "pure" because it doesn't credit the donor.

Tsadik is a teacher. He explains the traditional Jewish understanding of ritual, and he prizes it. He shares his research with us, and he likes to guide and warn other Judaica collectors of the pitfalls in collecting.

This book will bring many hours of pleasure to all of us who value the power of the Jewish object to recall the immediacy of Jewish everyday life.

Cissy Grossman, Ph.D.
New York City

INTRODUCTION

I struggled to come up with an appropriate introduction to my book, however after many rewrites, I realized that my sentiments are best summed up with what a nun wrote more than a hundred years ago in the introduction to her book.

Mary Hazelton Wade (1860-1936) was from Massachusetts and wrote a series of books for children titled *Our Little Cousin*, which charmingly explained through short stories the heritage and traditions of different ethnic peoples from around the world. In the preface to one of those books, *Our Little Jewish Cousin* (L.C. Page & Company, 1904), Ms. Wade wrote:

"In whatever direction you may travel—north, south, east, or west—you will doubtless meet some of your little black-eyed Jewish cousins. They live among us here in America. They also dwell in the countries far away across the wide ocean.

For many centuries they have been scattered far and wide. Their children learn to speak the language of the country where they happen to be born. They play the games and dress in the fashion of that country.

What is it that keeps them Jews? It is their religion, and their religion alone. It binds them as closely together now as it did in the days when they worshipped in the great temple at Jerusalem, two thousand years ago."

It is my hope that this book will help keep that bond an everlasting one.

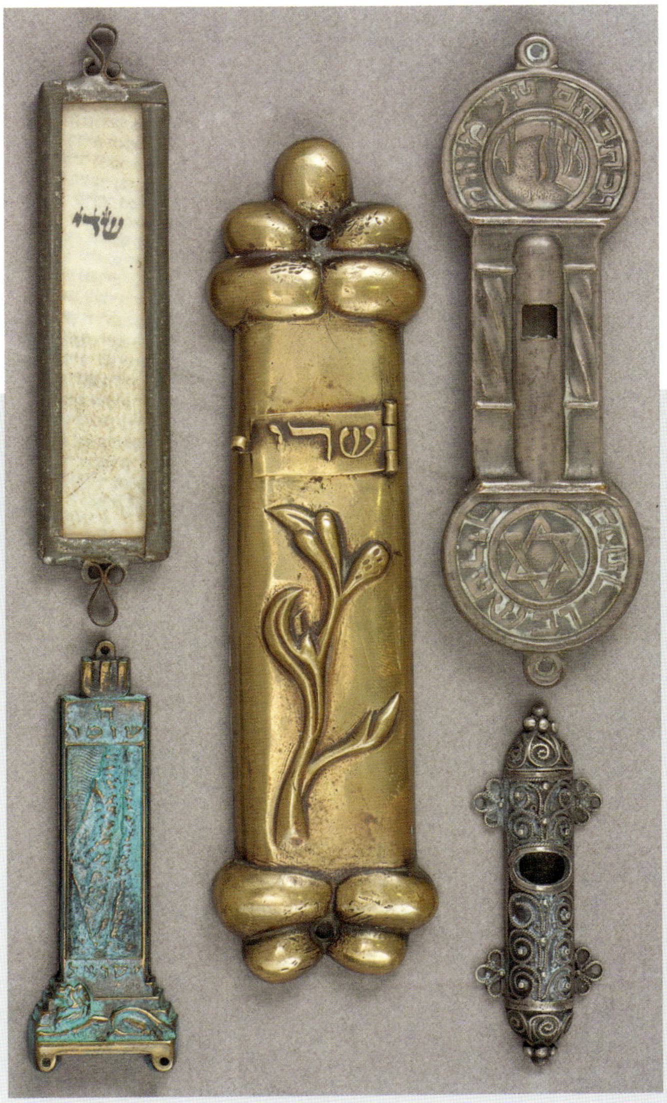

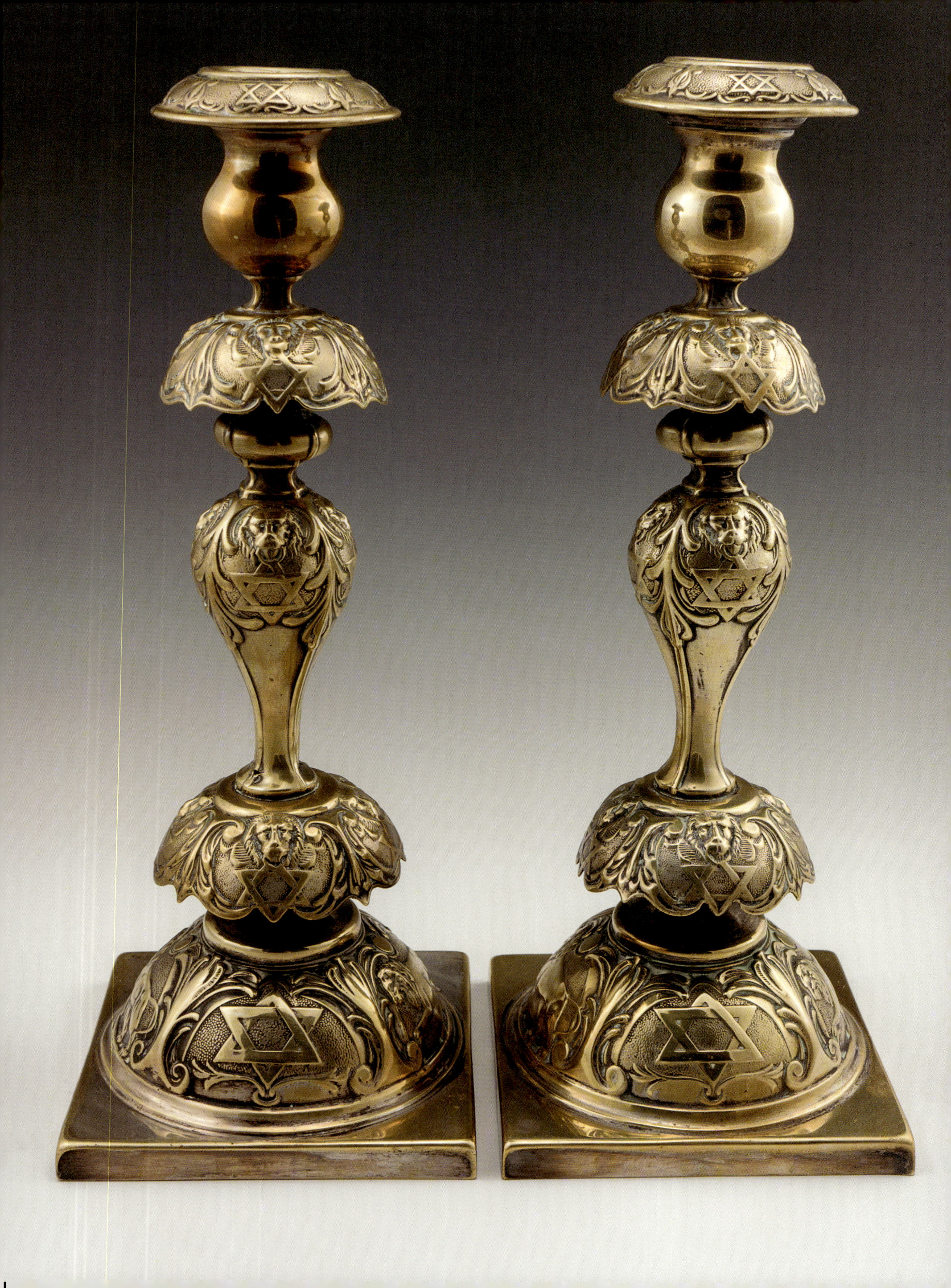

SABBATH & THE HOME

SABBATH CANDLESTICKS

Material: Brass
Origin: Warsaw, Poland, 1908
Hallmarks: "B. Henneberg Warszawa," "1908"
Dimensions: 13" x 5"

On Friday evening, two or more candles are lit, eighteen minutes before sundown. While candle lighting is traditionally done by the woman of the household, when no woman is present, it is done by a man. The purpose of lighting candles is twofold: to honor the Sabbath, and to create an atmosphere of shalom bayit (domestic harmony).

Rabbi Joseph Karo, sixteenth-century author of the *Shulchan Aruch (Code of Jewish Law)*, wrote that if a person were very poor and only had enough money to purchase the bare necessities for the Sabbath, candles were to take precedence over everything else.

These matching Sabbath candlesticks, impressed with lions and Stars of David, are the result of assembly-line production that was abundant in Warsaw during the end of the nineteenth and beginning of the twentieth centuries. To meet the demand of the Jewish population in Warsaw during this period (which at the time, numbered 350,000, second only to New York City as the greatest number of Jews in one city), factories such as Fraget, Henneberg, and Norblin began manufacturing all kinds of Jewish ceremonial objects that were affordable to the masses, the majority of which were issued in silver-plated brass.

While thousands of these Judaic-themed candlesticks were made during that time, finding a pair for sale today is not easy. When purchasing, look to see if the original drip pans with Star of David designs are present. Since they are removable, they are often missing or have been replaced with drip pans that do not have the Star of David motif.

SABBATH CANDELABRUM

Material: Brass
Origin: Poland, circa 1780
Dimensions: 18″ x 15″

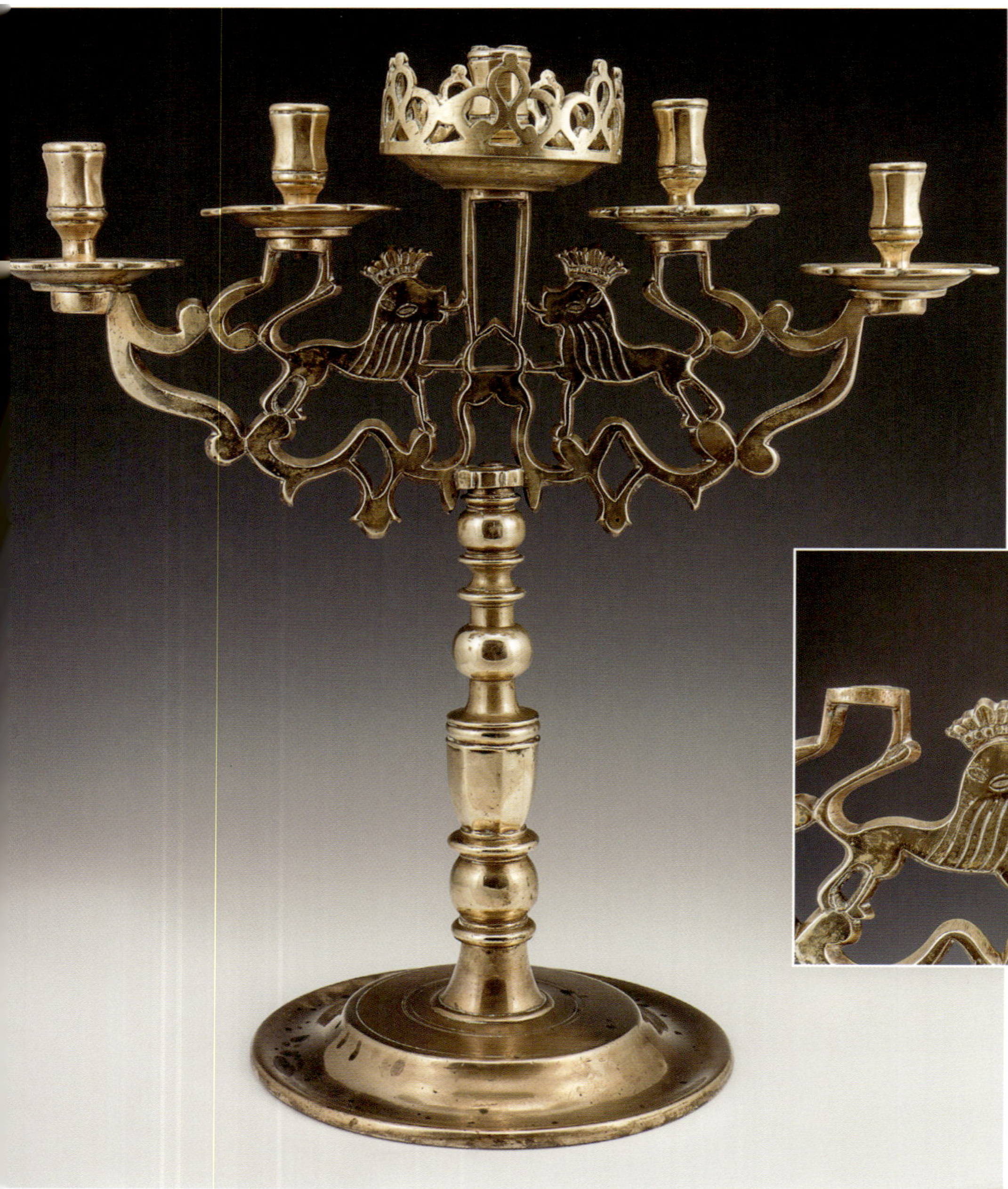

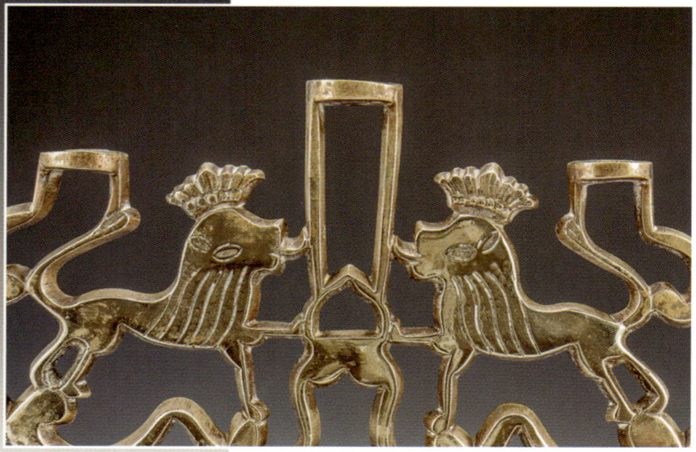

Although tradition states that two candles are lit for the Sabbath, among the Jews of Europe, this number increased to three, four, or five. This five-light candelabrum depicts a pair of crowned lions with forked tongues. Lions have, and continue to be, a popular representation of the Jewish nation, as worldwide Jewry (Ashkenazi/European at the very least) is assumed to be the remnants of the Biblical tribe of Judah, whose symbol was a lion. In Jewish iconography, this is known as Lions of Judah.

The immense heft, fine turning of the stem and base, thick threading of the screws, and quality of workmanship in the piercing and chasing of the lions indicates that this candelabrum is at least two hundred years old.

SABBATH CANDELABRUM

Material: Brass
Origin: Poland or USA, circa 1890
Dimensions: 19.5" x 14.5"

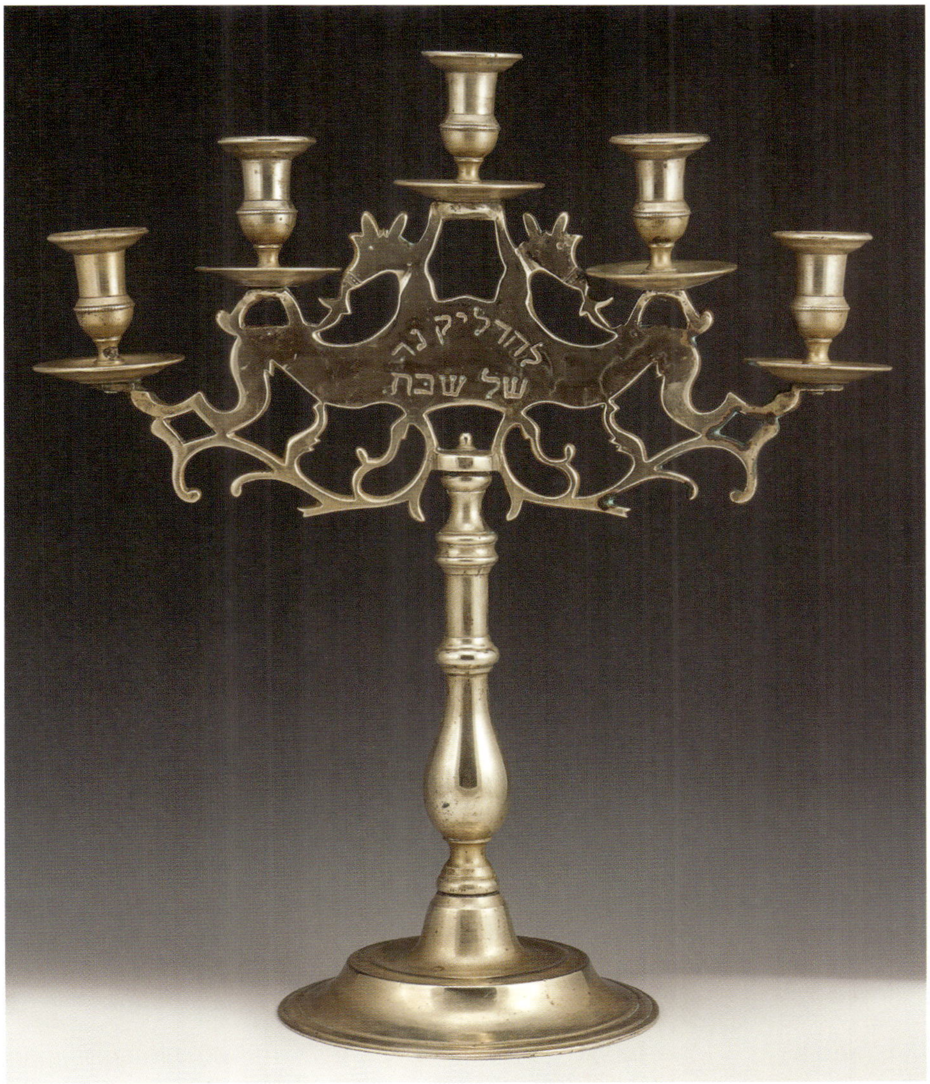

Here we have another five-light candelabrum, although this piece was manufactured more than one hundred years after the previously described example. Instead of Lions of Judah, a pair of deer are depicted with the phrase, in Hebrew: "To Kindle Light for the Holy Sabbath." This alludes to a verse from Psalm 42:2: "As the deer pants after water brooks, so does my soul pant after You, O G-d."

Although it has long been presumed that this candelabrum type hails from Poland, I find it troubling that no other examples are in European museums or ever appear for sale on that continent. However, this kind of piece regularly appears for sale in the United States of America. I contend that this is most likely American made, as there is a crudeness to the casting of the underside of the base that is found on other American brassware of the period. European brassware of the prewar era tends to be of a higher standard. The example shown here is the earliest type of this model found, with fine turning of the stem and base, detailed bobeches, and a substantial weight. More commonly found examples of this model are made of a lighter brass, with thin stems and smaller bases, and they date to the 1920s or later.

PAIR OF SABBATH CANDELABRA

Material: Brass
Origin: USA, circa 1925
Dimensions: 14" x 8"

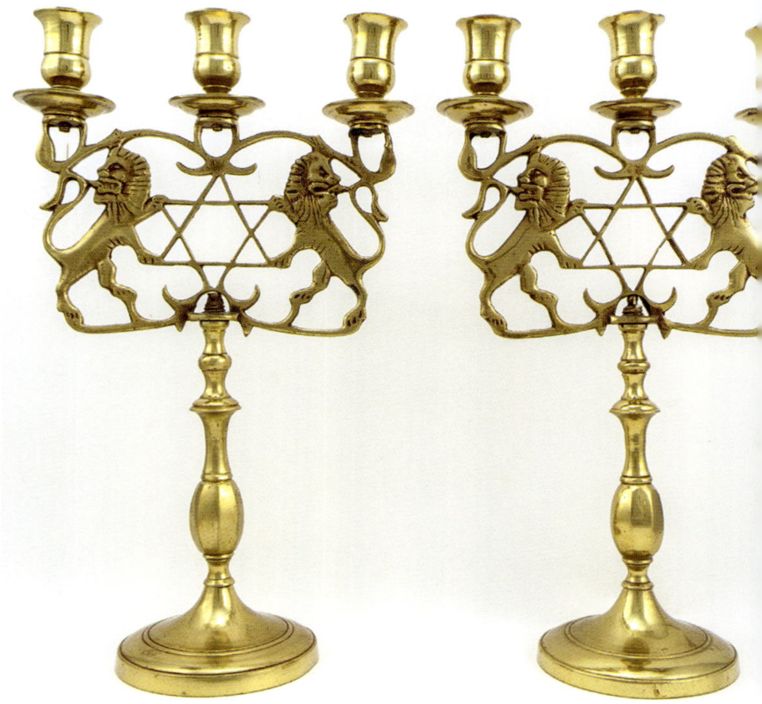

Until recently these candelabra were labeled as Polish in origin by most collectors and dealers in the Judaica field. Research has proven, however, that they are American, produced on the East Coast, likely in Connecticut or New Jersey, as both of these states were home to large brass foundries operating on a mass production scale during the early twentieth century. Since the candelabra are American in origin, many examples remain; single models and pairs appear frequently for sale at flea markets and antique shows around the country, as well as in antique stores (where they are often misrepresented as hailing from Poland).

SABBATH CANDLESTICK

Material: Marble
Origin: Cyprus, 1948 –1949
Dimensions: 6" x 6"

The British policy known as the White Paper of 1939 contained strict quotas for Jews who attempted to immigrate into Palestine. During the 1940s, camps were set up in Cyprus by the British government for the internment of Jews who violated this policy. During World War II, repeated requests to lift the immigration restrictions to save European Jews from certain death were ignored, and untold lives were lost. After the war ended, the British still enforced the White Paper, and Cyprus became home to thousands of Holocaust survivors caught trying to enter Palestine. Once again, Jews were kept under armed guard and behind barbed wire.

Life was not easy for the Jews held in Cyprus; living conditions were below that of German prisoners of war, as standards for POWs were set by the Geneva Conventions. Since there were no precepts for civilian prisoners, these European Jews were treated worse than their captured German oppressors.

Between 1948 and 1949, artistic detainees developed a unique genre of Judaica. From the local stone found on the grounds of the camp, a range of objects was carved, sometimes bearing motifs of tents, symbolizing the life of the interned. These objects were usually inscribed in Hebrew with the word "*Kafrisin*" (Cyprus).

This candlestick is one of those items. "*Shabbat Shalom*" flanks a Star of David with "*Kafrisin*" in its center, with two holes at top for wicks and oil.

During the years the camps of Cyprus were in operation, approximately 50,000 people were imprisoned and thousands of children were born.

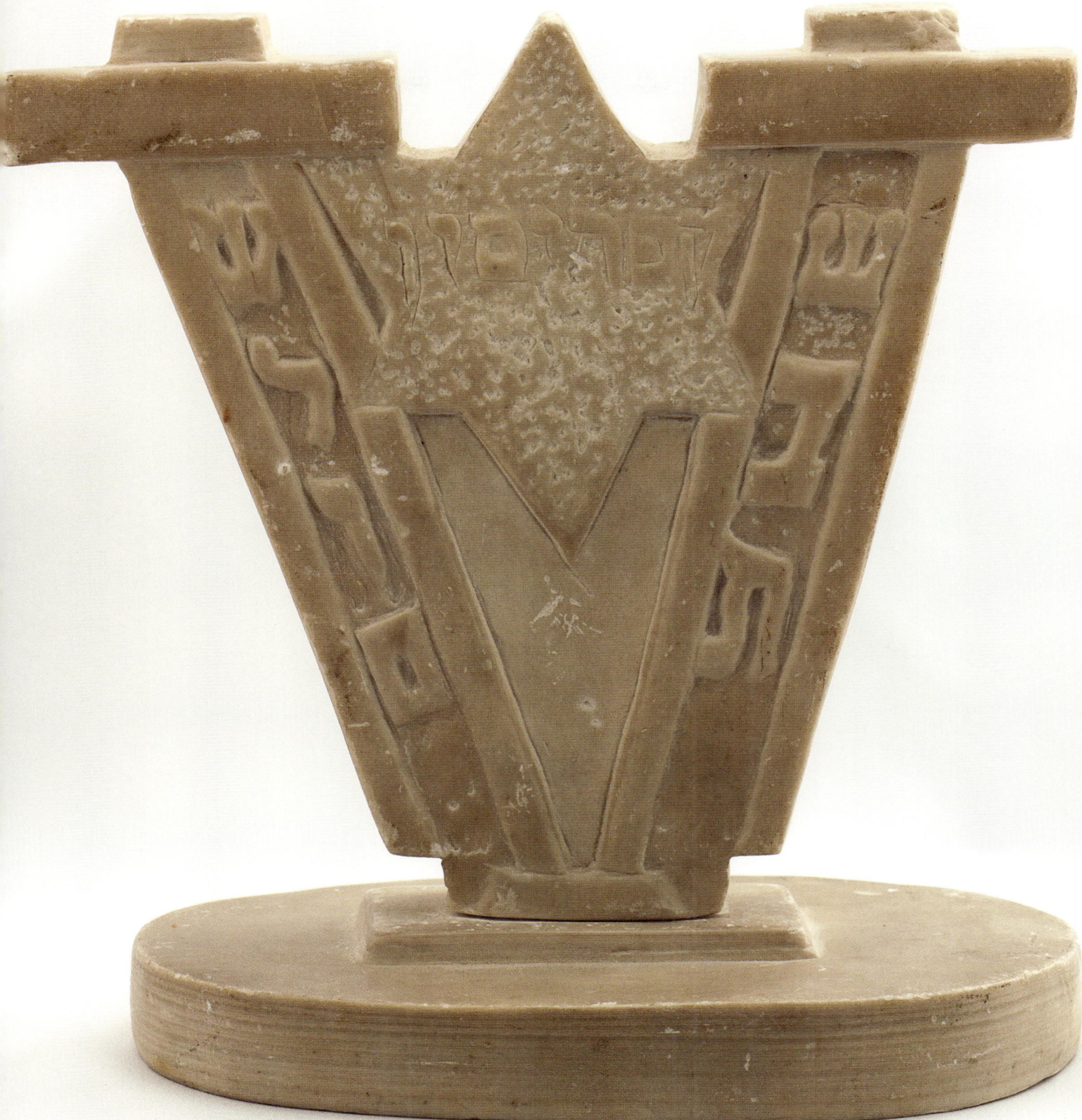

Even after the establishment of the State of Israel on May 14, 1948, the British government continued to hold 8,000 Jewish men of military age and 3,000 of their wives in order to prevent them from joining the 1948 Arab-Israeli War, known by Israelis as the War of Independence. In February 1949, the British government decided to recognize the State of Israel, and all prisoners in the Cyprus camps were released.

SABBATH PLATE

Material: Pewter
Origin: Germany, 1770
Dimensions: 13.75"

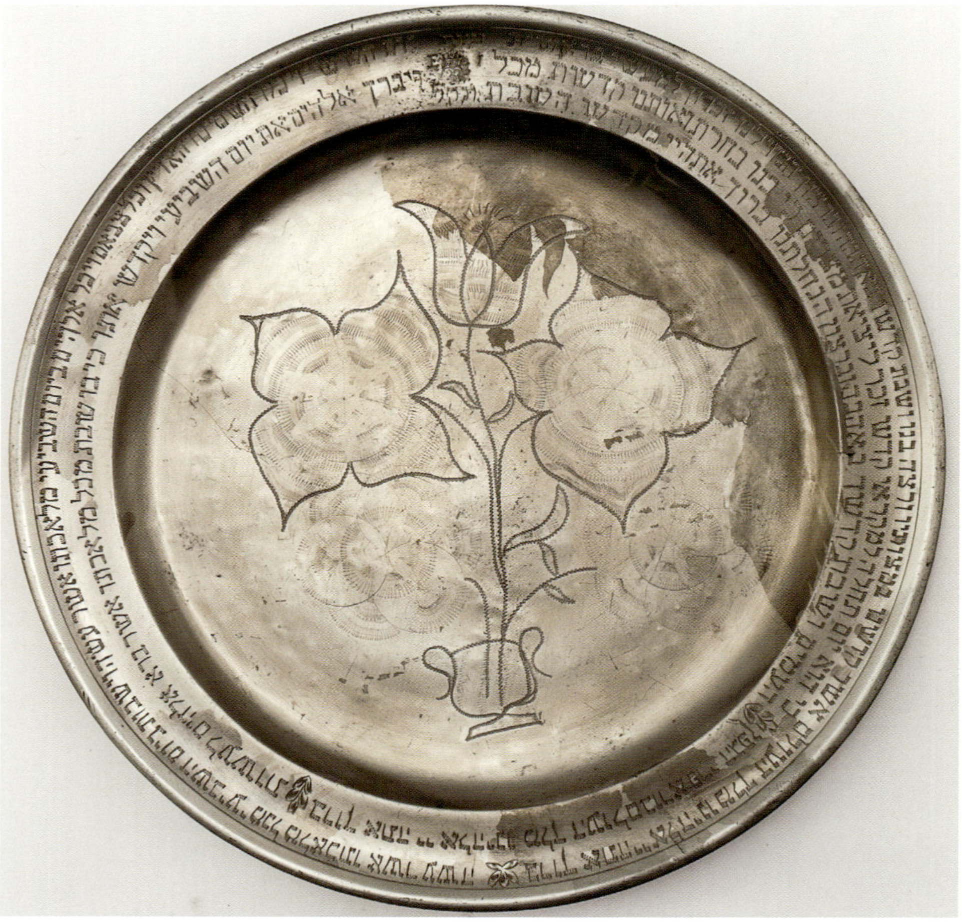

Pewter is commonly known as "poor man's silver," as when it is polished, it has the look and sheen of silver, though it is comprised mostly of tin. Pewter was the main tableware of Europe until the introduction of china. Because Jews were barred from joining guilds during this era in most of Europe, they could not make pewter items themselves. However, plain dishes could be purchased and a professional Jewish artisan hired to decorate the pewter object, copying Hebrew verses from prayer books and the Torah. Pewter is a soft metal and is easily engraved.

Not all Jewish pewter items were decorated by skilled artisans. Many plates were engraved by the "artist" of the family who owned the plate and were often crudely done, with little attention paid to proportion, line and form. Some are quite charming, however, and are sought after by the folk art enthusiast.

In the center of this tray are tulips in a vase, which was a typical decorative motif of eighteenth- and early nineteenth-century items from Germany and Holland. Engraved on the rim is the blessing made before drinking wine on Sabbath eve, which occurs Friday at sundown. This blessing is known as *Kiddush*. The large size of this plate indicates a probable use for challah bread, upon which a short blessing is said for, immediately following *Kiddush*. Included is a Hebrew date correlating to 1770.

I do not list the details of the hallmarks on any of the pewter plates featured in this book, as the only purpose a hallmark serves when dealing with Jewish pewter is to confirm the approximate date of engraving, nothing more. The collector of Jewish pewter must first and foremost become knowledgeable in the different styles of Hebrew engraving done on pewter in the eighteenth and nineteenth centuries, as there is much temptation among forgers to take an old pewter plate and newly engrave it with Hebrew, increasing the value of the formerly blank pewter piece perhaps as much as a hundred-fold. Generally, Hebrew engraving on pewter was done within fifty or sixty years of the manufacturing of the plate itself. If a pewter dish dates to about 1720, and the engraving appears to be of the style and quality of mid to late eighteenth-century Hebrew characters (and has appropriate wear), that fits. The collector should keep a watchful eye out for engraving that appears to date *earlier* than that of the pewter piece!

KIDDUSH CUP

Material: *Silver, partially gilt*
Origin: *Ukraine, circa 1830*
Hallmarks: *"12"*
Dimensions: *2.8" x 2.6"*

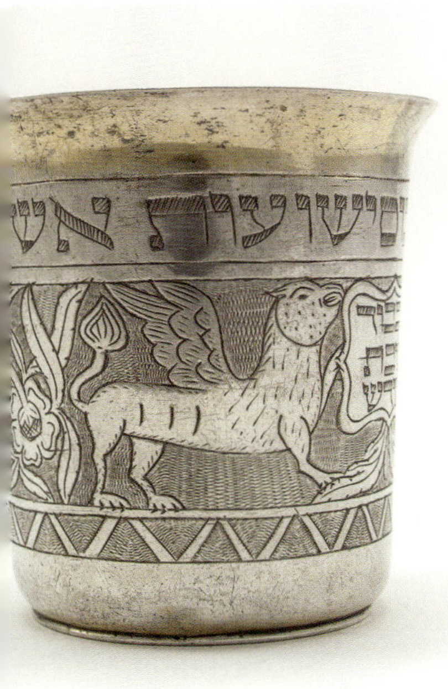

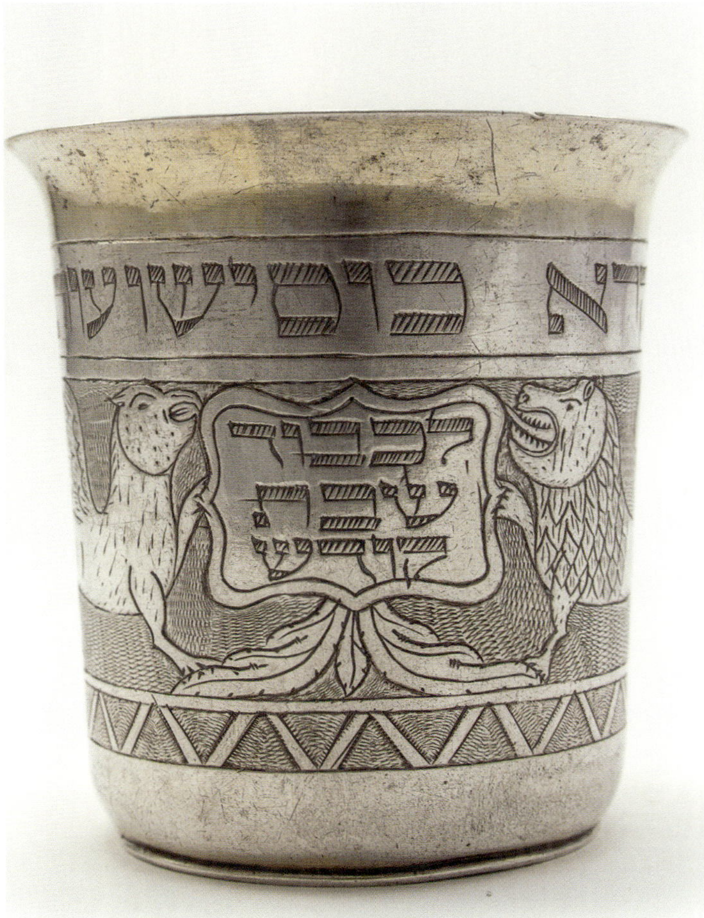

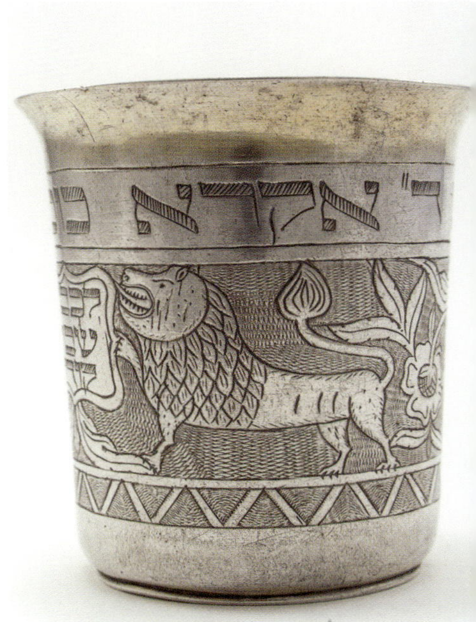

This cup features the classic Eastern European Jewish motifs of a lion and a griffin. Mythical creatures such as the griffin, unicorn, and Leviathan were used on a wide range of Judaic art in Eastern Europe; from ritual objects to gravestones to papercuts to the interiors of synagogues, where fantastically painted frescoes and lavishly carved Torah arks depicted these majestic beasts of fantasy.

This cup has the number "12" stamped on the underside of the base, signifying a silver content of 12 *lötig* (also known as "loth"), out of a possible total of 16 *lötig*, which equals 75% silver. Although cups of this shape and size with the "12" hallmark are often Polish in origin, the engraving style suggests this cup hails from the Ukraine, as the urn with sunflowers, the Hebrew letter "*daled*" for the abbreviation of "G-d," and the particularly ferocious lion are design elements found on other silver Jewish objects that were decorated in the territory that in the present day is the Ukraine.

This cup is a rare example of its genre for its combination of two types of engraved Hebrew sayings. The first, in the cartouche, reads, "In Honor of the Holy Sabbath," and the second, by the rim, states, "I will raise the cup of deliverance, and I shall invoke the Name of G-d" (Psalms 116:13). Generally only one of these declarations was engraved on European Kiddush cups, not both.

KIDDUSH CUPS

Material: Silver
Origin: Ukraine, circa 1840
Hallmarks: "12"
Dimensions: 1.5" – 1.75" x 1.25"

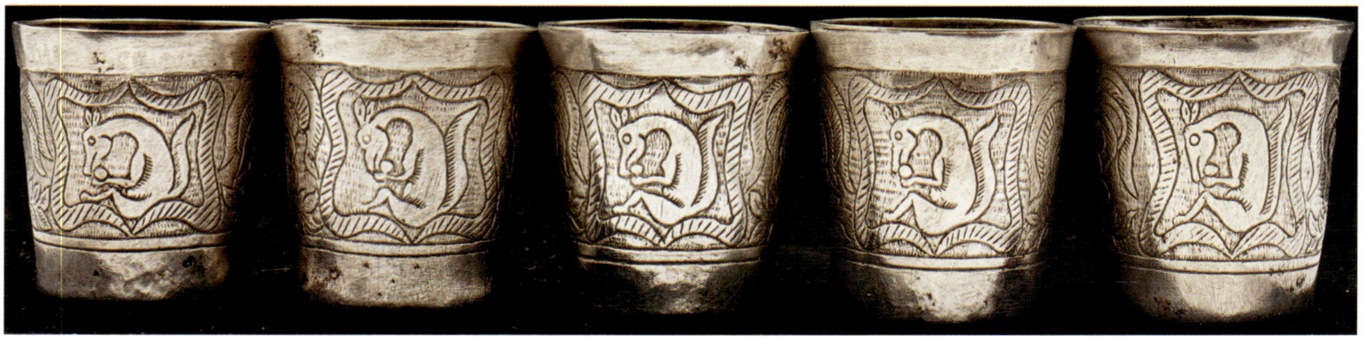

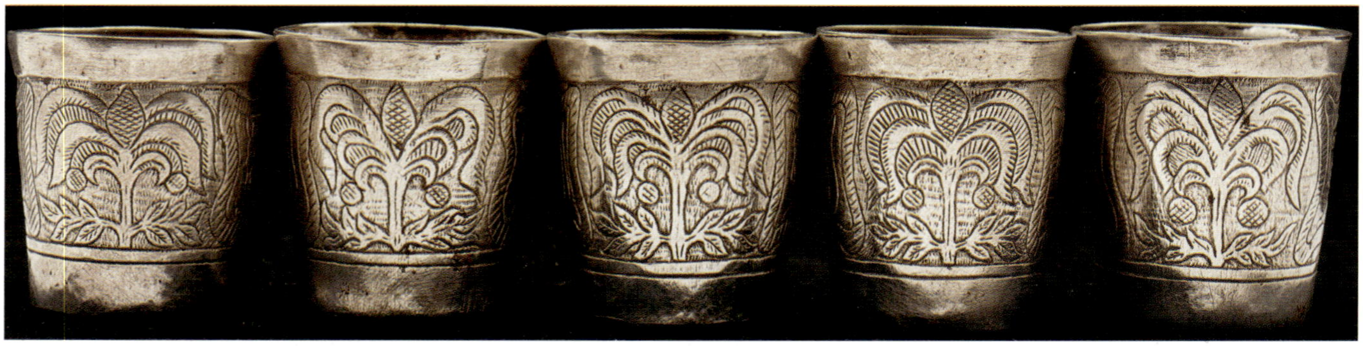

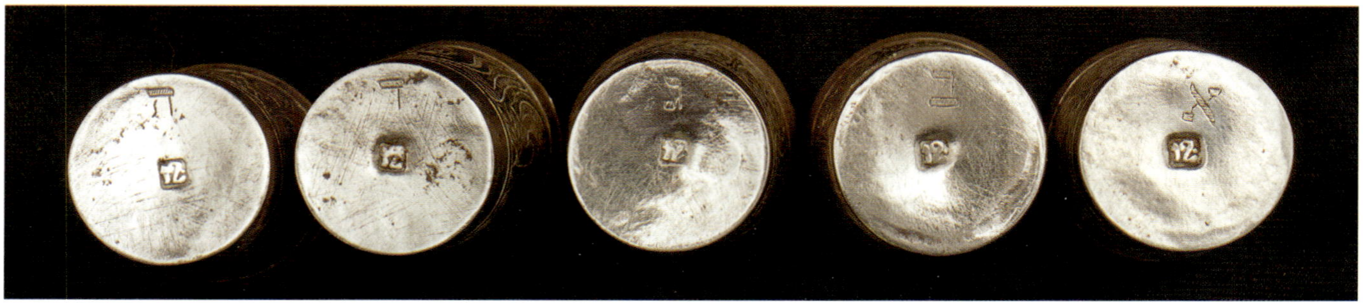

This is a highly unusual set of Kiddush cups for children. The cups are decorated with charming depictions of squirrels holding a nut and trees with low hanging fruit. Each cup has a different Hebrew letter engraved on its underside. In the Hebrew alphabet, letters also have a numerical value; the cups here have values of 1, 2, 3, 4, and 5 inscribed, so this was for a family of five children, each cup assigned to a specific child, probably by birth order. Notice how each consecutive cup is a bit larger than the previous one, so one can fit into the other for easy storage.

In the *Zohar*, a mystical commentary written about the Torah in the second century by the great sage Shimon bar Yochai, it states: "The words of the Torah are likened to a nut which has an outer shell, while its kernel is securely preserved inside." (Midrash HaNeelam, Ruth). Gershom Scholem (1897–1982), the preeminent modern scholar of Jewish mysticism, wrote in his book *On the Kabbalah and Its Symbolism* (Schocken Books, 1965): "The comparison of the Torah with a nut is not new in Jewish literature... the metaphor was particularly apt, because the nut was said to possess not only a hard outward shell, but also two finer inward coverings which protected the kernel."

The squirrels holding nuts under their chins, ready to break through to the kernel, could be a metaphor for attempting to uncover the different levels of understanding and beauty of the Torah.

The usage of squirrels as a decorative element on eighteenth- and nineteenth-century crafted Jewish objects was exclusive to the territory of Galicia, which is comprised of sections of modern-day Southern Poland and Western Ukraine. The rather primitive and robust engraving suggests that these cups originate from a rural area, likely in the Ukrainian part of Galicia.

KIDDUSH CUP / WINE CARAFE LABEL / CHALLAH KNIFE / FISH PLATE

Materials: Silver / Porcelain
Origin: Germany, circa 1900–1925
Hallmarks: "800" crescent moon & crown (silver items) / "Eamg Alt Schönwald Bavaria"
Dimensions: 3.75" x 2" / 3" x 2.5" / 11.25" x 1" / 10.25" x 15.9"

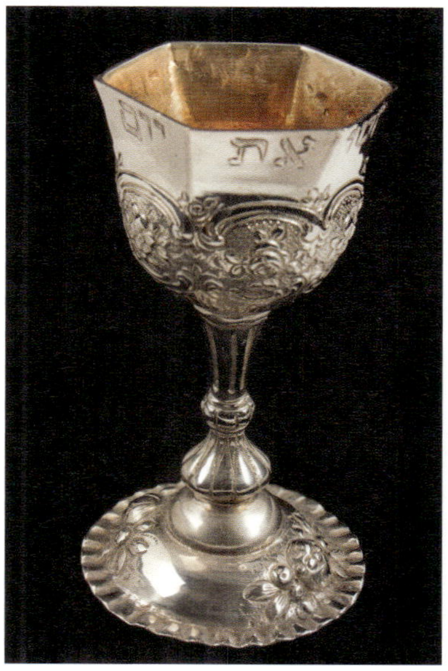

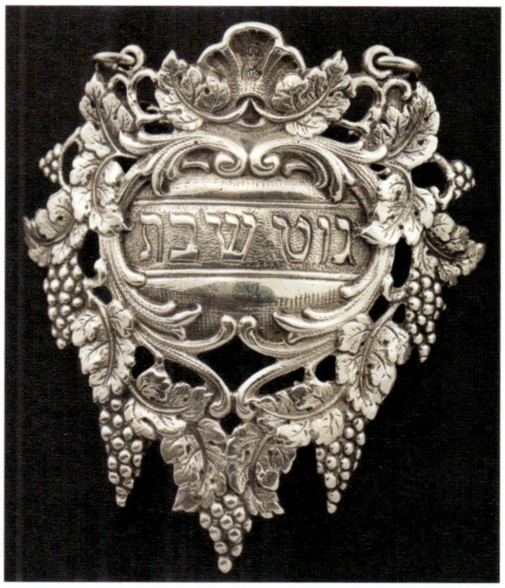

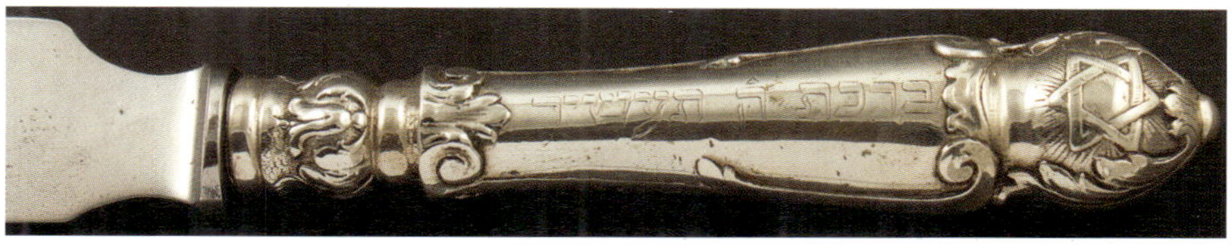

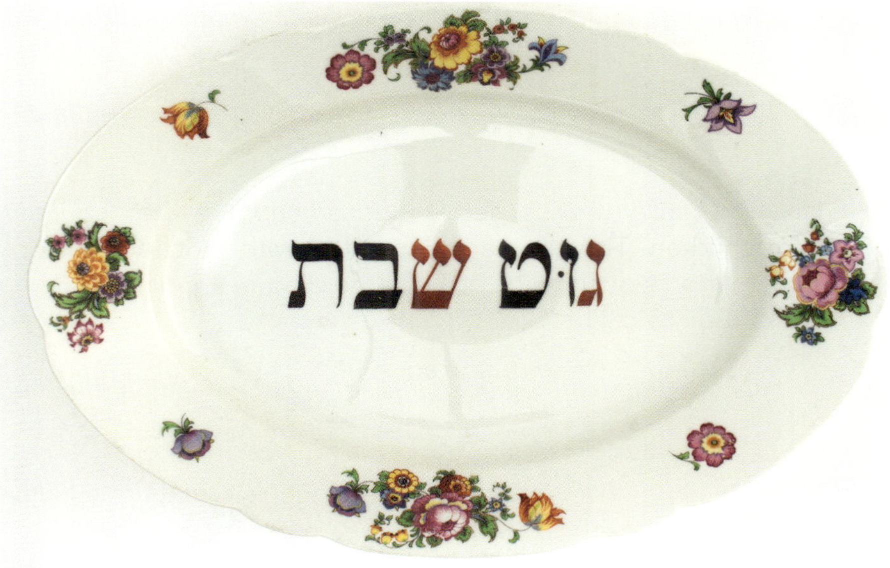

The objects shown here are what would typically be found on the Sabbath table of an upper class Jewish family living in Germany during the first quarter of the twentieth century.

The wine cup, its small size indicating its use was for a child, has the engraved verse: "Remember the Sabbath day, to keep it holy" (Exodus 20:8). Each of the cup's six sides has a word from this verse at top. Six- and eight-sided silver cups were favored by German Jews for the Sabbath and holidays during the eighteenth and nineteenth centuries. This cup, its form long out of fashion for German gentiles, was specifically made for German Jews, as a remembrance of the type of cup their great-grandparents would have owned.

The plaque was meant to be hung around a crystal decanter holding wine for the Sabbath. This plaque has the Yiddish phrase *Gut Shabbos* (Good Sabbath) cast in the center.

The knife was used for slicing the two loaves of Challah bread. Chased with a Star of David at its tip, one side of the engraved handle reads: "The blessing of The Lord makes one rich, while toil adds nothing," (Proverbs 10:22). The other side says: "Go your way, eat your bread with joy," (Ecclesiastes 9:7). The blade (not shown) is made of steel.

Around the year 200 CE, leading Rabbis deemed it meritorious for Jews to eat fish on the Sabbath, for among other reasons, the Sabbath is said to be an anticipation of the Messianic era, which will be inaugurated by the eating of the legendary fish, the Leviathan. The shape and size of this dish indicates it was for fish and has *Gut Shabbos* painted in the center.

KIDDUSH CUP

Material: Silver
Origin: Afghanistan, circa 1890
Dimensions: 1″ x 3.3″

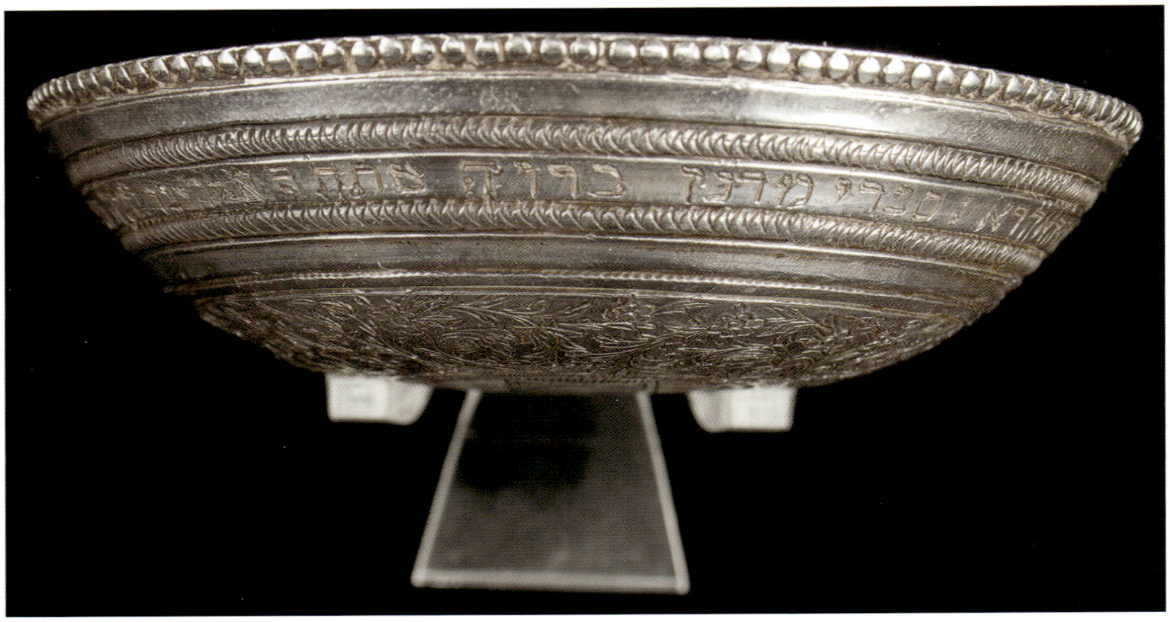

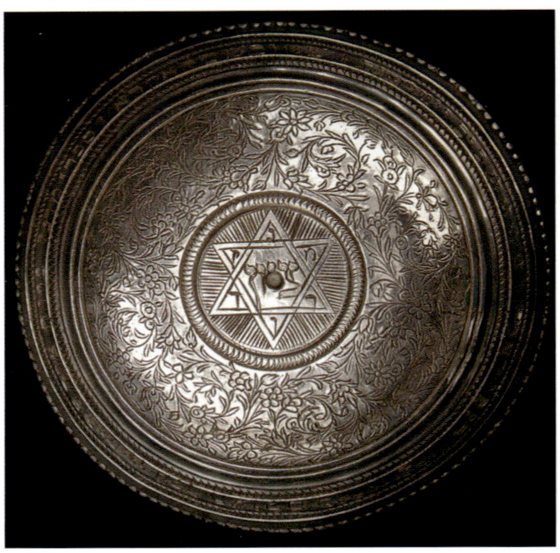

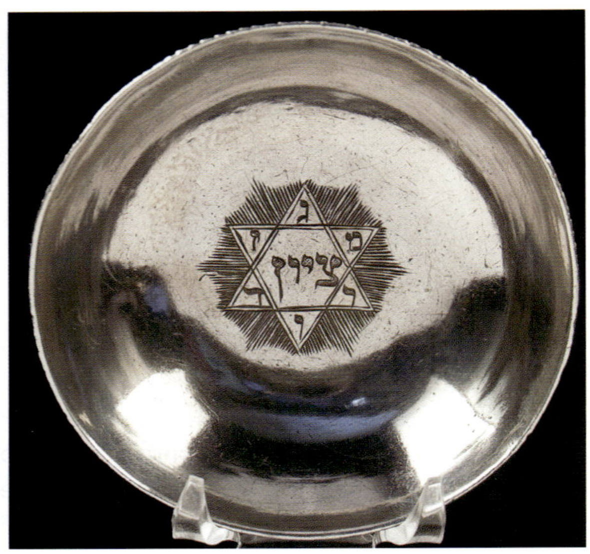

In areas such as Afghanistan, Iran, and Buchara (Uzbekistan), for many Jews, rather than fashioning a goblet or beaker for Kiddush, a bowl-shaped cup was used. This cup has decoration on both sides; the center of the shallow side is decorated with a Star of David. The Star of David bears the inscription "*Tzeeyon*" (Zion), as well as "*Magen David*" (Star of David).

The flat side of the cup is decorated with another Star of David in its center, which leads to a thick band of foliate designs. The outer rim says in Hebrew: "I will raise the cup of salvations, and I shall invoke the Name of G-d"; "By your leave, my masters"; "Blessed are You Hashem, our G-d, King of the universe, Who creates the fruit of the vine"; "Amen".

According to local traditions, bowl-shaped cups such as this sometimes had a matching saucer.

KIDDUSH CUP

Material: Silver
Origin: Israel, 1933–1948
Hallmarks: large letter "Vav", "Yerushalem" (in Hebrew), "925 Made in Palestine"
Artist: Attributed to Ludwig Wolpert
Dimensions: 3.25" x 3.3"

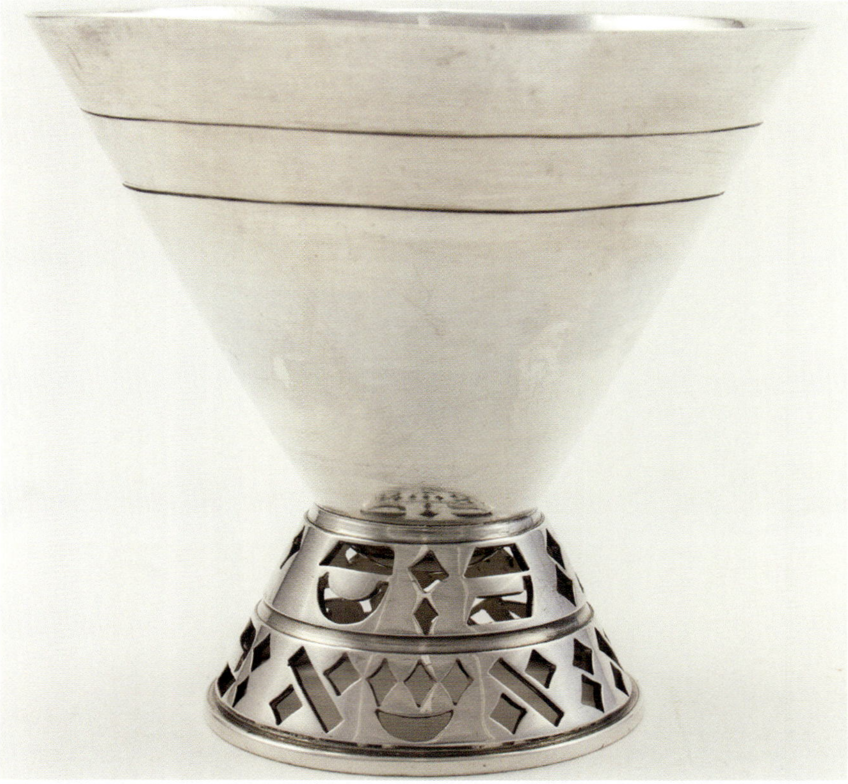

Ludwig Wolpert is widely regarded as the father of modern design in Jewish ceremonial art. He studied sculpture and metal work for eight years in Germany before immigrating to Israel in 1933. In Germany, he was influenced by the teachings of the Bauhaus school, which emphasized clean, simple lines and pure functionality. Wolpert was the first artist to integrate Hebrew letters into the design aspect of the object itself.

The form of this cup is recognizable to anyone familiar with the art deco movement of the 1920s and '30s, when cocktail glasses took this conical shape. Here Wolpert imitates the cocktail glass for the top half, but at the base, using the negative space, he incorporates in Hebrew: "I will raise the cup of deliverance and I shall invoke the Name of G-d."

The large Hebrew letter "*Vav*" hallmark stands for the first letter in the Hebrew spelling of Wolpert. In 1976, an exhibition on the works of Wolpert was held at the Jewish Museum of New York, and a worldwide search commenced for pieces that could be loaned for this occasion. Thirteen examples of Judaica by Wolpert made in Israel before May of 1948 were located; none were Kiddush cups.

In the Ludwig Wolpert Archives, stored at the Center for Jewish History in New York City, there appears an old black and white photograph depicting a "twin" to this cup, the only difference being that the Hebrew verses are solid, with empty space around. My attempts to locate that cup have been unsuccessful, making my cup the apparent lone survivor of this Wolpert design.

The unusual features of this cup, including an early implementation of cut-out verses in block typeface and the peculiar hallmark, suggest the possibility that it is a prototype, never meant to be sold.

HAVDALAH PLATE

Material: *Porcelain*
Origin: *Germany, circa 1900*
Hallmarks: *"H & Co. Bavaria", crown*
Dimensions: *9.5"*

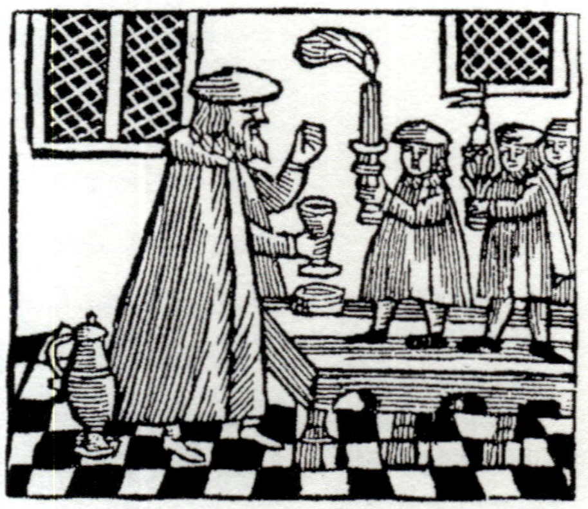

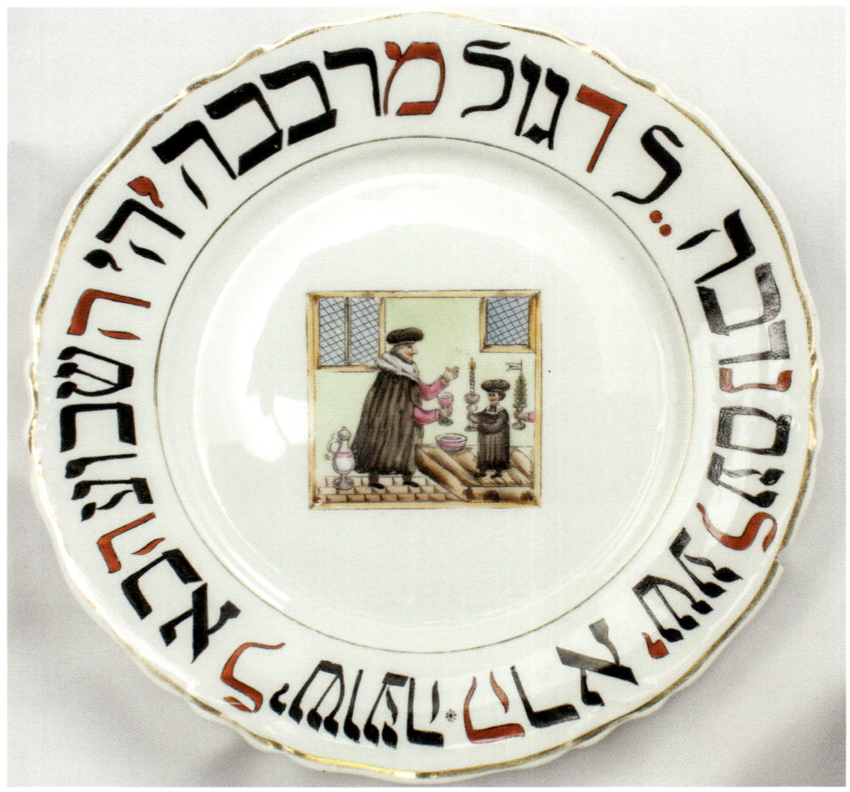

Havdalah is a ceremony recited at the conclusion of the Sabbath (Saturday sundown), which involves three items: a spice box, a lit twisted candle, and a cup of wine. After all the blessings are recited and most of the wine is consumed, the candle is extinguished by some drops of wine on a plate.

This plate differs from other known porcelain havdalah plates of the period, as the painted decoration in the center is most unusual. The Hebrew says "Give salvation to a generous nation that is dear and plentiful. May the coming week be good." In the center of the plate is a copy of a woodcut illustration from the 1623 work *Sefer Haminhagim* (Book of Customs), which depicts havdalah; the father holding the cup of wine, his young son holding the candle, and another child (in this image only the hand is seen) holding a spice box in tower form.

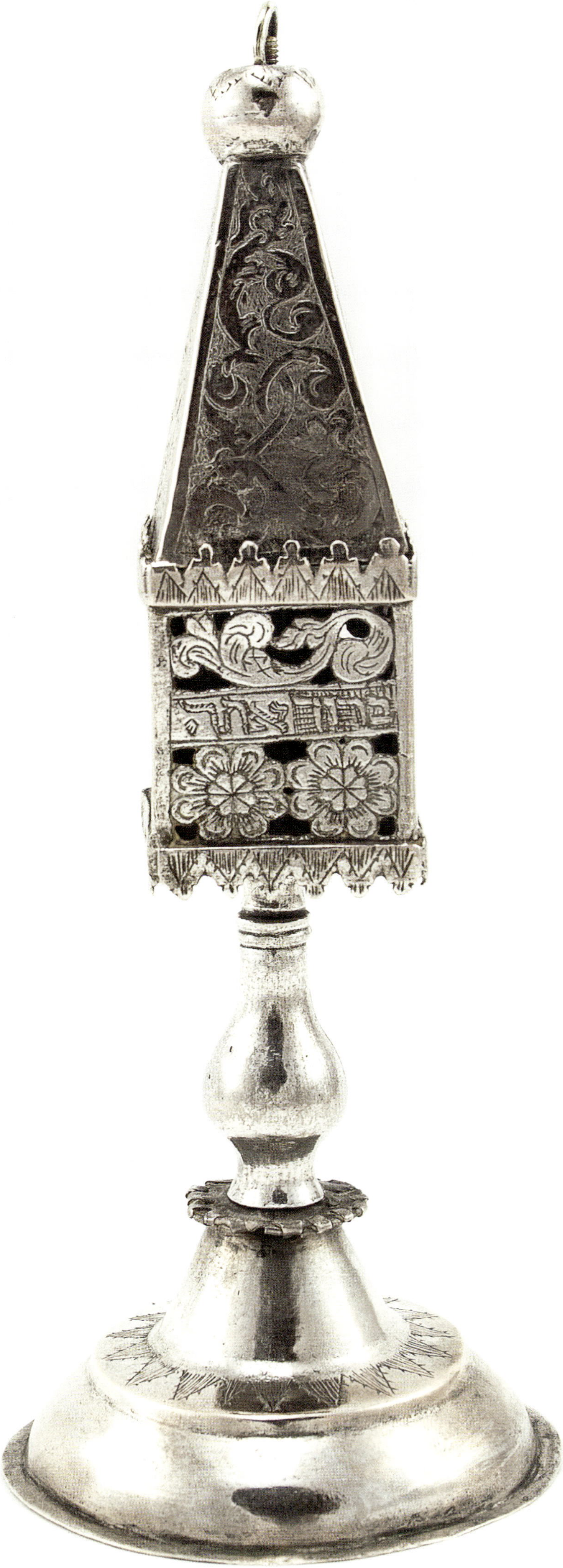

SPICE BOX

Material: Silver
Origin: Poland, eighteenth century
Dimensions: 5″ x 2.3″

Jewish spice boxes in tower form have been recorded as early as the sixteenth century. A generally held belief for why Jews began fashioning spice boxes as towers is that during the Middle Ages, spices were a precious commodity (often worth their weight in gold) and were kept in the tower of a city's fortification.

Another explanation of the tower shape traces it to this verse: "Like a bed of spices are His words at Sinai, like towers of perfume." (Song of Songs 5:13).

Here we have a typical eighteenth-century spice box in tower form, made of a grade of silver equaling about 70%, as opposed to the modern standard of silver, which is 92.5%, known as sterling. The pennant flag has been lost, and it has some repairs. This spice tower is unusual because of the engraved blessings of *havdalah* on each side of the tower. This was not the custom for Jewish spice towers; people tended to own a spice box in tower form (or fruit form, or flower form), or a spice box that was just a box, with Hebrew blessings engraved on it. The combination of the two on a piece from this early era is quite rare; there are a handful of silver spice towers with engraved blessings known (one in the collection of the Israel Museum) that date to the first half of the nineteenth century, but I am not aware of an eighteenth-century example aside from this one. The Hebrew is period to the piece, and most of the blessings are shortened to acronyms.

Many eighteenth- and early nineteenth-century silver Jewish objects from Poland are free of any hallmarks, as Jews were barred from joining the silver guilds of Poland until the second half of the nineteenth century. Familiarizing oneself with the look and feel of this type of silver is essential to distinguishing authentic pieces from forgeries.

SPICE BOX

Material: Wood
Origin: Poland, late nineteenth century
Dimensions: 9.5" x 1.6"

Jewish ceremonial objects made of wood hailing from prewar Europe are quite scarce, due to the immense destruction World War II brought to the Jews of that continent. Unlike metal objects, items from wood were easily destroyed. The Jewish Museum of Warsaw, for example, has a vast collection of silver and brass Judaica purchased in the 1950s and '60s (much from local junkyards at the cost of scrap); however, the museum does not own even one ritual object made of wood.

This piece is very unusual, as spice towers were fashioned in metals such as silver or brass and were rarely made of wood. With a great deal of skill, the artist of this work carved two separate pieces of wood, so that the entire top half can be lifted off and spices inserted. This tower, with its delicately carved spires, is topped by a flag that has a Star of David. Each side of the tower has a Star of David as well.

This example of Polish-Jewish woodcarving is intact only because it arrived at Ellis Island more than one hundred years ago. I purchased this tower and a carved wood mezuzah from an elderly woman who received them both as gifts from her mother-in-law on her wedding day in 1953. Her mother-in-law had owned them since she was a young woman. They were passed down from her grandfather, who carved them while living in Poland, the land of his birth, and later brought them with him to America. Sadly, the children and grandchildren of the elderly woman did not want the spice tower or mezuzah passed onto them, and some even suggested of the disposal of these precious objects to the trash. Fortunately the lady did not listen to them, as she felt the pieces must have had some monetary value due to their age.

A magnificently carved spice tower with a Star of David flag is on permanent display at the Jewish Museum of New York. It is also from Poland and dates to the nineteenth century.

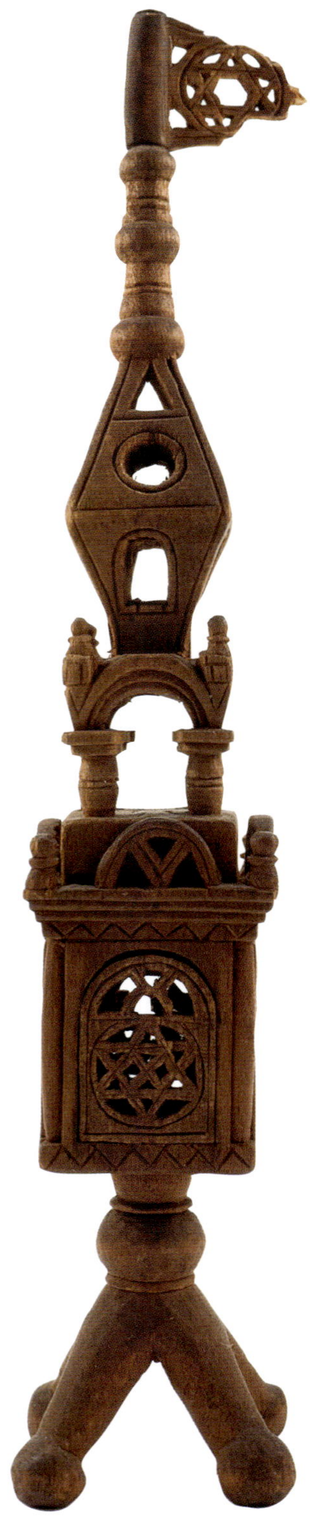

SPICE BOX

Material: Silver
Origin: Germany, circa 1890
Hallmarks: "800", crescent moon and crown
Dimensions: 7" x 1.5"

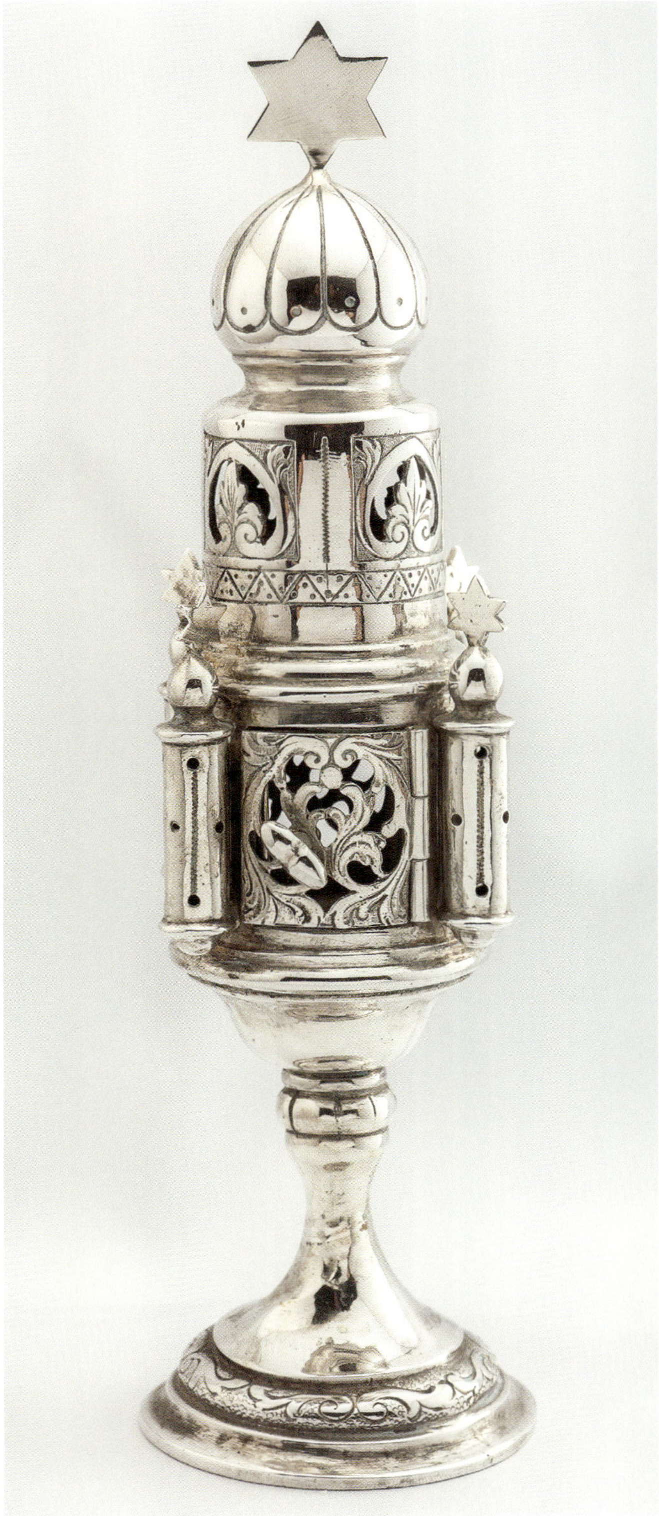

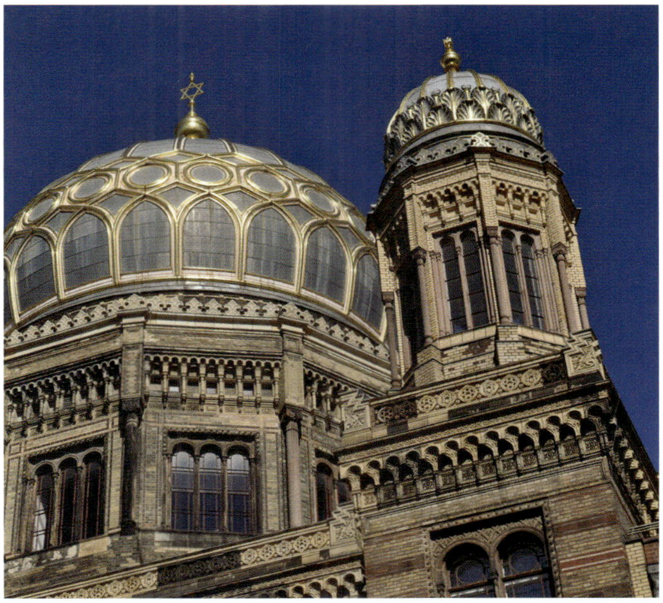

Photo (c) 2013 by Michael J. Brown.

Generally speaking, silver spice towers from Germany dating from 1886 (when the use of individual city marks were replaced by national marks of the crescent moon and crown) through the 1930s have survived in substantially large numbers. This model, however, is scarce. Its design imitates nineteenth-century European synagogues built in the style of Moorish Revival. Shown here is the Neue Synagoge in Berlin, built in 1866.

I bought this tower with the finial missing from the large dome in the center; I replaced it with a new Star of David.

SPICE BOXES

Materials: Silver / Wood
Origin: Germany, circa 1890 / Europe, 1786-1787
Hallmarks: "WK 800", crescent moon and crown
Dimensions: 2.75" x 2" / .75" x 2.75"

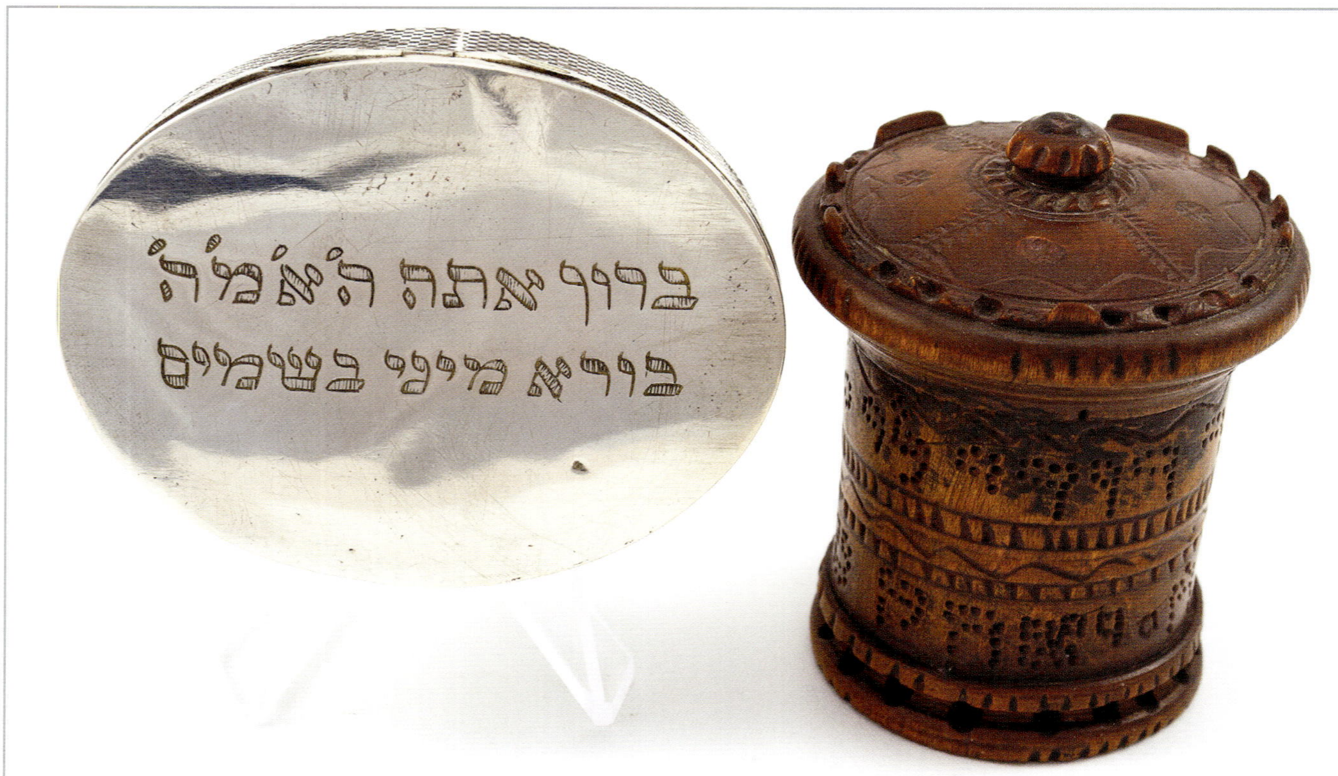

These containers are examples of how a secular item can be converted into a Jewish ceremonial object. The silver box was originally made for snuff or pills. An abbreviated blessing for spices was engraved on the lid. For the wood box, using a technique known as "pinpricking," the owner spelled out his name (Yitzchak Tvisk), the Hebrew year, and "A bag of myrrh is my beloved to me," (Song of Songs, 1:13).

The compact size of these spice boxes suggest they were for use while traveling. The employment of a verse from Song of Songs on a spice box is not known to me on any other examples. The wood box might not look like much, but it's a fascinating piece.

PLATE

Material: Ceramic
Origin: Moravia (Czech Republic), nineteenth century
Dimensions: 10"

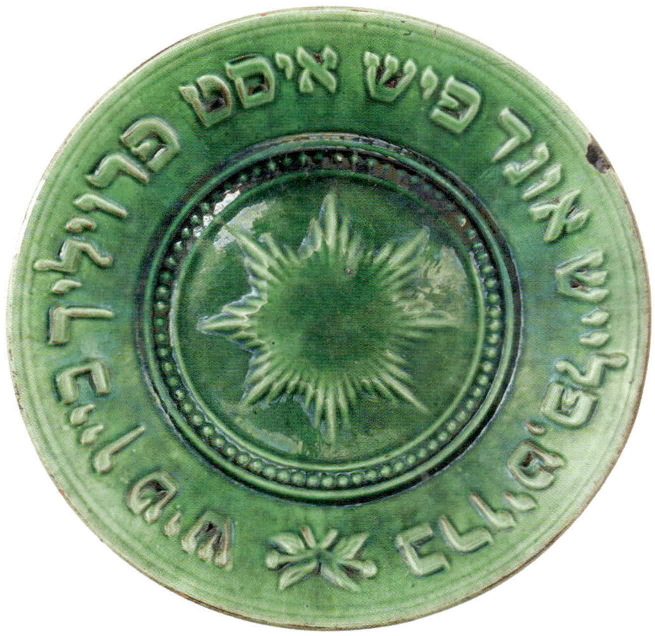

On the rim in Yiddish: "Bread, meat and fish brings happiness to the table."

MEZUZAH CASES

Material: Brass
Origin: Germany or The Netherlands, late nineteenth century / India, circa 1910
Dimensions: 8" x 1.2" / 6.7" x 2.25"

A mezuzah is a piece of parchment inscribed with verses from Deuteronomy 6:4-9 and 11:13-21, beginning with "Hear O Israel, The Lord your G-d, The Lord is One." The parchment is placed in a case and then affixed to the doorposts of a Jewish home to fulfill the Biblical commandment set down in Deuteronomy 6:9, "upon thy doorposts of your house." Over the centuries, designing and producing mezuzah cases has been elevated to an art form, with many cases having a small opening in the front so part of the parchment can be viewed.

The mezuzah case on the left (see page 26) has Hebrew verses cast in high relief. The first part of the Hebrew verses translates to: "G-d is my Protector, G-d is my shadow by my right hand. G-d will protect my goings and comings to life and to peace, forever," (Sefer Maharil, Lekutim 91, adapting Psalm 121:5) The second part states: "Anyone who is meticulous regarding the commandment of mezuzah will have length of days, as it is written 'So that your days will be numerous,' " (Tur Yoreh De'ah 285, referencing Deuteronomy 11:20).

Collectors, take note: Twentieth-century copies of this mezuzah case frequently appear for sale. Apparently they were cast directly off a nineteenth-century original. The copies tend to have a shorter length of as much as a quarter of an inch, the letters are in lower relief, and one or two letters by the edge may only be partially visible or altogether illegible.

There is a revered attitude toward many animals in India. Because of this, parchment was difficult

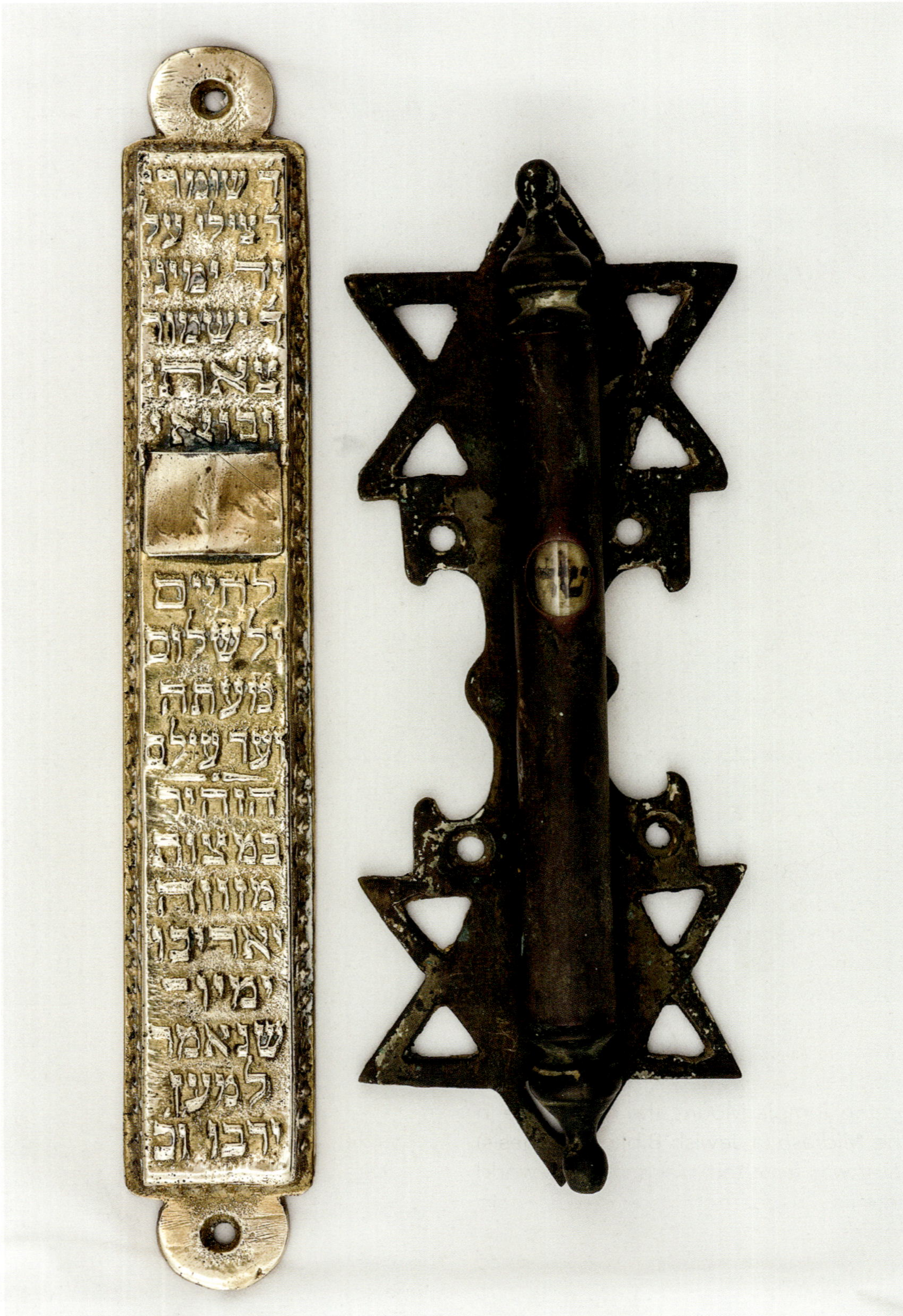

to obtain, so most Jewish homes only had one mezuzah, placed at the doorway of the main entrance. The second mezuzah case, with its bold Stars of David, is typical of Jewish ceremonial art from India; the usage of large Stars of David can be found on other Indian items such as menorahs and Torah ark curtains.

Be sure to check mezuzahs purporting to be antique and from India for appropriate wear and Old World construction, as reproductions, many authorized by the current Indian-Jewish community itself, regularly appear on the antiques market.

Material: Wood
Origin: Poland, late nineteenth century / Central Europe, eighteenth or nineteenth century
Dimensions: 6.75" x 1.75" / 6.25" x 2.25"

For the first case, two columns flank a crown; the columns represent the two front pillars of the First Temple in Jerusalem (built in 957 BCE by King Solomon), while the crown represents *Keter Torah* (Crown of Torah). A Star of David is at bottom. Depictions of the First Temple pillars continue to be a popular motif on contemporary mezuzah cases.

The second case is a spectacular example of European-Jewish woodcarving that details a myriad of images. Beginning at top: a pair of lion heads, a pair of rams, a dome with an opening underneath, pillars of the First Temple, a stonework design.

At first glance, the domed form and masonry motifs are puzzling. To be properly interpreted, familiarity with antique Hebrew books and maps is essential. During the eighteenth and nineteenth centuries, hand-illustrated and lithographed maps of the Holy Land, which included depictions of sacred Jewish sites, were popular among Jewish communities in Europe and the Middle East. The carver of this case, likely inspired by those maps, implements the two structures built on areas most important to Jews. The dome is the Dome of the Rock, a shrine for Muslims built at the end of the seventh century directly atop the Temple Mount, the holiest site in Judaism. The *Midrash* (a Jewish Biblical exegesis) explains that it was from this place that the world expanded into its present form, and this was where G-d gathered the dust he used to create the first man, Adam. The Torah records that G-d chose to rest His Divine Presence here; consequently, two Jewish temples were built on this location, where the dome now stands.

Illustrations of the Dome of the Rock appear on the title pages of printed Hebrew books dating back as early as the sixteenth century, where they are labeled "House of the Holy" or "Place of the Holy." The stonework represents the Western Wall, the sole remaining architectural element that has survived from the Second Temple.

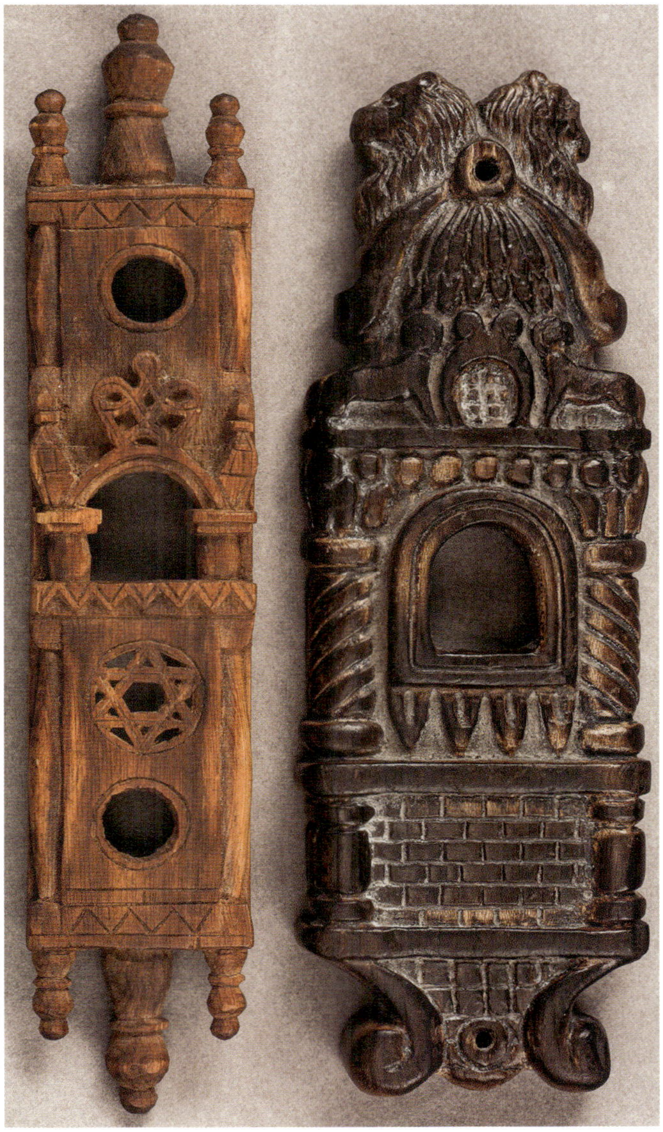

The pair of rams presumably signify the type of animals sacrificed on altars in the First and Second Temples, as well as possibly referencing Abraham sacrificing a ram instead of his son Isaac (Genesis 22: 1-24), and/or Moses sacrificing a pair of rams on the altar in the desert (Leviticus 8: 18-24). The lion heads are likely a metaphor for the phrase *Shomer Delatot Yisrael* (Gaurdian of the Doorways of Israel), as this makes up an acronym for one of the names of G-d, *Shaddai*, which is written on the section of parchment that is left exposed in the mezuzah case.

MEZUZAH CASES

Materials: Silver / Tin / Brass
Origin: Germany, circa 1925 (silver and tin cases) / Germany or Austria, circa 1915
Hallmarks: "Posen 800", crown | "800" crescent moon and crown
Dimensions: 3.5" x 1.5" / 3.5" x 1.5" / 3.85" x 1.5 / 2.8" x 1"

The first case, top left, was made by the silver firm Posen, which was founded by Lazarus Jacob Posen in 1834. Lazarus Posen manufactured secular silver goods for the general market, and upon his death in 1869, control of the business went to his widow, Bredina Wetzlar. Under her leadership and that of her son Jacob, Posen began producing Judaica. By the end of the nineteenth century, Posen became the largest supplier of silver Judaica in Europe. While menorahs, Sabbath articles, and Torah ornaments made by Posen appear on the market with regularity, Posen mezuzah cases are scarce. This case is embossed and chased with a sun, a rose, and a Star of David with rays emanating from it.

The second case, bottom left, although identical in origin, form, and workmanship to the Posen case, only has silver standard hallmarks and lacks a maker's mark.

The third case, top right, is from one of the eighty synagogues that were part of the city of Berlin before the Second World War, as it has Hebrew wording that reads "KK Berlin," meaning *Kehila Kedosha* (Holy Congregation) of Berlin. The case still contains the original parchment, as the hand-inked "*Shaddai*" can be seen through the small open space.

The fourth case, while having the same form as the silver examples, has a different style. This also depicts a sun with rays, however, the rest of the case has a playful *Jugendstil* design. *Jugendstil* was the German and Austrian version of art nouveau.

The sun motif on these mezuzah cases was perhaps inspired by this Biblical verse: "The sun set, and it was very dark. Behold—there was a smoky furnace and a torch of fire which passed between these pieces. On that day the Lord made a covenant with Abram," (Genesis 15: 17-18).

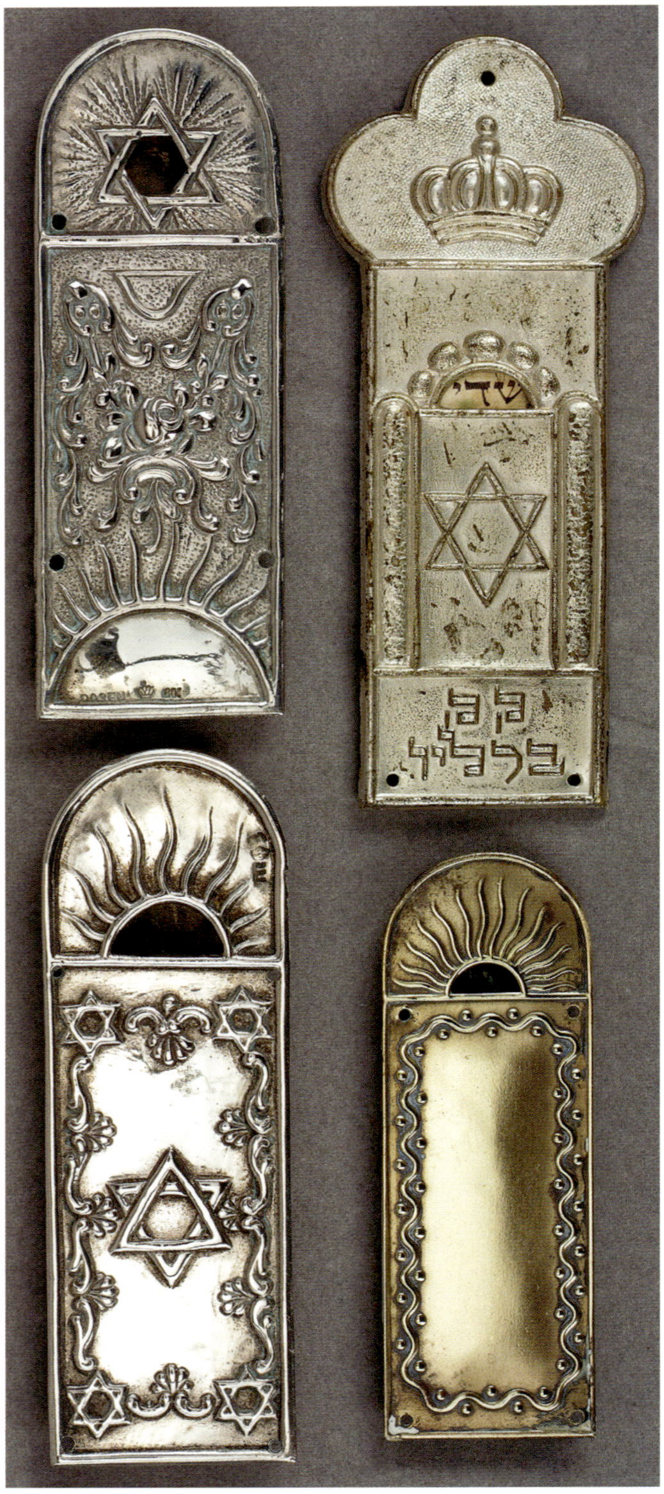

Materials: *Tin and glass / Brass / Brass / Tin-plated copper / Silver*
Origin: *Europe, nineteenth century / Israel. circa 1950 / The Netherlands, circa 1900 / Israel. 1940s / Israel. circa 1915*
Hallmarks: *"Pal-Bell Co Ltd. Made in Israel" / "MMACHE J17" / "sponbrass"/ "Bezalel"*
Dimensions: *4.25" x .9 / 3" x 1" / 6" x 1.5" / 4.5" x 1.8" / 2.5" x .9*

The case at top left is made of humble material, cut from strips of tin. Simply made cases from tin and wood were typical for the average nineteenth-century European Jew, as most were on the low end of society, economically. This example is one of a handful of published antique cases that I am aware of in which the entire length of the parchment can be viewed.

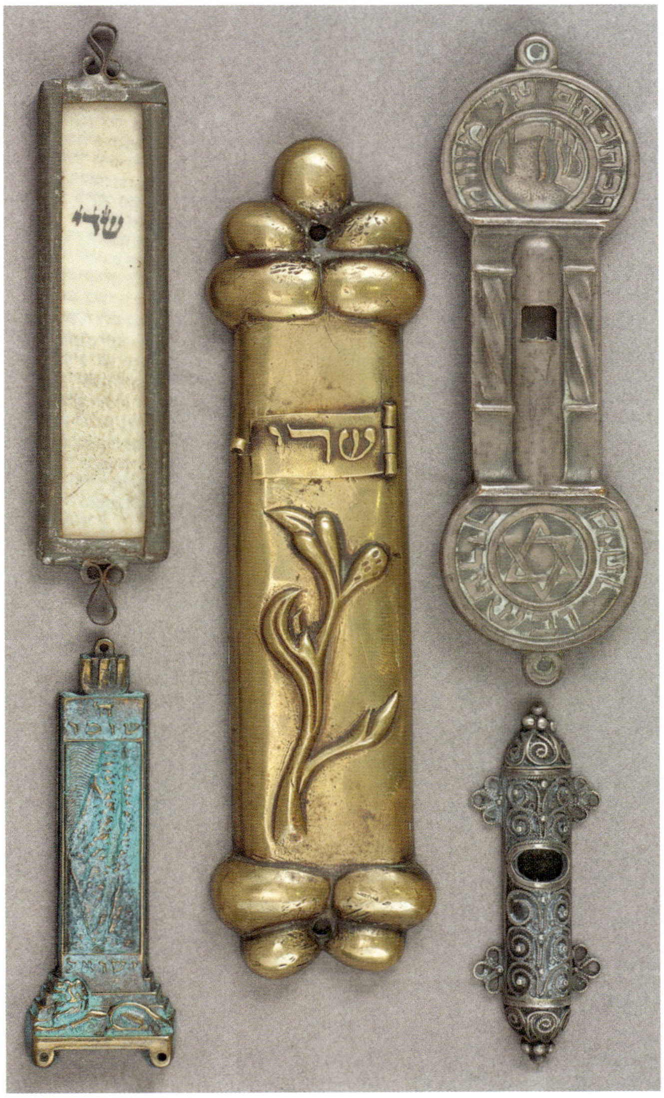

The case below that was made by the Pal-Bell company, a firm that manufactured secular items in brass and bronze as well as Judaica. Its founder, Maurice Ascalon, had formal artistic training in Brussels and Milan, and Pal-Bell began operations in Tel-Aviv under the name "Klein Komm." Pal-Bell items are known by their applied green verdigris, which gives them a centuries-old look, akin to objects from ancient times. This case depicts a reclining lion at bottom, a map of Israel, and in Hebrew "G-d is the Guardian of the Jewish people," topped by the Hebrew letter "*shin*," standing for *Shaddai*. The choice of imagery and Hebrew verse for this case, made approximately two years after Israel fought for its independence in 1948, is quite poignant.

The large case in the center, with its bulbous ends, slightly curved Hebrew letters making up the word "*Shaddai*," and prominent flower, makes it clear that its design was art nouveau-inspired (art nouveau is discussed in greater detail beginning on page 66, and a menorah is shown that is made by the same workshop from which this mezuzah case hails).

The case at top right has the two symbolic temple columns depicted. Starting at the rim of the top roundel and concluding below, from Deuteronomy 6:9: "And you shall write them upon thy doorposts of your house and on thy gates." In large letters it says, "*Shaddai*."

The vast majority of mezuzah cases produced by the Bezalel Academy of Arts and Crafts were made from thin sheets of brass or silver. This small silver case, bottom right, is atypical in this regard.

MIZRACH

Material: Brass
Origin: Munich, Germany circa 1925
Artist: Heinrich Schwed
Identifying Marks: Interlocking letters "HS," "M"
Dimensions: 10" x 8"

"*Mizrach*" is the Hebrew word for "east." East is the direction that most Jews in the Diaspora face during prayer, as Jewish law prescribes that Jews face the site of the ancient Temple in Jerusalem during prayer. As the vast majority of Jews in the Diaspora live west of Jerusalem, they face eastward during prayer.

It is customary in religious Jewish homes to mark a wall in the direction of east, to make sure people are facing the proper direction when praying at home. For this purpose, artistic wall plaques in every conceivable medium are created that feature the word "*mizrach*."

Were it not for the *Jugendstil* (German art nouveau) "line and ball" motif that decorates the border of this plaque, it could easily be mistaken as being made today, due to its very modern design.

Beginning at top center is the word "*mizrach*," flanked by a deer and an eagle. These animals are a reference to the verse: "Be bold as a leopard, light as an eagle, swift as a deer, and strong as a lion to do the will of your Father in Heaven," (Ethics of the Fathers 5:20).

Filling up most of the space of this plaque is a Star of David with rays emanating from it, along with a banner stating: "From the rising of the sun unto the going down thereof the Lord's name is to be praised," (Psalms 113:3).

At bottom center is the word "Jerusalem," flanked by two architectural scenes, one being the Tomb of Rachel and the other, the city walls and structures of Jerusalem, each titled as such in Hebrew.

Heinrich Schwed, the artist and maker of this *mizrach*, produced a variety of brass and aluminum dishes and trays decorated with Hebrew verses and Judaic motifs apropos for the Sabbath and Passover, as well as plates stating "*Mazel Tov*," for newlyweds.

The Nazis confiscated Schwed's business in 1938; shortly thereafter he, his wife and children fled to Buenos Aires.

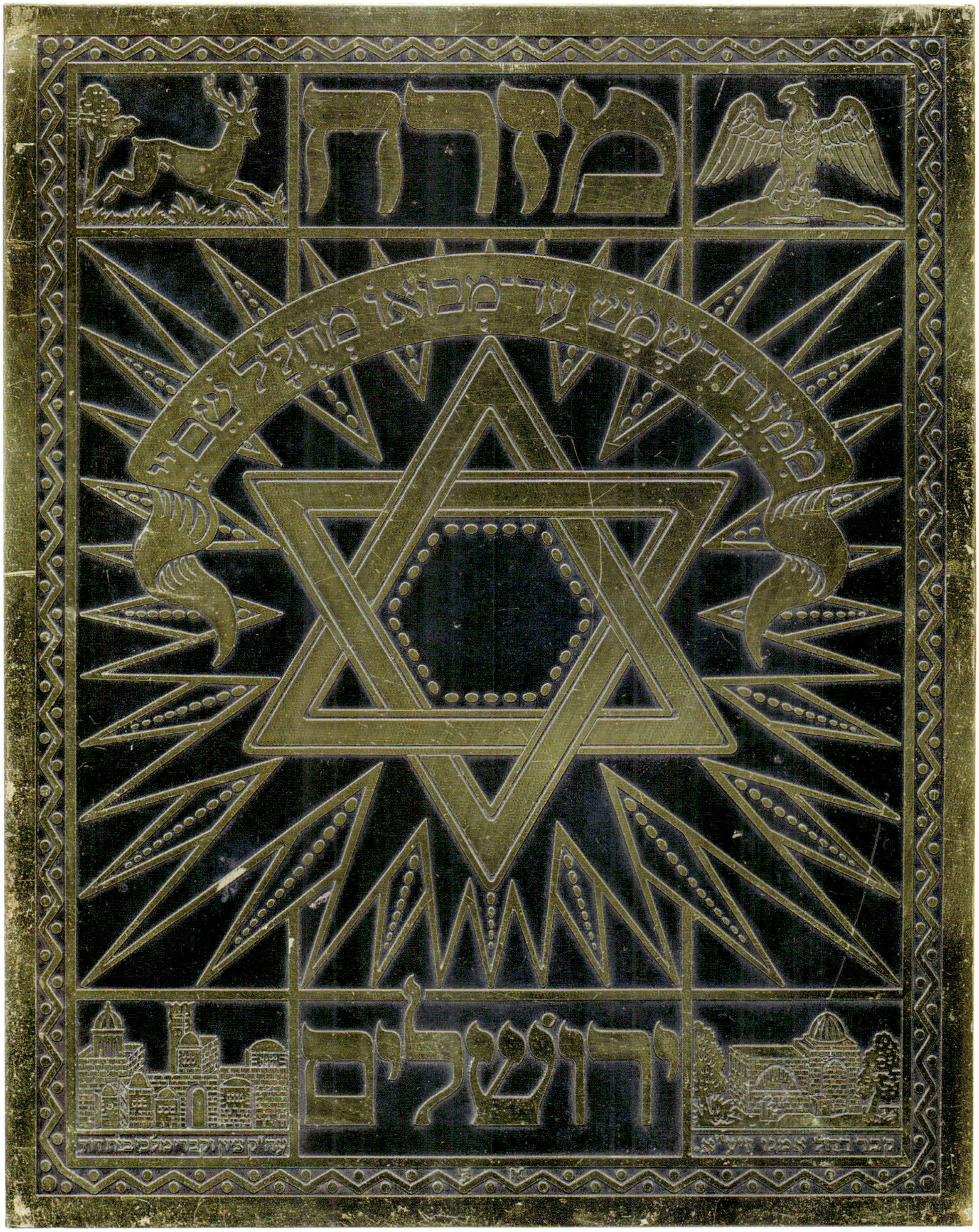
מזרח
ממזרח־שמש עד־מבואו מהלל שם ה׳
ירושלים

TEFILLIN BAGS

Materials: Velvet / Beadwork on cotton
Origin: Eastern Europe, circa 1890 / Israel, circa 1930 / Canada, circa 1875
Dimensions: 6.75" x 6.5" / 8" x 6" / 8" x 7"

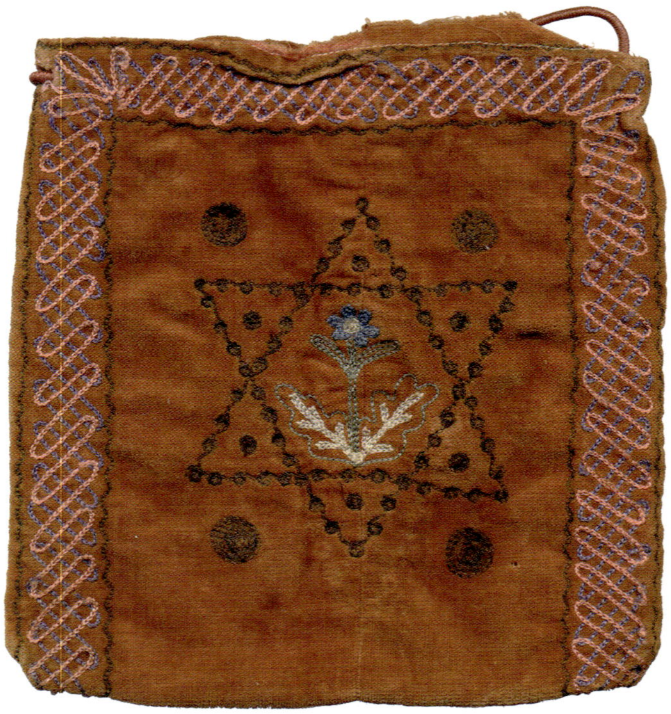

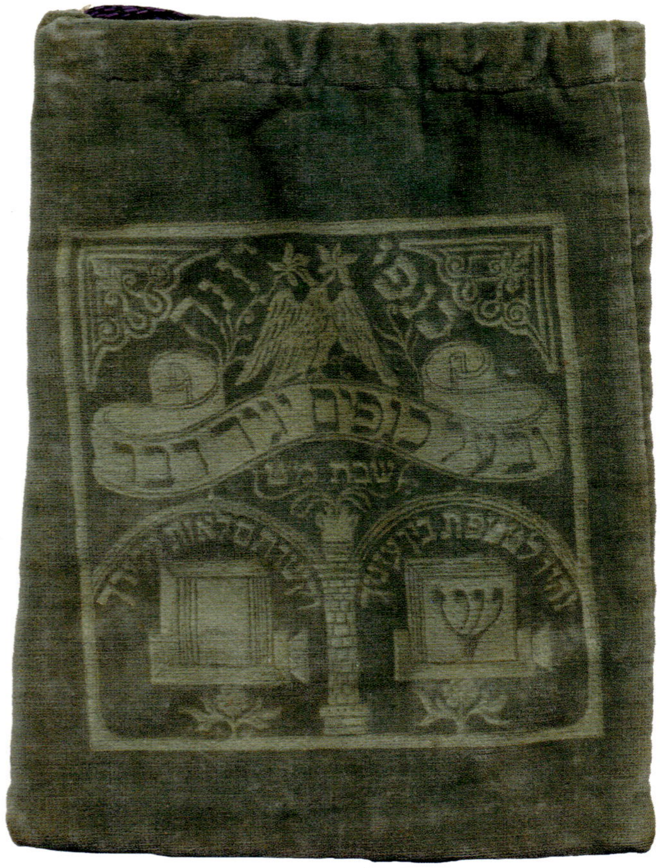

Tefillin, known in English as "phylacteries," are two black leather boxes containing scrolls of parchment inscribed with Biblical verses. The arm-*tefillin*, or *shel yad*, is worn on the upper arm, while the head-*tefillin*, or *shel rosh*, is placed above the forehead. They serve as a remembrance that G-d brought the Israelites out of Egypt. The sources provided for tefillin in the Torah are this verse: "[These words] must also be a sign on your arm and a reminder in the center of your head," (Exodus 13:9, repeated 13:16, Deuteronomy 6:8 and 11:18). *Tefillin* are worn during morning prayers by men, except on the Sabbath.

These pouches were made to hold *tefillin*. The first bag is a particularly pleasant example from Eastern Europe, showing a flower inside a Star of David. Its design reveals feminine undertones, as newly married Jewish women in prewar Europe often presented their husband with *tefillin* and *tallis* (prayer shawl) bags, with decorations sewn by them. The second bag is from Israel, displaying the *tefillin* cases themselves, along with a dove and the verse from Exodus 13:9. The third bag, made of beadwork on thick cotton, depicts the coats of arms of four provinces of Canada: Ontario, Nova Scotia, Quebec, and New Brunswick. The reverse has "*Tephilin*" embroidered in English above a decorative motif, and the owners initials "J.A.".

The last example is very interesting, as I am not aware of other Judaica with motifs specific to Canada.

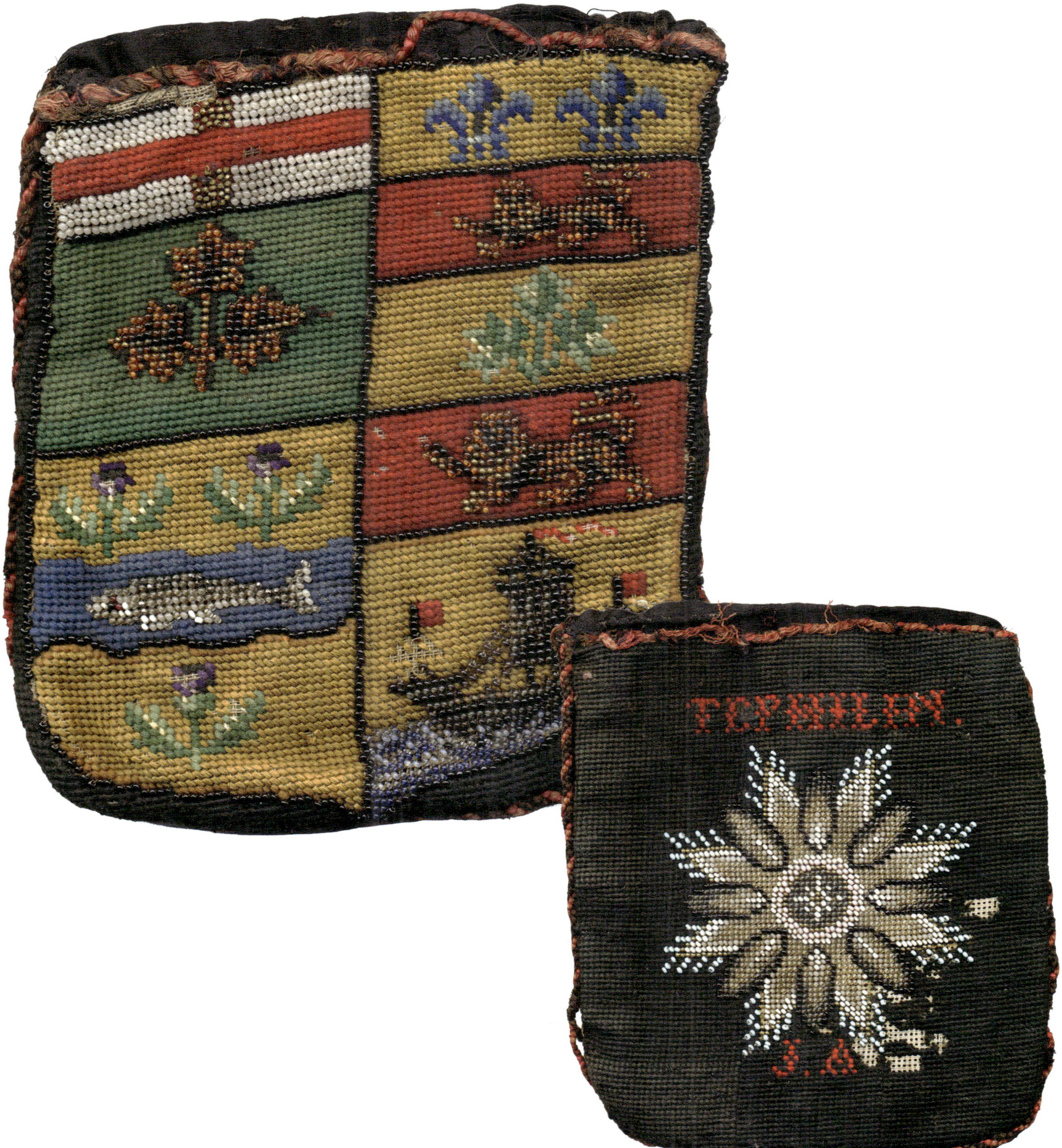

PLATE

Material: Pewter
Origin: Germany, circa 1780
Dimensions: 9.25"

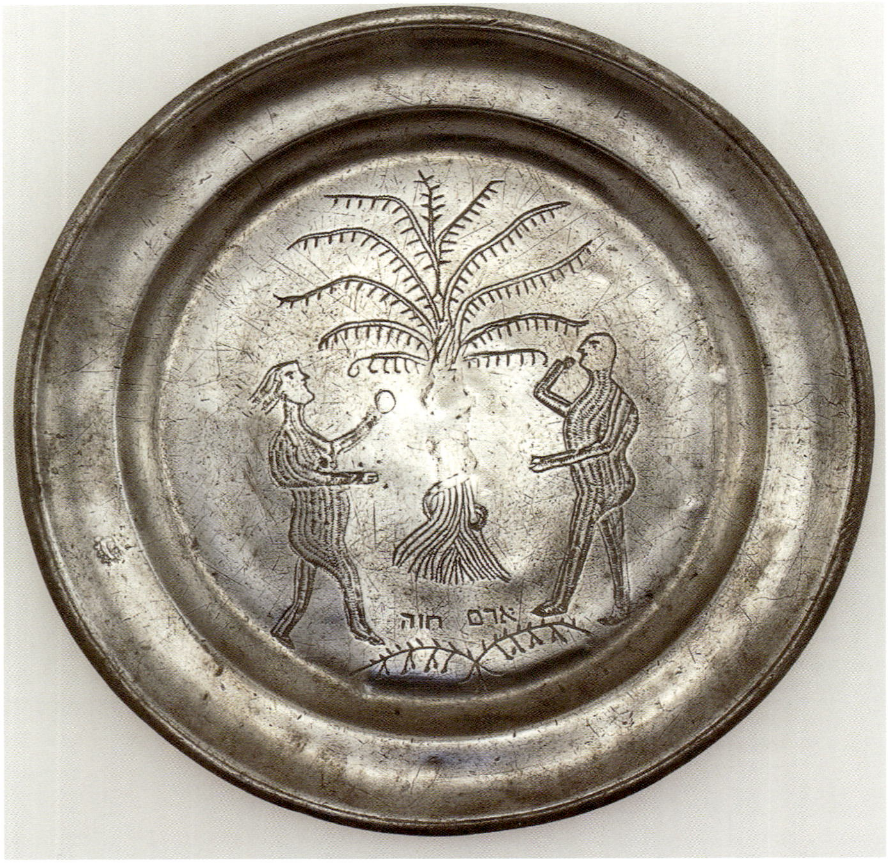

Unlike the pewter plate previously pictured and described, this plate has no references to the Sabbath and does not appear to have any ceremonial purpose. The function of this plate and the eleven plates shown subsequent to this one are unclear. Perhaps the intention was similar to that of a painting—to be displayed on a wall and enjoyed simply as decoration. It's educational as well, as the viewer becomes familiar with episodes of the Torah.

This plate shows Adam and Eve in the Garden of Eden, along with the serpent wrapped around the Tree of Knowledge. The depictions of Adam and Eve are extremely naive, as their bodies have no signs of gender specificity. The figure on the left (holding the forbidden fruit) with longer hair is titled in Hebrew "*Chava*" (Eve), and the figure on the right "*Odom*" (Adam).

Although the identity of the engraver of this Adam and Eve plate is not known, for the eleven plates and bowls on the following pages, it is apparent they were all executed by the same engraver, or possibly a close knit group of engravers working with each other in nineteenth-century Germany. More "Biblical dishes" from this artisan or group are in the collection of the Judaica Museum of Koln, Germany, and in the collection of Mishkan Le'Omanut Museum of Art, in Ein-Harod, Israel.

It is interesting to note that amongst German-speaking Jews of the eighteenth and nineteenth centuries, depictions of Adam and Eve sometimes appear on objects used for Passover, such as pewter trays that have the order of the Passover service engraved on them, as well as *Sederzwehl* (Seder towels), which are embroidered strips of cloth used for washing the hands during this holiday.

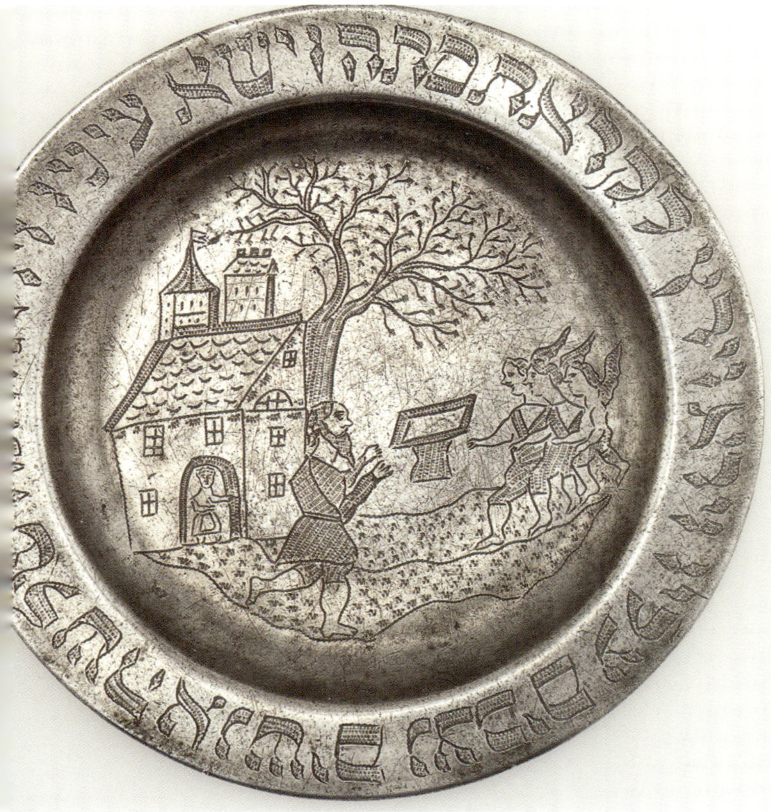

PLATE

Material: Pewter
Origin: Germany, nineteenth century
Dimensions: 9.25"

In the center, Sarah stands in the doorway of her house (with tiled roof and chimney!), while Abraham runs to greet three angels. In the background is a table under a tree.

On the rim in Hebrew: "[Abraham] lifted his eyes and he saw three strangers standing a short distance from him. When he saw [them] from the entrance of his tent, he ran to greet them," (Genesis 18:2).

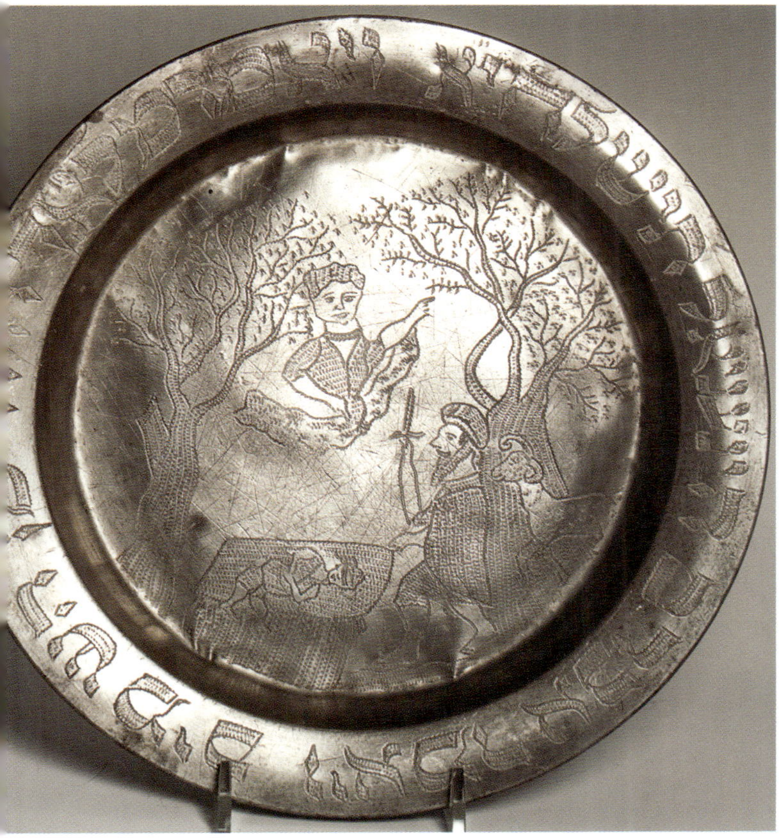

BOWL

Material: Pewter
Origin: Germany, nineteenth century
Dimensions: 9"

Abraham is about to sacrifice his son Isaac on an altar, when an angel appears to stop him.

On the rim in Hebrew: "And an angel of G-d called to him from heaven, and said, 'Abram![sic] [Abraham!]', and he said, 'Here I am.'" "And he said, "Do not stretch out [your hand against the lad]," (Genesis 22:11-12).

BOWL

Material: Pewter
Origin: Germany, nineteenth century
Dimensions: 8.75"

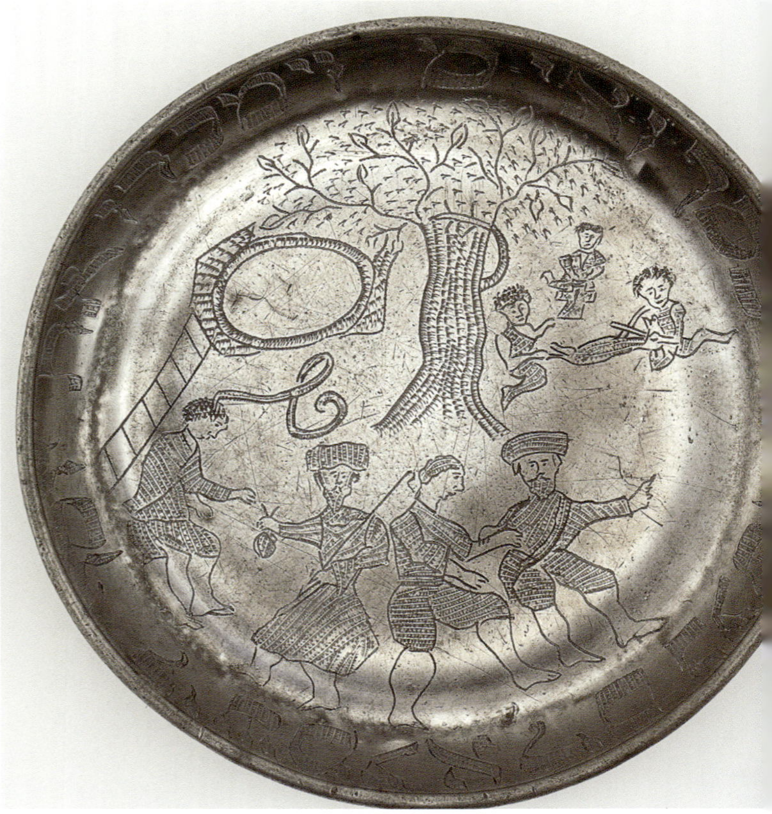

There are two Midianite Arabs with hats: One leads Joseph away, another pays. In the background is a pit with a ladder and snake, beneath the tree on the right, three of Joseph's brothers slaughter a goat to stain the coat of many colors.

On the rim in Hebrew: "They sold Joseph to the Arabs for twenty pieces of silver," (Genesis 37:28).

BOWL

Material: Pewter
Origin: Germany, nineteenth century
Dimensions: 8.75"

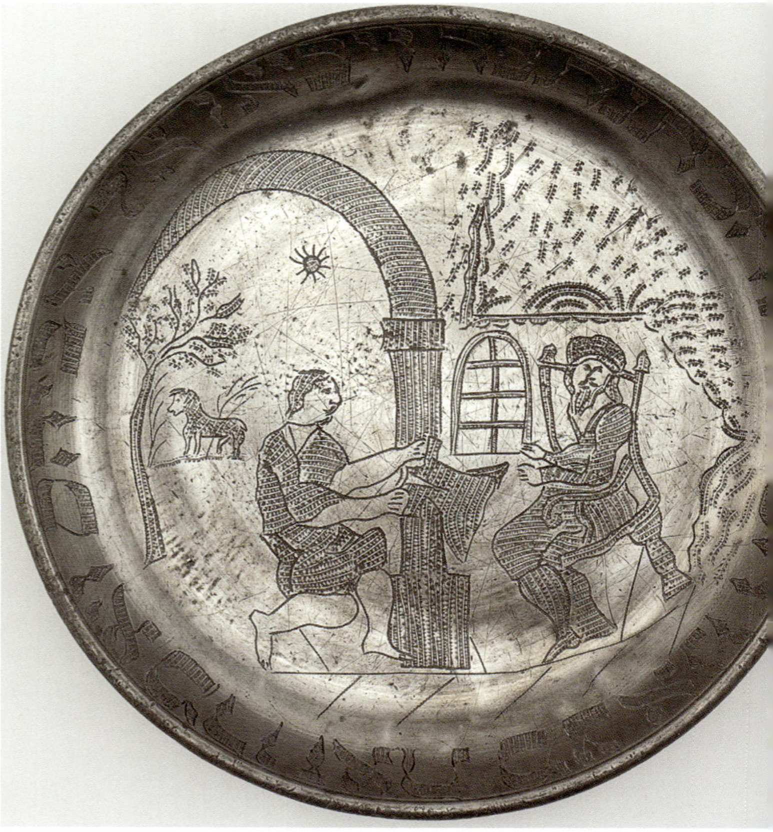

Jacob is seated, and one of his sons is showing him the bloodied coat of many colors that belonged to Joseph. There is a background landscape with an animal, tree, and sun.

On the rim in Hebrew: "It was brought to their father. 'We found this coat,'" (Genesis 37:32).

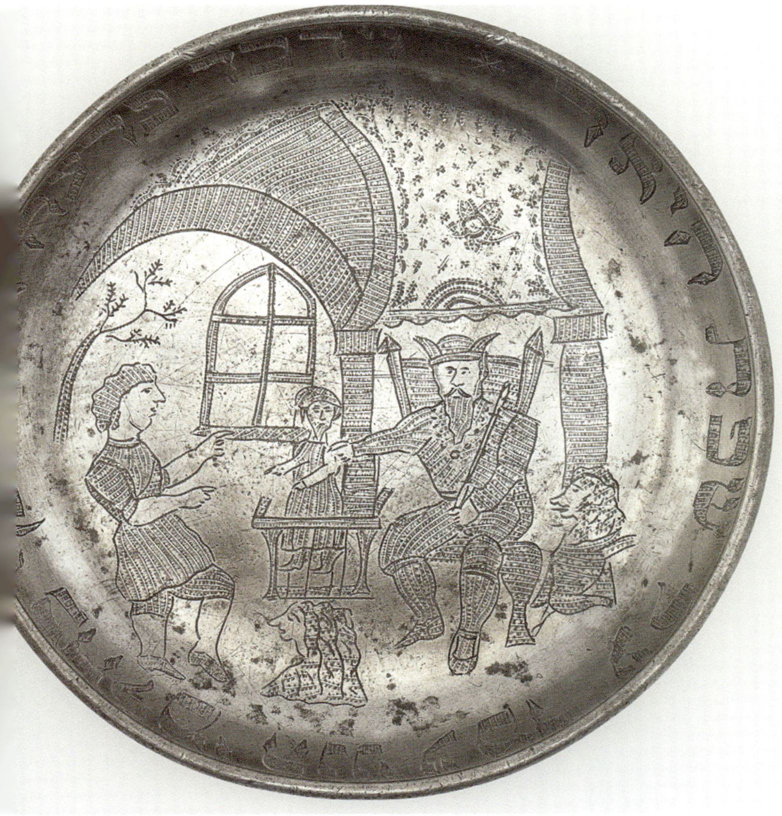

BOWL

Material: Pewter
Origin: Germany, nineteenth century
Dimensions: 8.75"

Pharaoh is on the throne, pointing to a small figure behind bars. He is flanked by a lion and advisors of the court. Joseph motions as he explains Pharaoh's dreams.

On the rim in Hebrew: "Pharaoh related it to Joseph: 'In my dream, I was standing on the bank of the Nile,' " (Genesis 41:17).

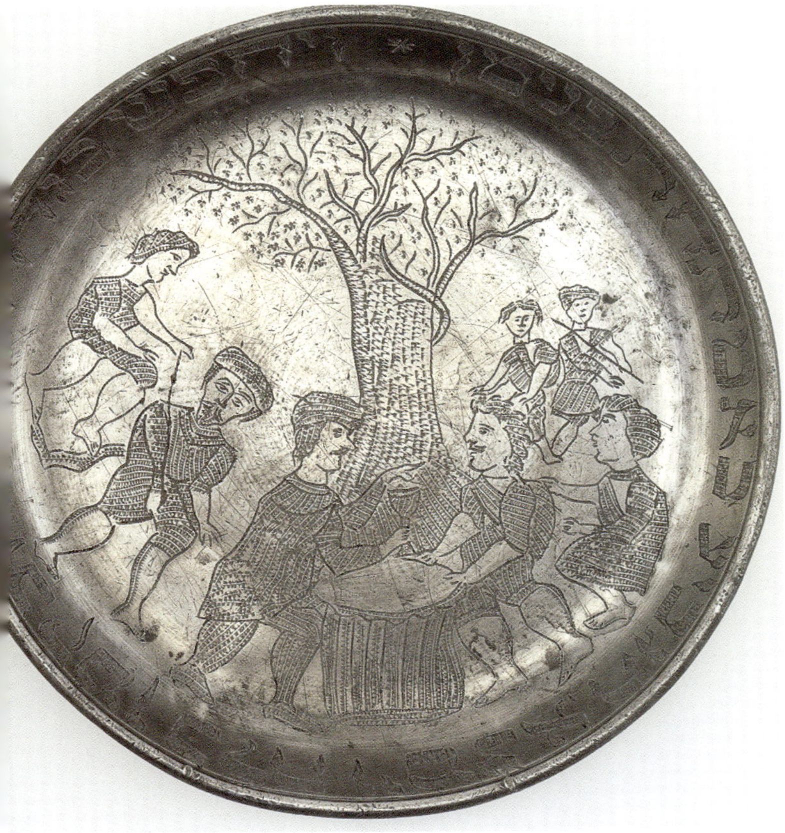

BOWL

Material: Pewter
Origin: Germany, nineteenth century
Dimensions: 8.75"

Joseph's brothers are stunned, as Egyptians (with mustaches) discover the goblet in Benjamin's pack.

On the rim in Hebrew: "[The overseer] inspected each one, beginning with the oldest and ending with the youngest. The chalice was found in Benjamin's pack," (Genesis 44:12).

PLATE

Material: Pewter
Origin: Germany, nineteenth century
Dimensions: 9.25"

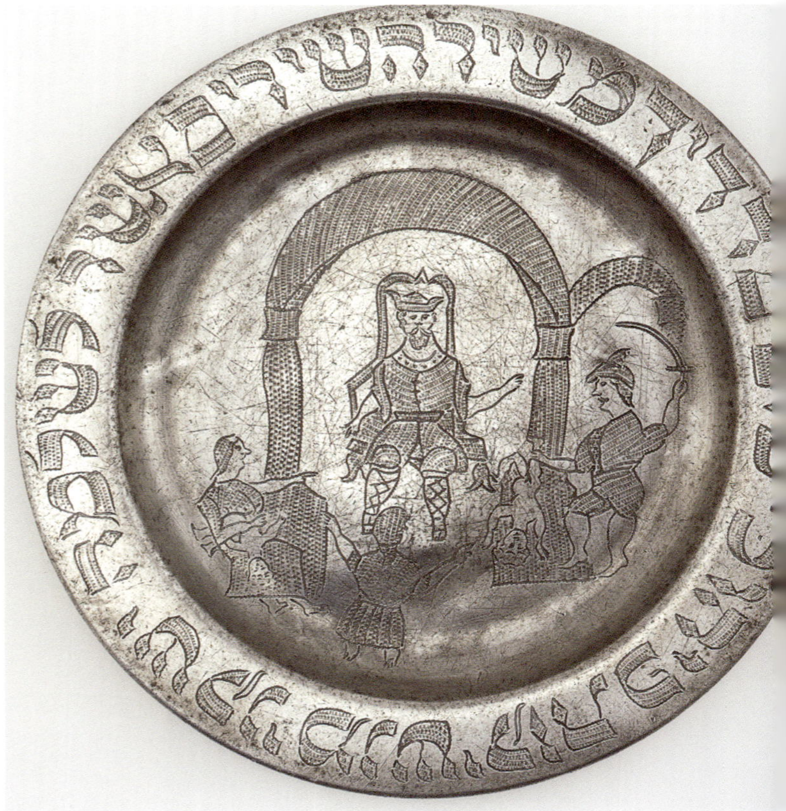

King Solomon on his throne commands a soldier to split a baby in two, as the false mother holds a dead child and the real mother waves her arms about hysterically.

On the rim in Hebrew: "The song that excels all songs dedicated to G-d, the King to Whom peace belongs. Communicate Your innermost wisdom to me again in loving closeness, for Your friendship is dearer than all earthly delights," (Song of Songs 1:1-2, indirect reference to works of Solomon).

PLATE

Material: Pewter
Origin: Germany, nineteenth century
Dimensions: 9"

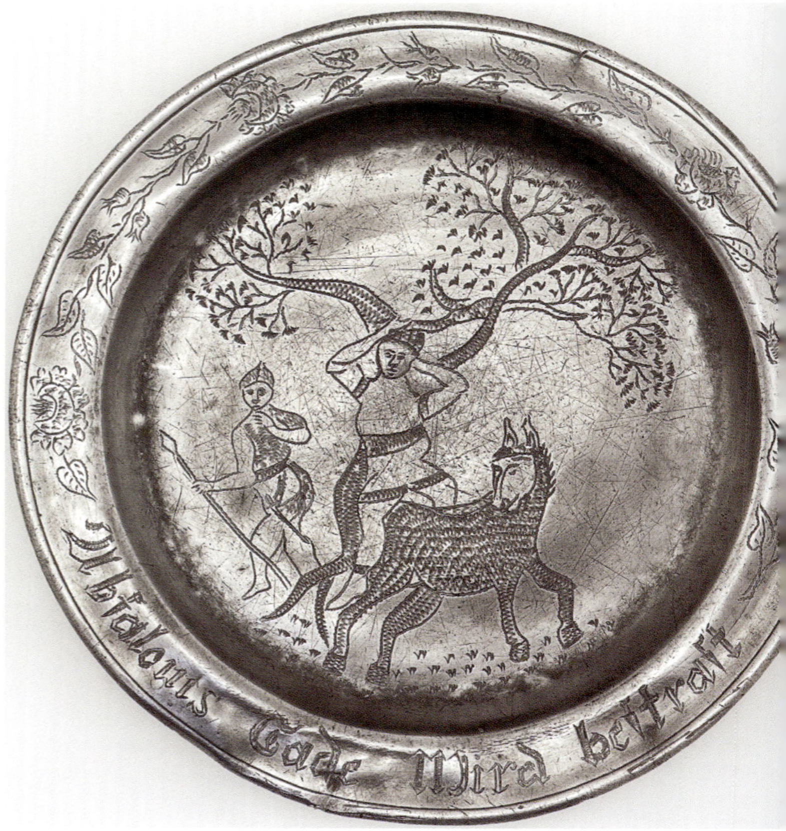

The glorious hair of Avshalom is caught in a tree; he is on his horse with a frightened soldier in the background.

On the rim in German: "Avshalom is hanged in an oak." (Samuel II 18:10).

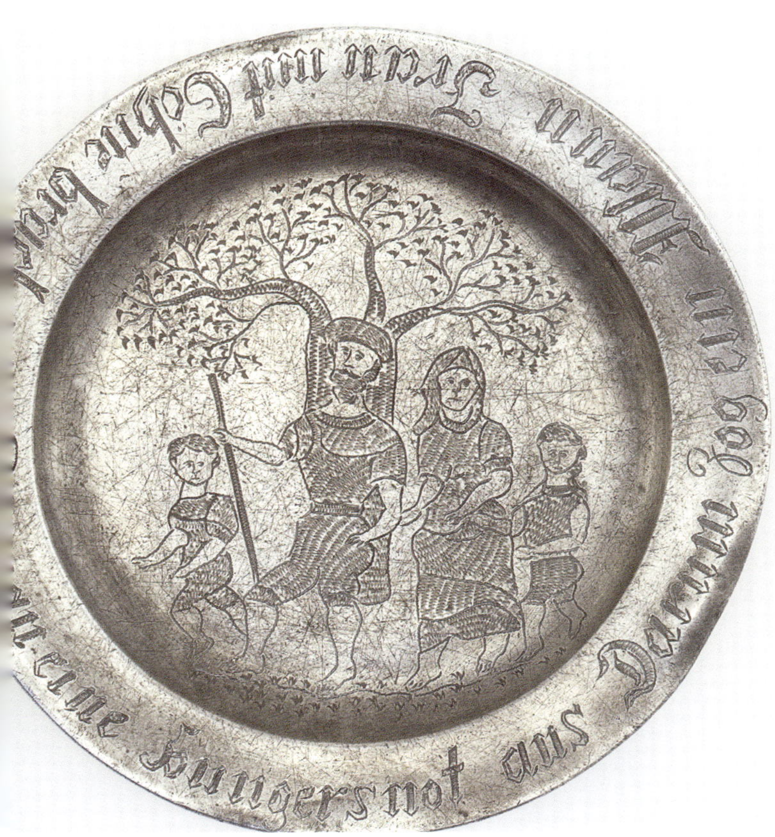

PLATE

Material: Pewter
Origin: Germany, nineteenth century
Dimensions: 8.75"

Elimelech, his wife Naomi, and their two sons Machlon and Kilion are walking.

On the rim in German: "And a man went from Bethlehem in Judah to sojourn in the fields of Moab, he, his wife, and his two sons," (Ruth 1:1).

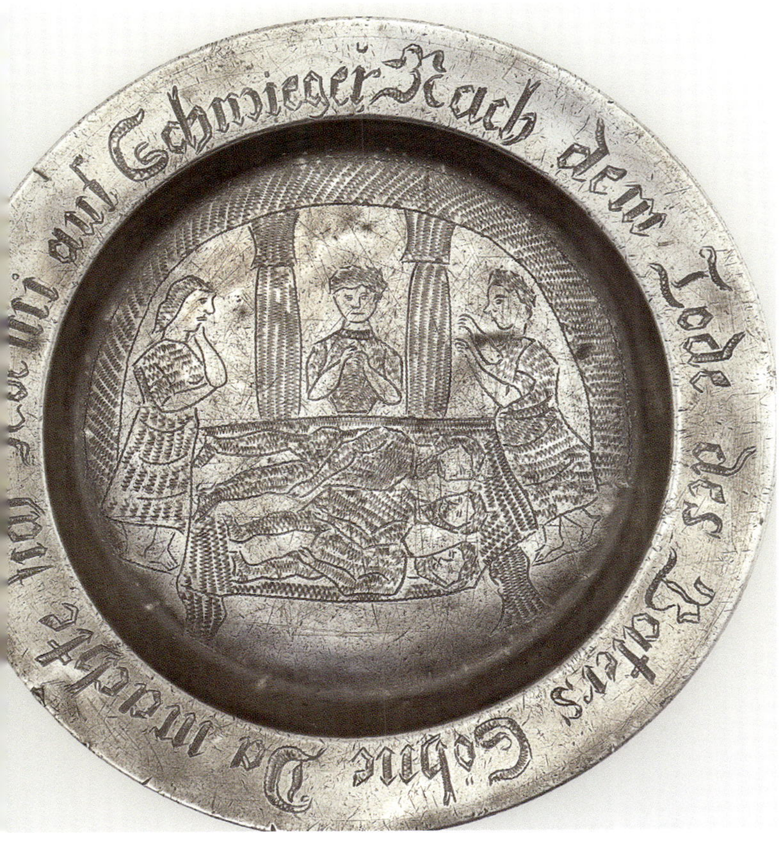

PLATE

Material: Pewter
Origin: Germany, nineteenth century
Dimensions: 9"

Naomi, Orpah, and Ruth are shown with sad expressions above three corpses lying on a bed (their deceased husbands).

On the rim in German: "Naomi lost her children and husband,." (paraphrase of Ruth 1:5).

PLATE

Material: *Pewter*
Origin: *Germany, nineteenth century*
Dimensions: *9"*

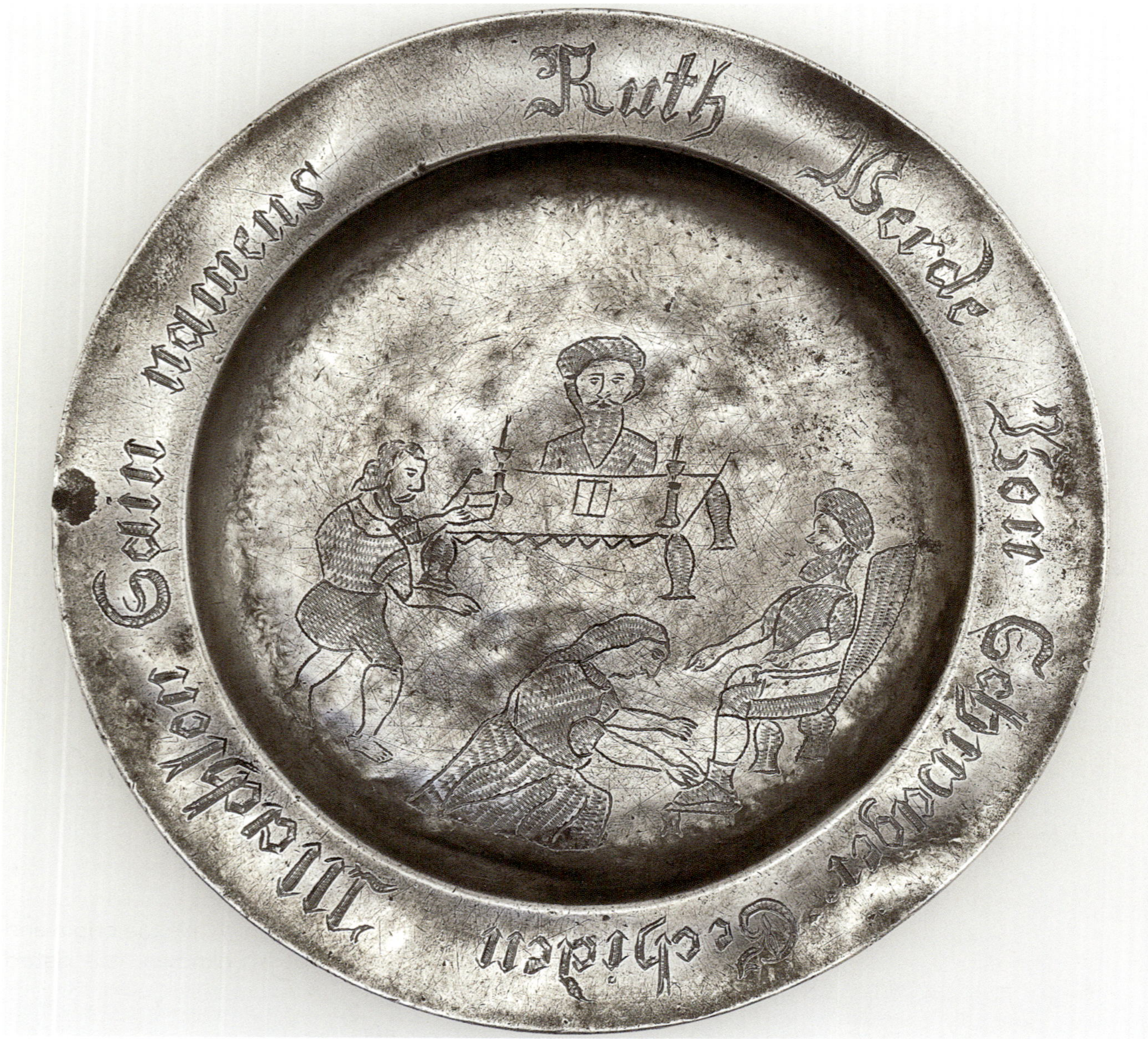

Rabbi at table oversees the *halitzah* ceremony as a woman removes her brother-in-law's shoe.

On the rim in German: paraphrase of Ruth 1:5.

This plate is very interesting, as this scene, while alluded to in the text, did not actually occur, since Ruth was redeemed by her husband's relative Boaz and therefore did not require *halitzah*.

Origin: Alsace, France, eighteenth century
Medium: Oil on Wood Panel
Artist: Unknown
Dimensions: 6.25" x 9.75"

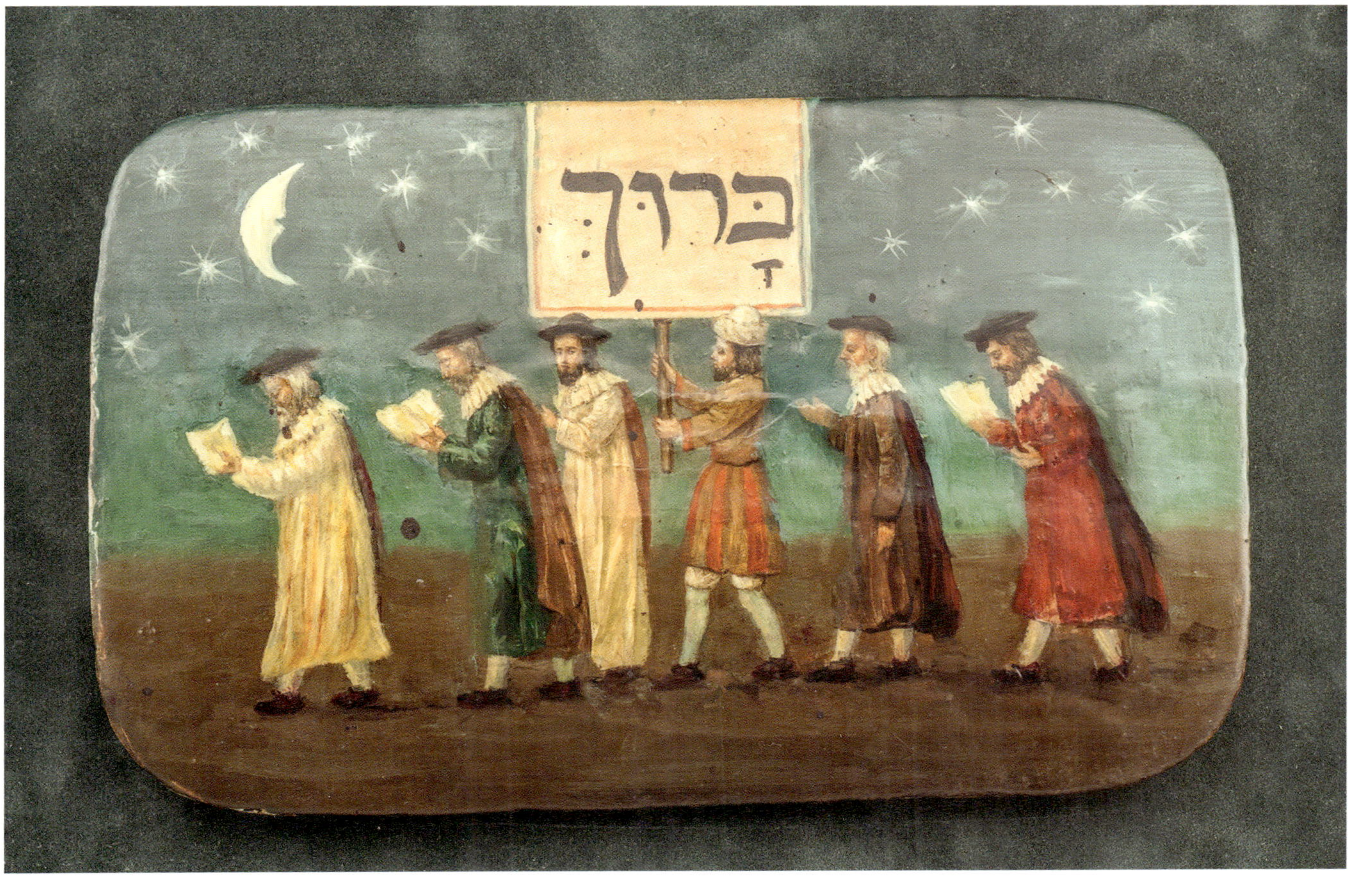

This painting shows the ritual of *Kiddush Levana* (Sanctification of the Moon), which is done on the first day of every month in the Hebrew calendar, marked by the appearance of the New Moon. The figure in the center holds a banner with the word *"Baruch"* (Blessing).

It is the high level of artistry that leads me to believe this originates from Alsace. It has that certain *je ne sais quoi* that those immersed in the field of antique Judaica have come to recognize as a particularly sophisticated level of craftsmanship that so many Jewish items from Alsace have, which makes them relatively easy to identify as hailing from this region in Europe.

An identically configured *Kiddush Levana* scene can be seen in an illustrated manuscript in the collection of The Jewish Museum of Budapest. There, the male figures are simply rendered and drawn in a naive manner, as opposed to the highly detailed, lifelike men depicted in this painting. While the origin and artist of that manuscript is unknown, it is dated 1763. It is likely that the manuscript illustration and this painting are copies of an older work that was well known in European Jewish artist circles of the eighteenth century. That older work is apparently now lost.

At first glance, the condition of my painting appears remarkably well preserved; however, when inspected under UV light, it is apparent there was a severe crack in the center of the wood and subsequent restoration has occurred, including touch-ups to the paint of the damaged area, as well as a coating of varnish over the entire piece. Nevertheless, it stands as a noteworthy survivor of a very old painting with Judaic subject matter.

PAINTING

Medium: Oil on Canvas
Origin: Europe, 1918
Artist: Attributed to Mane Katz
Identifying Marks: On reverse: "No. 123 / 1918 / S.I. Goldern", "'Rabbiner', M. Katz"
Dimensions: 14.1" x 16"

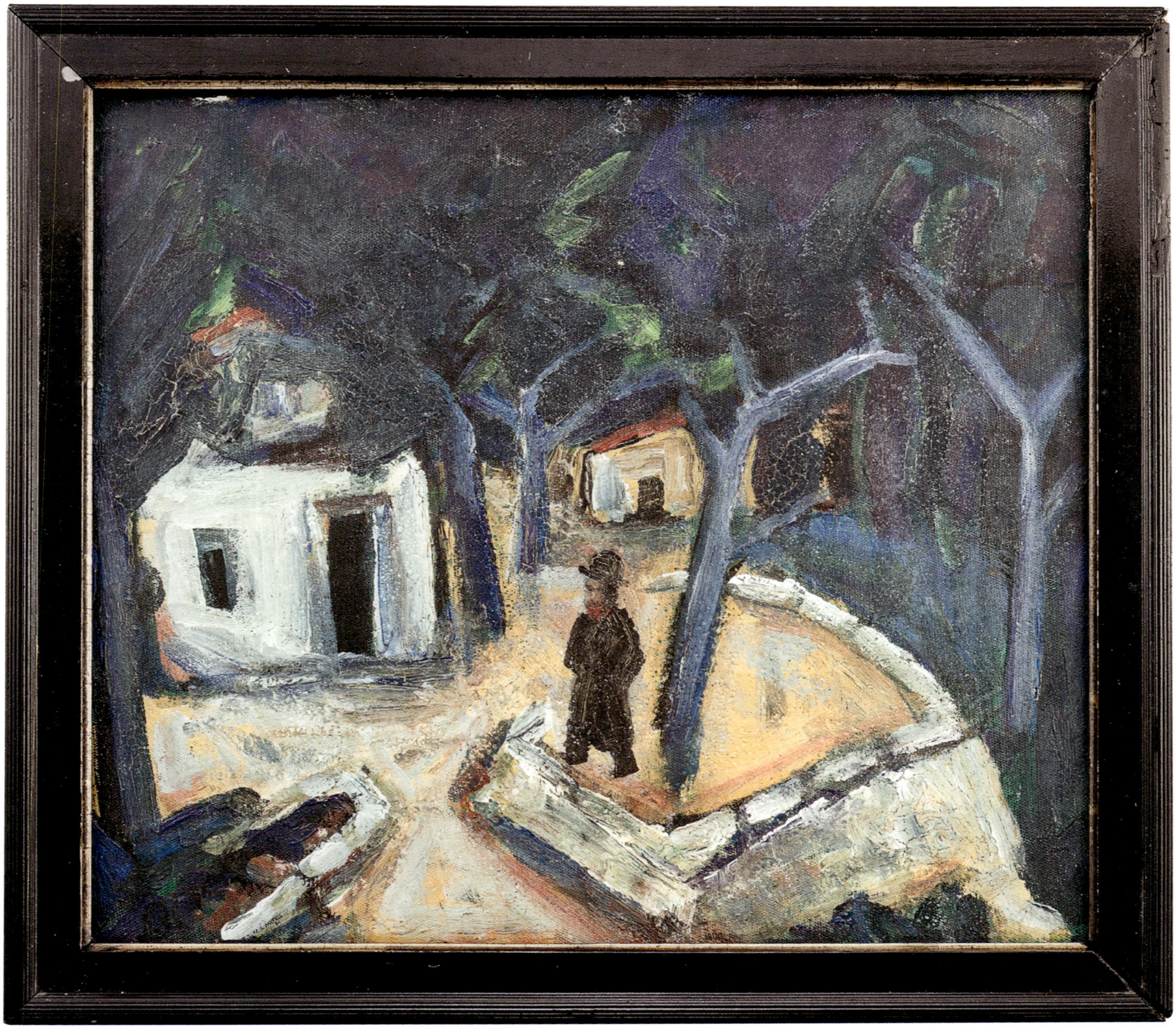

The field of collecting paintings by listed artists is very different from collecting antique objects. With the vast majority of objects, their origin and approximate age can be determined in a variety of ways, including wear, craftsmanship, and material. For the most part, reproductions and forgeries of antique objects can be spotted when handled by competent museum or auction house employees who have years of training and experience in handling objects similar or identical to those which the maker of the forgery is trying to pass itself off as. When presented with a painting, though, the question of provenance is first and foremost and is demanded when dealing with a noteworthy artist. Only after the area of provenance is taken into account are examinations of the composition, signature, and materials undertaken.

Mane Katz is one of the most famous painters of Jewish subject matter of the twentieth century; his works are held in high regard in both museums and private collections. In 1970, a two volume set of all the known works of Mane Katz was published in England. Compilations such as this, called a *catalog raisonné*, are the result of the author of these books doing exhaustive research, tracking down hundreds of paintings held in museums and collections worldwide. Paintings that appear on the market that purport to be from an artist but are not listed in such a catalog, if it exists, are held to a high level of suspicion. As you may have guessed, this painting is not in the *catalog raisonné* of Mane Katz.

I bought this painting at an auction house in Germany as part of a sale comprised of several estates. So, for all intensive purposes, this painting has no provenance to speak of. The next step is to examine the material; all art experts agree that the canvas, paint, and stretcher that were used for this painting are old. I believe the evaluation of the department head of twentieth-century paintings at a major auction house in New York said it best: "It is impossible for this to have been created after 1920, as the paint and stretcher used here were practically obsolete after that date."

From that statement alone, it would mean that this painting could indeed correlate to a date of 1918. The next step is to look at the style and examine the brush strokes. Does this painting have similarities to other known works of Mane Katz?

The red-bearded rabbi with round hat, in addition to the window and doors on the houses, are identical stylistic matches to many other paintings by Katz, as is the overall theme of the painting, which depicts a scene of Eastern European *shtetl* (Jewish town) life. The lack of a signature is not worrisome, as a number of Mane Katz paintings are unsigned. The brush strokes appear to be in his vein as well, including Katz's typical flourishes of thick impasto.

There is, however, one glaring difference between this painting and the others known; those blue trees. The trees are done in the style of "German Expressionism" that was popular for a short period during the early twentieth century. Other Mane Katz paintings do not have this strong of an influence from that movement. How can this be explained?

First, I attempted to compare this painting to other Mane Katz paintings done during this era and lo and behold, none are known! There is one painting done in 1911 by Mane Katz that is wholly unlike other works of his, which is to be expected, as he was only seventeen years old at that time and had yet to find his "voice." His next earliest known painting is from 1922 and is done in a Cubist manner. In fact, a large number of his works from the 1920s are unrecognizable to what is known today as a "Mane Katz"; many are done in a variety of styles, and can be seen as being directly influenced by artists such as Gauguin and Cezanne.

Mane Katz visited Paris in 1913, which was the center of the art world. It was there that he was exposed to a myriad of different styles of painting that were in fashion at the time, including Cubism, Fauvism, and in all likelihood, German Expressionism. Like other artists early in their careers, many of the paintings Katz did in the 1920s reflect him experimenting with the different styles of art he was exposed to in Paris and attempting to use them in his own work.

Even though I believe this is probably, if not certainly, an early work by Mane Katz, the lack of provenance and the absence of this painting from the *catalog raisonné* present a problem for me in the "art world." Of the ten or so experts I have shown this to, it has been a 50/50 split in opinion; some agree with me that this is a Mane Katz, others do not. Regardless of what the "experts" say, I enjoy having this *shtetl*-themed painting in my collection.

CHARITY BOXES

Materials: Tin / Brass and leather / Tin
Origin: USA, 1915 / Germany, circa 1930 / England, circa 1915
Identifying Marks: "Am. Can. Co. 70-A 12-15" / "John J. Moser Berlin" / "Tree of Life College, Thrawl St., London"
Dimensions: 4" x 3" / 4.6" x 3" / 4.75" x 3.4"

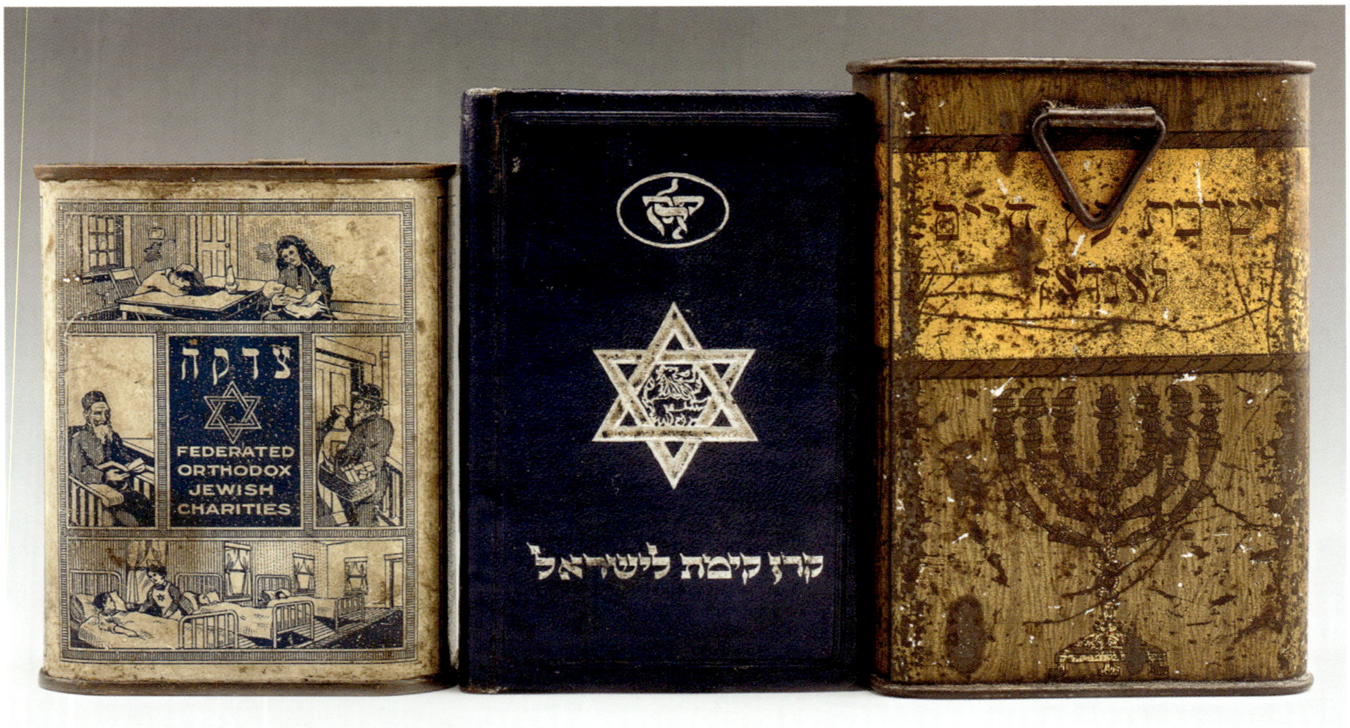

The Federated Orthodox Jewish Charities, founded in 1911 and based in Chicago, was an umbrella group for twelve different Jewish charities. The graphics on the box at left convey this message of funds being appropriated to multiple charitable organizations; on each narrow side of the box, all twelve charities are listed in English and Yiddish, including "Immediate Relief Society," "Jewish Consumptives Relief Society," "Free Burial Society," and "Shelter Home for Strangers." In 1922 the FOJC merged with Associated Jewish Charities and from then on was known as Jewish Charities of Chicago.

The Jewish National Fund, established in 1902 and continuing to operate today, is for Israel. Jewish children all over the world have been collecting for the JNF since its inception; most Jews in the United States are familiar with the tin "Blue Box," in which funds are collected at home, synagogue, and Hebrew school. This box is an example from Germany, which up until World War II, was a leader in donations to the JNF from countries that had significant Jewish populations. Instead of a cheaply made tin box, this box is heavy brass encased in blue leather. It resembles a book and has a round hole on the underside so bills can be rolled in. The side shown here has the monogram of the JNF in Hebrew inside a circle, a Star of David with a lion inside it, and "Jewish National Fund" at bottom. The other side has a map of Israel.

The last box, at right, is for Yeshiva Etz Chaim, a Rabbinical college established in 1903 in England, marking the first Yeshiva that opened in England. It depicts a facsimile of the Temple Menorah from an ancient ruin. This seemingly odd choice of imagery on a charity box may be explained by widely publicized discoveries of ancient sites in the Middle East by archaeologists at the turn of the twentieth century.

Material: Tin
Origin: USA, 1920s-30s
Dimensions: 3.1" x 3.3"

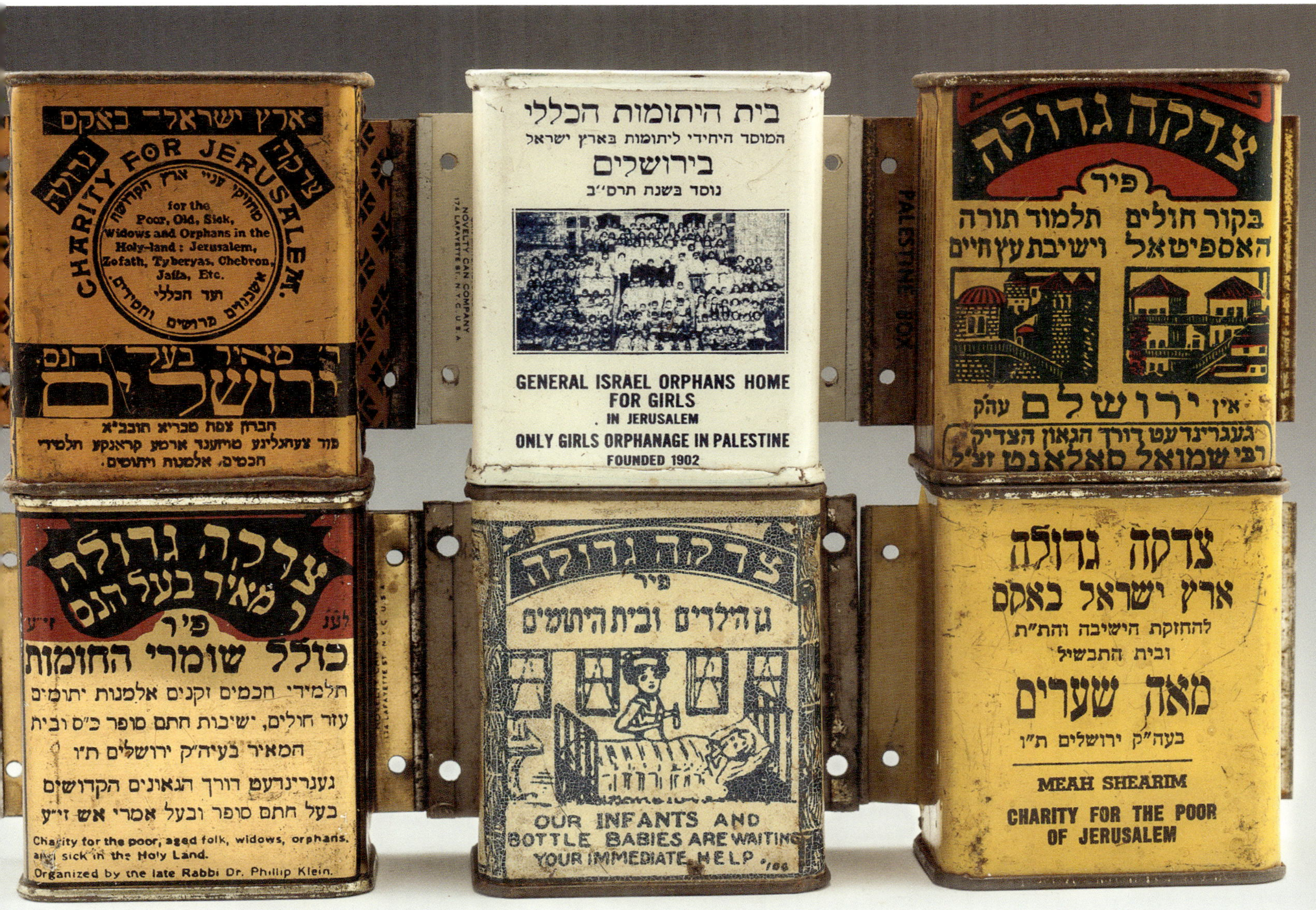

CHARITY BOX

Material: Silver
Origin: USA, circa 1925
Hallmarks: "Sterling," monogram of the Henckel company
Dimensions: 3" x 2.25"

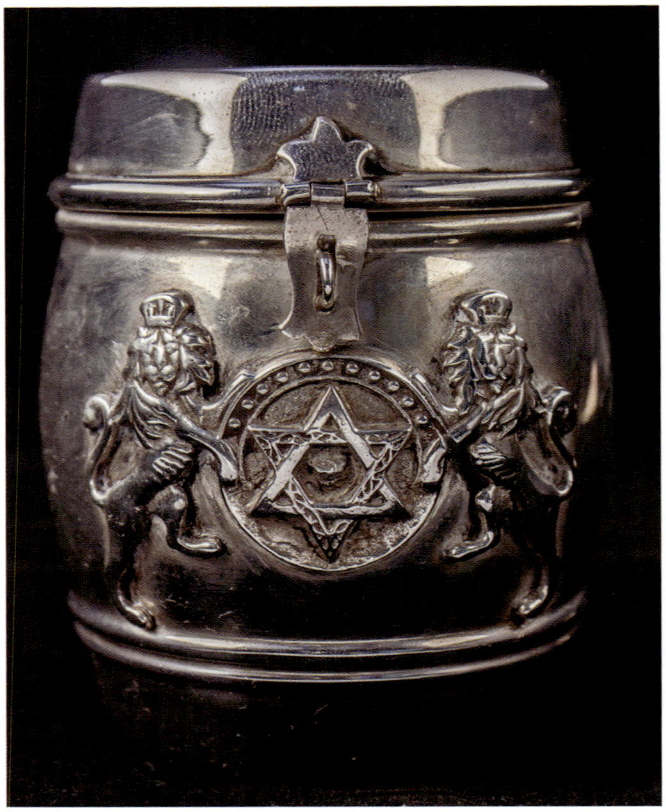

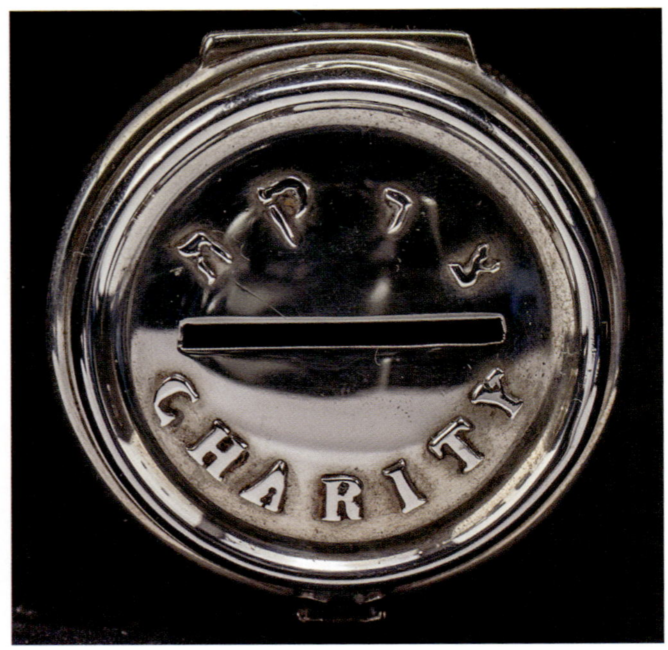

With the exception of the tin can pictured at bottom center of the photo showing six tin cans, these charities were for the poor of Jerusalem. They were made to be hung on the wall of a home or institution.

The George A. Henckel company was a silver workshop operating in New York City beginning in 1909, whose hallmark ceased to be used by 1940, as it was absorbed into another company. The barrel shaped box was made by the Henckel firm, but it is unlikely the decoration was done by them. Normally it would be worrisome to find Jewish-themed appliqué on what was originally a secular piece, but the style and manner in which the ornamentation was executed here is in perfect keeping with typical American Judaica design of the 1920s; in particular, the crowned Lions of Judah holding the Star of David are exactly how they should be from this region and era.

A likely scenario in the creation of this piece was that someone wanted a charity box made, either for a child (due to its small size), or for adult use, where it was placed next to the Sabbath candlesticks, so charity could be given right before the lighting of the candles Friday at sundown. Someone during the 1920s bought a silver barrel-shaped box with lid, latch, and slot (of whose original purpose was that of a still bank) and hired a skilled New York silversmith of the era to add Judaic elements so it could be transformed into a charity box.

PASSOVER

SEDER TRAY

Material: Pewter
Origin: Germany, 1774-1775
Artist: "Schulberr"
Dimensions: 14"

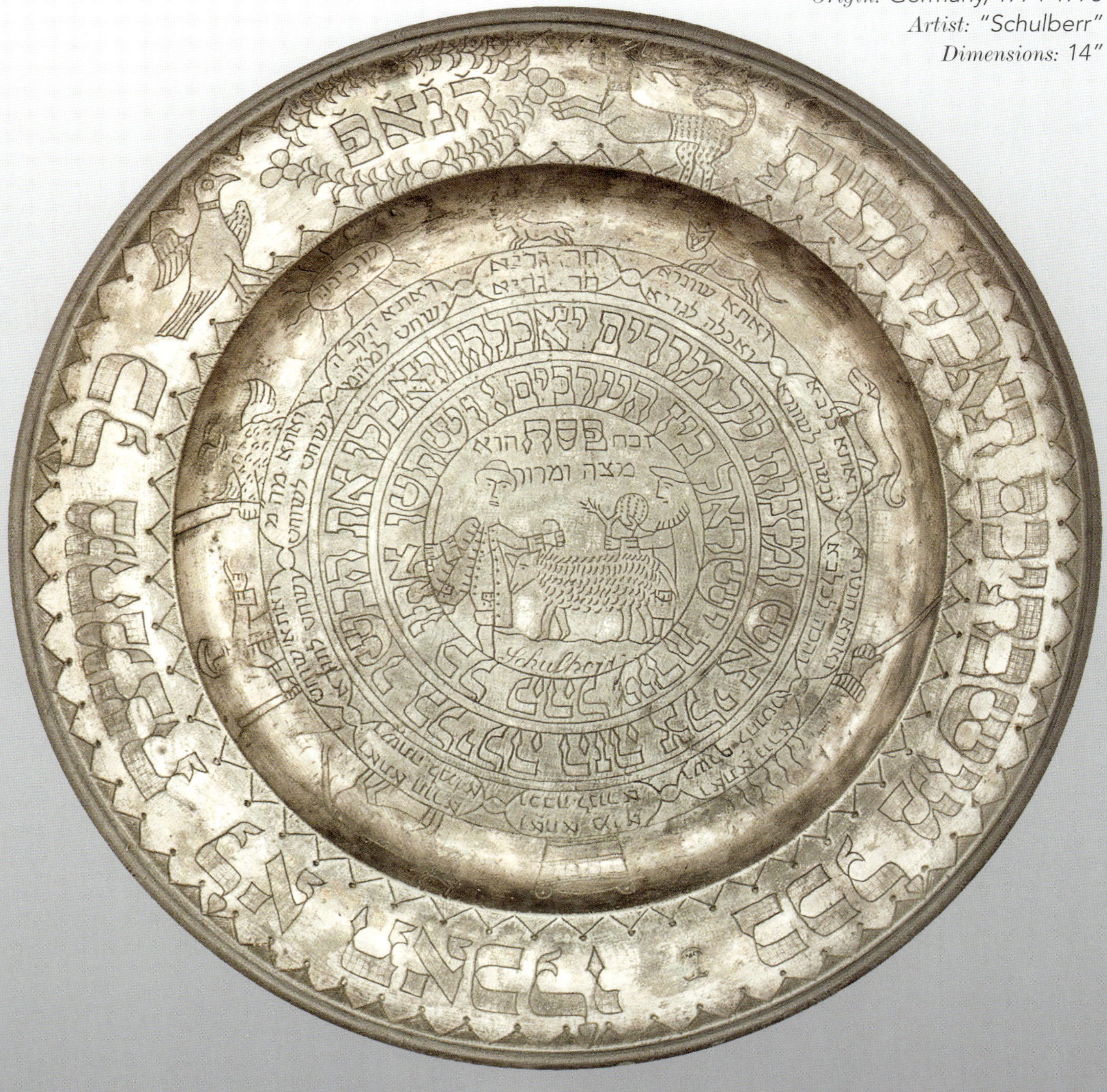

As with the pewter plates pictured and described previously, this plate was engraved by a professional artisan. Pewter Passover plates decorated by these skilled engravers can vary in terms of quality; some plates might be simple, having the word "Passover" in the center of the plate and the order of the Seder on the rim. Finer still are plates with these elements along with a pictorial scene copied from a *Haggadah*. The quality of these plates can reach even higher, having elaborate decoration, until the entire plate is filled with Hebrew verses and scenes relating to Passover; the best of these plates combine an excellent balance between calligraphic and pictorial decoration. Between approximately 1750 and 1800 is when these "high end" types of Passover plates were engraved by independent artisans or those employed in workshops.

The plate featured on these pages is a "high end" piece. The outer rim has the verse "You must not eat anything leavened. In all the areas where you live, eat matzahs," (Exodus 12:20). A deer and bird flank two sets of initials, which likely represent that of a husband and wife, the owners of this plate. The inner rim has the Passover rhyme "*Chad Gadya*" ("One Little Goat") depicted, with the goat, cat, dog, stick, fire, water, ox, butcher, Angel of Death and G-d himself, represented by the word "*Shechinah*" (Divine Spirit) inside a circle with rays emanating from it. Under each illustration is the beginning of that particular verse. Then, these two verses: "The entire community of Israel shall then slaughter (their sacrifices) in the afternoon"; "Eat the [sacrificial] meat during the night, roasted over fire. Eat it with matzah and bitter herbs," (Exodus 12: 6-8). In the center it shows two men: The one on the right is in the traditional synagogue dress of eighteenth-century German Jews, which was a flat round hat, sleeveless gown, and frilled collar. Next to him is written: "Matzah, Bitter Herbs," as that is what he is holding in each hand. The man on the left holds a lamb (representing the Paschal lamb) by a leash in one hand, and a butchers knife in the other. Above both men it reads: "The Passover service," (Exodus 12:27). The engraver of this piece signs his name in cursive English script "Schulberr," underneath the lamb.

This should be the conclusion of the decoration of this plate. Incredibly, the reverse is engraved as well. The rim has the verse: "From the 14th day of the first month in the evening, until the night of the 21st day of the month, you must eat [only] matzahs," (Exodus 12:18). In the center, it says in a mixture of Hebrew and German: "This is a wedding gift from the cantor" ("einwarf" is old German for "wedding gift"), and then "in order of the small counting." This last statement is an indication to add up the numerical value of the Hebrew letters from "This is a wedding gift..." to discover the Hebrew year of the wedding, which when tallied equals the period between September 1774 and September 1775.

Shown is a close up of one the letters on the rim. Notice the level of workmanship in the letter. This style of engraving is known as cross hatching or basket weaving. All the rim letters engraved on both the obverse and reverse of the plate were executed in this high standard. The amount of labor put into decorating this plate is staggering, as to complete just one of those Hebrew letters would take about an hour.

There are probably a few hundred pewter Passover plates scattered across the globe in museums and private collections, perhaps even as much as a thousand. This is the only pewter Passover plate known where the reverse side has been engraved.

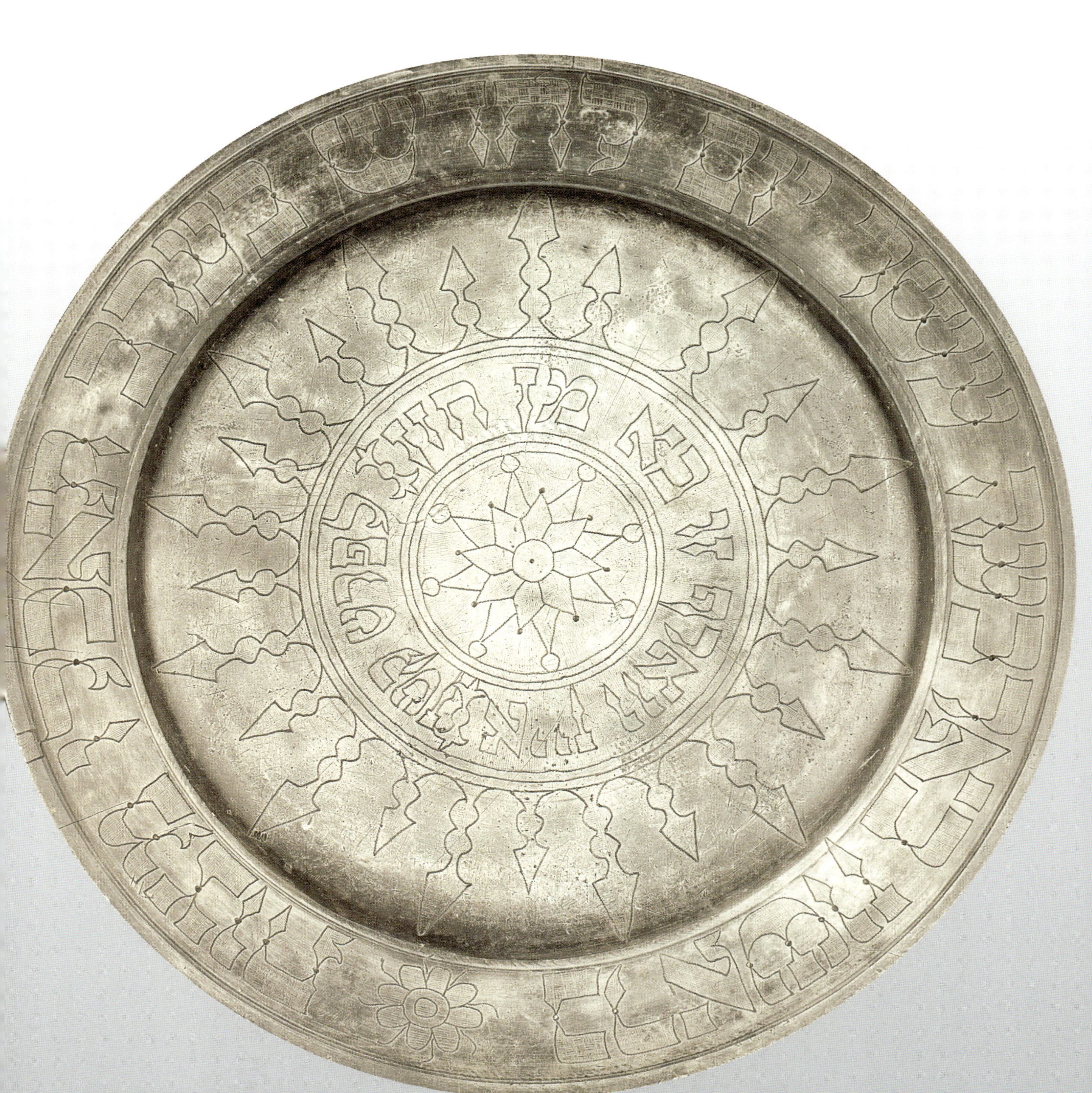

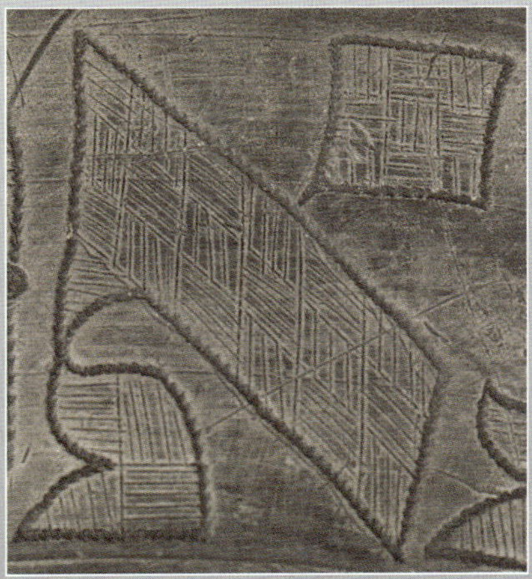

SEDER TRAY

Material: Pewter
Origin: Austrian-controlled Bohemia (Czech Republic), eighteenth century
Dimensions: 12"

The quality of the engraving on this piece is average at best. It was mostly likely "home decorated." The plate has the order of the Seder on the rim and the phrase "Passover Matzah Bitter Herbs" in the center of a two-headed bird (looking more like a chicken than the eagle it is supposed to represent), along with two sets of initials (or possibly the date, as the letters correlate to 1750-1751; however, it is an aberrant way of displaying a Hebrew date).

At first glance, this plate appears quite ordinary. The double-headed eagle was the crest of a number of European countries and is found on many examples of antique pewter Passover plates, as some Jewish engravers liked to show loyalty to their respective country by including its national crest as a decorative motif on the object. However, upon closer inspection, it can be deduced that the engraver of this plate was an especially religious Jew.

The crest of the Austrian Empire was a double-headed eagle; its left claw grasped a sword, its right held a scepter, and atop the eagle's head was a crown. Here, however, the scepter and crown are transformed into flowers, leaving only the left claw accurate, holding the sword. Why this curious change?

Symbolism is the answer. The scepter in the right claw is supposed to be topped by a Christian cross. With other pewter Passover plates engraved with the double-headed eagle that reside in the collections of the Jewish museums of London and Budapest, this conflict was resolved by a nondescript staff in the right claw, but even that was deemed too literal for this artisan, so he made the scepter into a flower. As for the crown, it's obvious: There is only one crown for one king and that king is certainly not the human ruler of a plot of land, but G-d himself, *the* King. So, the crown is turned into a flower as well.

The engraver of this plate must have been pleased with himself, as his patriotism was kept intact without sacrificing the commitment to his faith.

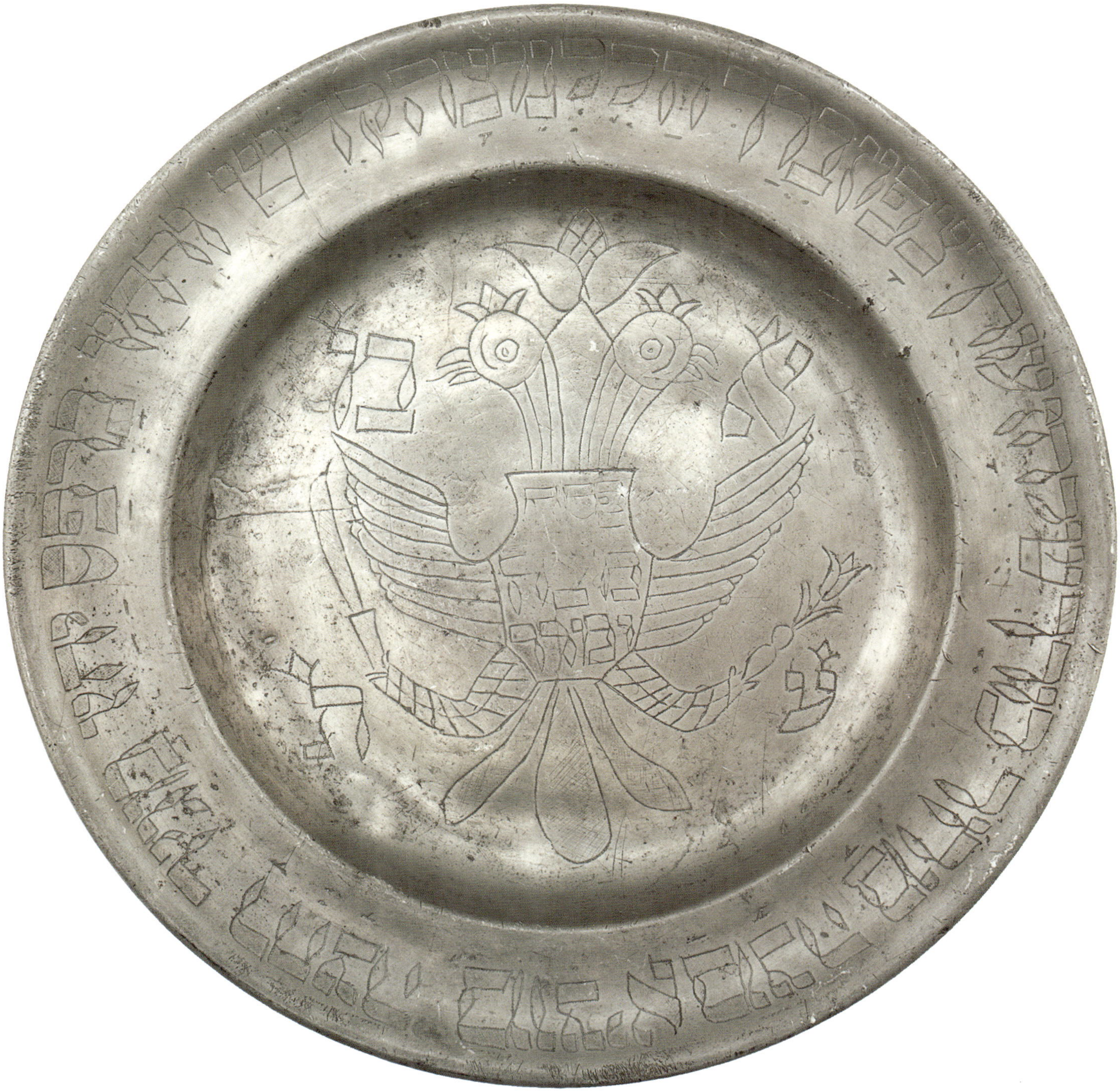

SEDER TRAY

Material: Copper
Origin: Austro-Hungarian Empire, circa 1890
Hallmarks: "BD," Diana head
Dimensions: 12.25"

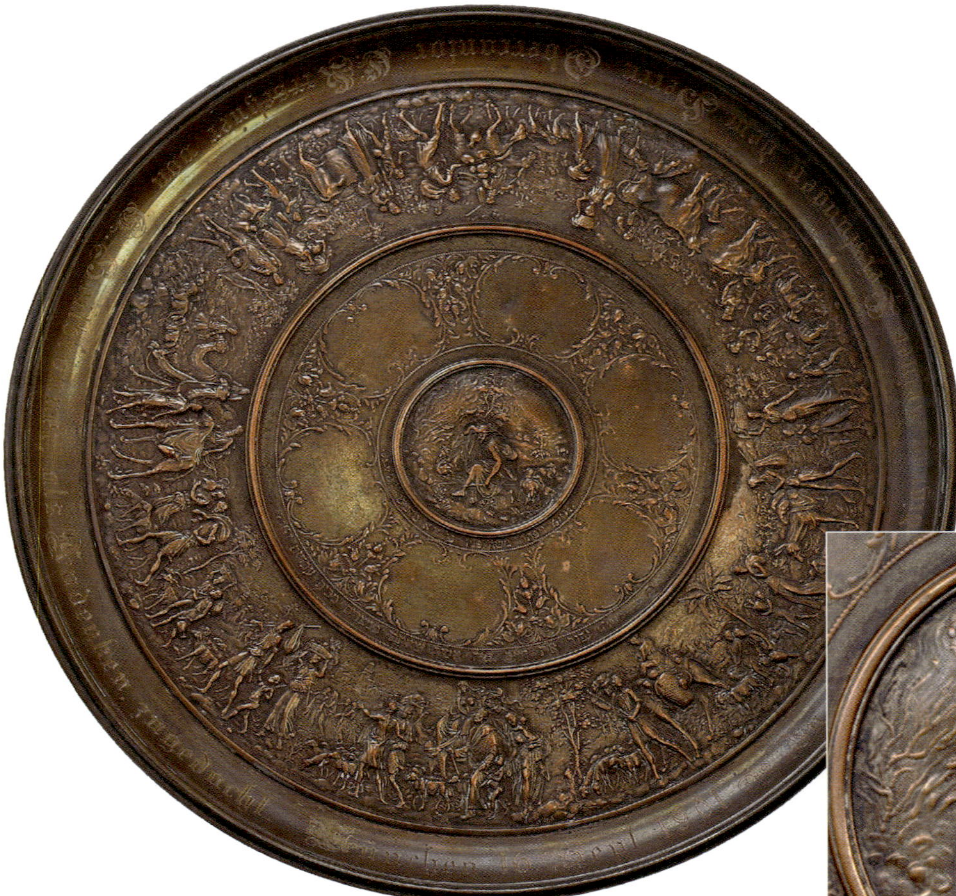

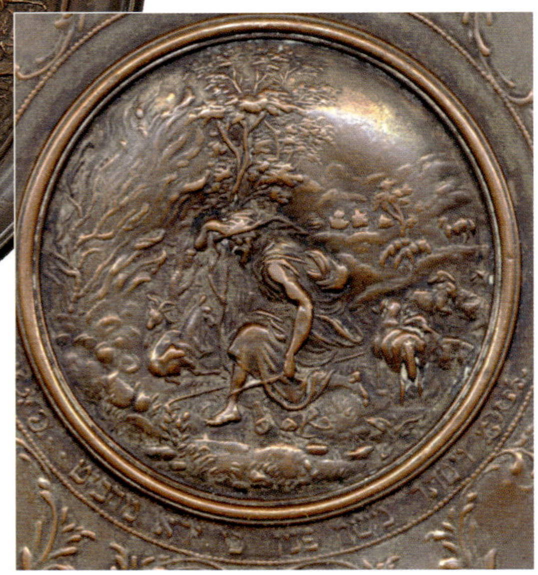

This Seder tray is a prime example of the high level of design and production many Central European Jews desired in the creation of their ritual items during the nineteenth and early twentieth centuries. When high end manufacturing occurs, what follows is the adaptation of the latest fashions of the time. This tray, with its beading, palmettes, and other restrained foliate borders, indicates it was designed in the style of Grecian Revival, which was popular in the decorative arts of Europe during the second half of the nineteenth century. It is expertly manufactured, likely using the method of electroplating.

The center of the tray has Moses kneeling by the burning bush and underneath him is the Hebrew verse: "Moses hid his face, since he was afraid to look," (Exodus 3:6). Then there are six spaces for the ritual foods, and underneath them: "Remember this day as [the time] you left Egypt, the place of slavery," (Exodus 12:3).

The outer rim depicts the exodus from Egypt; men, women and children are clutching belongings, riding camels, and prodding livestock along.

There is an engraved presentation on the rim in German to Emanuel Kirschner, the last chief cantor of the main synagogue of Munich before the Second World War began. He was also a preeminent composer of religious music in prewar Germany. The presentation is dated September 16, 1901.

Material: Copper
Origin: Jerusalem, Israel circa 1935
Hallmarks: In Hebrew "Yerushalem" (Jerusalem), large letter "Gimmel"
Dimensions: 16.75"

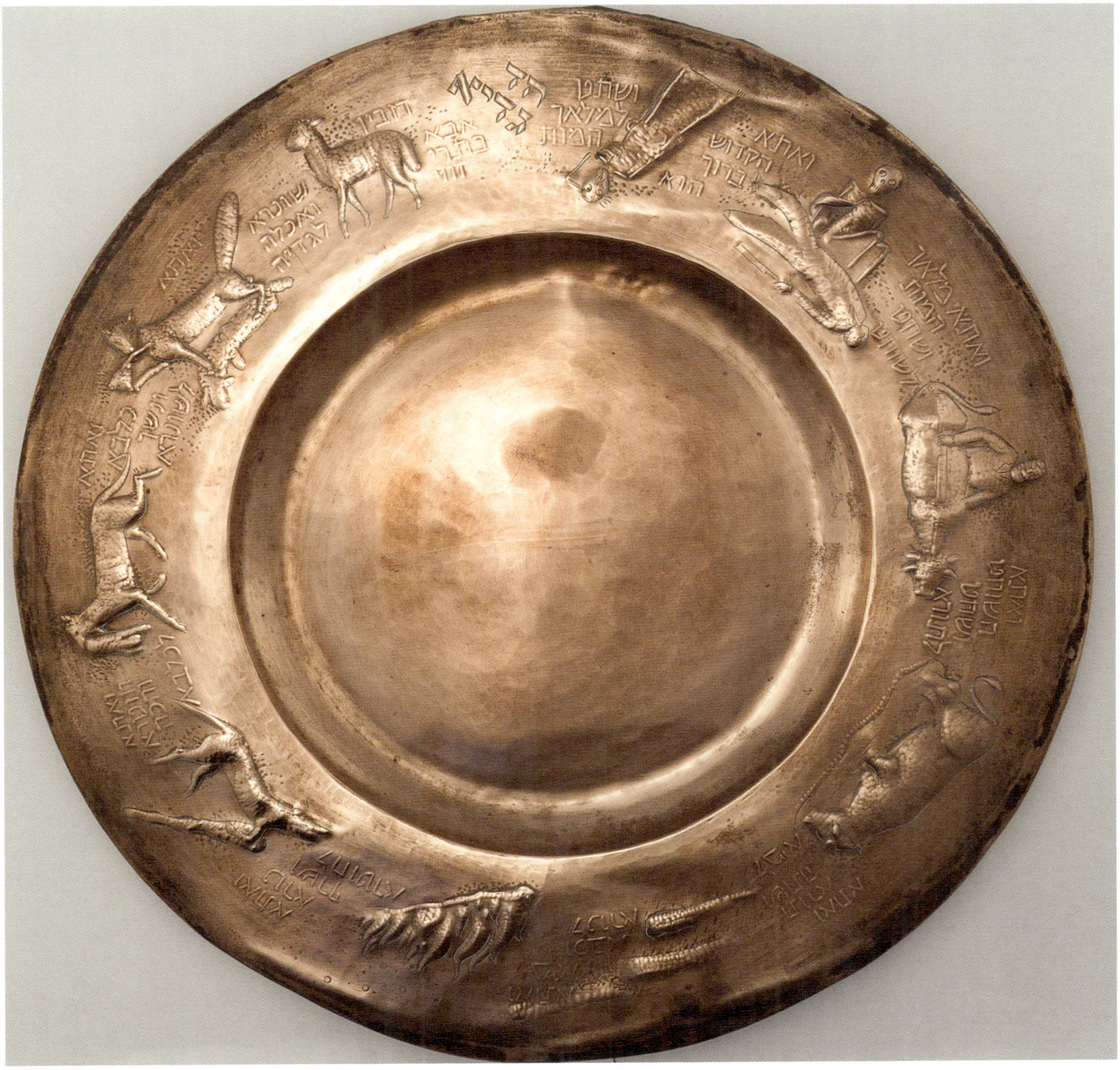

Unlike the previous Seder trays, this plate was entirely made by hand. First, the artist hammered the copper, giving it a textured look and feel. Then, using small tools on the reverse side, the artisan slowly and carefully tapped out a design that appeared on the obverse side, in raised relief. This technique is known as *repoussé*. The wide rim has the Passover rhyme "*Chad Gadya*" ("One Little Goat") depicted, with each figure appropriately titled in Hebrew for all the characters in the rhyme.

I do not know the identity of nor am I aware of other wares from the artist or workshop that has the "Gimmel" hallmark, which is too bad, as this piece is well executed.

SEDER TRAY DISHES

Material: *Porcelain*
Origin: *Germany, nineteenth century*
Dimensions: *3"*

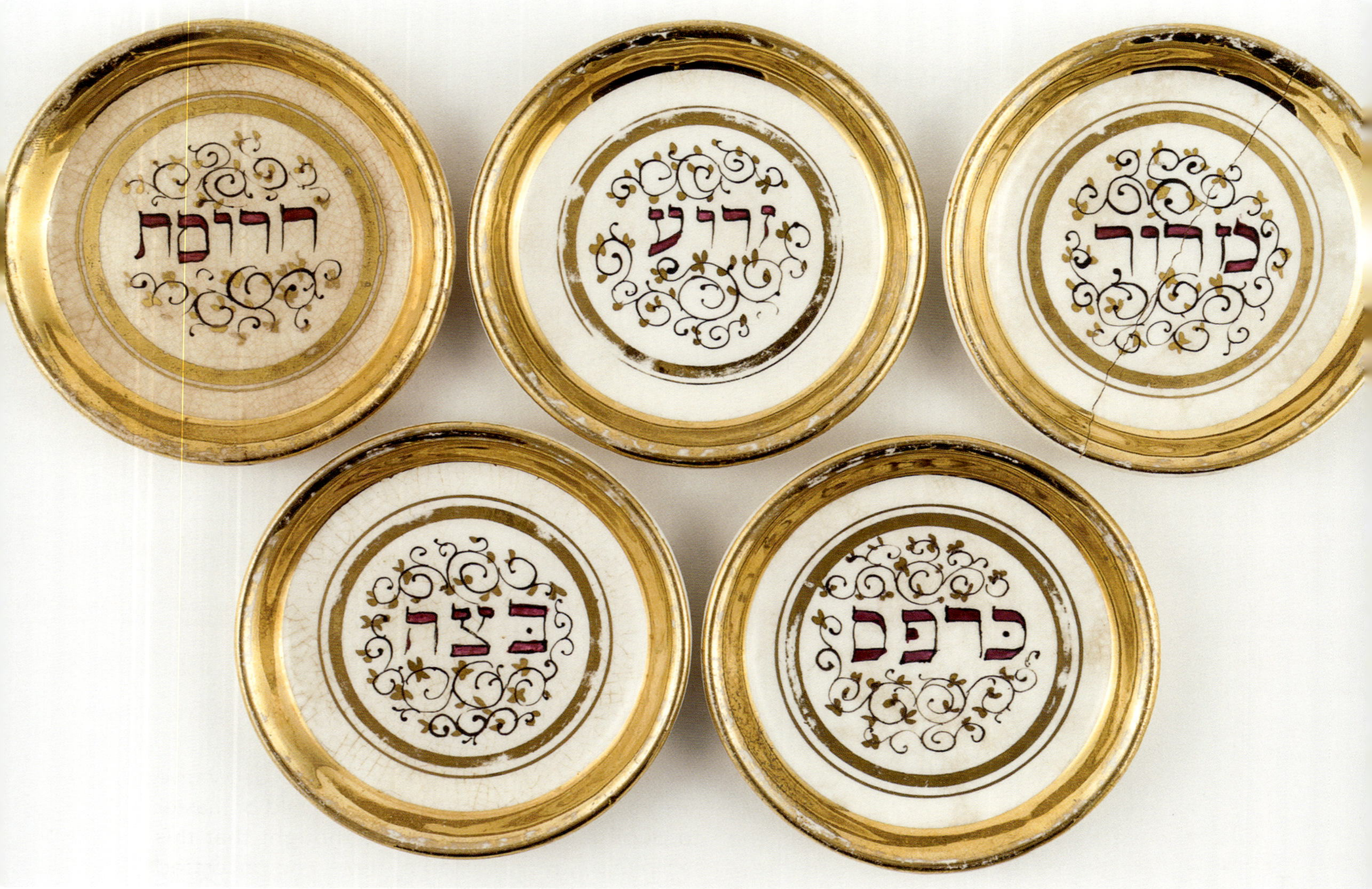

An integral part of the Passover service is the Seder tray, upon which the ceremonial foodstuffs are placed. Here, unadorned gilt porcelain dishes were painted in Hebrew, each labeled appropriately: "Bitter Herbs," "Shankbone," "Egg," "Vegetable," "The Mixture." Unfortunately, the tray itself has been lost, and only these small dishes remain.

MATZAH BAG / MATZAH COVER

Materials: *Cotton / Metallic thread on velvet*
Origin: *Hungary, circa 1900 / Eastern Europe, nineteenth century*
Dimensions: *15" x 14" / 16.25"*

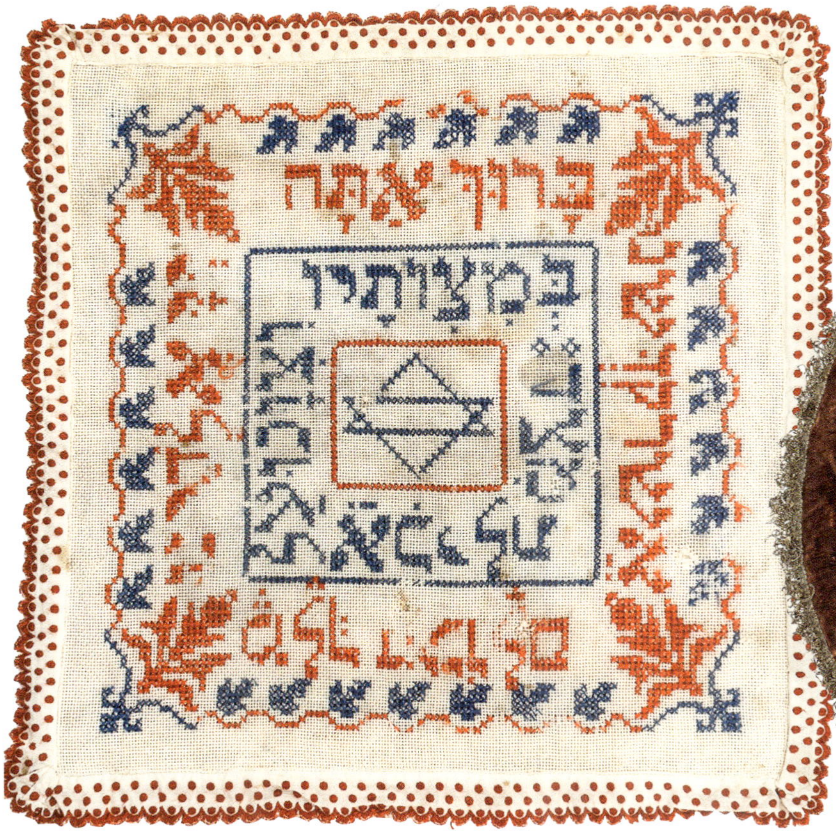

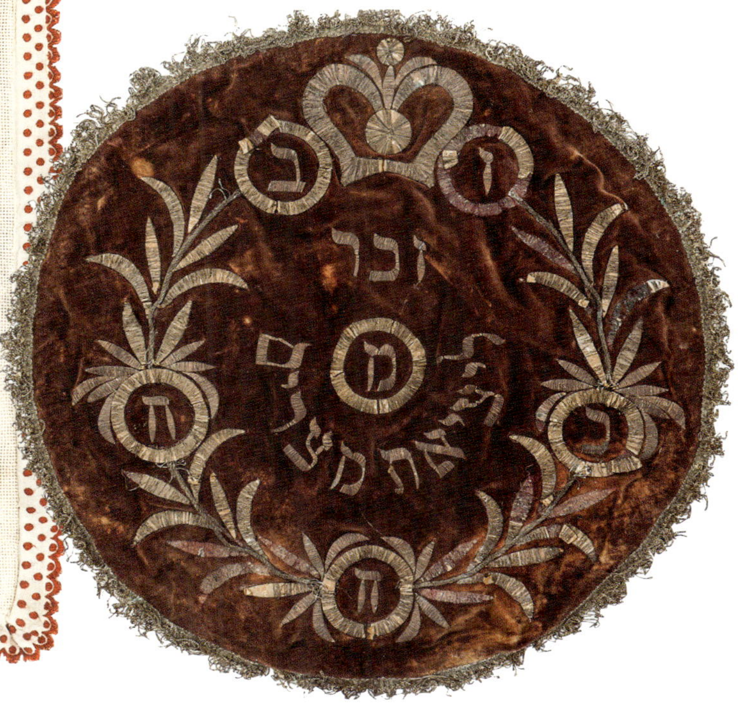

The needlepoint bag has three strips of cotton attached; each strip has a slit for insertion of one matzah for use during the Seder. The blessing over the matzah is written in Hebrew, ending in the center around a Star of David. These types of handmade matzah bags and covers were very popular in Europe; the majority of examples found are from Hungary and Romania, either in needlepoint or silk. This piece is a bit different than the norm, as the design motif of a Star of David in the center is atypical.

Sewing metallic thread on material was a highly skilled craft in Europe that was exclusive to Jews and is known as *Spanier Arbeit*, Yiddish for "Spanish Handwork." This title is derived from the Jews who fled Spain during the Inquisition, who were masters of this technique. Thousands of these Spanish-Jewish refugees settled across Europe, and those who possessed this complex skill of the decorative arts passed it down from parent to child or master to pupil for generations. It is thought that this technique was originated by Jews who decorated textiles for the Second Temple, in 515 BCE.

Generally, *Spanier Arbeit* was implemented solely on items for the synagogue, such as the Torah ark curtain. Here, however, we have a matzah cover done in this manner. The artist imitates the Seder tray, with six circles for the specific ritual foods, labeled with the first letter of that food in Hebrew. The center circle placement is for the bitter herbs and around it are the words: "Remember our exodus from Egypt." This is topped by a crown (of Torah).

Although it is difficult to ascertain the exact country of origin for this piece, the overall style is reminiscent of *Spanier Arbeit* from Poland.

SOUP TUREEN

Material: Ceramic
Origin: Strasbourg, France, circa 1790
Dimensions: 6.5" x 7.5"

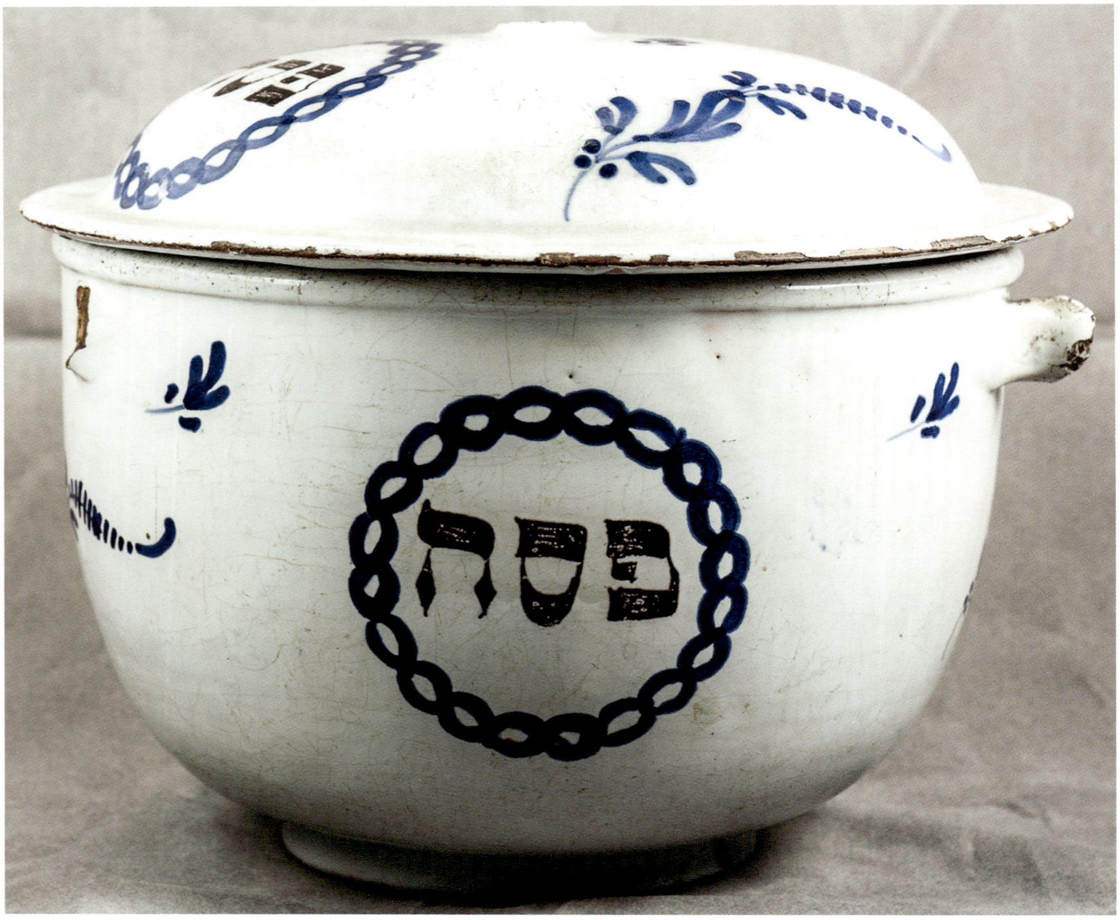

Passover is also known as the "Feast of Unleavened Bread." Due to the frantic nature of the exodus from Egypt, the Hebrews could not take the time to let their breads rise before baking. As a result, during this holiday, there are strict prohibitions against eating or owning foods with leavening or yeast, which is one of the reasons why matzah is eaten during Passover.

A special set of dishes is taken out once a year to serve meals and ensure no contamination from even the tiniest bit of bread during Passover. This tureen for soup is one of these dishes, as hand-painted in bold black Hebrew lettering is the word *Pesach* (Passover), both on the lid and the bowl.

This tureen, made of fine tin-glazed pottery known as faience, is an example of the mass-produced faience ware made in Strasbourg during the eighteenth and early part of the nineteenth centuries. Strasbourg is the capital and principal city of the Alsace region in northeastern France, consequently many Alsatian-Jewish families owned these white bodied dishes with blue floral motifs having the word *Pesach,* to be used only during Passover. The Hebrew lettering was done at the same time that the lid and bowl were painted, as it is underneath the translucent glaze.

Despite the fact that the condition of this piece has much to be desired, it is a rare, if not sole survivor of this type of tableware, as even though plates and bowls of this well-known French-Jewish model exist today in substantial numbers, I am not aware of another tureen aside from this example.

SALT WATER CONTAINER AND SPOON

Material: Porcelain
Origin: USA, circa 1925
Hallmarks: "3H.4667/H.B" (tureen) / harp with Star of David (spoon)
Dimensions: 6.2" x 3.5" / 1.5" x 7.5"

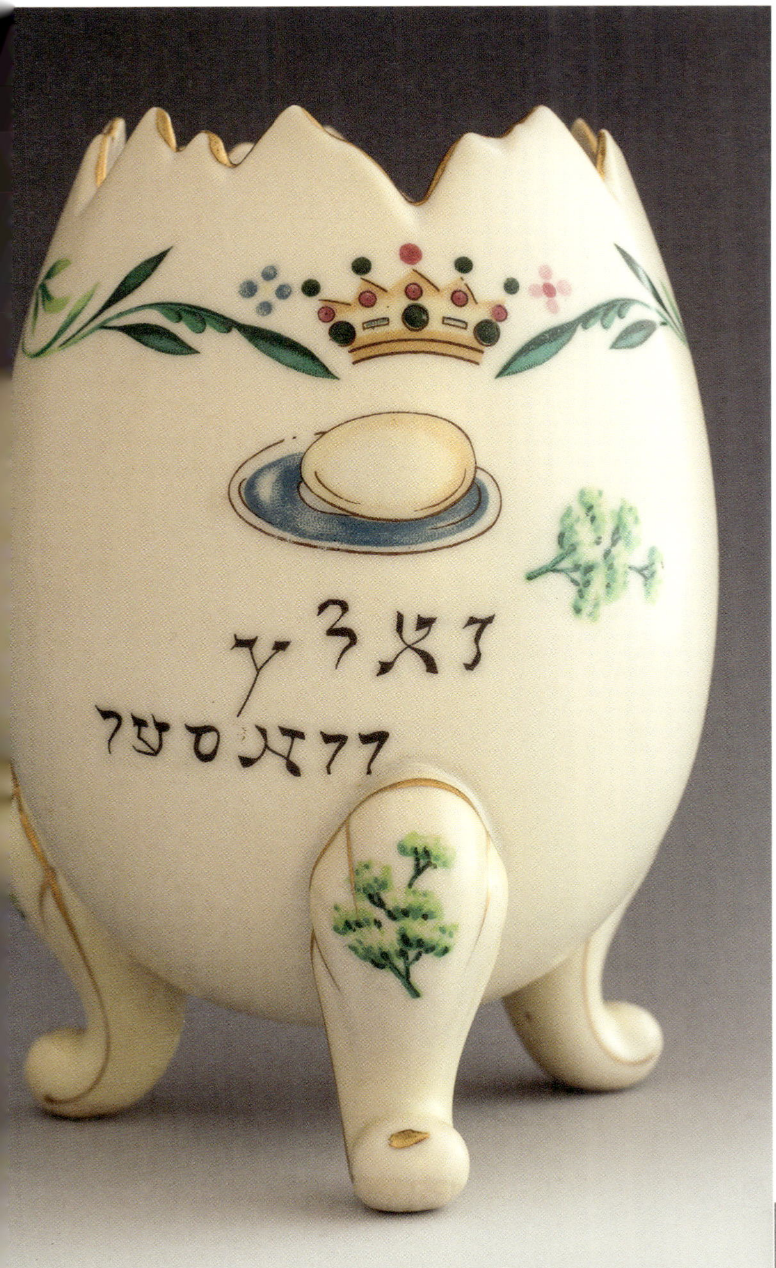

The use of salt water for the dipping of ceremonial foodstuffs is central to the Seder meal. The egg dipped in salt water is a symbol of the Temple festival offerings and of prosperity and fertility.

This salt water container is in the form of an egg resting on three feet, decorated with an egg beneath a crown, parsley, leafy stems, and the Yiddish inscription "*zalz vasser*" (salt water). The other side of the container has an open book inscribed in Hebrew: "How is this night different from all other nights?"

Apparently this set was decorated in one of two ways. The first, shown here, is in a matte glaze, and the spoon is painted and hallmarked. The other type of set has a glossy glaze, and the spoon is plain and unmarked. That other set is found quite frequently, unlike the pairing shown here. Because of the stark contrast in the numbers of pieces found between this type of set and the other one, it is possible the other set is a later version, perhaps even made during the postwar period. This is all pure speculation, however, simply based on my own experience dealing with these particular pieces.

The bowl and spoon shown here are interesting for their high level of quality, which is not the norm when encountering mass-produced items for the American-Jewish market during the early twentieth century.

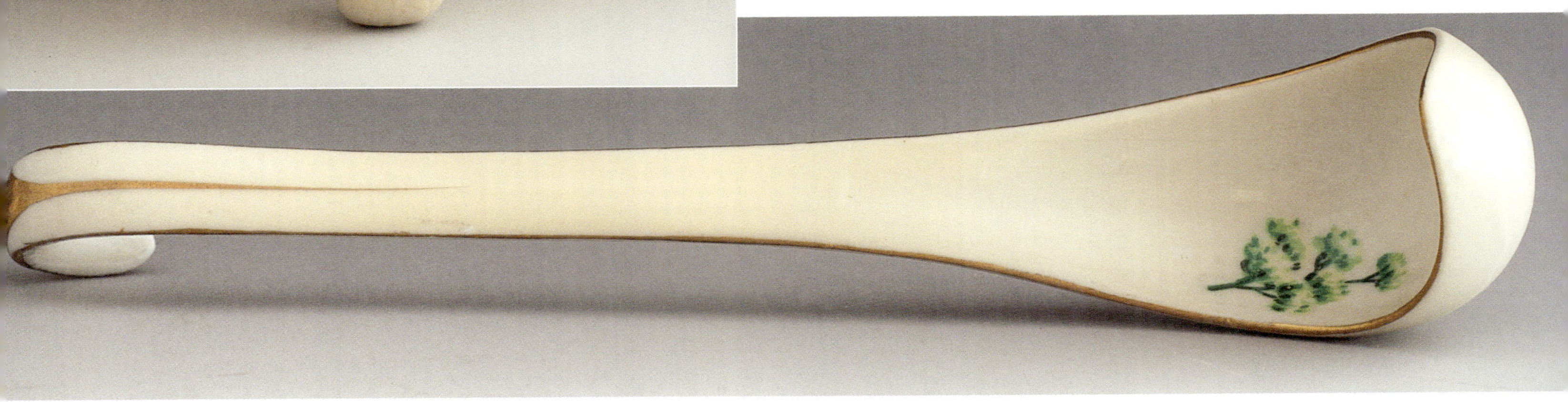

MORTAR FOR CHAROSET

Material: *Brass*
Origin: *Morocco or Israel, circa 1940*
Dimensions: *5.25" x 5.5"*

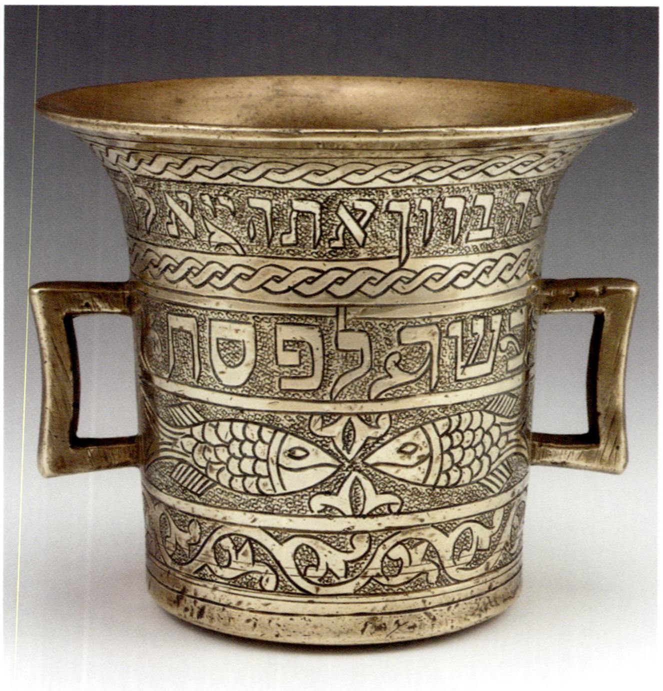

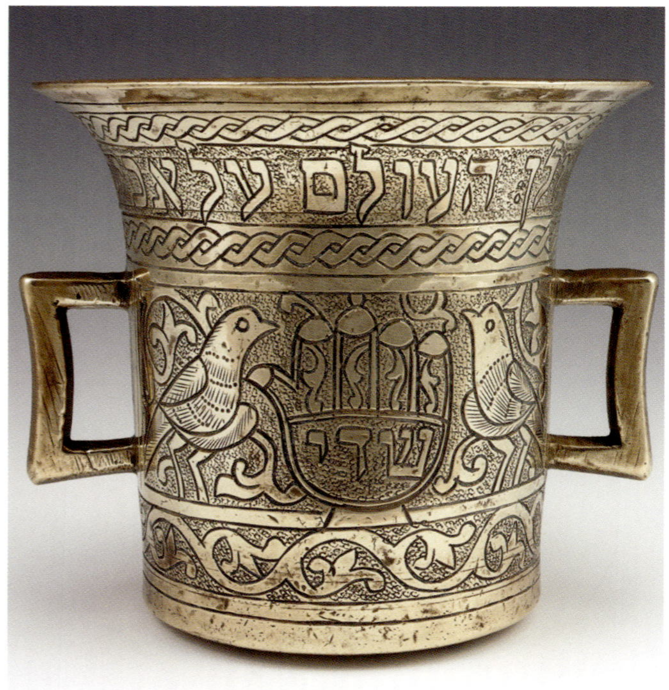

The history of using a mortar to grind and mix food or ingredients goes back thousands of years and is mentioned in the Torah: "The manna was like coriander seed with a pearl-like luster. The people could simply go for a stroll and gather it. They would then grind it in a hand-mill or crush it in a mortar, cooking it in a pan and making it into cakes," (Numbers 11:8-9).

This mortar dates to the nineteenth century. Around 1940, a Moroccan Jew residing either in Morocco or Israel chose to put it to use for Passover, to make *charoset*, and had it engraved appropriately. *Charoset* is a sweet, dark-colored, lumpy paste served during the Seder. Its color and texture recalls the mortar (no pun intended) with which the Israelites bonded bricks when they were enslaved in Egypt. A typical *charoset* is made up of nuts, apples, cinnamon, and sweet wine; ingredients mentioned by King Solomon in the Song of Songs as recalling the attributes of the Jewish people themselves.

The mortar is engraved with the blessing of the matzah by the rim (as *charoset* is eaten with matzah during the Seder meal), "Kosher for Passover" above two smiling fish, and doves flanking a *hamsa* with "*Shaddai*" in the center of it, all motifs popular with Moroccan-Jewish artists (the *hamsa* is discussed in detail on page 102).

For a mouth-watering recipe of *charoset*, go to the end of this book!

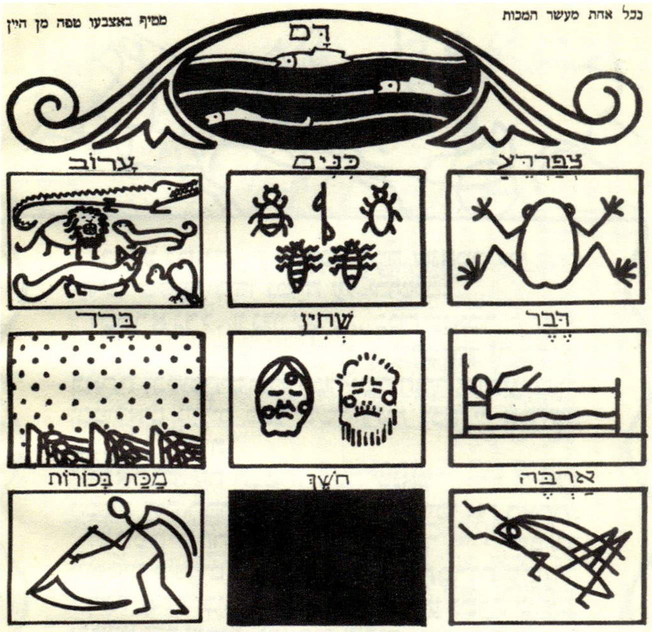

HAGGADAH

Material: Paper
Origin: Berlin, Germany 1927
Artist: Otto Geismar
Dimensions: 8.6″ x 7″

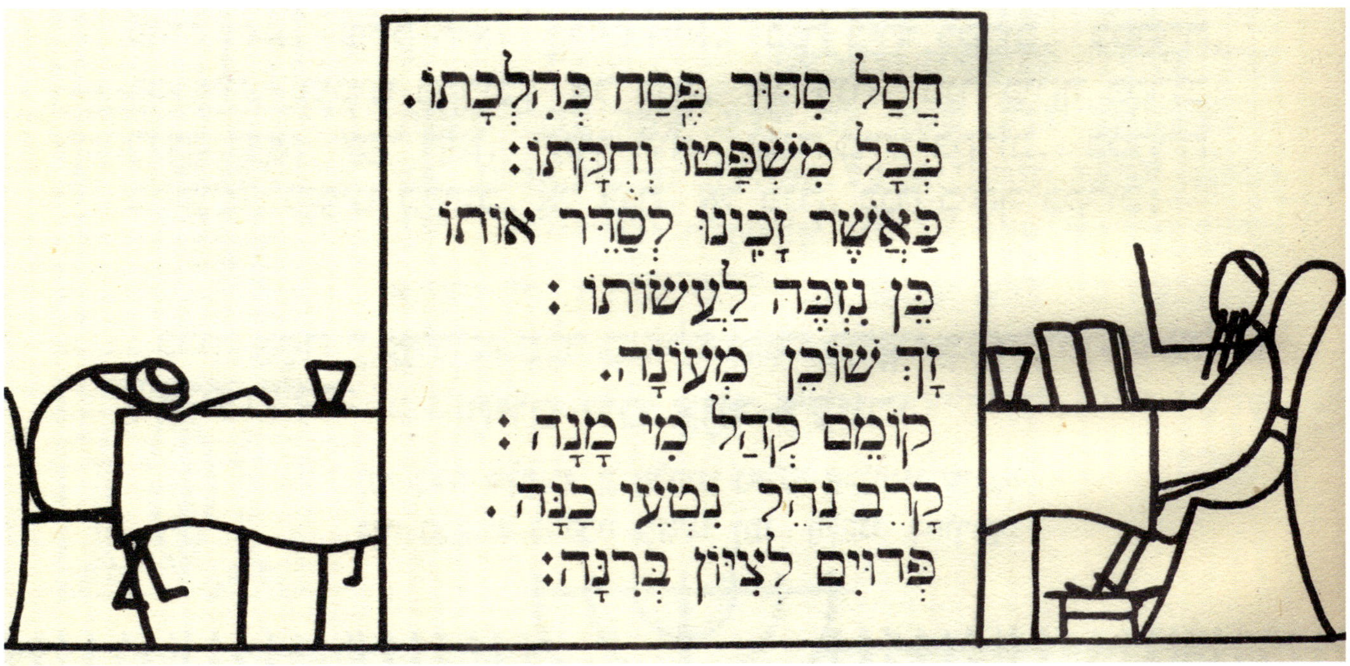

The word *Haggadah* means "telling," which is a fulfillment of the Biblical commandment from Exodus 13:8: "On that day, you must tell your child, 'It is because of this that G-d acted for me when I left Egypt.'" The Haggadah was compiled sometime between the years 200 and 500 of the Common Era; the earliest surviving example of a Haggadah is from the tenth century.

The depictions in this Haggadah were done by Otto Geismar in prewar Germany. All of his charming illustrations give the viewer a clear understanding of the specific portion of the Haggadah that is being discussed. Shown are his depictions of the Ten Plagues and the last page in the Haggadah.

Typically, the Seder service concludes well after midnight, and here Geismar shows his sense of humor; on the right is a bearded figure with skullcap, his arm lifted as if he is reading aloud, while at the other end of the table another man has his back bent, his head resting on his arm, apparently asleep due to the late hour.

These minimalist stick figures by Otto Geismar are ahead of their time, and came sixty years before similarly conceived figural depictions were done by the artist Keith Haring, who would achieve worldwide acclaim for his works.

CHANUKAH

CHANUKAH MENORAHS

Material: *Brass*
Origin: *Galicia or Ukraine, circa 1880 / Galicia or Ukraine, circa 1915*
Dimensions: *5.5" x 5.75" / 6.5" x 6.25"*

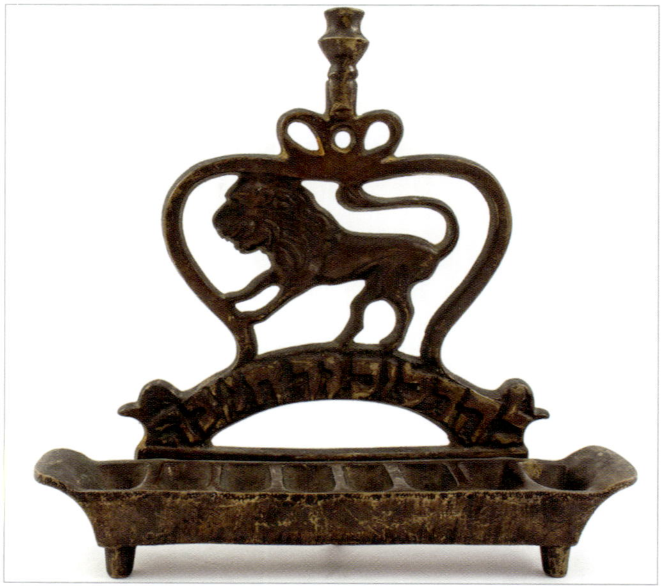

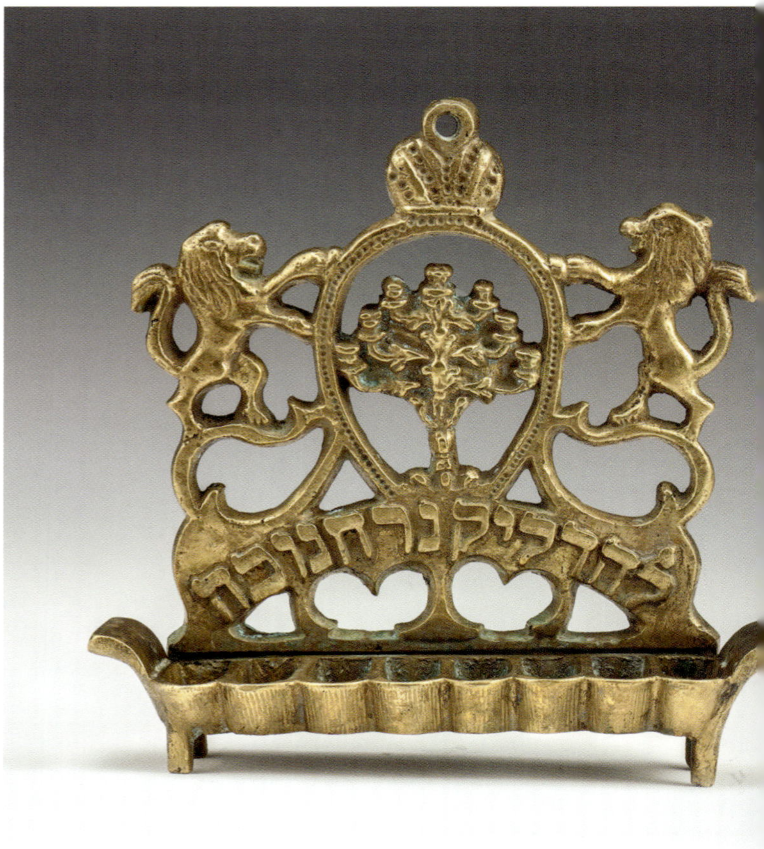

Both the menorahs shown here, as well as the five menorahs on the following three pages, were made by sand casting. These menorahs were cast repeatedly, spanning from the eighteenth until the early twentieth century. Generally, the heavier and more finely cast the menorah, the earlier the date of manufacture. When possible, check the threading of any screws on the piece; they should be of different lengths and uneven. It is invaluable to have hands-on experience with these types of menorahs to be able to differentiate between authentic, old examples and post-1945 copies.

These menorahs are classic examples from this region of Europe. Both say in Hebrew: "To light the flame (of) Chanukah." One shows a rampant lion and has a warm, dark patina. The other has Lions of Judah flanking the Temple menorah, with a Crown of Torah at top. The backplate design of this menorah is found as a decorative element on large, six-foot high synagogue menorahs from Galicia and the Ukraine that date back as early as the seventeenth century.

Material: Brass
Origin: Galicia or Ukraine, eighteenth and nineteenth centuries / Galicia or Ukraine, nineteenth and twentieth centuries
Dimensions: 9" x 10" / 5.75" x 7.25"

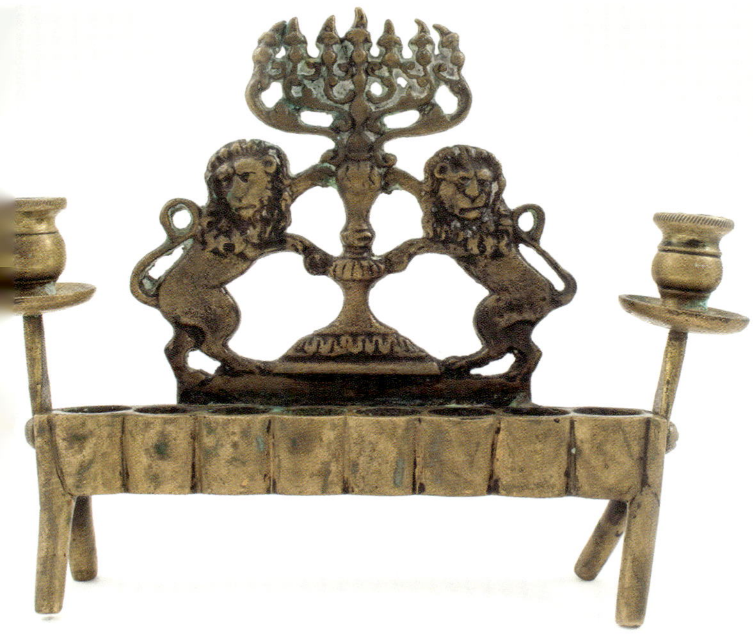

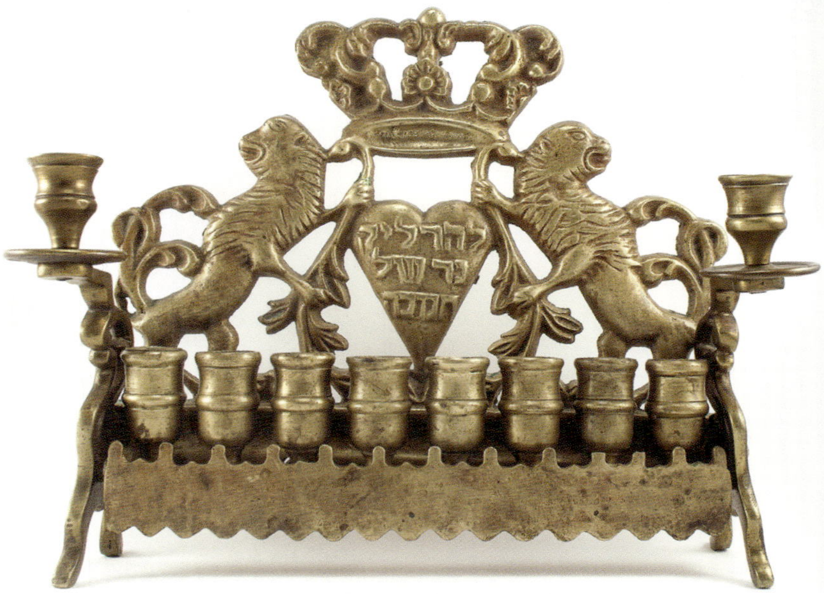

For most people, being married is an essential part of life. In the field of antiques, however, when you hear someone say "that piece is a marriage," the statement freezes collectors and dealers in their tracks; it's as close to vulgarity as you can get. A "married piece" is when an object is not entirely original: One part is from one period in time, and then a significant portion was added to the object during another period (decades or even centuries later), either to replace a damaged or missing part, or to make a vast improvement in the function or design of said object. Sophisticated collectors tend to stay away from married pieces, as the value of such items can be as little as 10% of the value of an all-original piece.

Occasionally, however, a married piece can be of such charm that the value is elevated to what the piece would be if it were entirely original. That is the case with the menorah pictured at top left. The backplate is eighteenth century and is a well-known design of Lions of Judah flanking a representation of the Temple Menorah. At some point the oil wells that were connected to the backplate were lost or damaged, and during the late eighteenth or early nineteenth century, someone had a new set of oil wells made, to make it once again a fully functional Chanukah menorah.

The other menorah is another well-known model. Lions of Judah flank a heart motif, of which its interior reads: "To light the flame of Chanukah." This is all topped by a Crown of Torah. The legs seem to be buckling under the weight of the menorah because when I bought the menorah, the legs and servant lights were missing. I "married" new legs to the piece but they were from a later (and thereby thinner casting) example of this menorah. The lack of original legs does hurt the value, which is perhaps 25% less than what this menorah would be worth if it had its original legs.

CHANUKAH MENORAHS

Material: Brass
Origin: Galicia or Ukraine, late eighteenth century / Galicia or Ukraine, early nineteenth century
Dimensions: 4.5" x 6" / 6.5" x 6"

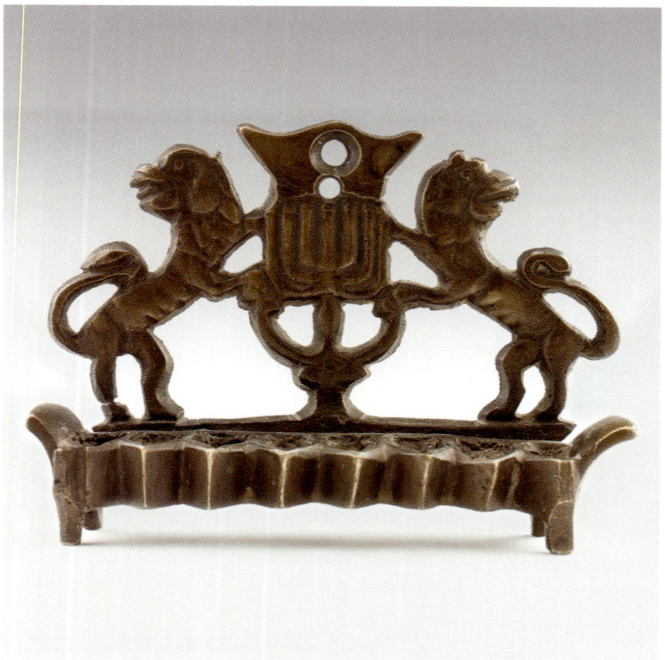

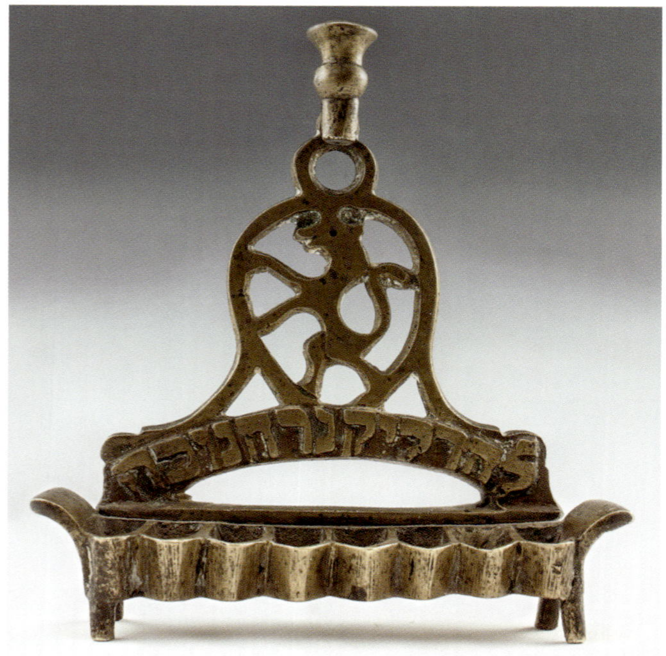

The menorah above (left) is a bit primitive in its design, which for me, only adds to its appeal. Two Lions of Judah flank a representation of the Temple Menorah. The large hole was created so the piece could be hung on a wall, as there was a tradition in Europe of hanging Chanukah menorahs in the home during the 357 days of the year when they were not used. The smaller hole is for the servant light, which is now missing.

The other menorah shows a smiling lion standing on its hind legs, above the Hebrew legend: "To light the flame (of) Chanukah."

CHANUKAH MENORAH

Material: Brass
Origin: Kiev, Ukraine, circa 1800
Dimensions: 6" x 6.75"

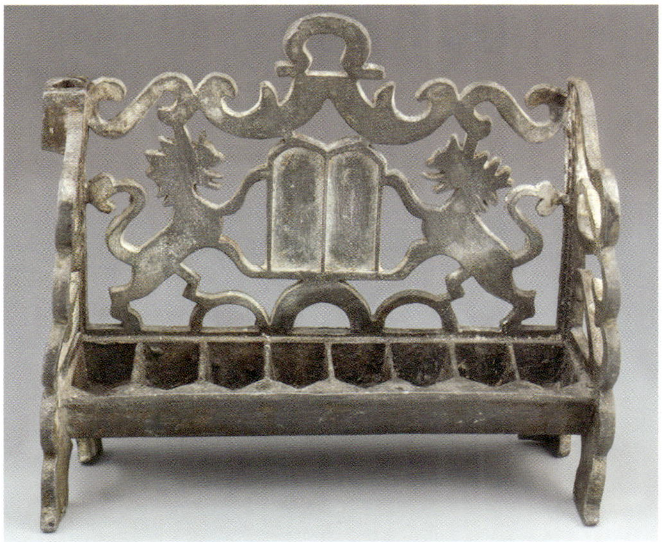

This menorah is fascinating, as I am unaware of other examples of this model, either in private or public collections (including museums worldwide). Purportedly, this menorah was found in the burnt-out ruins of a synagogue in Kiev.

Lions of Judah flank The Ten Commandments. The lions have forked tongues and are surprisingly abstract in their form. The sides of the menorah have representations of snakes.

CHANUKAH MENORAH

Material: Brass
Origin: Galicia or Ukraine, circa 1910
Dimensions: 6" x 6.6"

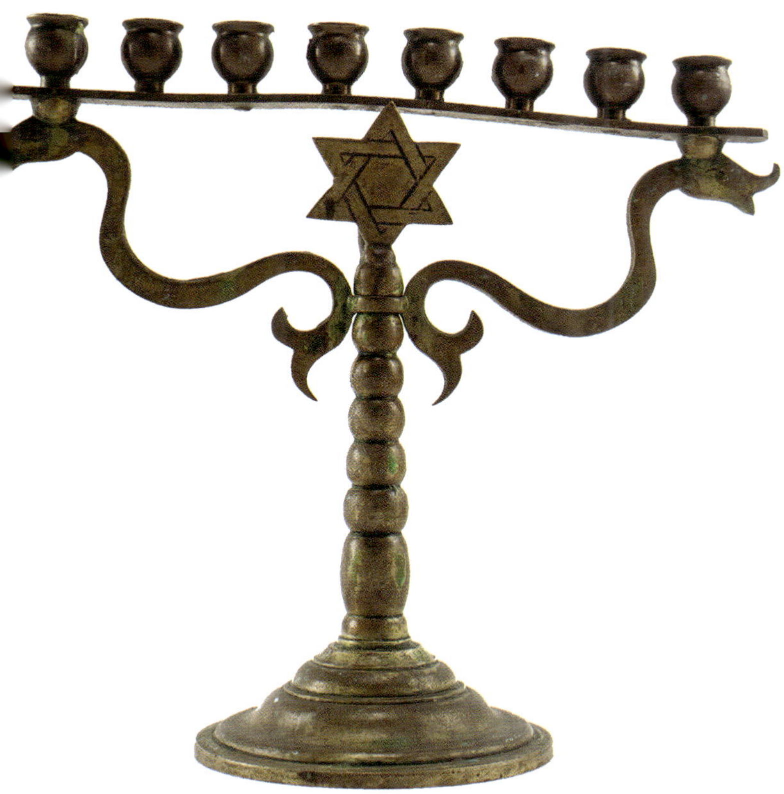

Two snakes flank a Star of David, while remnants of the servant light are attached on the reverse side. The snake may appear here as a symbol of eternity and redemption in Jewish art. The use of this motif on a Chanukah menorah is meaningful as the holiday marks the rededication of the Temple, representing the reemergence of the Jewish state. Snakes as a central symbol on Chanukah menorahs are exclusive to menorahs from Galicia and the Ukraine.

Menorahs identical to this one must have been assembled by the maker of this piece; however, I am unaware of other examples.

CHANUKAH MENORAHS

Materials: *Brass / Silver-plated Brass*
Origin: *Stuttgart, Germany, circa 1900 / Warsaw, Poland ,circa 1900*
Hallmarks: *"Johs. Rominger Hofl. Stuttgart" / "Norblin & Co. Galw Warszawa"*
Dimensions: *6.5" x 7" / 6" x 8"*

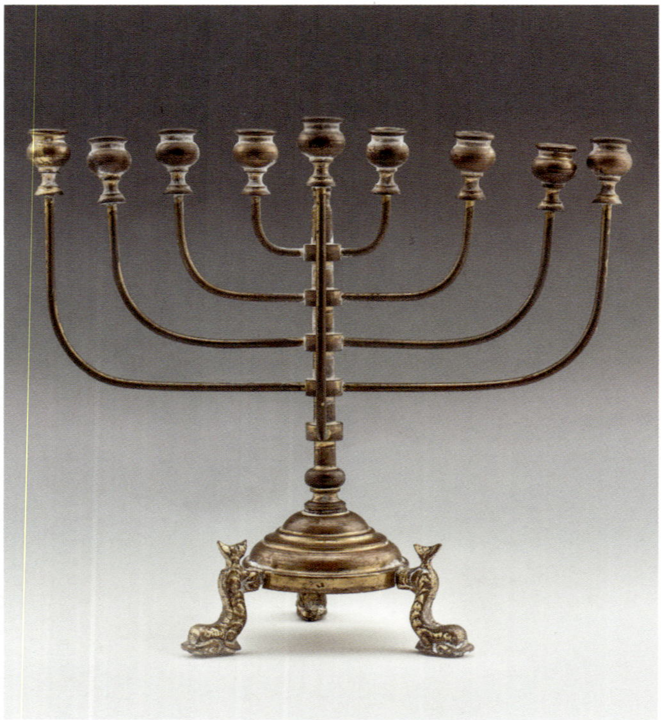

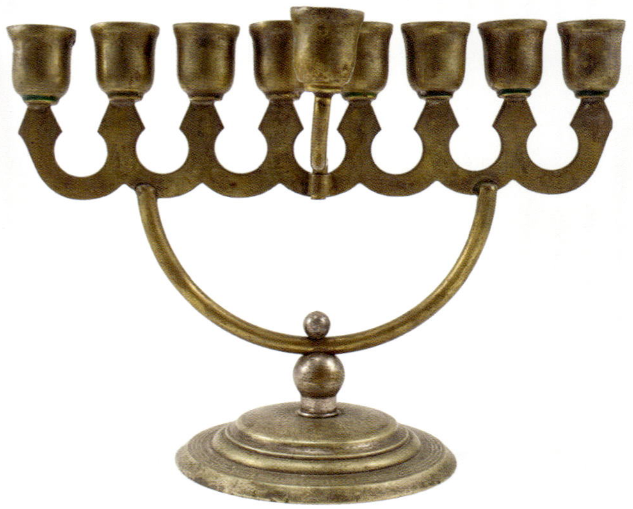

The first menorah stands apart from other brass menorahs made in Germany during this era because the base is elegantly elevated by three feet in the shape of fully formed dolphins. Other than this piece, only brass menorahs from the Netherlands had feet in the shape of dolphins, but those menorahs have a completely different design overall. They are at least double the size of this one.

The second menorah is a result of the mass-produced Judaica objects industry of Warsaw that was marketed toward the large prewar Jewish population that resided there. Typically, menorahs made by various Warsaw factories were of the type that had a backplate and oil sockets attached at the bottom; this example is unusual in that its form is free-standing.

Material: Brass
Origin: Italy, circa 1915 / Italy, circa 1880
Dimensions: 16" x 12" / 5" x 5.5"

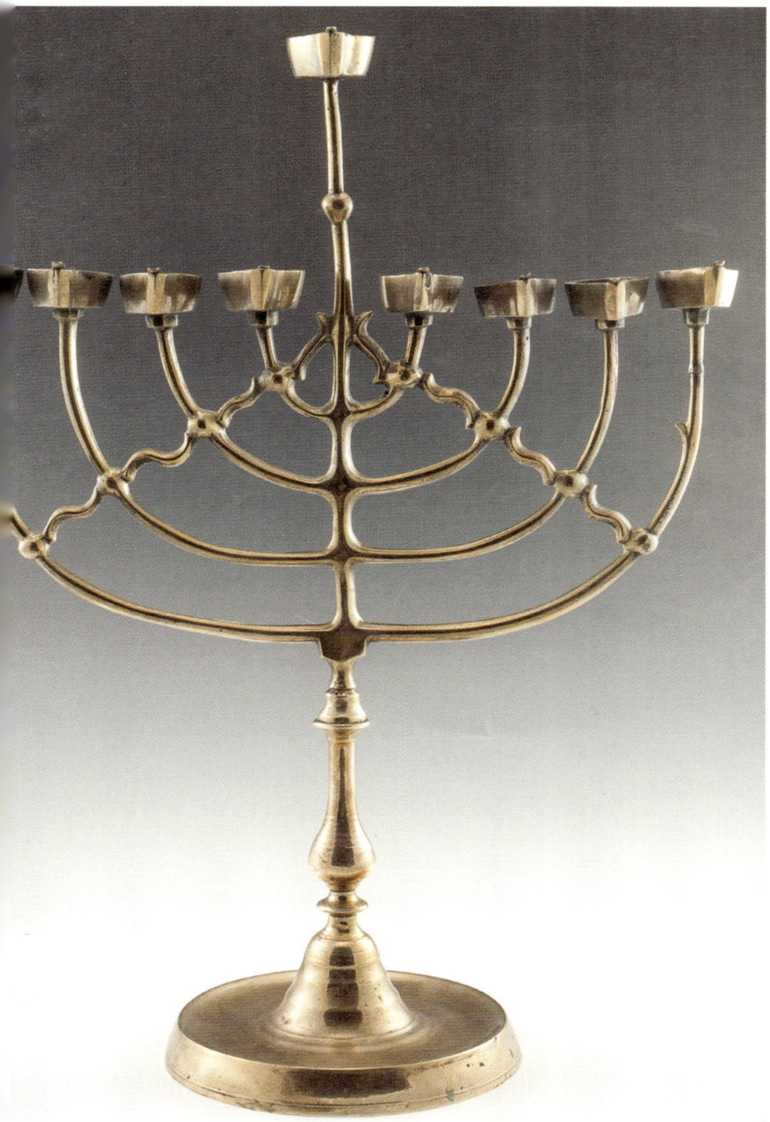

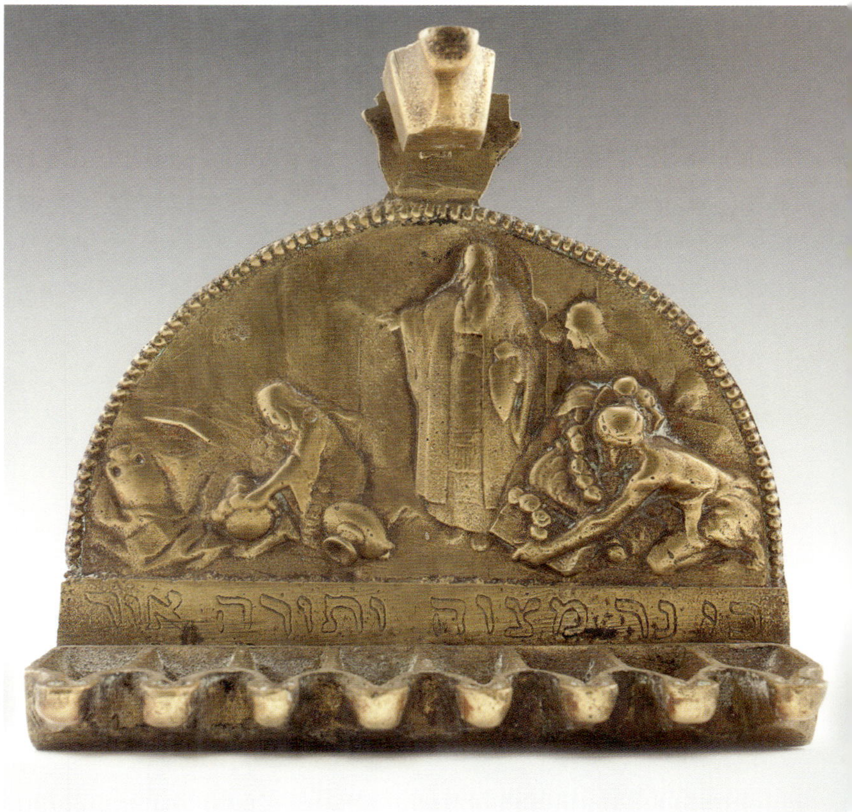

This small menorah above is big in design. The scene depicted is of the Maccabees cleansing the Temple. The standing bearded figure with his arm extended is the *Kohen Gadol* (the High Priest of the Temple). The Hebrew inscription reads: "For the Commandment is a lamp, and the Torah is a light," (Proverbs 6:23).

The other menorah, at left, is of a classic Italian design, with older examples dating as far back as the early eighteenth century on display at numerous Jewish museums in Italy.

CHANUKAH MENORAHS

Material: Brass
Origin: The Netherlands, circa 1900 / Russia, circa 1910
Hallmarks: "MMJ21"
Dimensions: 6.75" x 12" / 10" x 9.5"

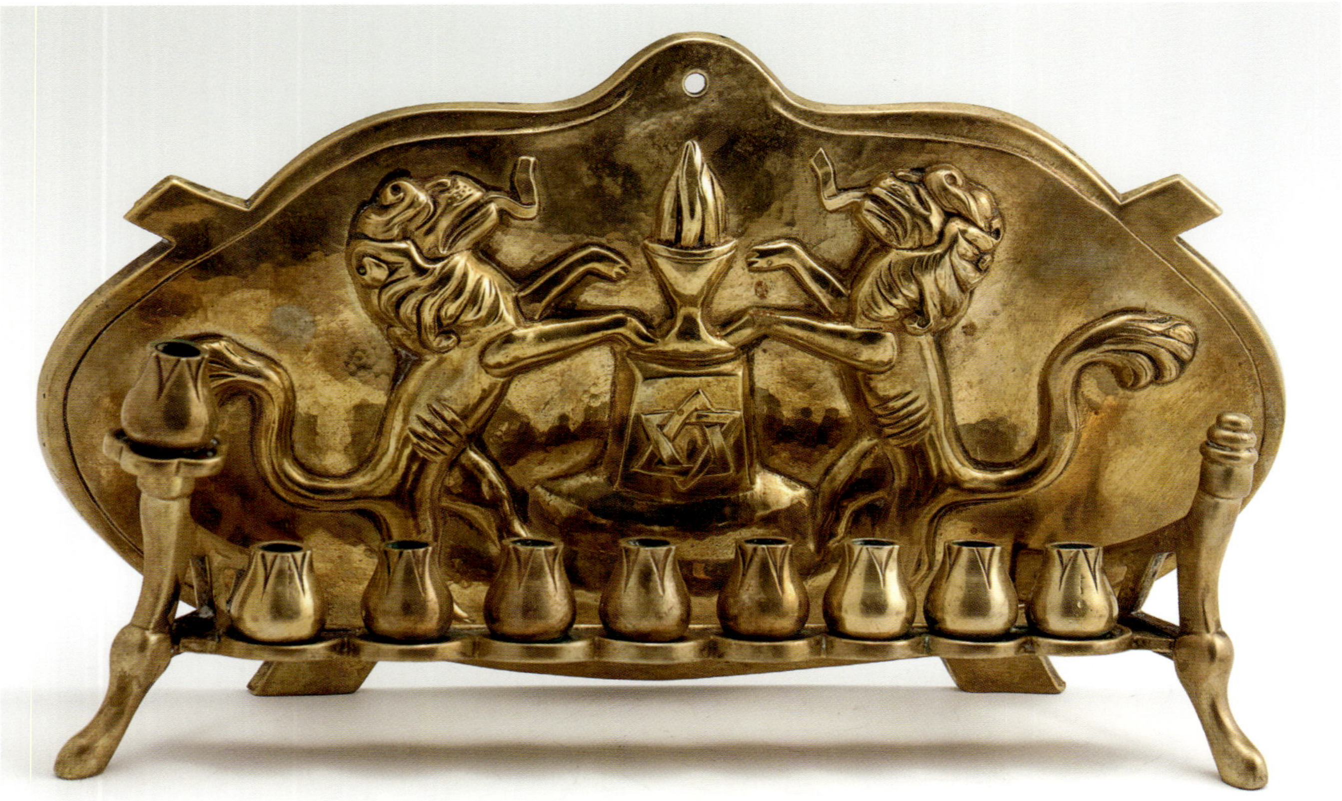

The menorah with vines shown at right is in the style known as art nouveau. Art nouveau came into fashion in 1880 and ceased to be used by 1920. It is characterized by flowing, curvilinear designs meshing with floral and other plant motifs. From the smallest button to grand architectural structures, countries such as France, England, and Spain incorporated art nouveau design into much of what they created for use in daily life. It was possible to live in an art nouveau house with art nouveau furniture, silverware, dishes, etc.

Apart from the standard-shaped candle holders, this menorah implements the art nouveau aesthetic; notice the vine-like shaft, with leaves attached to its sides, stems included. Working down to the base, more leaves are found, ending in a slightly elevated tripod base, reminiscent of a tree.

Art nouveau had very little impact on design elements in Judaica, therefore Jewish objects done in the art nouveau style are scarce. You are much more likely to find Judaica done in the *Jugendstil* (German for "Youth Style") manner. *Jugendstil* can sometimes be mistaken for art nouveau, but it tends to be more formal and less fluid in its designs.

The other menorah has only a hint of art nouveau influence; the candle holders are in the shape of lotus flowers. The rest of the menorah depicts Lions of Judah flanking a representation of the incense altar in the ancient Temple in Jerusalem. Here, the "holy fire" symbolizes the miracle of the Chanukah celebration.

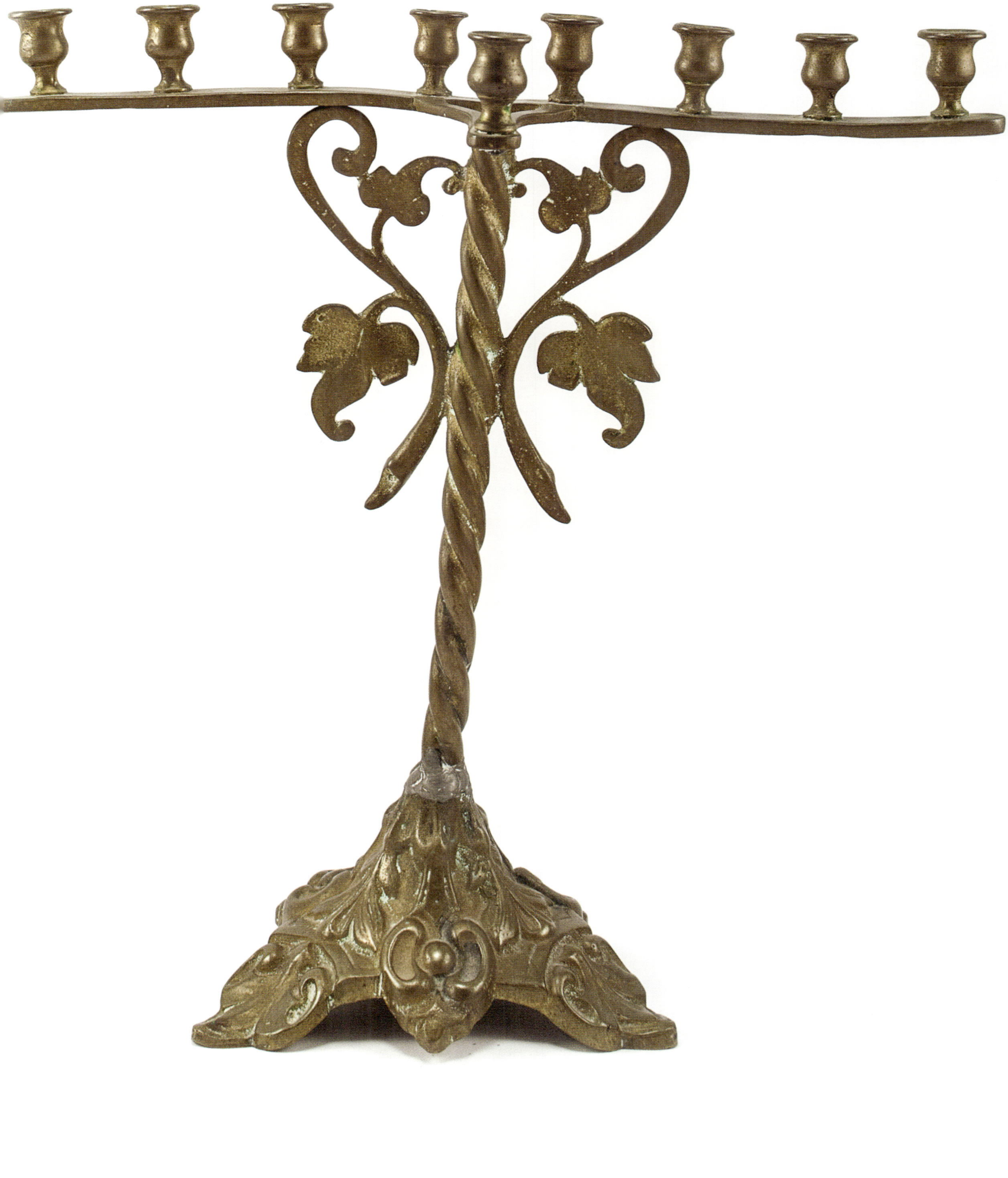

CHANUKAH MENORAH

Material: *Brass*
Origin: *USA, circa 1920*
Hallmarks: *"Der Tog," in Yiddish*
Dimensions: *11.5" x 11.5"*

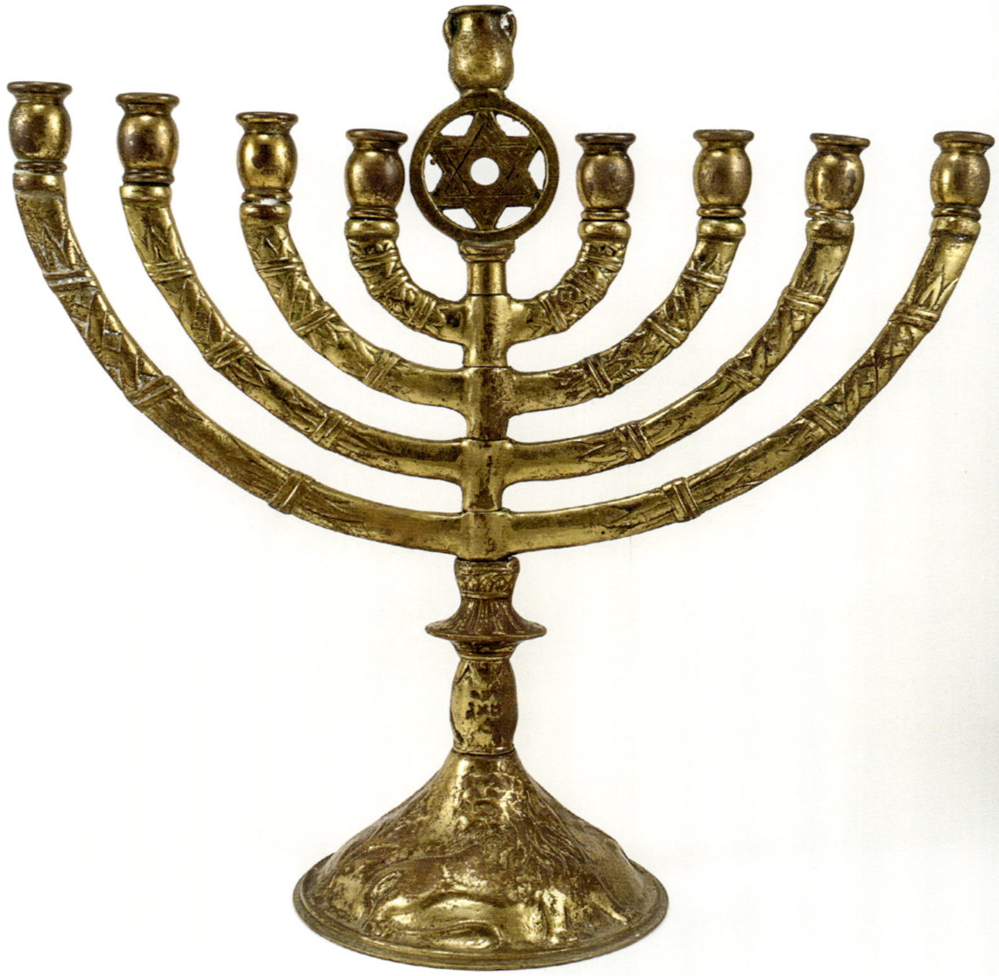

At the turn of the twentieth century in New York, a number of newspapers sprang up to meet the needs of newly arrived Jewish immigrants from Europe who wanted to read current events in the one language shared by them all, Yiddish. One of those newspapers was *Der Tog* (Yiddish for "The Day"), which was very popular and gained a large audience. This menorah was most likely a promotional item of sorts, perhaps received after paying for a subscription to the paper. The menorah is large and heavy, with the servant light cast in the shape of a two-handled jug, referencing the one cruse of pure oil that was found in the Second Temple in Jerusalem, as in the days of antiquity, valuable liquids such as wine and oil were stored in large clay jugs. A ferocious Lion of Judah adorns the base.

I have seen quite a few of these *Der Tog* menorahs over the years, although to my knowledge, this is the first time a photo of this menorah has been published. Another example of this menorah can be spotted in a few scenes of the critically acclaimed 2009 Coen brothers movie *A Serious Man*.

If you have relatives who were European immigrants and lived in New York in the 1920s, check "grandma's attic," as perhaps you might find your own *Der Tog* menorah resting in a trunk, waiting for you to put it to good use on Chanukah.

Material: Brass
Origin: Germany, circa 1930
Dimensions: 12.5" x 9.75" / 18" x 11.5"

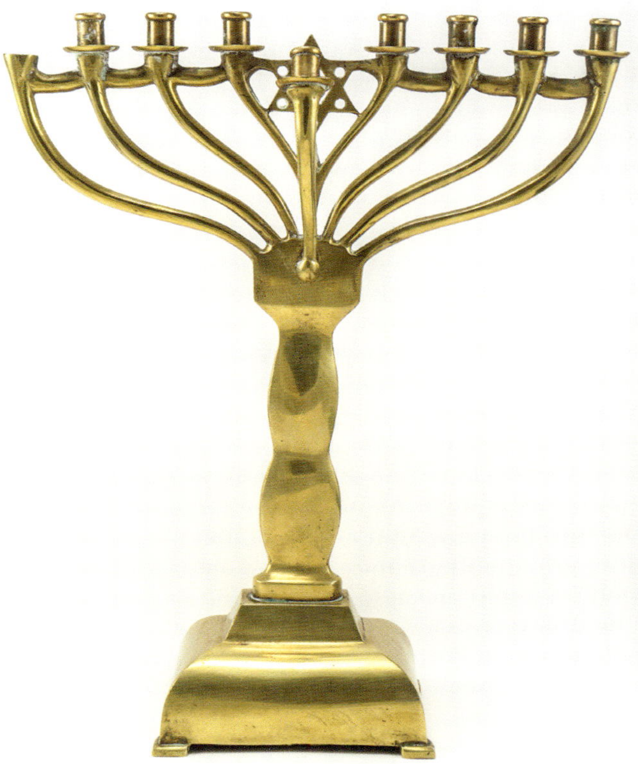

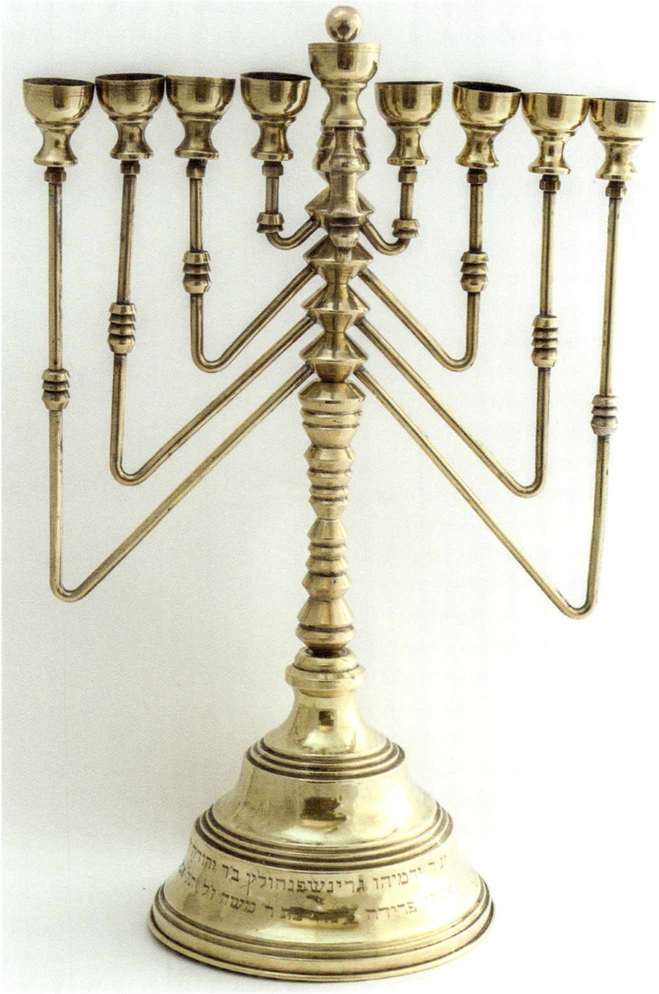

The base of the menorah at left echoes the style of eighteenth- and nineteenth-century German menorahs, but the similarities end there. The wavy shaft works its way up to curved arms connected to each other by a dollop of metal, centered by a Star of David. This design is a direct influence from the art deco movement, which emphasized sweeping curves, unlike art nouveau, which emphasized sinuous curves derived from nature.

The second menorah is noteworthy in that it displays the impression the Machine Age had on the decorative arts. Items designed in this manner are a reflection of the power and influence that machines had on daily life, starting at the onset of World War I. From household items such as the radio and telephone to vehicles such as airplanes, the Machine Age was an explosion of mechanical advances on the world that were here to stay.

The circular base, with its streamlined design, sets the tone for the shaft, which is made up of chunks of metal reminiscent of nuts and bolts. The curved arms have smaller versions of this decorative element, ending with half-cups that could be yet another part of some type of mechanization.

The base has a Hebrew dedication to a synagogue in Tel-Aviv, from which this menorah was donated to by its owner, likely a refugee from Nazi Germany.

CHANUKAH MENORAH

Material: *Brass*
Origin: *Israel, circa 1950*
Dimensions: *7" x 8.6"*

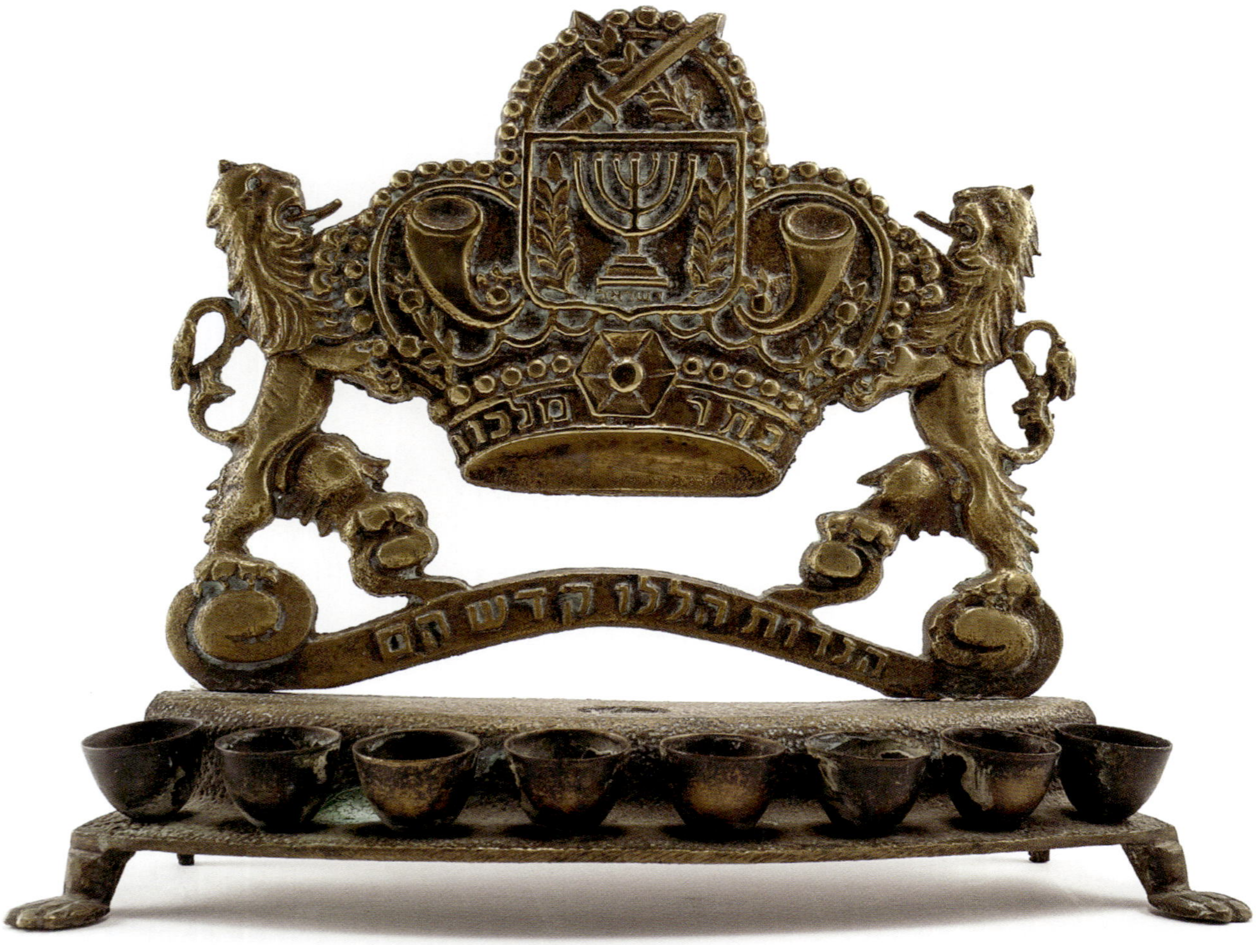

This menorah beautifully combines the observance of Chanukah with celebrating the founding of the State of Israel. Lions of Judah uphold a crown labeled "Crown of Government" in Hebrew. In the center of the crown is the state seal of Israel: the Temple Menorah between two olive branches and the Hebrew word *Yisrael.* Two *shofars* flank the state seal, as if to announce that a new chapter in modern history has arrived; a Jewish-controlled land of Israel. Atop the state seal is a sword crossed over an olive branch, which is a symbol of the Israeli Defense Forces. At bottom by the oil wells is the reference to Chanukah: "These lights are holy."

Due to a lack of any hallmark, the maker of this menorah is unknown, although Israeli collectors have surmised that this menorah and others like it were made by the company Keter Israel.

CHANUKAH MENORAH

Material: Silver
Origin: Hungary, circa 1920
Hallmarks: "JS," "P," "Torv Ved" (protected by law), Diana head
Dimensions: 5.5" x 7.5"

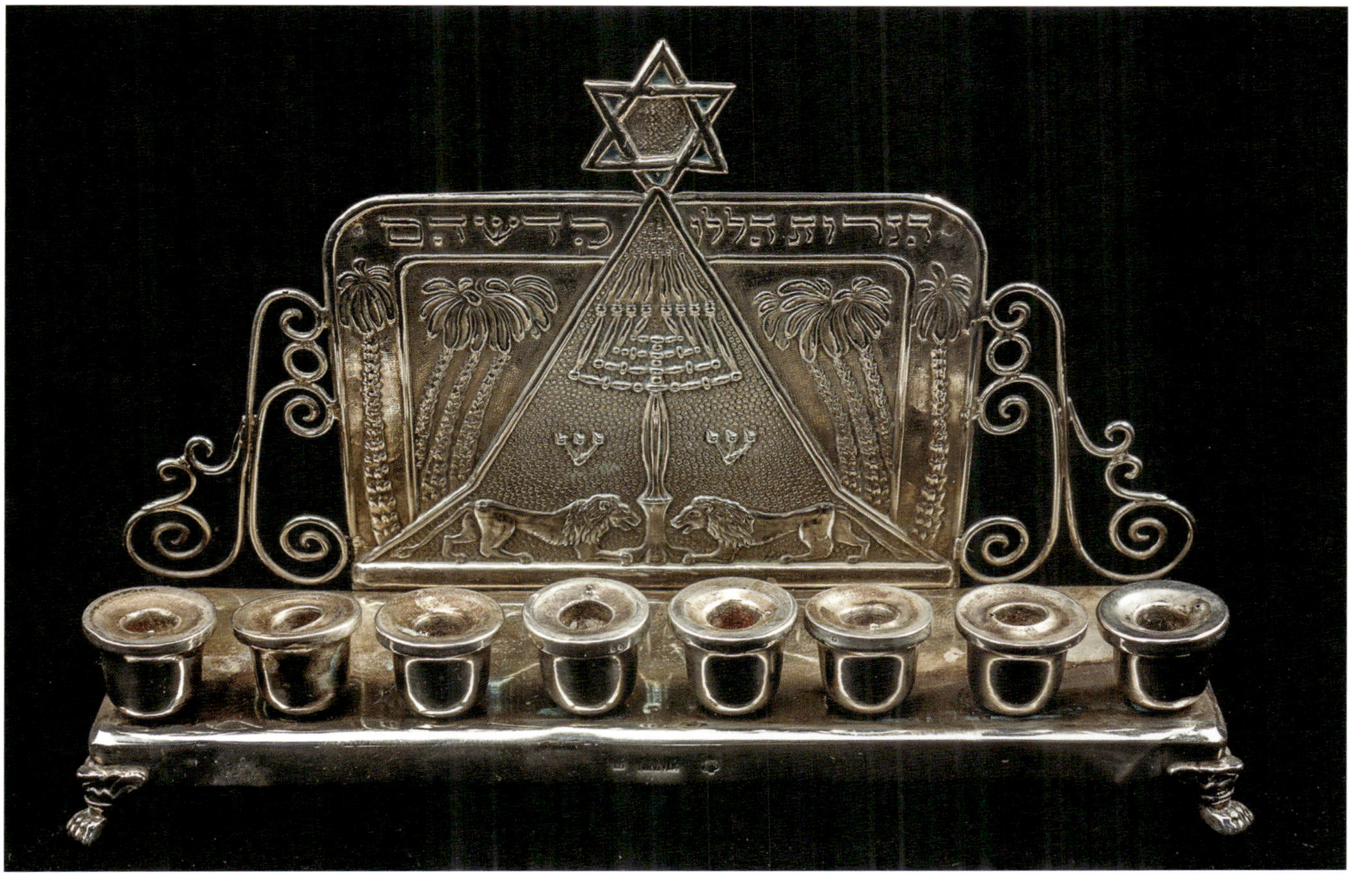

This menorah is an interesting combination of two distinctly different styles of design that were combined to form one piece. The row of oil sockets with paw feet is a basic design element of European menorahs that were used throughout the eighteenth and nineteenth centuries. The backplate, however, is more in keeping with early twentieth-century design from Israel, specifically crafts produced at the Bezalel Academy of Arts & Crafts in Jerusalem (see page 110). The crouching lions in particular are identical to lions found on menorahs made by Bezalel around 1915.

The artist of this piece, residing in Hungary, was likely directly influenced by Bezalel objects he saw in person. Boris Schatz, the founder of Bezalel, made it a point to bring his wares to the attention of the large Jewish communities that were spread across Europe and the Americas in the 1910s and '20s. Bezalel exhibitions were held in numerous European cities such as Prague, Berlin, Vienna, and Warsaw.

At top in Hebrew is "These lights are holy," with a Star of David. The palm trees represent the Garden of Eden, a motif popular on nineteenth- and early twentieth-century European menorahs. The meaning of the two large "*shin*" letters above the lions is unclear.

CHANUKAH MENORAHS

Material: Silver
Origin: Vienna, Austria, circa 1925 / Germany, circa 1930
Hallmarks: "Bottwin Wein," "HB 800," toucan head / "835," crescent moon and crown, workshop monogram of Oskar Haegele
Dimensions: 5.25" x 5.5" / 6" x 7.1"

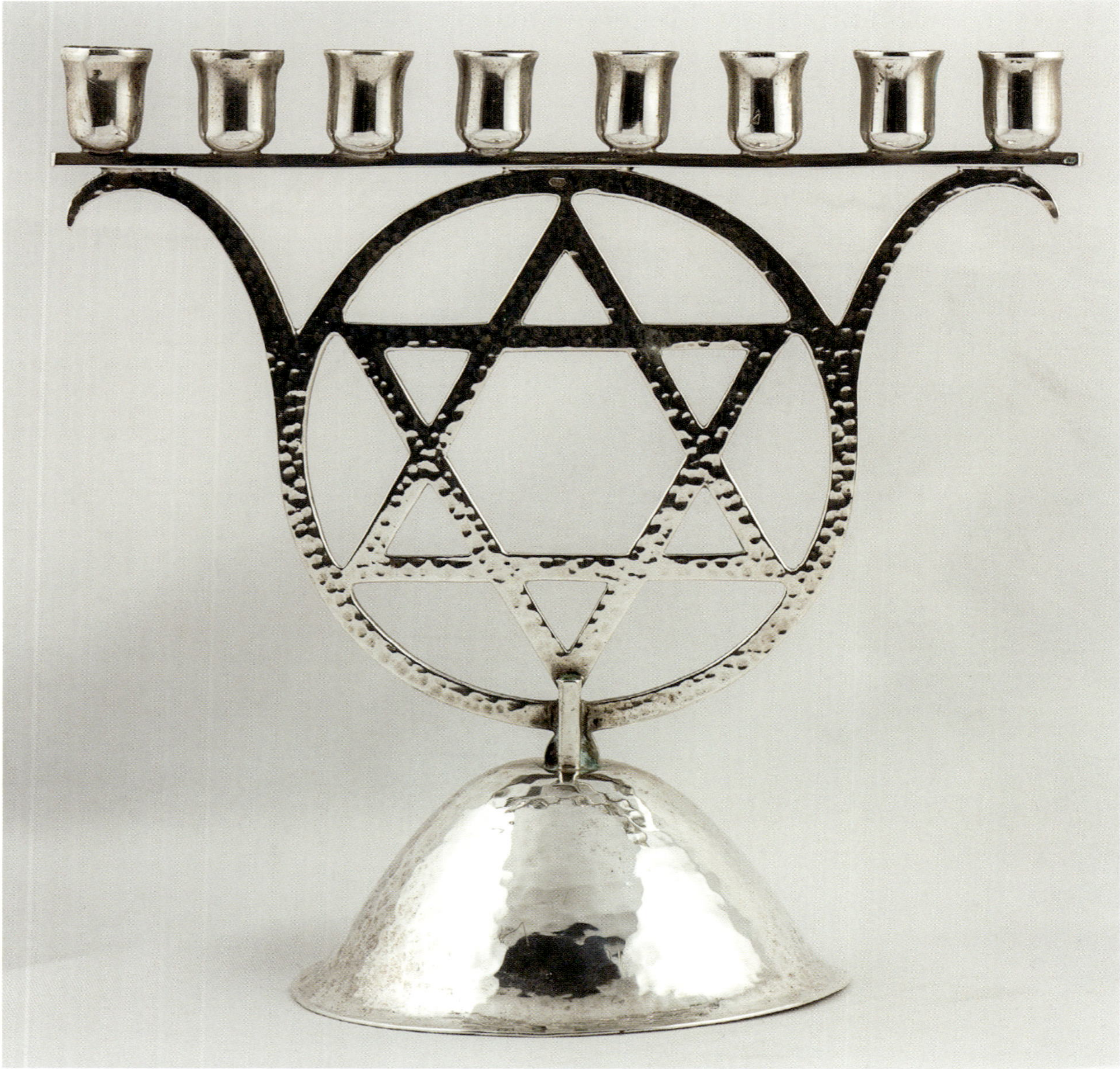

These two menorahs are examples of how crafts designed by large workshops can influence independent artisans operating in the same regional area.

Apart from the cups, the menorah above is entirely hand-hammered. Silver objects such as vases, pitchers, and candlesticks were made in an identical manner to this menorah at the Wiener Werkstatte ("Viennese Workshops," 1903-1931), which sought to make high-quality products for a select market who could afford them. The pieces from the Wiener Werkstatte had simple shapes, minimal decoration, and geometric patterning.

The menorah at right has the Bauhaus aesthetic as the foundation of its design. The Bauhaus (1919-1933) was Germany's foremost school of

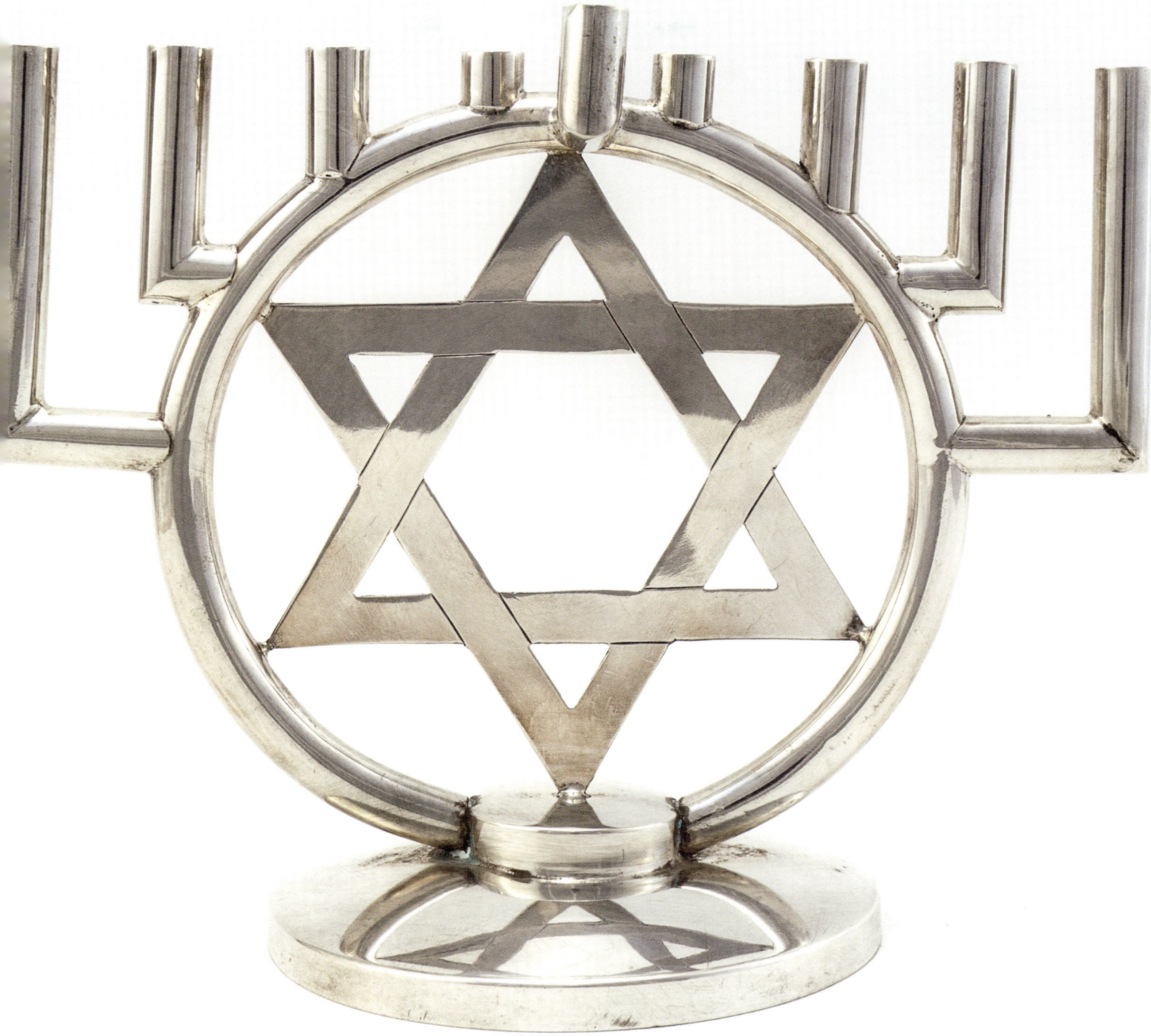

contemporary art and architecture until it was closed down by the Nazi regime. It stressed sleek, elegant proportions, unadorned/polished surfaces, little ornamentation, and geometric forms. This menorah has a large Star of David at its center; around it is a graceful circle of tubular structure from which angled arms emerge, all resting on a disc-shaped base. Although Bauhaus was concurrent with and formed part of the art deco movement, items done in the style of the Bauhaus have design elements specific to that art movement, unlike other seemingly similar pieces inspired by the broad category that is art deco. German Chanukah menorahs made in the manner of the Bauhaus are rare.

CHANUKAH MENORAHS

Material: Silver
Origin: Germany, circa 1925 / Germany, circa 1930
Hallmarks: "800," crescent moon and crown / "900," crescent moon and crown, "richter-engel original handarbeit" workshop monogram
Dimensions: 5.5" x 5.5" / 5.5" x 6.25

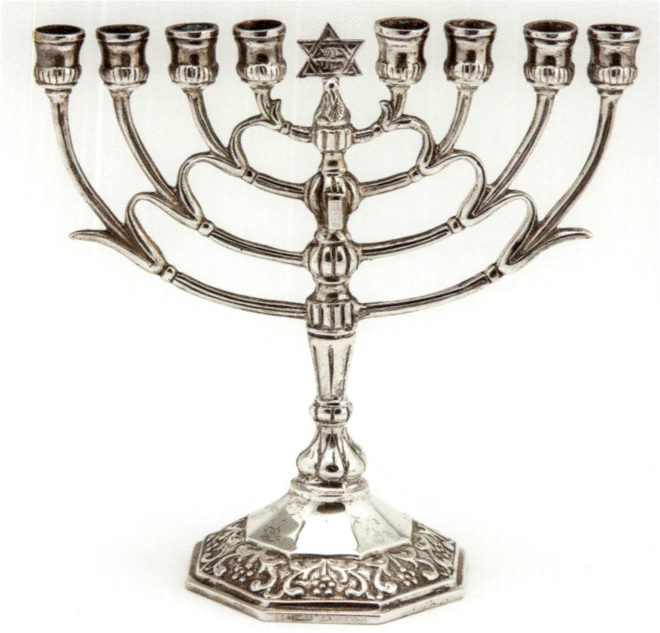

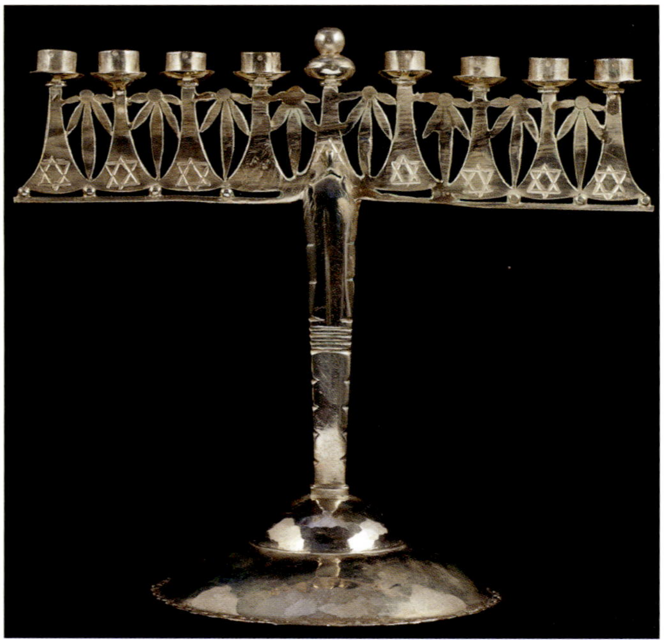

At first glance, the menorah at left appears comparable to other menorahs of the era, as much is standard: the cups, Star of David finial with "Light of Chanukah" engraved in Hebrew in the center, and finally, the acanthus leaf decoration and octagon base. Many German menorahs were made with arms that had a repeating pattern of flower buds, as it references the description of the making of the Temple Menorah, as written in Exodus 25:31: "Make a Menorah out of pure gold. The Menorah shall be formed by hammering it. Its base, stem, and [decorative] cups, spheres and flowers must be hammered out of a [single piece of gold]."

The designer of this menorah makes a simple but powerful artistic change with a flourish: He has each arm have only one flower bud, and starting from the middle, as the arms get longer, these buds become larger, and every bud on each separate arm is connected to a bud either above or beneath it.

The second menorah is a curiosity of sorts. The shaft and base are beautifully executed. There is light hand-hammering on the base that references the Arts and Crafts movement, while the shaft is art deco. However, the cut-out pattern of palm leaves and engraved Stars of David are of a lower standard; the engraving in particular is sloppy and crude. Yet the cups, finial, and small balls by the end of the leaves are well done—the balls cite the influence of the Secession, yet another art trend.

Whatever the reason may be for the apparent contradiction in the quality of workmanship, this is an interesting rarity, as I am not aware of other Judaica made by this firm.

CHANUKAH MENORAHS

Material: Iron
Origin: Germany, circa 1910 / USA, circa 1920
Dimensions: 11.75" x 12.25" / 12.25" x 12.25"

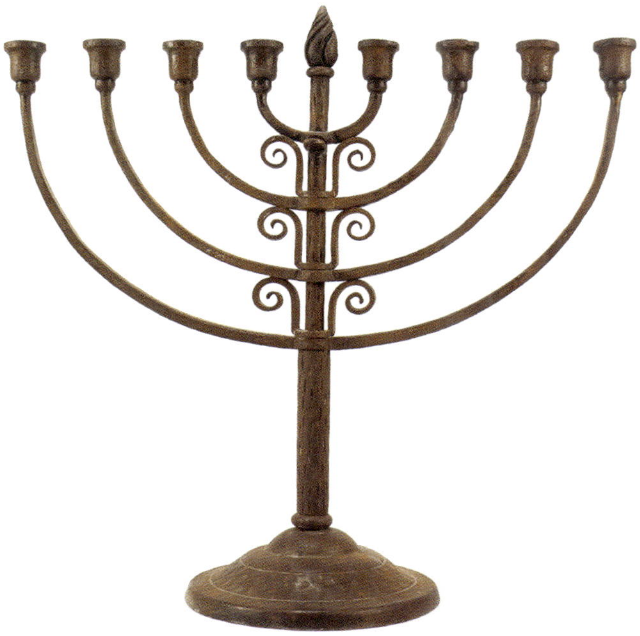

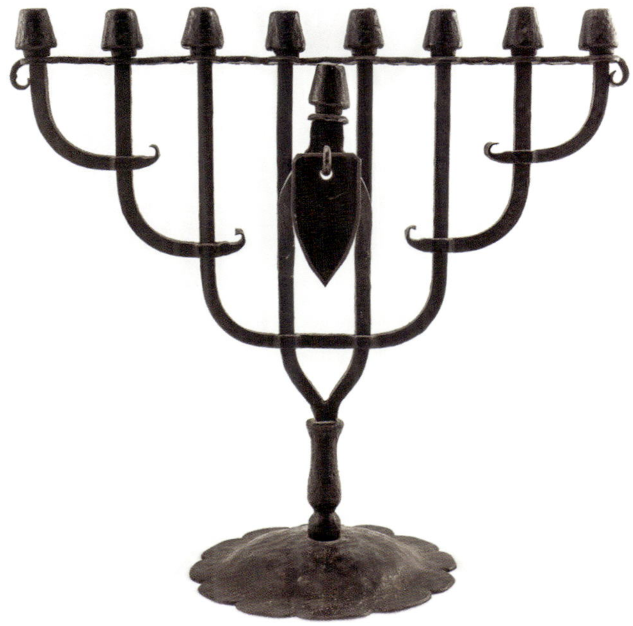

These menorahs are examples of Judaica done in the style known as Arts and Crafts. The Arts and Crafts movement originated in England in the 1860s and ended around 1920, having spread its influence throughout Europe and the United States. This trend is defined as a return to making items by hand; it encouraged originality and simplicity of form and favored the use of local natural materials, such as iron.

Both menorahs shown are completely hand-wrought. For the menorah at left, the base has one section that is hand-hammered, which was a primary design aspect of the Arts and Crafts style. The shaft is covered in notches, another expression of Arts and Crafts. The flame finial points the origin of this menorah to Germany.

The menorah at right appears to have been made in the United States, as identically designed seven-light examples in silver were popular as presentation gifts to members of the B'nai B'rith in the 1930s and '40s and appear on the market fairly regularly. Those silver candelabra were made by Robert Sturm, a silversmith from Cincinnati, Ohio, who worked in the Arts and Crafts style from the early 1900s through the 1930s. Either Sturm made this nine-light iron menorah, or he borrowed its design to implement in his manufacturing of seven-light candelabra in silver.

Jewish ritual objects made in the Arts and Crafts manner are rare, as this decorative style had little impact on Judaica design.

CHANUKAH MENORAH

Material: Iron
Origin: Prague, Austro-Hungarian Empire (Czech Republic), second half of the nineteenth century
Dimensions: 20" x 19"

As a general rule, iron and steel are never used as materials for a Jewish ceremonial object, as those metals are too closely associated with war. When they are found in a Judaic capacity, they are usually employed as an architectural element of some manner, such as gates for a synagogue or cemetery. Massive, heavy charity boxes from iron are sometimes found as well. The one exception to the tradition of banning iron from ceremonial objects (charity boxes are not ceremonial objects) are menorahs. Perhaps this allowance was made because Chanukah is not a holiday derived from the Torah. Whatever the reason, ceremonial items such as Kiddush cups or Torah pointers are never made of iron, only menorahs.

Shown here is one of a matching pair of Chanukah menorahs I own. It was made for use in a synagogue, as each menorah was originally positioned on a pedestal year-round, flanking the *amud,* which is the desk set before the ark from which the cantor reads the prayers aloud for the congregation.

The pointed holders on this menorah are known as "prickets," and were used for large candles. Candelabra with prickets were very popular in Germany but are also found on antique pieces from the Netherlands and the region that is today the Czech Republic. Even though the country with the largest amount of iron candelabra (both secular and Jewish) is Germany, the Star of David points to Prague as its origin. Synagogue menorahs made of iron with such large, prominent Stars of David were found only in Prague.

The menorah retains traces of gilding, as when new this was entirely covered in gilt, giving the appearance that it was made of gold, akin to the Temple Menorah of antiquity.

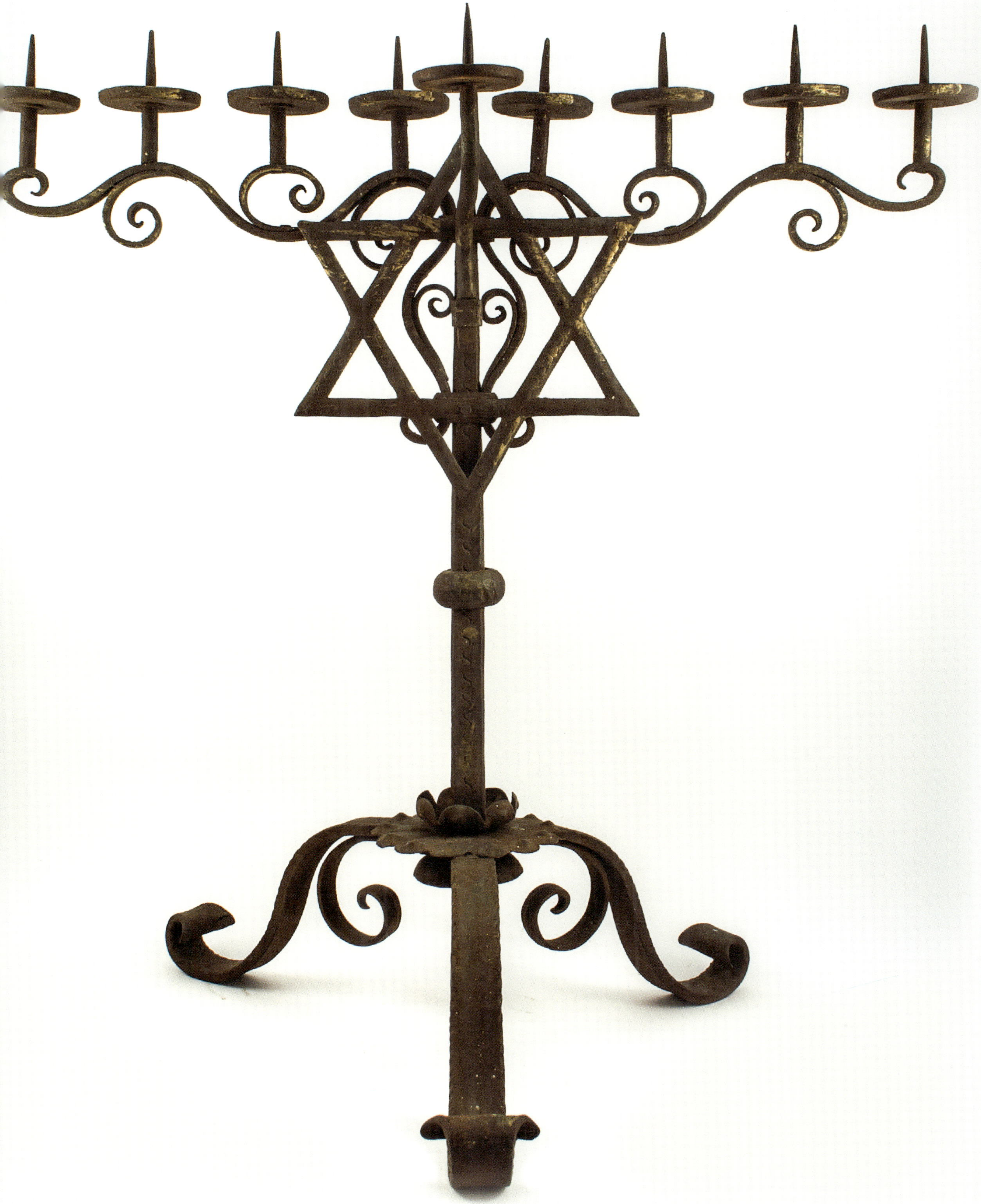

CHANUKAH MENORAH

Material: Iron
Origin: France, circa 1925–1935
Dimensions: 19.75″ x 21.75″

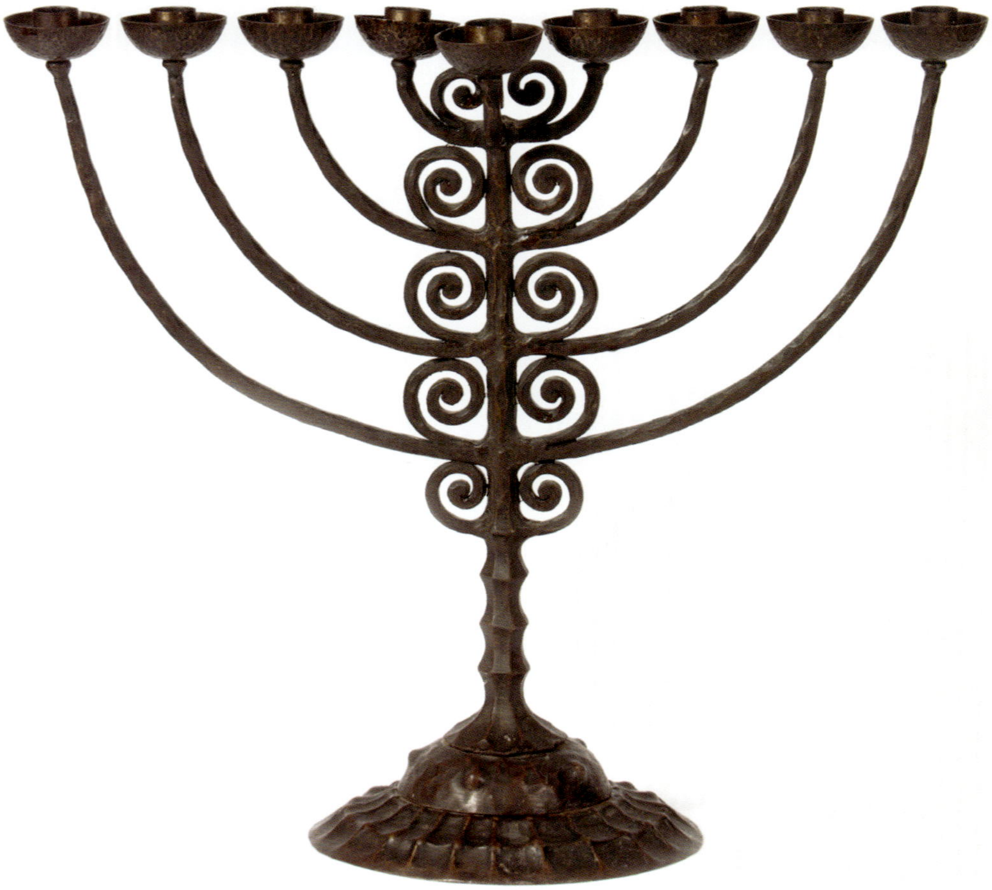

To the casual observer, this menorah may appear to have been done in the Arts and Crafts style; upon close examination, however, it is determined that this is an unmistakable piece of French art deco ironwork.

The Exposition Internationale des Arts Décoratifs et Industriels Modernes (International Exposition of Modern Industrial and Decorative Arts) was a world's fair held in Paris, France, from April to October 1925. The term "art deco" was derived by shortening the words "*arts décoratifs.*" Visitors to the exhibition were entranced by the "*moderne*" design, and businessmen were quick to return to their factories and incorporate the styles they saw at the fair into their own wares. Among the exhibitors was Edgar Brandt, an innovative master of ironwork.

The person who fabricated this massive menorah clearly was influenced by Brandt, as the beaten-edged, flattened scrollwork and applied patina are features that are prominent in some of his works. The thumbprint-depression styled base is pure French deco.

As was the fashion in prewar Europe among the Jewish upper class, many decorated their homes with multiple menorahs. It's easy to envision a wealthy Jew in the south of France hiring a skilled artisan familiar with iron to forge a Brandt-like menorah for celebrating the holiday outdoors, on the terrace of his home.

This menorah is a rare example of French art deco Judaica.

Materials: Olivewood and white metal / Ceramic
Origin: Israel, 1930s
Hallmarks: "Dov Brunsht, Totzeret-Yisrael, Yaffo*Tel-Aviv" (in Hebrew), "Palestine" / "Eretz – Yisrael" (in Hebrew), "Made in Palestine," monogram of the Kadar company
Dimensions: 9.25" x 7.25" / 8.5" x 13.5"

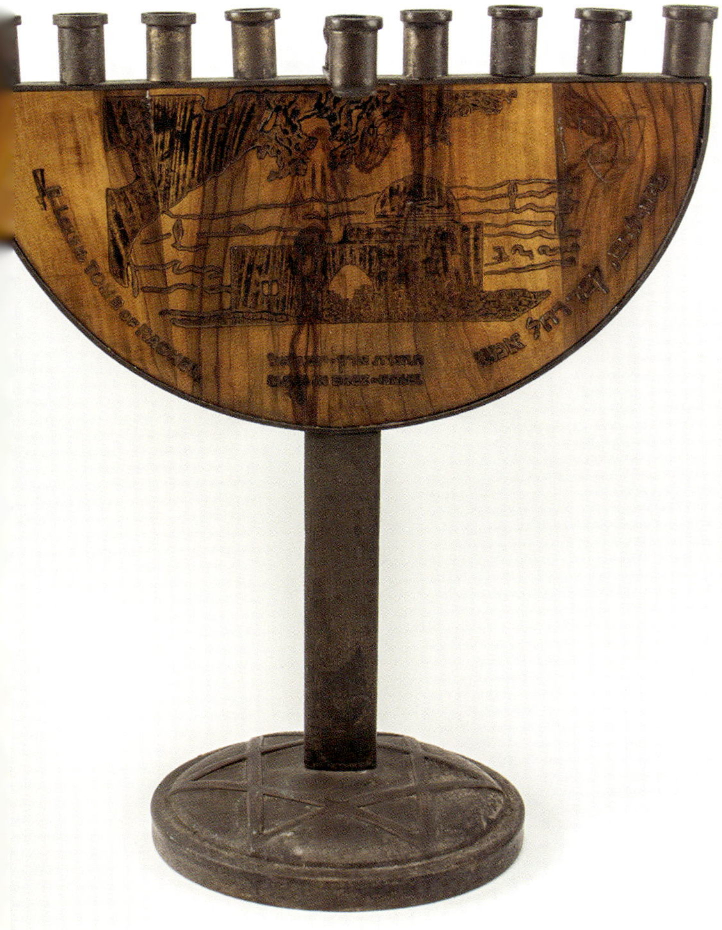

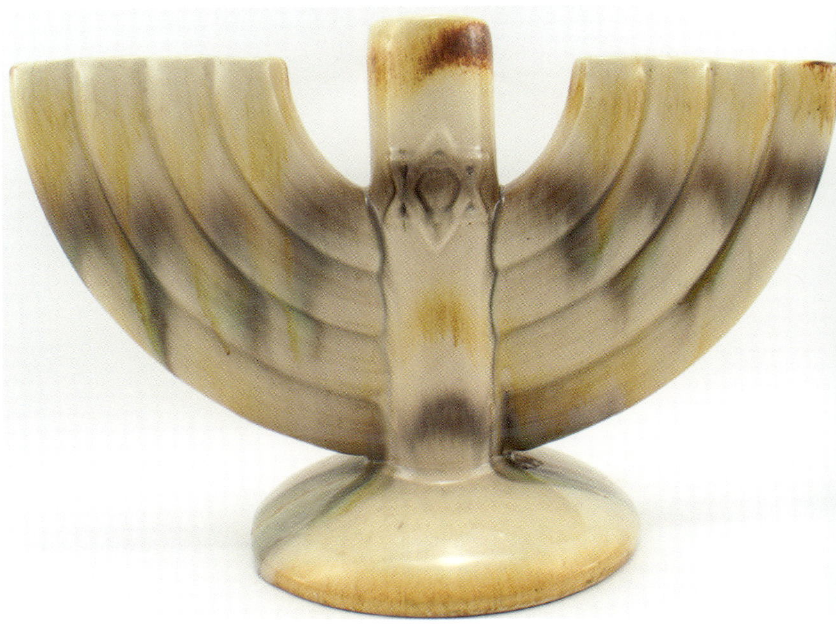

Olivewood is native to Israel and was used as a material for all types of objects imaginable, including many items specifically designed for the tourist and export market.

The center of the menorah at top is made of olivewood, with an engraving of the Tomb of Rachel, and is titled as such in Hebrew and English. The rest of the piece is made of metal, with a Star of David on its base. The overall design of the piece, with its half moon shaped middle, shaft with rounded edges, and sleek cups, was influenced by the art deco movement.

The Bauhaus school of art and architecture was deemed degenerate by the Nazis, who subsequently closed its doors in 1933. Yet in Tel-Aviv throughout the 1930s, the building of Bauhaus-inspired architecture was in full swing, giving the city a very modern look. The ceramic menorah, created in Israel at the same time as this architecture, follows most of the Bauhaus principals of design, but to be perfectly accurate this would be described as art deco in form. Its proportions and streamlined appearance are marvelous. It was made by the Kadar company, which continued producing Judaica made from ceramic throughout the 1940s and '50s; however, the art deco-inspired design in their items appears to have ended by 1940.

Tel-Aviv has the largest amount of surviving Bauhaus-inspired architecture in the world today, totaling more that 1,500 buildings. In 2003 the United Nations designated the city of Tel-Aviv a World Heritage site because of this.

CHANUKAH MENORAH

Material: Wood
Origin: Poland or Ukraine, circa 1900
Dimensions: 10" x 11.75"

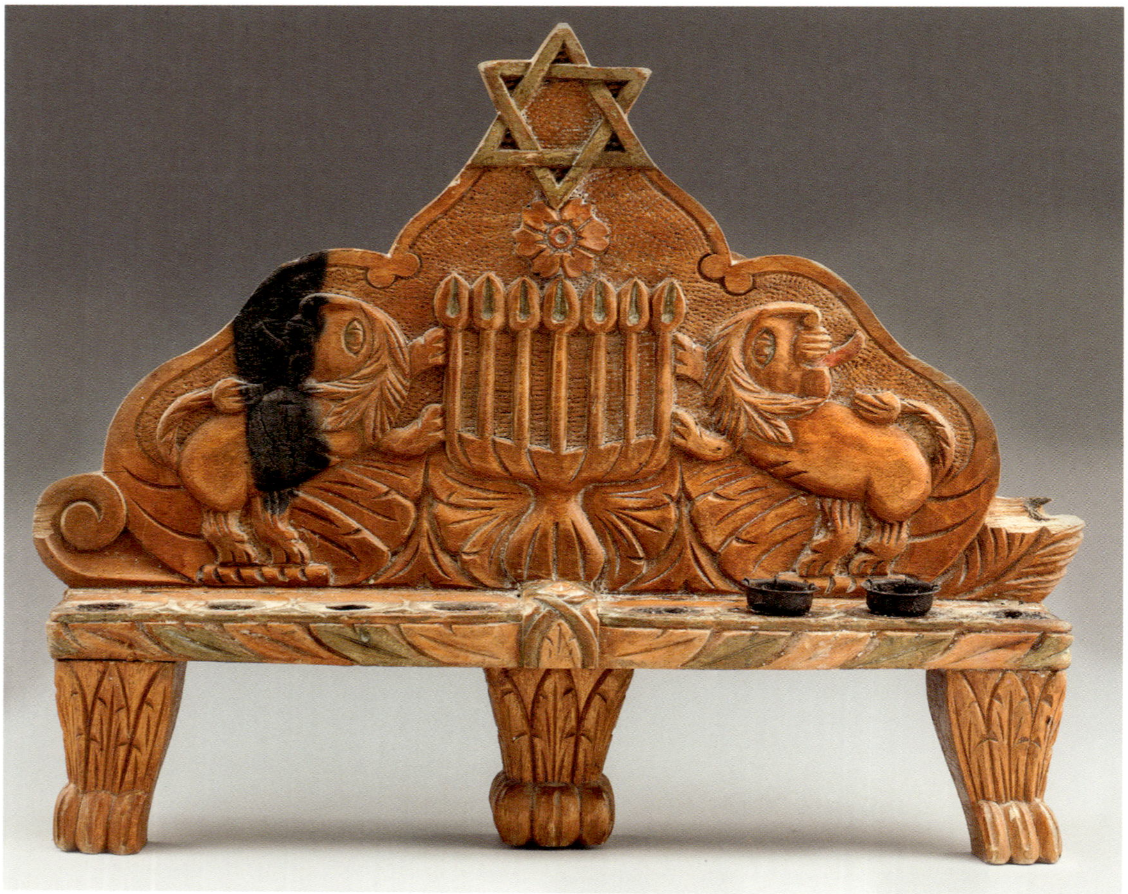

It is highly unusual to find a menorah made entirely of wood for obvious reasons; in fact this menorah has suffered "burn trauma" on its left side!

Even though it may seem illogical to make a menorah solely from wood, a handful of examples made in prewar Europe do exist and are in museums. None, however, are even remotely similar in design to this piece.

All of the stylistic elements of this menorah are found in Jewish art of Eastern Europe: the open flower bud at top; the depiction of the Temple Menorah with closed flower buds as the lamps themselves; and lastly the lions, with their forked tongues and peculiar placement of the eyes.

The backplate of the menorah is expertly carved and a graceful balance is achieved, even with so many motifs represented in such close proximity to one another. This was originally painted at parts. The tongue from the lion on the right still retains some red paint, and the Star of David has some gold. The servant light was located on the right side but has since broken off. The legs are carved in the form of paw feet and uphold a plinth with holes for the placement of oil. The reverse features a worn and rusted iron hook so this menorah could be hung on a wall during the rest of the year, as was customary in European Jewish households. Two tin oil receptacles remain.

In Eastern Europe there was a tradition of highly skilled Jewish woodcarving dating back hundreds of years. Less than half a century after this menorah was made, that world disappeared forever.

DREIDELS AND CHANUKAH MENORAH BACKPLATE

Materials: Brass, Silver / Lead / Bone / Wood / Lead
Origin: Israel, circa 1925 / Europe, circa 1890 / Israel, circa 1920 / Ukraine, circa 1900
Hallmarks: "Bezalel Jerusalem" in Hebrew (top row of dreidels)
Dimensions: 1" x 1" – 2.25" x 1" / 2.75" x 5.75"

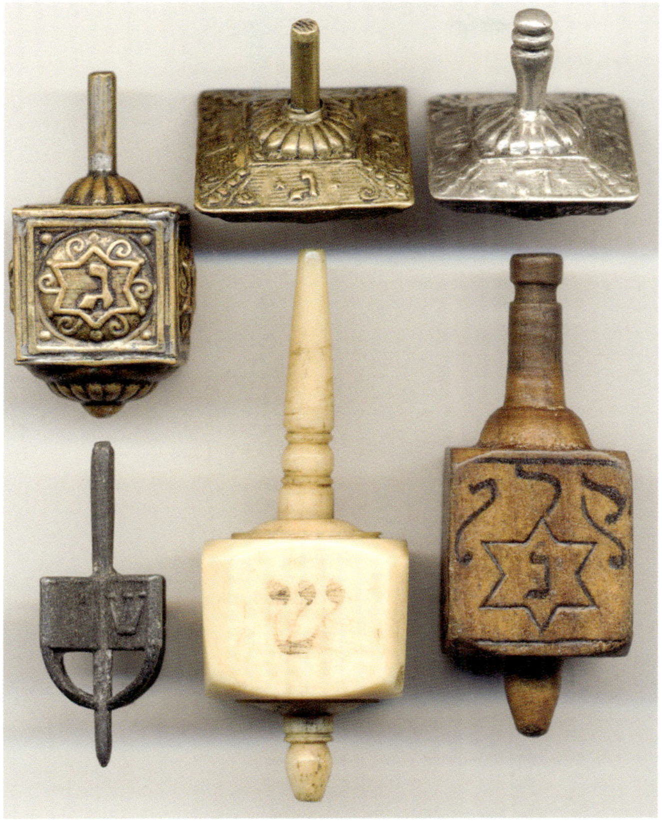

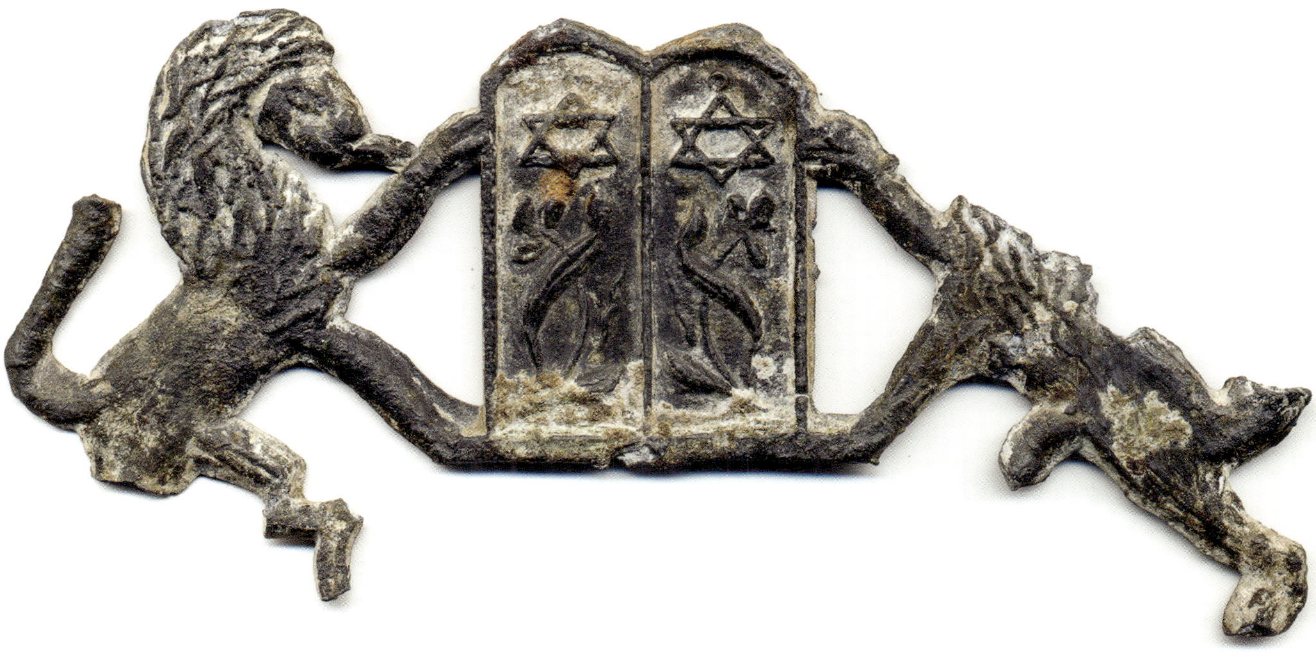

The top row of dreidels were made by the Bezalel School of Arts and Crafts. The small lead dreidel at bottom left is most likely from Germany, while the hand-carved and turned bone dreidel probably hails from Russia. The wood dreidel was issued by the Jewish National Fund and given away to children; each side has one of the Hebrew words of "Jewish National Fund" as well as "Jerusalem."

The lead piece was most likely the backplate of a menorah. It was sold to me as "found in a trunk of junk" in a flea market in Kiev, Ukraine

DREIDELS

Material: *Lead*
Origin: *Poland, circa 1900*
Dimensions: *.5" x .5"*

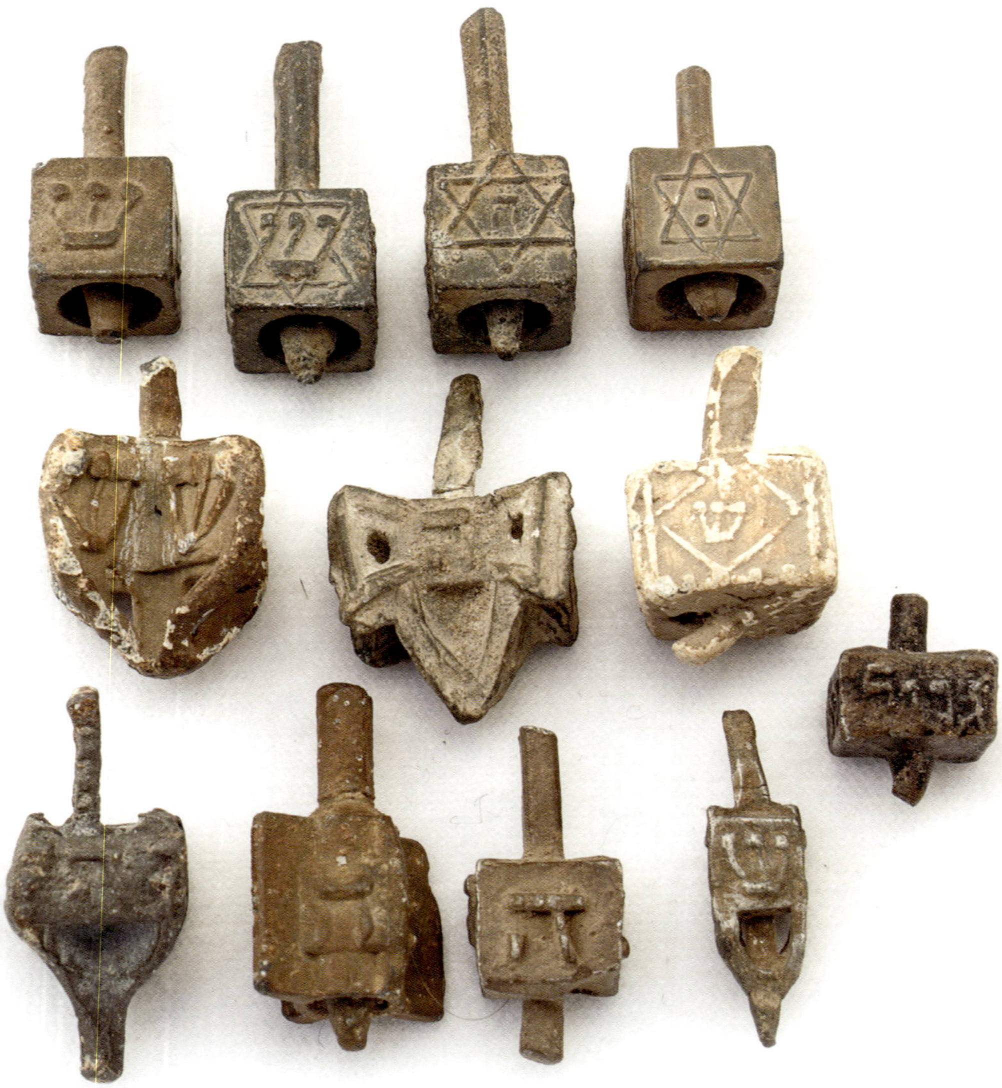

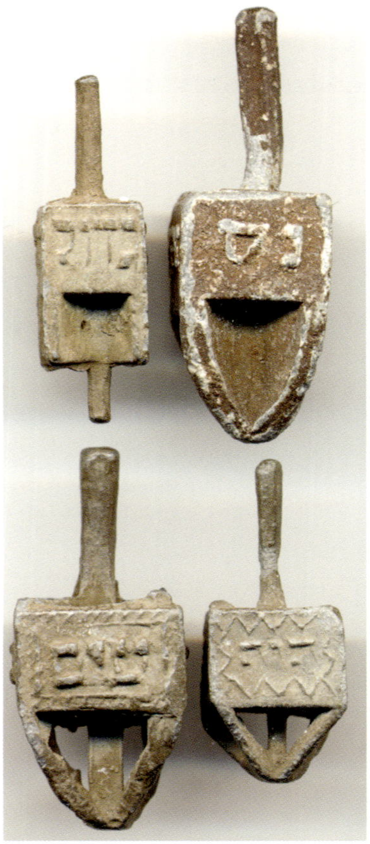

In 1939, Poland was home to the largest Jewish population of any country in the world (including the United States, with an estimated 3,300,000 Jews residing there). During World War II, approximately 3,000,000 Polish Jews were murdered, leaving only 300,000 left in 1945.

These dreidels were unearthed after roadwork construction began on Zgierska street in the city of Lodz during the 1950s.

Printed in The United States of America

PURIM

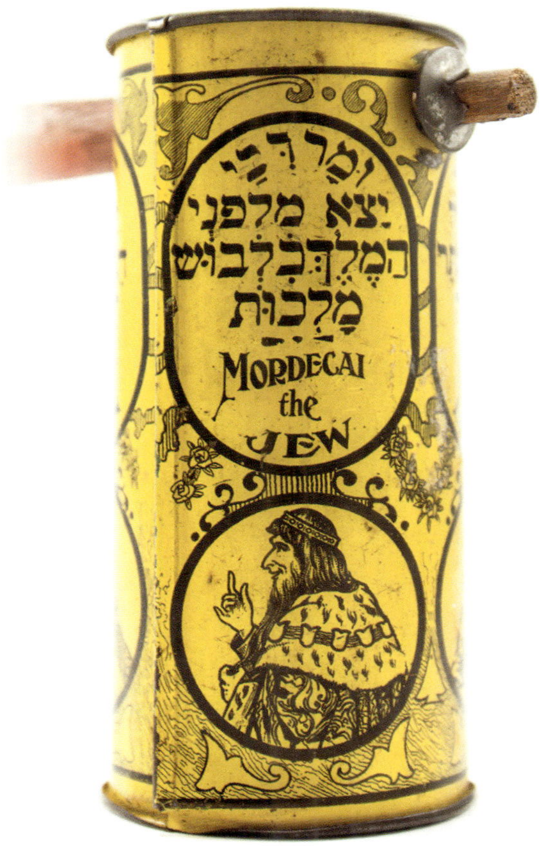

PURIM GRAGGER

Materials: Tin and wood
Origin: USA, circa 1920
Dimensions: 3.75" x 4.75"

On the holiday of Purim, when the Book of Esther is read aloud in the synagogue and the name "Haman" is said, a big ruckus ensues, with a stomping of feet and spinning of *graggers* (rattlers, noisemakers). Haman plotted to have all the Jews of ancient Persia killed during the sixth century BCE. He was the vizier under King Achashveyrosh (in most English texts this is generally spelled "Ahasuerus"; I have used a transliteration of the original Hebrew to spell it here).

This *gragger* has the names and portraits of the main characters of the Purim story lithographed on tin, along with excerpted verses in Hebrew from the Book of Esther that correlate to that person.

The portraits of Haman and Mordechai are curious, if not a bit disturbing. Haman was an evil man, and while he is shown in medieval armor —looking quite gentile to be sure—he does not look evil but instead has a strong, heroic look about him. Mordechai, who is titled "Mordecai the Jew," resembles Shakespeare's Shylock more than the humble, pious figure in the Book of Esther; he is shown with a hooked nose and luxurious fur stole and gives a seemingly conspiratorial crook of the finger along with a wry smile. Even the caption "the Jew," is a bit off-putting. It is likely that these images were drawn and titled by a gentile.

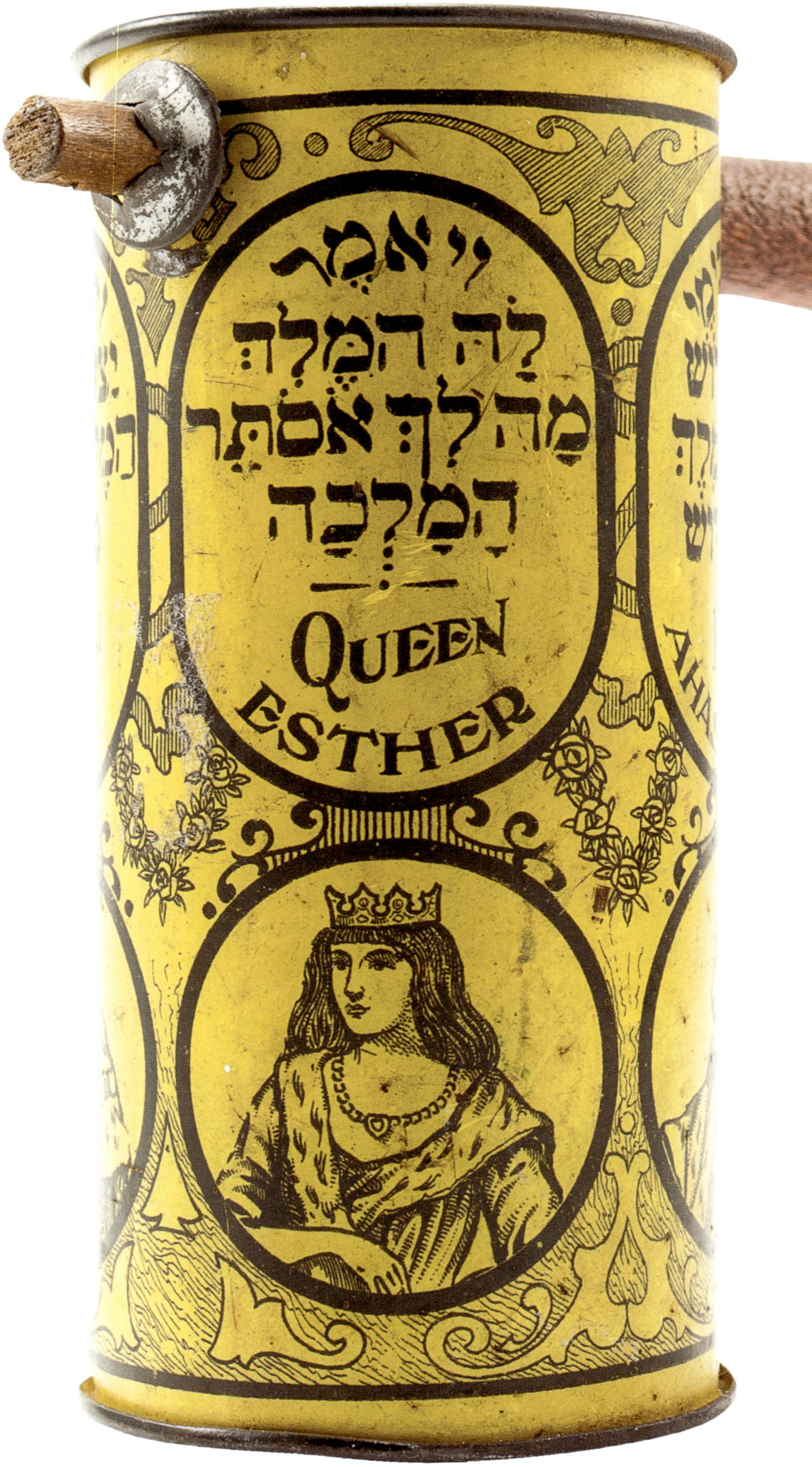
ויאמר
לה המלך
מה לך אסתר
המלכה
QUEEN
ESTHER

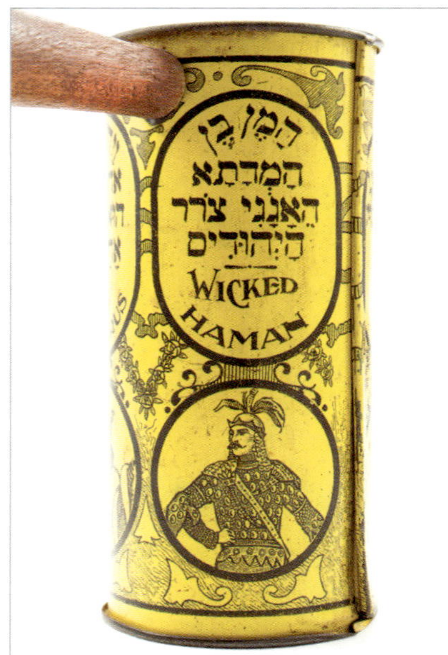
המן בן
המדתא
האגגי צרר
היהודים
WICKED
HAMAN

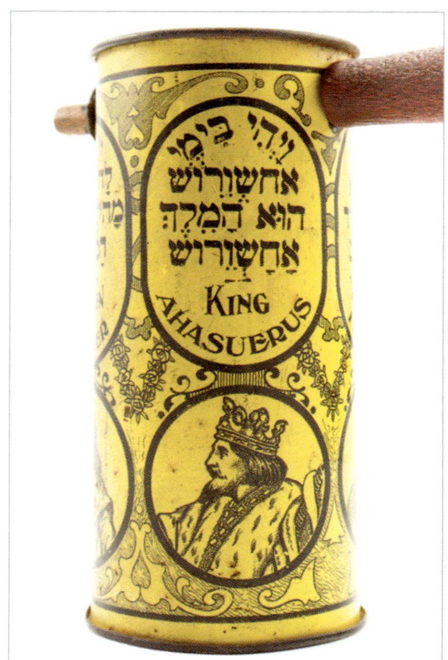
ויהי בימי
אחשורוש
הוא המלך
אחשורוש
KING
AHASUERUS

PURIM DRINKING MUG

Materials: Ceramic and pewter
Origin: Bohemian region of the Austro-Hungarian Empire (Czech Republic), circa 1905
Artist: "SPJ"
Dimensions: 7.25" x 5.6" (including handle)

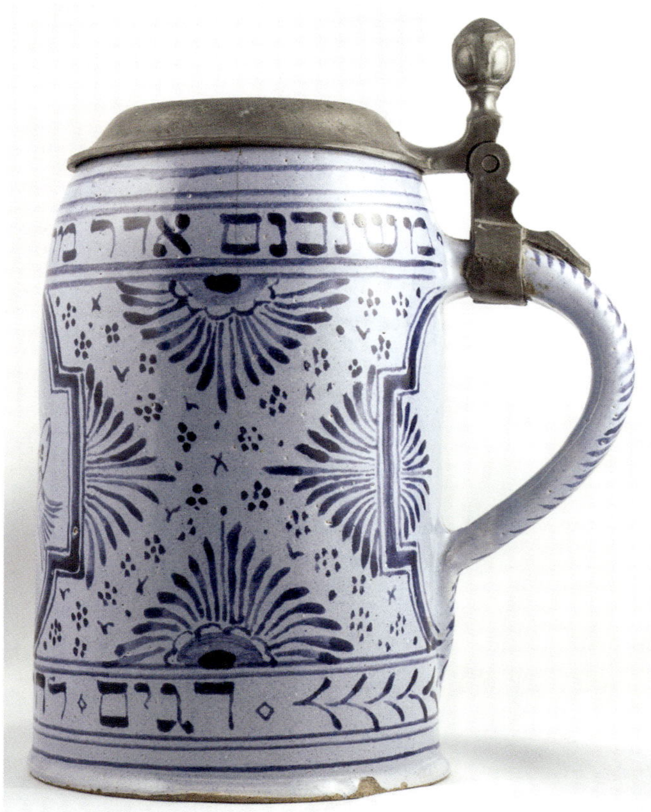

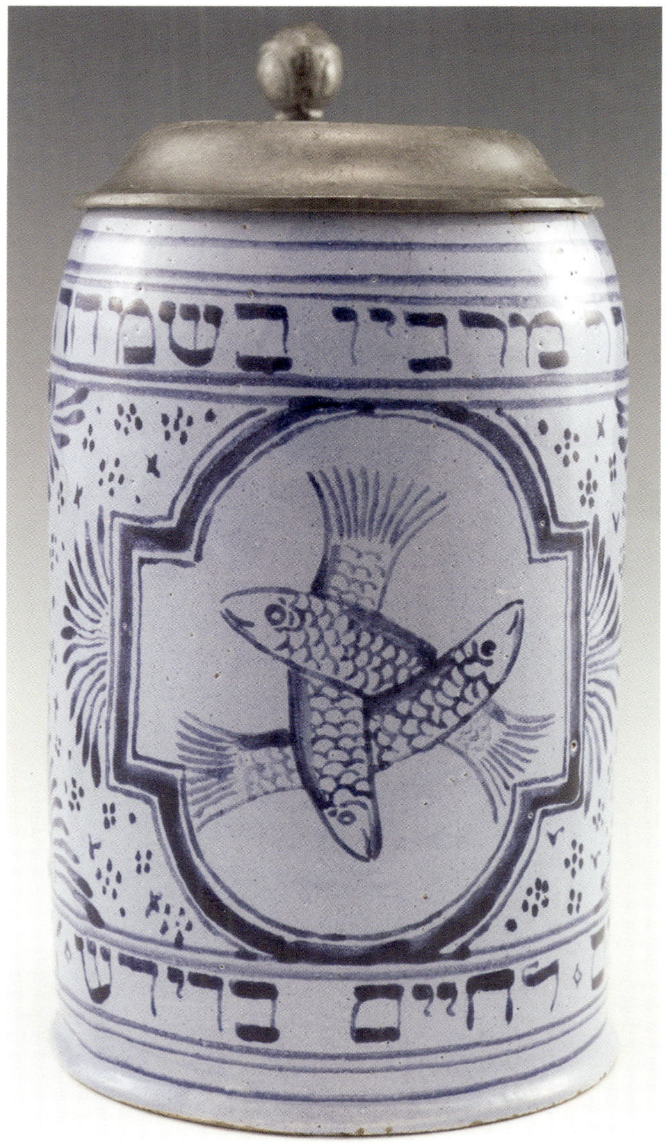

"It is one's duty to become intoxicated with wine on Purim until one cannot tell the difference between 'cursed be Haman' and 'blessed be Mordechai' " (Babylonian Talmud, Megillah 7b).

The central fish motif is symbolic of Purim, as this holiday occurs during the Hebrew month of Adar, who zodiacal symbol is fish. Fish also designate abundance, fertility, and good luck. At top in Hebrew, it says: "With the entrance of Adar rejoicing is increased." Continuing at bottom:"Luck of Adar, (luck of) fish," and finally "*L'Chayim Bridis,*" a toast half in Yiddish ("To life, brothers!").

Drinking utensils specifically associated with Purim are very rare. While a few pewter wine flagons and silver wine cups for Purim are scattered across Jewish museum collections around the world, this is the only known vessel made for drinking beer that was decorated for this holiday.

This stein was likely a unique commission for a beer-loving Bohemian Jew to be used on this festive holiday that encourages mild inebriation.

PURIM PLATE

Material: Pewter
Origin: England, 1750
Dimensions: 9.5"

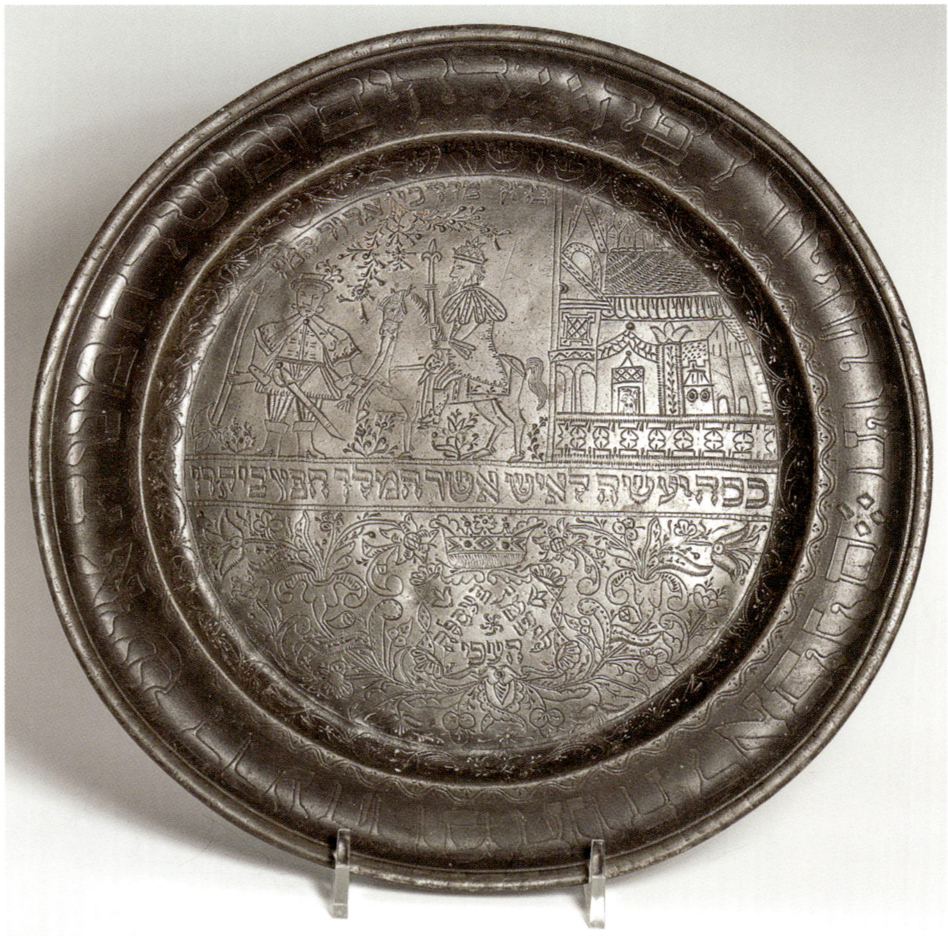

On the day of Purim, after The Book of Esther is read in the synagogue, it is customary to send at least two gifts of food to friends or neighbors and to give money to at least two poor people. This tradition originates directly from this verse: "As the days on which the Jews had rest from their enemies, and the month which had been transformed for them from one of sorrow to gladness, and from mourning to festivity; they were to observe them as days of feasting and gladness, and for sending delicacies to one another, and gifts to the poor," (Esther 9:22).

This plate was used for the purpose of *shalach manos* (sending delicacies), which is the giving of tasty food to a friend or neighbor. In Central Europe, nuts and candied or dried fruit were the usual treats extended.

At the center of the plate, wicked Haman is leading righteous Mordechai on horseback. The verse that describes this scene (Esther 6:9) is engraved below. Atop Mordechai and Haman is: "Blessed be Mordechai, cursed be Haman." To the right of Mordechai is the royal palace (complete with tiny soldier guarding the entrance), titled "Shushan."

On the plate rim is the latter part of the verse from Esther 9:22, along with a Hebrew date equivalent to the year 1750. At bottom is the name of the couple who gave this gift of food; displayed in a cartouche is "Lipman / Pessaleh Hychi."

This plate has an outstanding provenance; it was featured at the Anglo-Jewish Historical Exhibition of 1887, held at the Royal Albert Hall in London and is pictured and described in the catalog of that event. The plate bears an English hallmark dating from the last quarter of the 17th century.

Jewish ceremonial objects hailing from mid-18th-century England are quite rare, as the total Jewish population of England at this time numbered only 8,000 souls.

A fascinating aspect of this plate is the depiction of the Hebrew date, as the letters are spelled out phonetically. I cannot locate any other examples of a Hebrew date written this way on a piece of Judaica. Intriguing!

SUCCOT

ETROG BOXES

Material: Olivewood
Origin: Israel, circa 1910 / Israel, circa 1940
Marks: "Jerusalem" stamped in Hebrew and English / applied paper label stating "Mininbergs' Institute of Palestine Art Tel-Aviv"
Dimensions: 3.25" x 6" / 3.25" x 6.5"

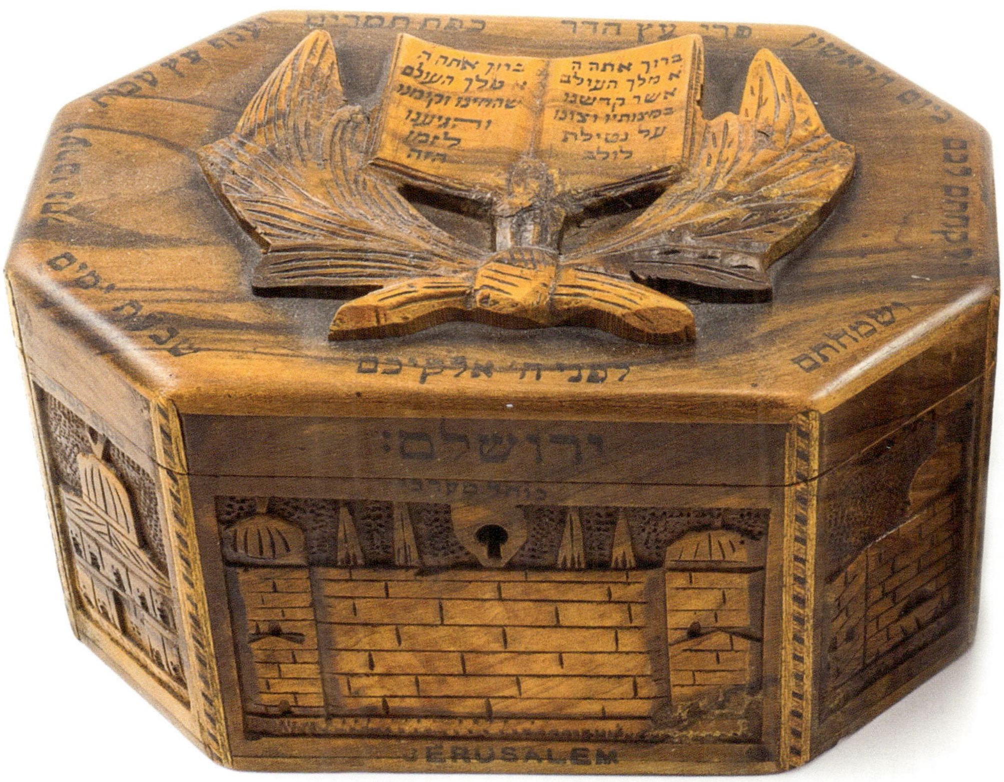

An etrog is a medium-sized citrus fruit used with a *lulav* (a bundle consisting of myrtle, willow and date palm branches) during rituals on the holiday of Succot. In English, it is known as a citron, and in scientific literature it is cited as an etrog citron.

The box above has a carving of an open book on its lid upon which are two prayers related to Succot. Around the edge of the lid it says: "On the first day, you must take for yourself a fruit of the citron tree, an unopened palm frond, myrtle branches, and willows

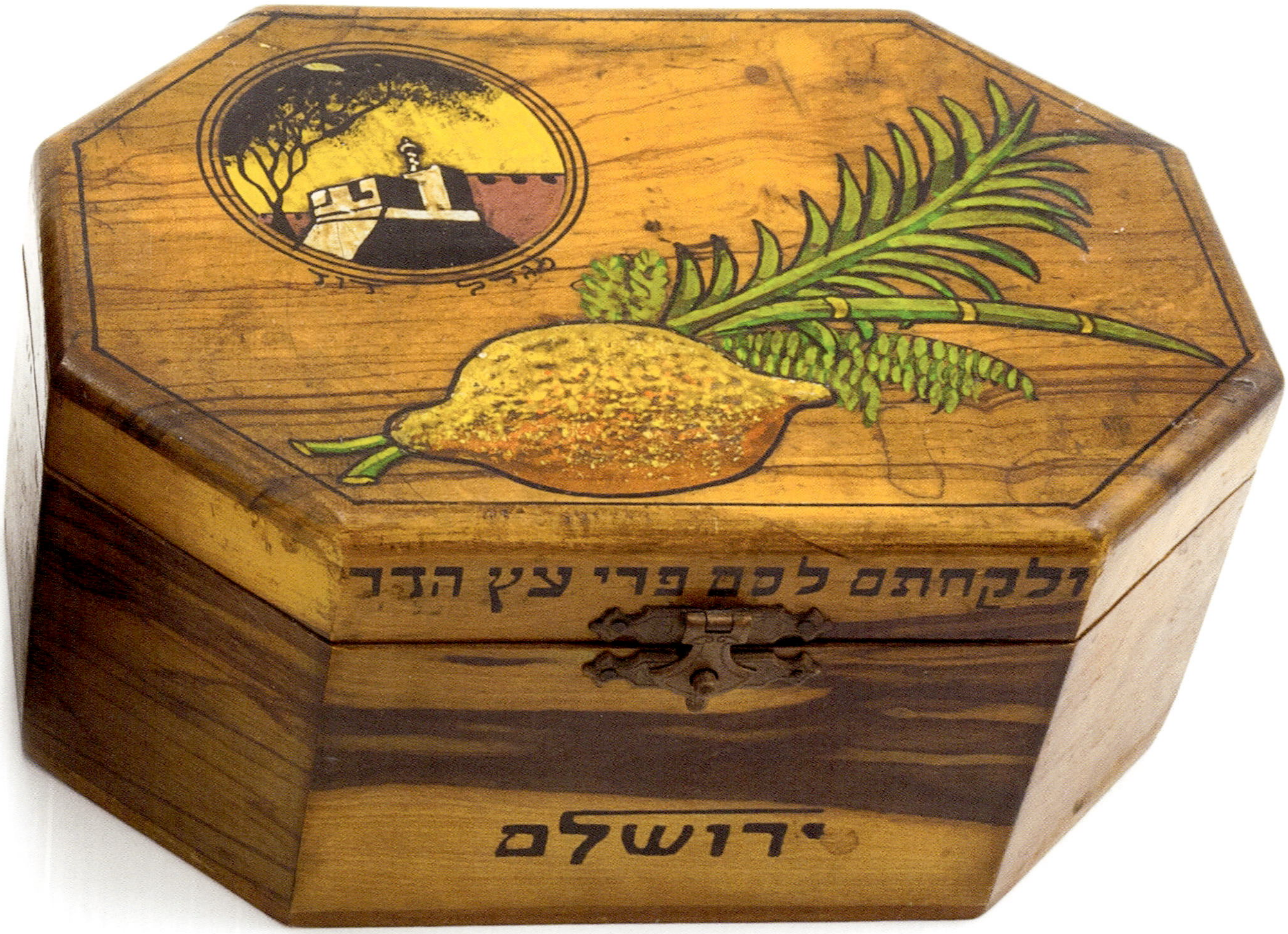

[that grow near] the brook. You shall rejoice before G-d for seven days,"(Leviticus 23:40).

Around the sides of the box are eight different carved scenes of ancient sites of Israel, titled as such in Hebrew: "The Western Wall," "[Tomb of] Rachel our Mother," "[Tomb of] Zechariah the Prophet," "Tombs of the House of David," "Tombs of the Patriarchs," "Tomb of Samuel," "Gravesite of Avshalom," "Temple Mount."

The second box, above, was made approximately thirty years later than the first box. Painted pictures are used instead of carved wood. The main scene is of the *lulav* and *etrog*, and the minor scene shows the Tower of David. The first third of the verse from Leviticus is written, along with "Jerusalem."

Olivewood etrog boxes from Jerusalem were made in tremendous quantities and finding old examples to purchase today is not difficult.

BIRTH & MARRIAGE

AMULETS FOR BABIES AND CHILDREN

Materials: Brass / Lead / Tin
Origin: Iran, late nineteenth century / Poland, nineteenth century, Jerusalem, circa 1890
Dimensions: 35 mm – 41 mm, 1.6" x 1.1"

Protective amulets are objects that are worn and believed to ward off evil by means of semi-religious powers. The earliest evidence of amulets in Judaism has been traced back to the year 1230, in which *Sefer Raziel*, a handbook for writers of amulets, was composed by Rabbi Eliezer of Worms, Germany.

The heart-shaped amulet (see page 90 for all amulets) has the phrase "G-d is my Protector," along with the names of three angels: "Senoy, Sansenoy, Semangelof." This amulet and the other amulets that state they were made for babies were placed around the neck of a newborn boy until he was circumcised, and if for a girl, was worn for twenty days after she was born.

The next two amulets have identical writing and symbols, including fish (signifying good luck and fertility). The first has a large letter "*hey*" (for "Hashem," G-d) and a sunflower inside the letter. The square-shaped amulet has Lions of Judah flanking the letter "*hey*," topped by a Crown of Torah.

Obverse: "This boy should grow up to learn Torah, get married, and do good deeds."

Reverse: "May it be Your will Hashem our G-d and G-d of our forefathers, you should save the babies of Israel that they should not get diphtheria, and should grow to Torah, and you should protect them with mercy, amen."

The fourth amulet states on its reverse it was for a girl, while the obverse has a pair of candlesticks flanking the "*hey*." This matches the motif of Sabbath candlesticks that is often found on nineteenth-century European Jewish gravestones for women.

The last two amulets have blessings and names of angels, along with the priestly hands inside the letter "hey" on one obverse. The reverse sides depict the Western Wall and Tomb of Rachel. One blessing reads: "This boy should be protected from the evil eye and all diseases."

The ring made of tin says "*mazel tov*" (good luck). In *Kultura I Sztuka Ludu Zydowskiego Na Zemiach Polskich. Zbiory Maksymiljana Goldsteina*, published in 1935, author Dr. Karol Dresdner states European mazel tov rings were used the same way in which amulets were.

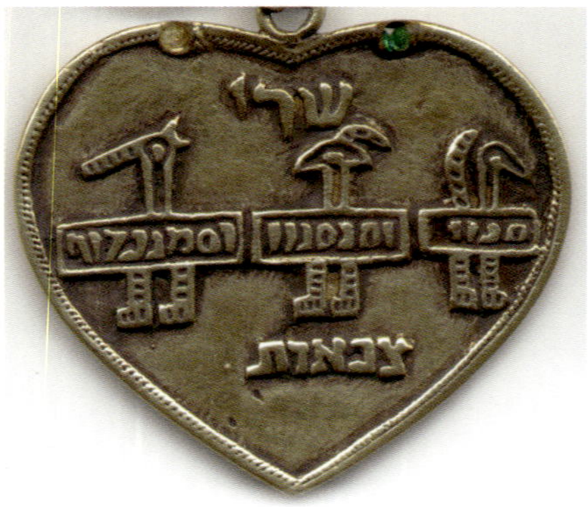
שדי
צבאות
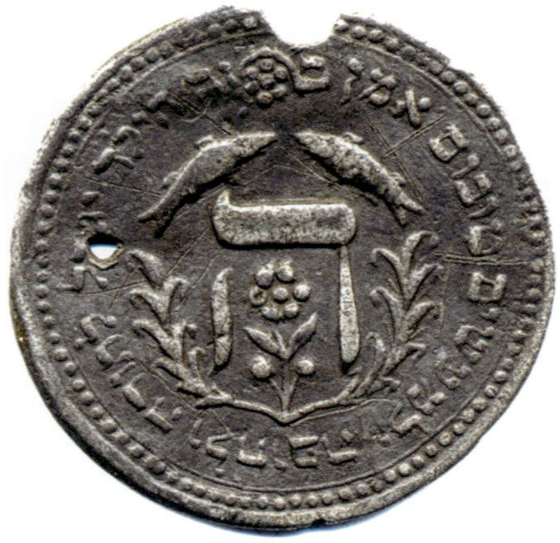
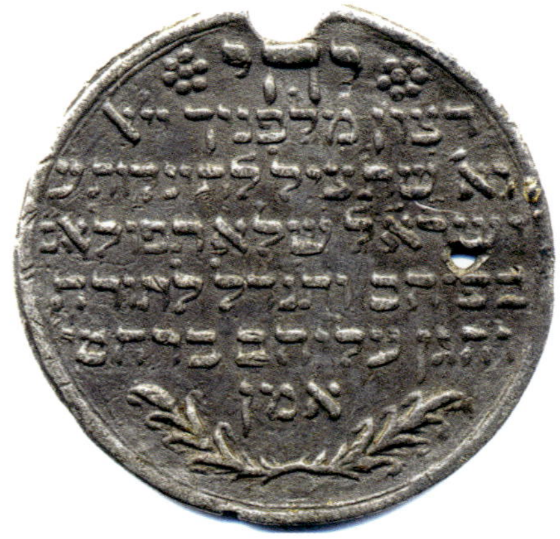
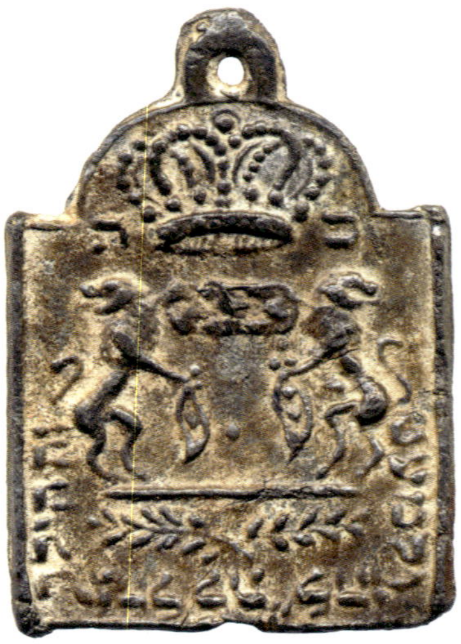
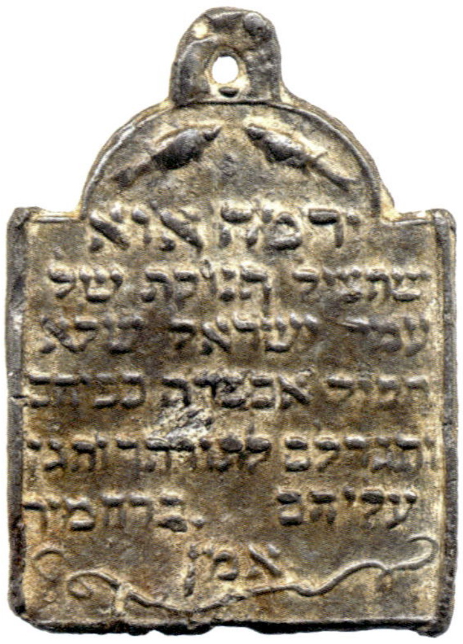
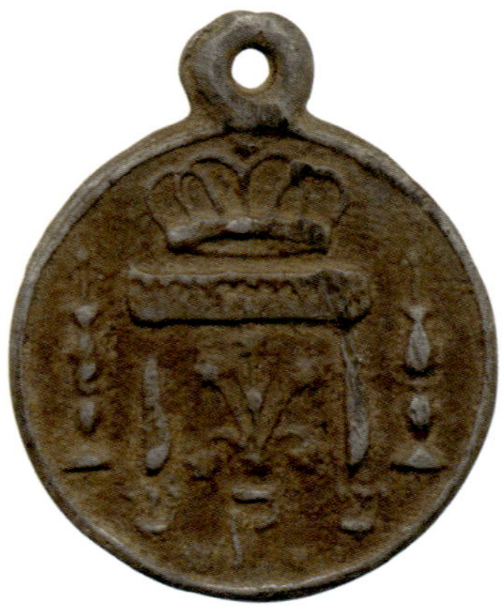
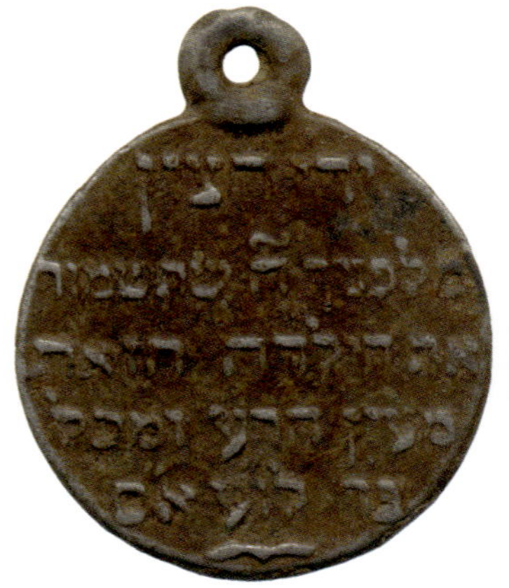
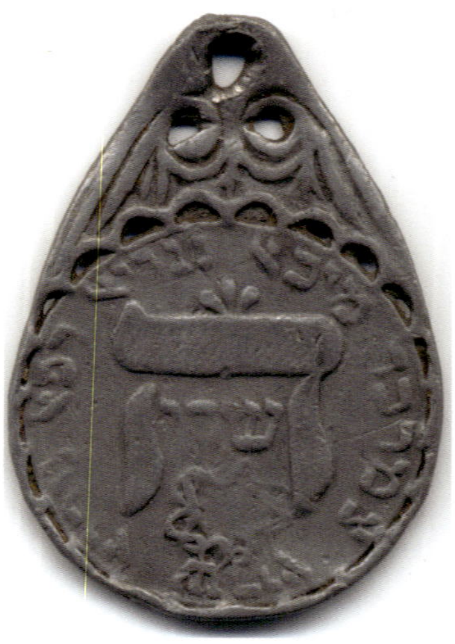
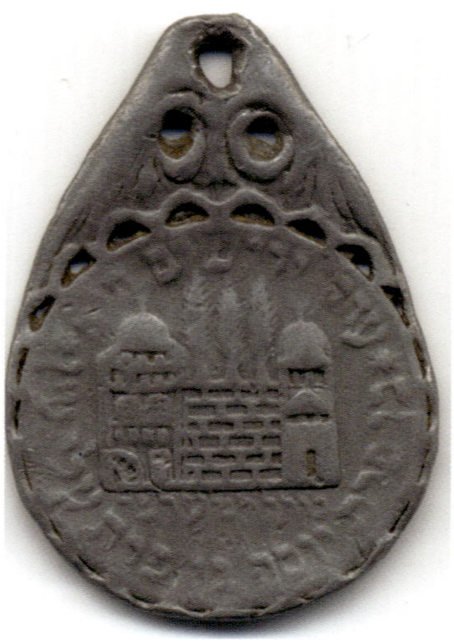
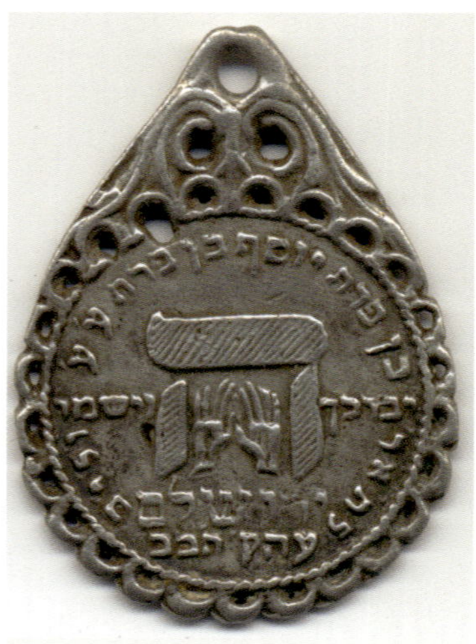
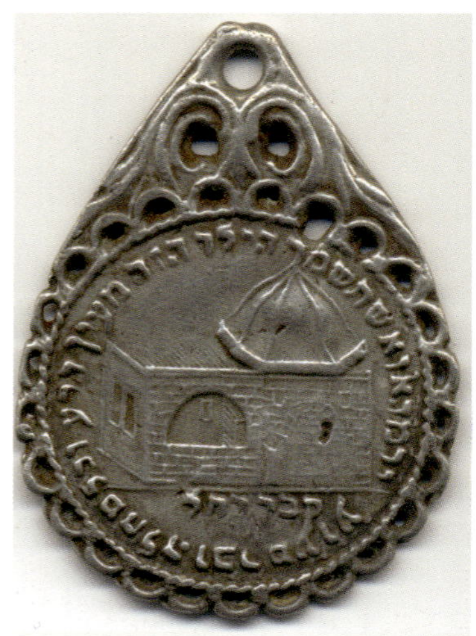
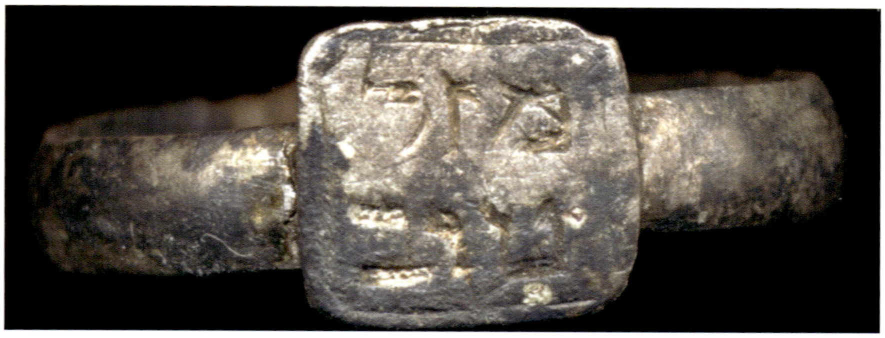

CIRCUMCISION KNIFE BOX

Material: Wood
Origin: Dolyna, Ukraine, 1827 -1828
Artist: Moshe Yosef Maisels
Dimensions: 1.5″ x 11″

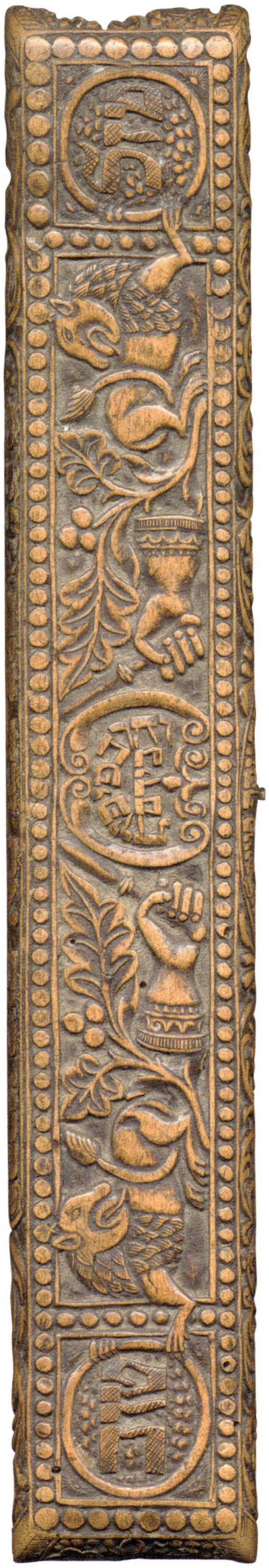

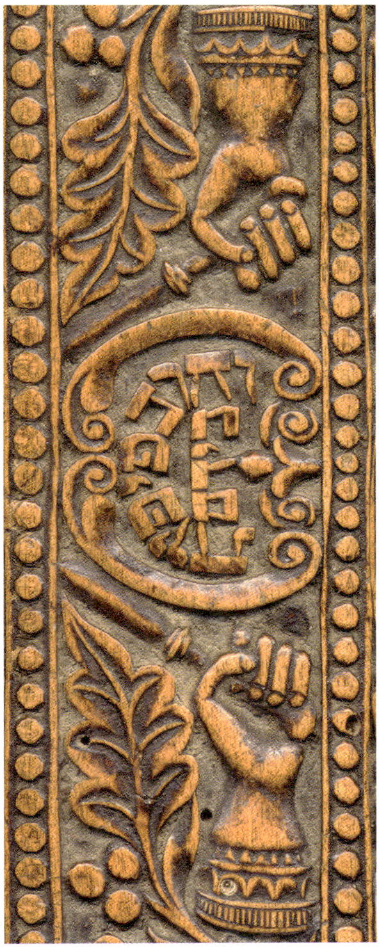

Detail

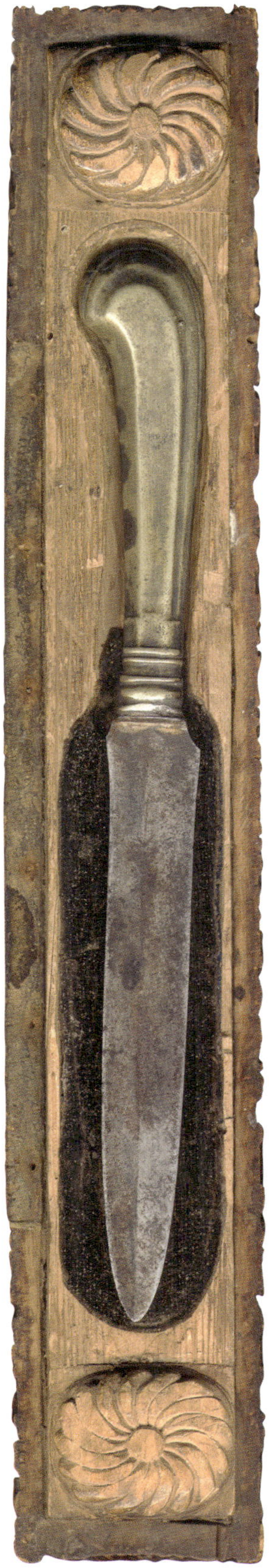

"G-d said to Abraham, 'And as for you, you shall keep My covenant—you and your offspring after you throughout their generations. This is My covenant which you shall keep between Me and you and your offspring after you: Every male among you shall be circumcised. You shall circumcise the flesh of your foreskin, and that shall be the sign of the covenant between Me and you. At the age of eight days every male shall be circumcised, throughout your generations,' " (Genesis 17:9-12).

This lavishly carved box was created to house the knife for the circumcision ceremony. The lid has the words "*mazel*" (luck), and "*tov*" (good), at opposite ends, with each word being flanked by a Lion of Judah. Toward the center, a pair of hands holding knives flank the words "*v'cherev pipiyot biyadam*" (a double-edged sword in your hands), which references the double-edged knives used in circumcising so there is no chance of the dull side being used during this delicate procedure. The origin of the phrase "*v'cherev pipiyot biyadam*" is found in Psalms 149:6, as a weapon the righteous would use to fight their enemies.

On the reverse side of the box, it reads: "*kayem es valad hazeh*" (give this newborn sustenance). Here, there are also notches above all except one of the Hebrew letters of those words, which signifies that when adding up the numerical value of the letters, the Jewish year (5)588 is revealed, which equals the period of September 1827 through September 1828, indicated by the appropriate "date words" of the abbreviated "*leprat katan*" (in order of the small counting) and stressed by the word *leprat* that precedes the beginning of the phrase "*kayem es valad hazeh.*" Signed on the front above a sunflower motif is "the humble Moshe Yosef Maisels from Dolyna."

Decorative elements of tree branches, leaves, berries and flowers are used to fill space; there is no unadorned place on the box. Even the side edges of this narrow box are carved; they depict a two-handled basket holding a plant. *Horror vacui* (fear of emptiness) is the art term for this tendency, which is characteristic of primitive art, as well as folk art. The brass hook that would have been used to close the box is missing, and only the latch remains (in the center of the box, underneath the artist's signature). The blade of the knife is a later replacement, and possibly the handle is as well. From the internal space left, it is clear the first blade was large, as this box was designed to close tightly around the original knife.

The tradition of masterful Jewish woodcarving from Central and Eastern Europe dates back to at least the seventeenth century. The interior of the synagogue, specifically Torah arks, would be densely carved and decorated with animals, fruit, foliage, and Hebrew verses. In countries such as Poland, Lithuania, and the Ukraine, most of the synagogues themselves were constructed of wood. The territory that had the most prolific Jewish woodcarvers of synagogue interiors was Galicia, a heavily forested region with a large Jewish population. The wooden Torah arks in this area had the most resplendent decoration of all the synagogues of Europe. Due to the destruction of World War II, however, only a handful of wooden synagogues still exist. Today we know of the formerly large number of these magnificently carved Torah arks of Galicia from photographs taken before the war.

This circumcision knife box from the Ukraine (then Galicia) is part of that centuries-old woodcarving heritage. While no other works by Moshe Yosef Maisels of Dolyna are known, two works by a descendant of his, Yecheskel Yehoshua Maisels of Dolyna, are. Both pieces are cases to house the scroll of Esther for reading on the holiday of Purim. One case, dated 1913, belongs to the Hebrew manuscript collector Rene Braginsky, while the other Esther scroll case, dated 1892 and originally owned by Baron Rothschild, is currently on long-term loan to the Judisches Museum der Schweiz, in Basel, Switzerland. Along with the corresponding signature of the artist's surname and city, the carving style on the Esther scroll cases are an identical match to those on this box, down to the leaf and berry motifs. Although there are no records of a woodcarving dynasty known as the "Maisels of Dolyna," because of the survival of this circumcision knife box and the aforementioned scroll cases, for a few generations at the very least, that is exactly what they were.

This is the only carved wood circumcision knife box known, making this a unique treasure.

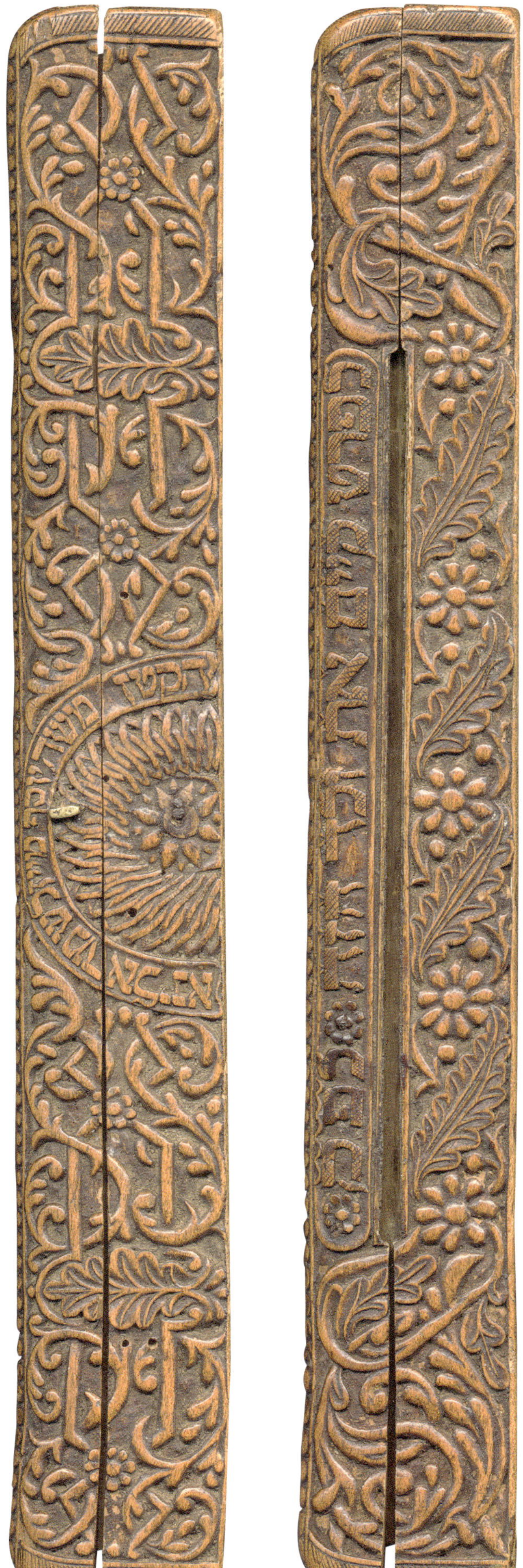

MARRIAGE CUPS

Material: Silver
Origin: Germany, circa 1925
Hallmarks: "800," crescent moon and crown
Dimensions: 3" x 2.6" (each cup)

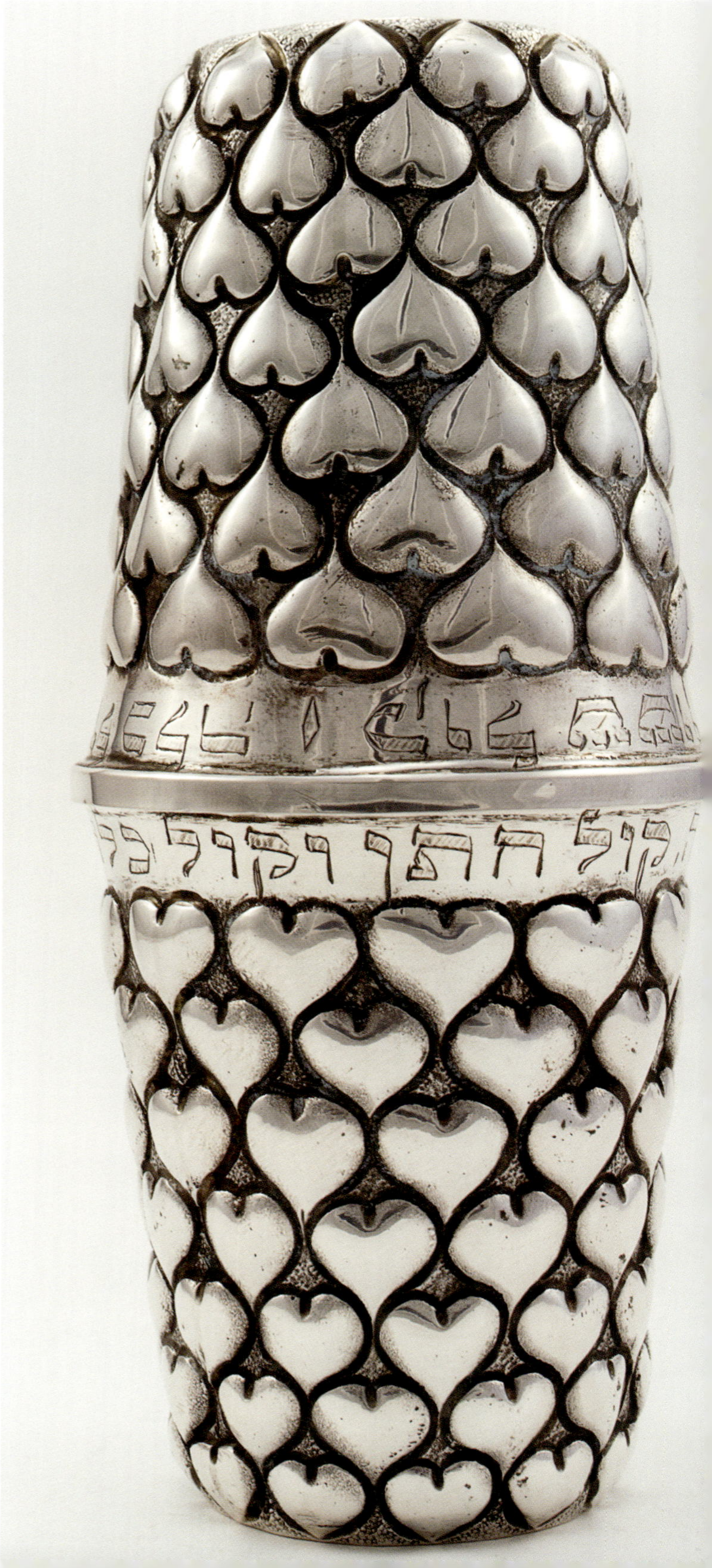

Two cups of wine are used in a Jewish wedding ceremony. The first cup accompanies the betrothal blessing. After this is recited, the groom drinks some wine, then he passes the cup to his bride so she may drink. After the giving of the ring and reading of the marriage contract, the *Sheva Brachos* (Seven Blessings) are recited over a newly refilled cup, the second cup of wine. At the conclusion of the blessings, again, the groom drinks and then passes the cup to the bride so she may drink.

But while there are two times during the traditional marriage ceremony that wine is drunk, *only one cup* is actually used, and it is shared by the groom and bride. So, for what purpose was this "double cup" made?

In Germany there was a tradition among the gentile population to have a silver "double cup," at the wedding ceremony, so that it could come apart and the bride and groom could toast each other. This tradition of non-Jewish origin was assimilated by many Jews residing in Germany and its surrounding area between the eighteenth and early twentieth centuries. Jews would purchase these secular double cups and have them engraved appropriately in Hebrew. On each of the cup rims it reads: "The sound of joy and the sound of gladness, the sound of the groom and the sound of the bride," (Jeremiah 7:34).

Double cups engraved with Hebrew relating to the wedding ceremony only hail from Germany and Austria. While they are quite attractive, there is no actual ceremonial purpose for using both cups, as one is sufficient. They would make a nice gift for the newlyweds, however.

THE SYNAGOGUE

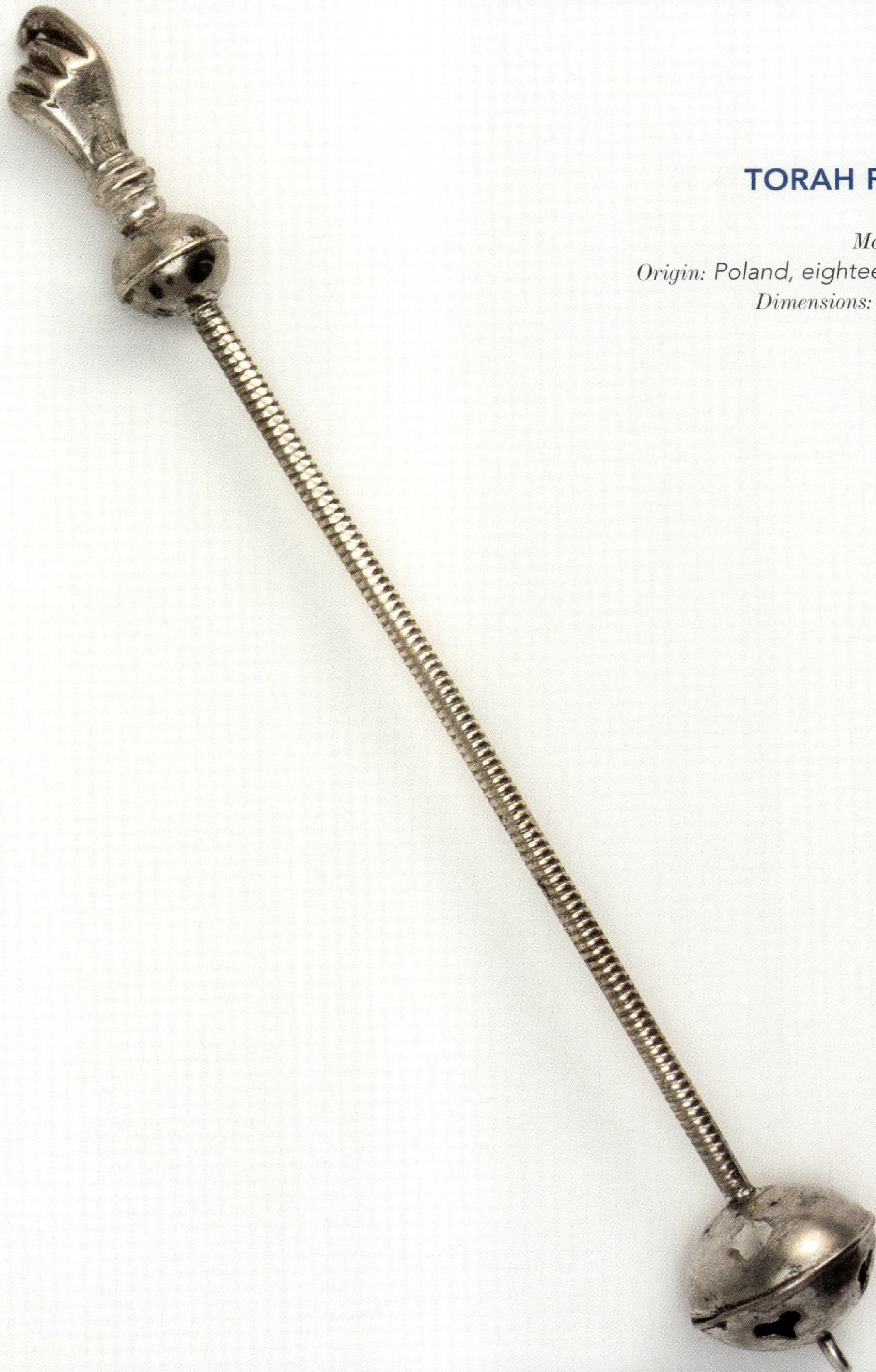

TORAH POINTER

Material: Silver
Origin: Poland, eighteenth century
Dimensions: 1.25″ x 9.6″

When reading from a Torah scroll, a pointer, or as it is referred to in Hebrew, *yad* (literally "hand"), is used so the letters of the scroll do not get dirty or smudged, as our hands always excrete oils, which can damage the ink and the scroll itself. It takes a year to have a Torah scroll written, all by hand with a quill, by one scribe, at a cost of tens of thousands of dollars. When the scroll is closed, the Torah pointer is hung by a chain or rope from the staves of the scroll and placed in the ark.

Overall, the design and construction of this pointer (see page 95) is typical for silver Torah pointers from eighteenth-century Poland. It is comprised of low-grade silver, likely 65% or even less. Eighteenth-century Polish craftsmen often used an alloy of silver mixed with copper, sometimes amalgamating as much as 50% of copper into the silver. When this kind of silver becomes tarnished, orange highlights appear.

The feature that makes this pointer unusual is the decorative piercing of hearts at the end. While the hearts motif is charming and has strong visual appeal, it is likely there is a deeper meaning here, perhaps to convey to the user of the pointer that he should have a love for the Torah he is reading.

TORAH POINTER

Material: Brass
Origin: United States, circa 1810–1850
Dimensions: 2" x 15"

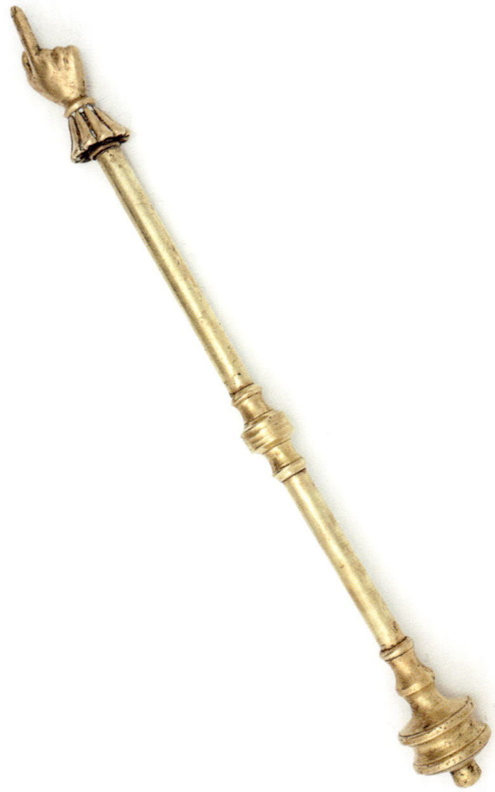

This large pointer was found in Pennsylvania. Aside from the hand itself, the rest of the pointer has parts that are identical to late eighteenth- and early nineteenth-century American brassware; the overall design appears to match the Federalist period of about 1810. The shaft and end piece display excellent craftsmanship; they were manufactured by being turned on a lathe. Upon close examination, however, it is ascertained that the hand was not made at the same time as the rest of the pointer, even though it does have wear and is finely molded, having been expertly cast using the lost wax method.

A possible explanation for the origin of this item might be as follows: An early nineteenth-century synagogue congregation located in an area of the eastern United States wanted to add a pointer to their inventory of Torah ornaments. Old implements of brassware were located (a fireplace poker for example) and were given to a local craftsman, who then fashioned a hand that matched the rest of the pieces in size and proportion.

Jewish ceremonial art from the United States of America that pre-dates the Civil War is extremely rare. In 1848, there were only 50,000 Jews in this country, which is tiny when compared to the total U.S. population of 1850, which numbered more than 23,000,000. The first significant wave of Jewish immigration did not occur until the 1860s, when 150,000 German and Polish Jews landed on our shores. Following that, between 1880 and 1914, more than 2,000,000 Russian Jews arrived in the United States, the largest Jewish immigrant wave to ever come to the nation.

TORAH POINTER

Materials: *Brass and silver*
Origin: *Europe or United States, circa 1910*
Dimensions: *1" x 9.5"*

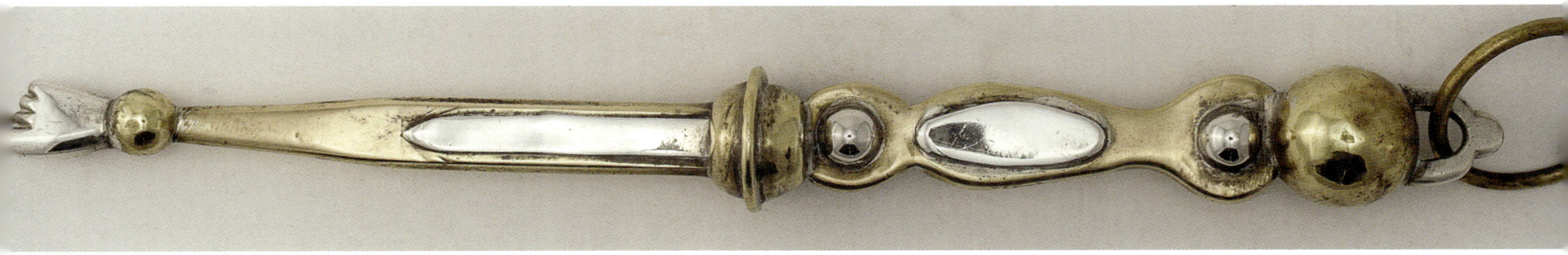

The entire design of this pointer was made in the style of the Arts and Crafts movement. A characteristic of many Arts and Crafts pieces was the usage of "mixed metals," which meant using at least two different metals and fashioning both of them to create one piece but showcasing each metal in its own right. Here we have a silver hand, a flat brass shaft inlaid with a silver strapwork design, and a brass ball-shaped end with a silver loop attached, holding a brass chain.

Because there are no hallmarks and no design elements pointing to a specific country of origin, it is difficult to state exactly where this was made. In all likelihood it is German, as the majority of surviving Jewish ceremonial art fashioned in the Arts and Crafts style hails from there, but the United Kingdom or the United States are plausible countries of origin as well.

I am not aware of other Torah pointers even remotely similar to this one, as all the elements of this pointer were made purely in the style of the Arts and Crafts movement. Aside from being a rare Jewish ceremonial object of its type, this pointer is a remarkable piece of Arts and Crafts metalwork, both in its design and execution.

TORAH POINTERS

Material: Brass
Origin: Morocco, circa 1915 / Djerba or Morocco, circa 1900
Dimensions: 1.75" x 6.75" / 1.75" x 10.5"

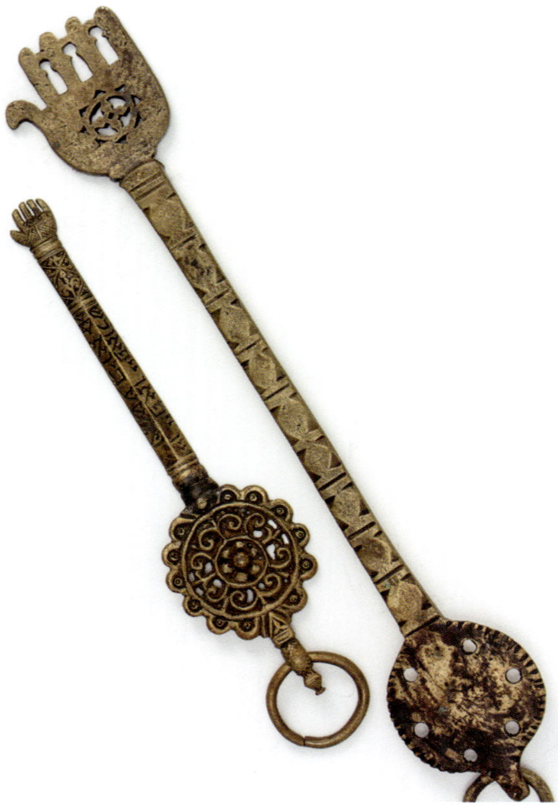

The small pointer is well cast and exquisitely chased; it is made of two pieces of brass that connect to each other with handmade pins, which were then soldered. One side has an engraved dedication, while the other side depicts a bird, a motif typically found in the design of functional objects made and used by Moroccan Jewry.

The large pointer was forged from one piece of brass that is nearly a quarter of an inch thick. Completely fashioned by hand, this was hammered, carved and pierced by someone who was a master craftsman in metalwork.

The hand of this pointer is in the form of a hamsa, a palm shape that is used for good luck among Muslims and Sephardic Jews. There is a finely cut rosette in the center of the palm. The *qewas del-biban* dividing the fingers of the hand reveals the influence that the surrounding Islamic culture had on the Jewish maker of this pointer. *Qewas del-biban* are keyhole-shaped arched doorways (also known as a "Moorish arch" and "horseshoe arch"), which are emblematic of Islamic architecture. Keyhole arches are commonly found as a motif on Middle Eastern Chanukah menorahs, but this is the only Torah pointer I am aware of that incorporated keyhole arches into its design.

In addition to their widespread architectural use across the Muslim world, keyhole arches became popular in Western countries at the time of the Moorish Revival movement. For example, they were widely used in Moorish Revival-styled synagogues.

A few other Torah pointers I have seen that were identified as hailing from the Island of Djerba had the same repeating "bar pattern" going across the center of the pointer. More research is needed, however, before I can state with certainty that this does indeed originate from Djerba.

TORAH POINTER

Material: Wood
Origin: Ancona, Italy, eighteenth century
Artist: Yosef Delmedigo
Dimensions: 1.5" x 13"

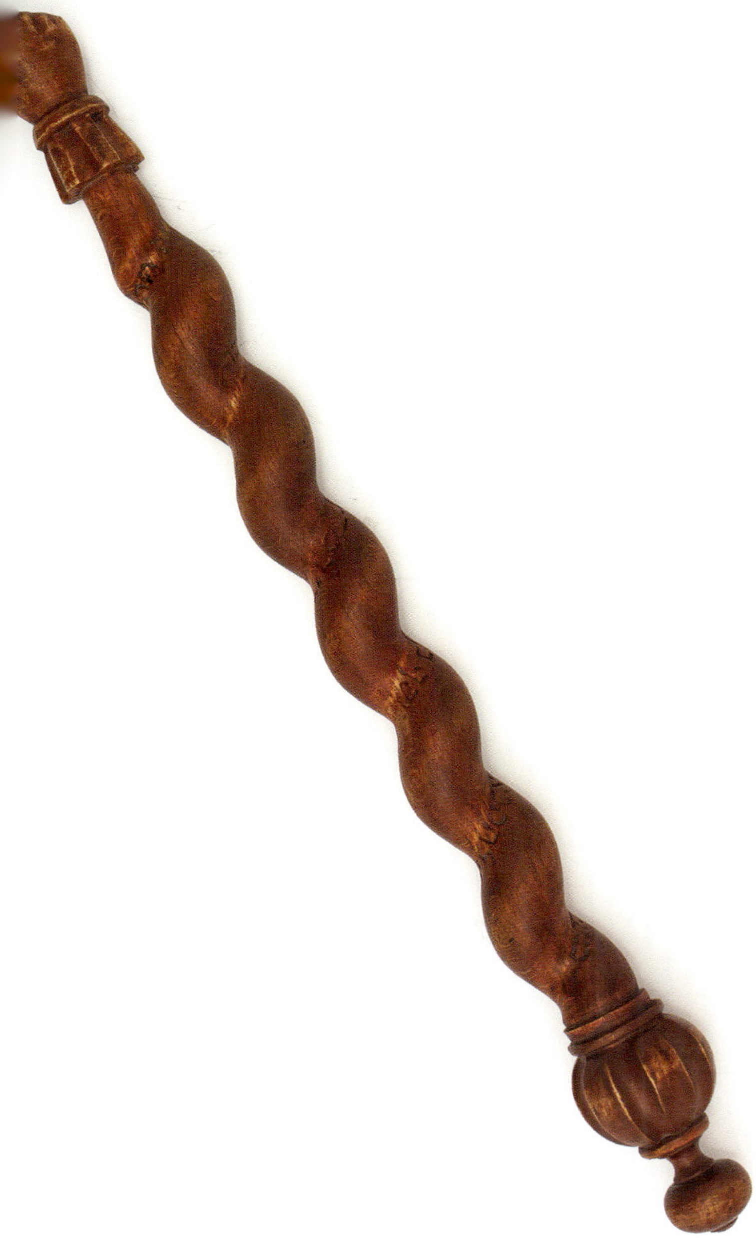

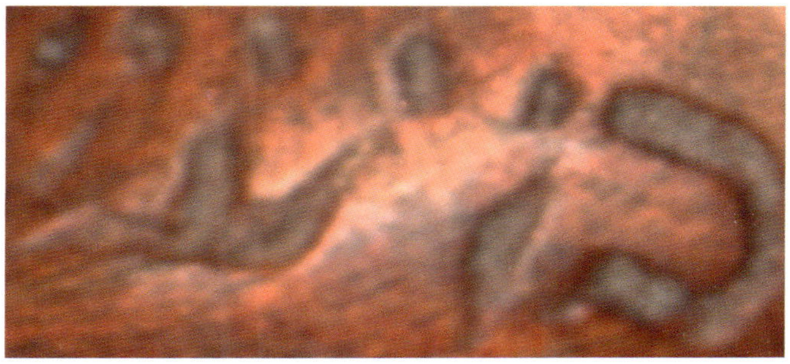

This pointer was carved from a single piece of wood and then stained. There is deep engraving of Hebrew throughout the shaft that reads: "Made by my hands, and not to boast, I am the humble Yosef, the oldest son of Yochanan Delmedigo of Ancona." One twist part of the shaft is skipped and left blank, then underneath the cuff of the hand, by the last twist part, written in the opposite direction (toward the hand), it says: "This is the Torah, the Torah of Moshe" (Moses).

There were two noteworthy Jews with the surname "Delmedigo": One was Eliyahu Delmedigo (1460-1497), a philosopher and Talmudist; the other was Yosef Delmedigo (1591-1655), a rabbi, philosopher, mathematician, and astronomer. Both of these men came from the Greek island of Crete, and each spent many years studying in Padua, Italy. Since "Delmedigo" is a very uncommon Jewish surname (even among Mediterranean Jews), it is quite possible that the person who fashioned this pointer is a descendent of either of these men.

The craftsmanship of this pointer is of the highest level; in particular, the quality of the engraved Hebrew is exquisite.

TORAH POINTER

Material: *Olivewood*
Origin: *Israel, circa 1910*
Identifying Marks: *"Jerusalem" in Hebrew*
Dimensions: *1.5" x 12.5"*

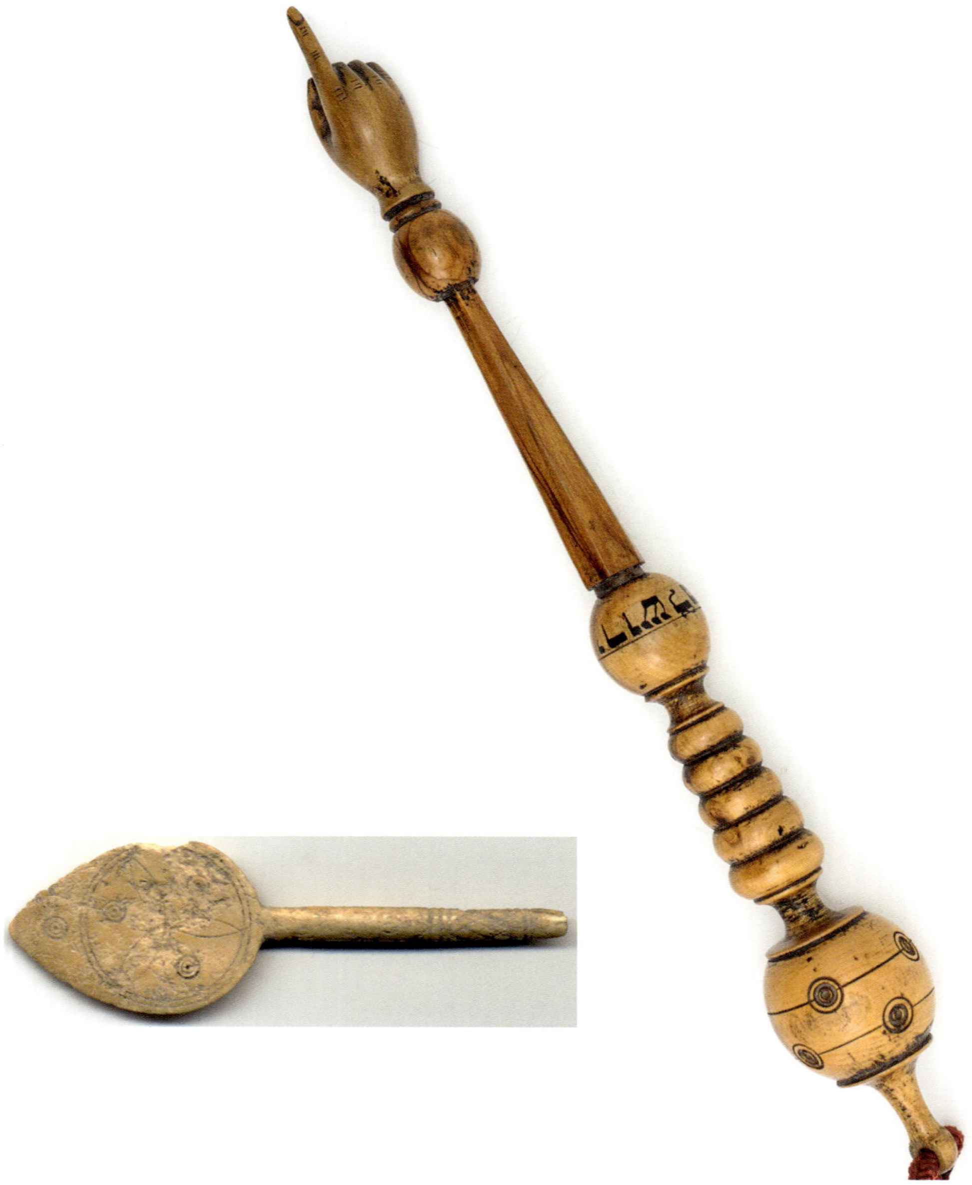

This pointer was fashioned from a single piece of wood. Noteworthy is the skillfully carved hand, which shows details such as fingernails. The center of the pointer has "Jerusalem" hand-inked (as opposed to stamped, which most olivewood objects of a ceremonial nature tend to be). The end has a cloth rope for hanging from the scroll when put in the ark.

The large ball shape at the end of the pointer has a repeating pattern design of circles; this exact decoration is found on items from antiquity dating to more than two thousand years ago. Due to the enormous number of ancient items that were being unearthed in the Middle East during the late nineteenth and early twentieth centuries, design aspects of these objects began being filtered down to the public consciousness, as discoveries were appearing in museum exhibits and for sale in tourist shops. For olivewood items made in Jerusalem between 1880 and 1930, many pieces appear with this circular motif from antiquity.

Shown also is a fragment of a cosmetic item made from bone, with this same circular motif. It was found in Israel and dates from the first or second century of the Common Era.

TORAH CROWN

Material: Silver
Origin: Poland, circa 1885
Hallmarks: "84" on each arm
Dimensions: 12" x 10.5"

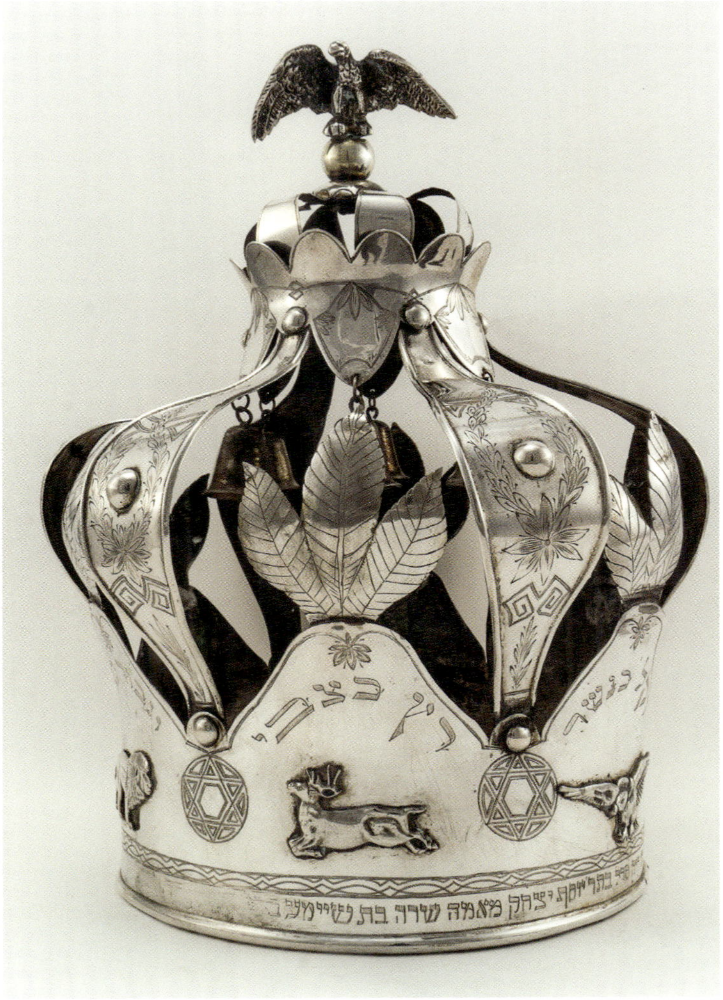

Unlike the Torah pointer, which has an important function during the synagogue service, the Torah crown is purely decorative. The crown is placed on the tops of the staves to which the scroll is attached. The custom of using crowns to adorn Torah scrolls is documented as early as the twelfth century, where the 1159 inventory of the Cairo Genizah (a storage room that held almost 200,000 manuscripts, located in the Ben Ezra Synagogue of Fustat, Egypt, discovered in 1864), lists four crowns of different metals given to a synagogue in Israel.

This crown is particularly attractive due to the animals and symbols that adorn the base that reference this verse: "Be bold as a leopard, light as an eagle, swift as a deer, and strong as a lion to do the will of your Father in Heaven," (Ethics of the Fathers 5:20). The leopard, eagle, deer, and lion are portrayed in the form of applied silver plaques; above each animal is part of the verse relating to them. For example, the deer is in mid-jump, and above it, it says "swift as a deer." In addition to the animals, there are plaques in the form of the hands of the *Cohanim* (symbol of the Priesthood), for the "to do the will" part of the verse, and the Ten Commandments for "your Father in Heaven."

The foliage between the arms of the crown, engraving, eagle finial, hallmarks, and overall construction point to Poland as the country of origin. There is an inscription at the rim of the base that was done at a later date, which donates this crown to a synagogue in Jerusalem.

TORAH FINIALS

Material: Olivewood
Origin: Israel circa 1930
Identifying Marks: "Jerusalem" in Hebrew
Dimensions: 9.5" x 4.1"

Like the Torah crown, finials are used to adorn the Torah scroll. The earliest example of Torah finials that have survived the millennia are from the Spanish realm; a fifteenth-century pair from the Jewish community of Camarata in Sicily, which, unfortunately, are now used as stave ends in the Cathedral of Palma de Majorca.

Objects made from olivewood for every use imaginable were produced in tremendous quantities for the tourist market of Jerusalem. The one item rarely seen are Torah finials. The few that are known are all similar in form and are spool-shaped.

These finials are the creations of a gifted artisan. The top of the finials are in the form of a *hamsa*, which is the Arabic word for "five," and refers to the number of fingers on the hand. The *hamsa* was used by both Jews and Muslims in the Middle East as a symbol that could ward off the notorious "evil eye." *Hamsa* are often found as amulets and wall hangings for the home.

Each fingertip has roses painted in fine detail. Both sides of the *hamsa* form are beautifully carved with ancient sites of Jerusalem and are appropriately titled as such; the sides shown here are of the Tomb of the Patriarchs and The Western Wall. At the very bottom by the opening, "Jerusalem" is hand-inked. The reverse sides (not shown) are carved with The Tomb of Rachel and The Tomb of Samuel the Prophet.

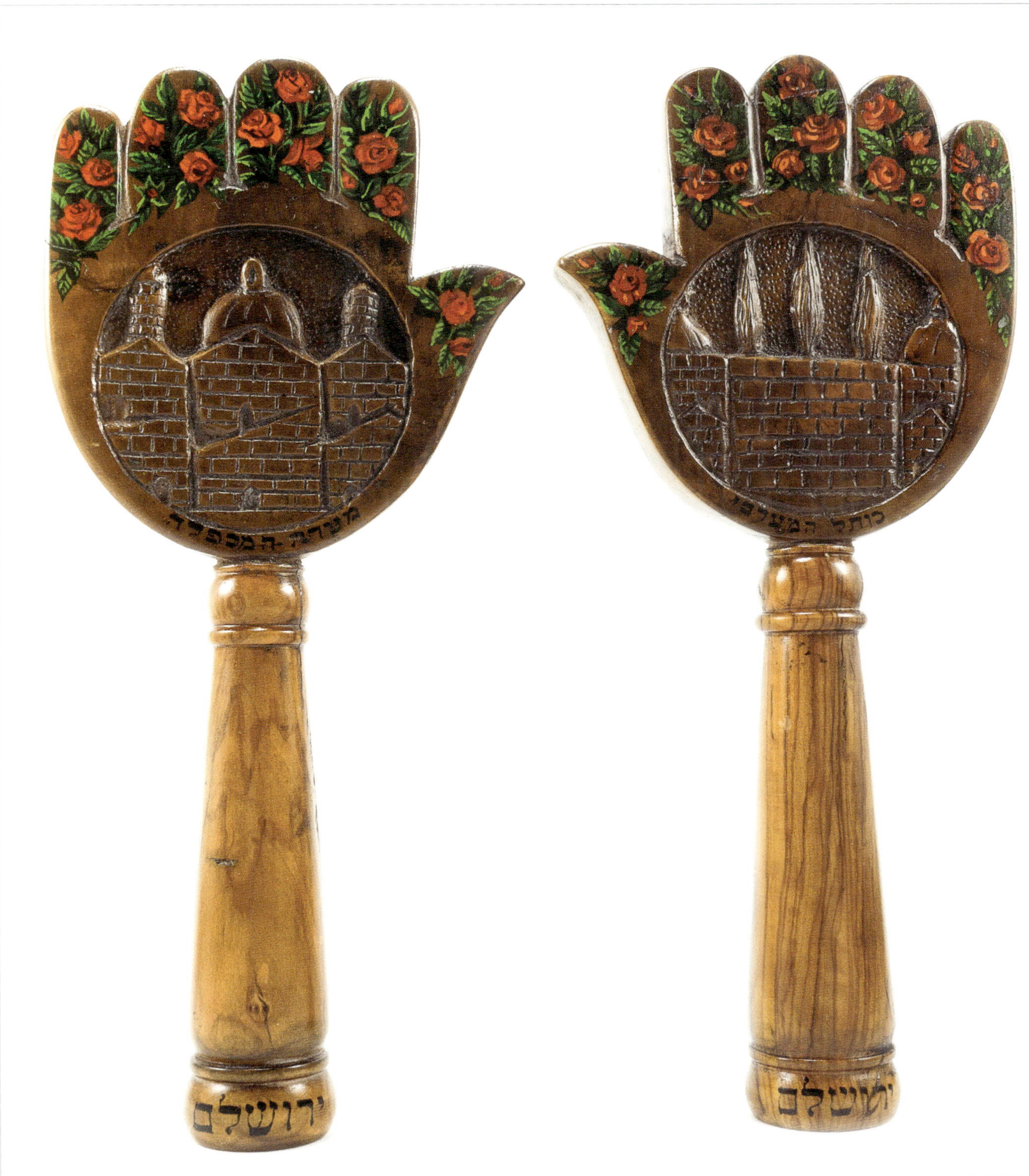
מערת-המכפלה
ירושלם
כותל המערבי
ירושלם

TORAH SHIELDS

Materials: *Copper / Silver*
Origin: *Galicia (Southern Poland & Western Ukraine), circa 1760 / circa 1780*
Dimensions: *3.5" x 3" / 5.1" x 4.75"*

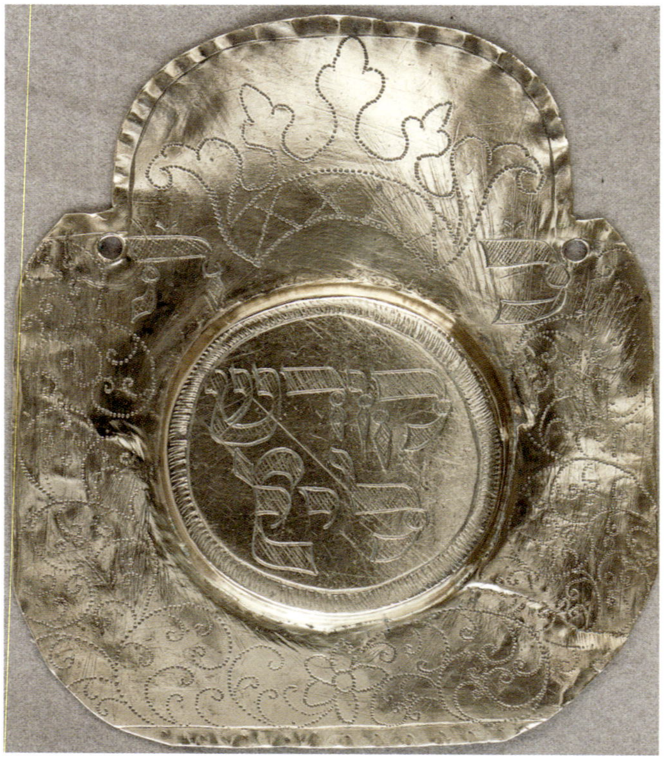

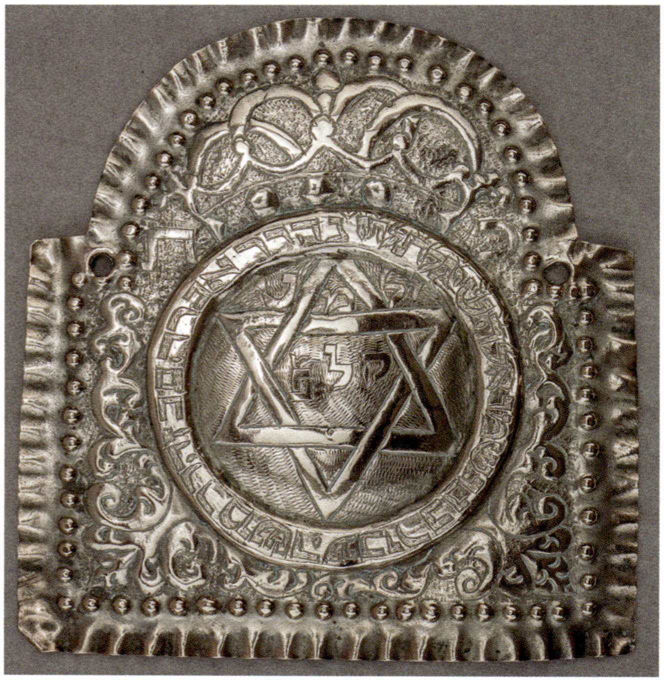

Generally, the Torah shield serves an important function: On it are the words "Sabbath" or "Passover" or another holiday, so the person taking a particular Torah scroll out of the ark to be read would know which Torah would be rolled to the appropriate place for the reading of the day. Sometimes Torah shields had small removable plaques with the names of holidays and Sabbath on them, so the shield could be "suited up" for the right day.

The one exception to the standard, purposeful shields are the modest-sized shields from Galicia dating from the eighteenth and early nineteenth centuries. These shields never had removable plaques on them with "Sabbath" or holidays inscribed. They were only decorative, there to enhance the beauty of the Torah scroll, like the Torah crown and finials. These shields were usually donated to celebrate a circumcision or for the one-year anniversary of a child's birth.

One shield simply states "Holy to G-d" in the center. Above that is a crown with the letters *"chaf taf"* flanking it, for *Keter Torah* (Crown of Torah).

This shield has had its side edges trimmed at some point. Even when taking this trimming into account, it is clear the shield was only a bit larger than it is now, as the original crimping has been retained at its top and bottom. A possible explanation for its incredibly compact size is that it was used for a small-sized Torah scroll, perhaps for a scroll that belonged to a *shteeble*, a Yiddish word meaning a private house where prayers are said with a group of little more than ten men, as opposed to services held at a synagogue.

The other Torah shield is a more typical-sized example from this era and region, although the Star of David motif on this early a piece of Judaica is most unusual.

The heavily abbreviated dedication on this shield reads: "The donation of Rabbi Avraham, elder son of Rabbi Moshe, for his son Shmuel, his name will be praised by G-d, in exile we pray, in remembrance, (the boy should be), close to G-d and do good deeds." A Crown of Torah is above with the letters *"chaf taf."*

TORAH SHIELD

Material: Silver
Origin: Poland circa 1770
Dimensions: 9.75" x 6.75"

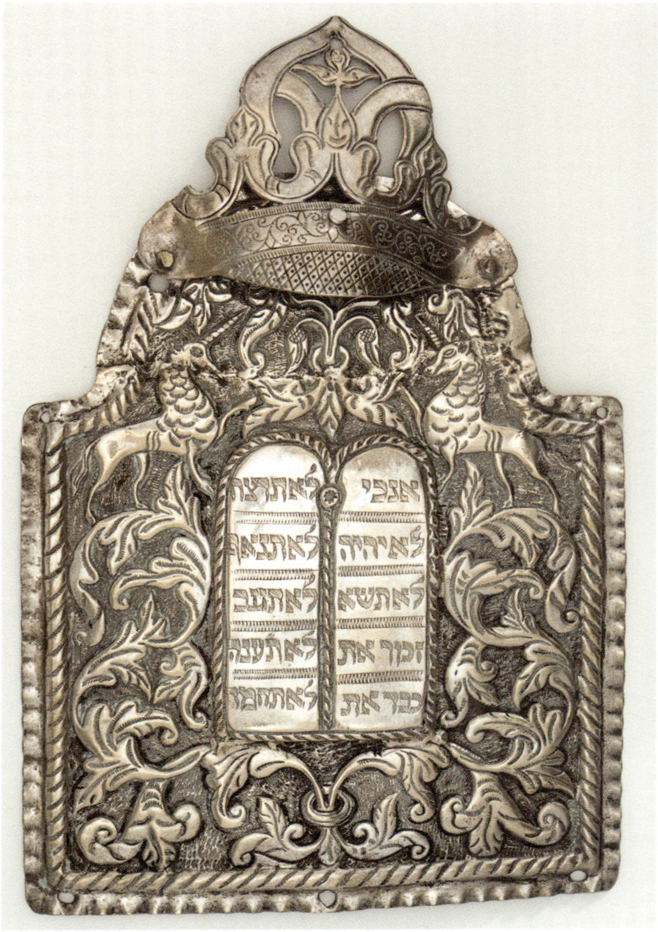

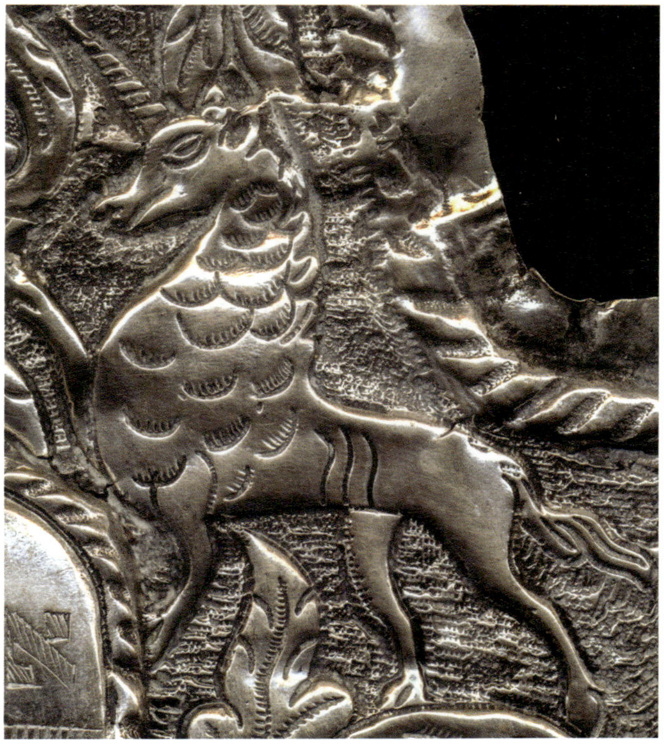

This shield is decorated with a pair of unicorns above The Ten Commandments. Was the unicorn truly a mythological creature, or did it actually exist?

The *re'em* is mentioned in many places in the Bible, described as a "great horned mammal." The Talmud states that this animal was too large to fit into Noah's ark, but survived the flood by grasping onto the ark with its horn.

Then there is the *tachash*, a colorful animal with a single horn on its forehead that appeared only once, in the desert, so Moses could use its skin to cover the Tabernacle (Babylonian Talmud, Shabbos 28b).

The mammal called a *keresh* is mentioned having one horn and is kosher to eat (Babylonian Talmud, Chullin 59b).

Parts of the Kabbalah reference unicorn-like animals living under the earth.

TORAH ARK CURTAIN

Material: Metallic thread on velvet
Origin: Poland circa 1885
Dimensions: 51.75" x 34"

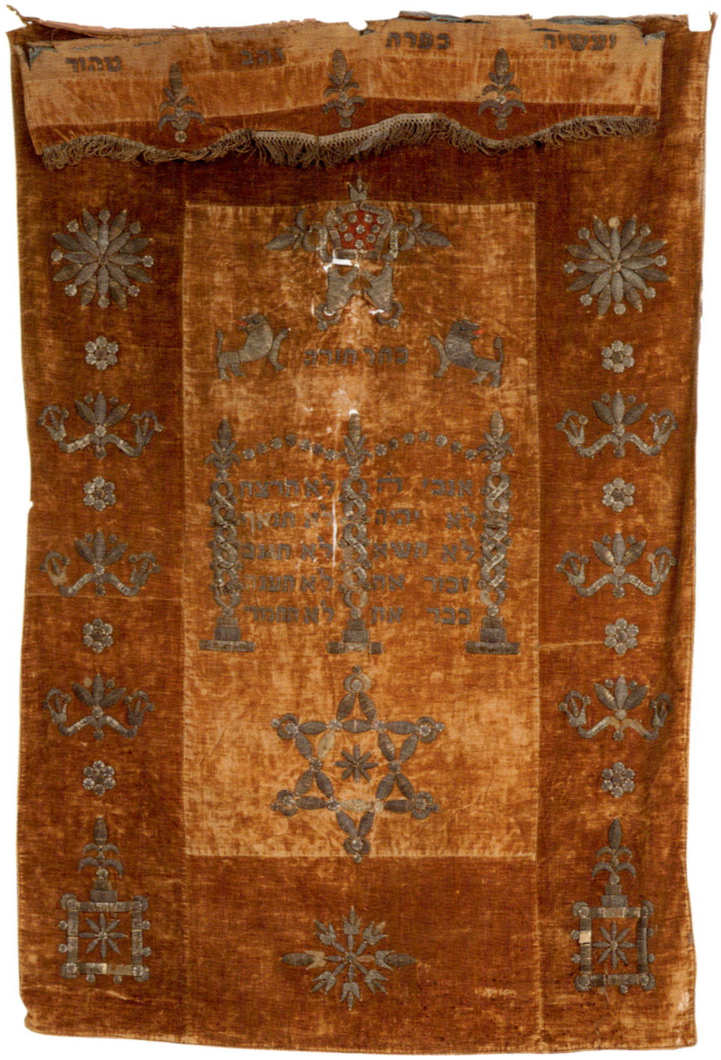

This ornate curtain is used to cover the ark in the synagogue, which houses the Torah scrolls. The curtain, or *parochet,* corresponds to the veil that was before the Holy of Holies in The First Temple. This *parochet* is made using the technique of *Spanier Arbeit*, (Spanish Handwork), which is the Yiddish term for sewing metallic thread on velvet.

Beginning at the very top, it reads: "Make a golden cover for the ark," (Exodus 25:17). Below that is a crown, the "priestly hands," and two Lions of Judah flanking the phrase "Crown of Torah." Then there are the Ten Commandments separated by Solomon's pillars, akin to the pillars seen on mezuzahs that reference The First Temple. Finally, there is a large Star of David.

Besides the intricate and delicate handwork of this piece, what attracted me to it was the absence of what is found on the vast majority of surviving European Torah curtains: Dedications. On every *parochet* I have encountered, there are dedications by the person or family who supplied the funds to have the *parochet* made for the synagogue ark. Sometimes these dedications are very long, perhaps filling up half the space of the curtain itself. To me, this *parochet* is "pure" design-wise, in that the only Hebrew words on it relate to G-d and the Torah.

SYNAGOGUE SCONCES

Material: Iron
Origin: France (?), circa 1895
Dimensions: 10.5" x 15.75"

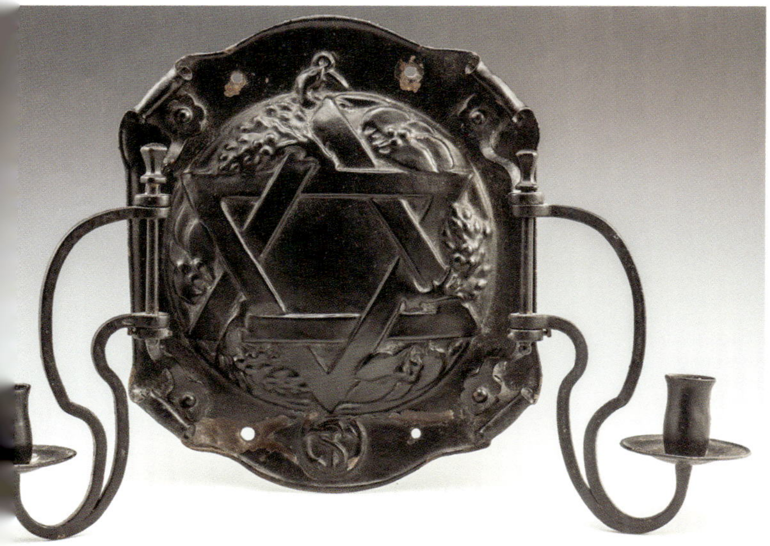

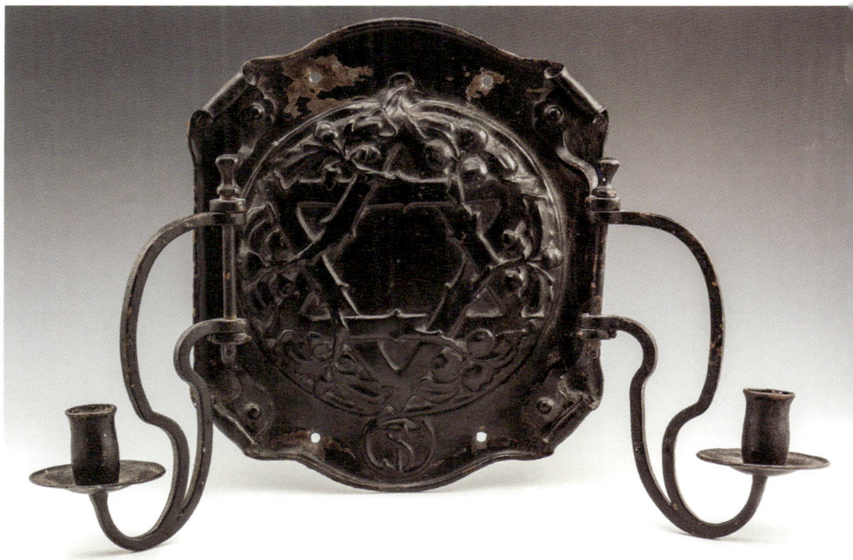

These sconces, likely a unique commission, are from a high end foundry, as the quality of design, casting, and assemblage is most impressive. The sconces would probably have hung by the inside doors of the synagogue that open up to the sanctuary itself.

While the main design element is a large Star of David, there are leaves, flowers, berries, and fruit that undulate within the lines of the Star, and each sconce has different patterns using these components from nature. These motif configurations are a direct influence from the art nouveau movement. There are two intertwined English characters, "ST", that are located underneath the Star. These letters could be the initials of the name of the synagogue itself ("*Shaarei Tefillah,*" for example) or of the firm that made these sconces.

SYNAGOGUE CHARITY BOX

Material: Iron
Origin: Hungary, circa 1900
Dimensions: 10.5" x 18.25"

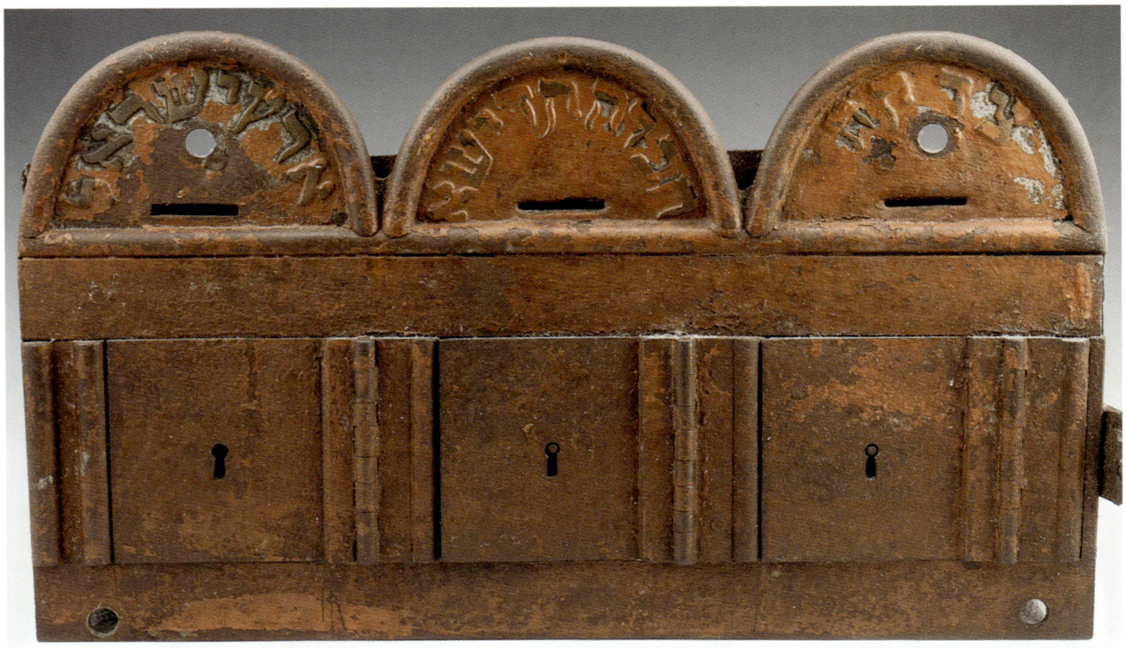

This massive iron charity box was constructed in a manner exclusive to European charity boxes, of which older examples date as far back as the eighteenth century. This was located in the wall of the synagogue itself, either indoors or outdoors by the entrance. Synagogue charity boxes like this might have slots for as many as a dozen different charities. This example has three slots that are titled in Hebrew: "Charity," "Burial Society," "Land of Israel," with each fund having its own separate compartment and locked door.

This type of synagogue charity box is still being manufactured for the remnants of Chassidic sects that survived the Holocaust and have relocated to the United States and Israel. The containers of today are made of plastic.

LAVER

Material: Copper
Origin: Poland or Ukraine, 1839 - 1840
Dimensions: 6" x 6.5" (including handles)

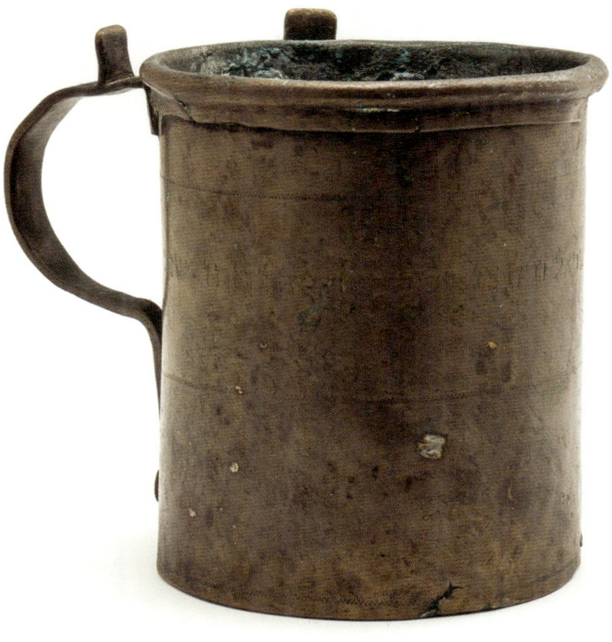

Featuring simple wriggle-work engraving, two excerpts of Biblical verses in Hebrew decorate this cup for washing hands. The first, "thus shall you bless the Children of Israel" (Numbers 6:23), refers to G-d telling Moses that Aaron (the first *Cohen Gadol*, or High Priest) and his sons should bless the Israelites.

The second excerpt, "they shall wash their hands so they should not die" (Exodus 30:21), again references Aaron and his sons, so they should be cleansed before making an offering to G-d at the altar.

After the conclusion of the second verse, the Hebrew date equaling September 1839 to September 1840 is stated, indicating when this cup was donated to a synagogue.

Because the engraved excerpts discuss *Cohanim* (Priests), this washing cup was only to be used by synagogue congregants of Cohanic heritage, as it is they who must wash their hands before performing the *Birkat Cohanim* (Priestly Blessing) for the rest of the congregation on certain holidays. *Cohanim*, meaning descendants of Aaron and his sons, make up between three and five percent of the Jewish population.

As with pewter plates and all types of silver objects, there is great temptation among forgers to purchase an old European copper laver for a very minimal amount, and, with a bit of engraving, greatly increase its value, due to the scarcity of surviving lavers from prewar Europe that have authentic, period Hebrew engravings, which sometimes include vegetal and animal motifs. Especially talented forgers engage in the time-consuming craft of chasing; that is, hammering a seemingly appropriate Hebrew verse and/or animal figures on to a laver.

The worn laver shown here might not be the most pleasing to the eye, but it is an example bearing honest Hebrew engraving. One should be on guard if offered an elaborately decorated laver, as nearly all such types are forgeries copied from books that show examples held in museums, or are "fantasy pieces" of craftsmen who think themselves to be quite clever, presenting a "newly discovered" treasure to an increasingly hungry, yet often naive, collecting public.

THE BEZALEL SCHOOL

BEZALEL CATALOGUE

Material: Paper
Origin: New York, 1926
Artist: Reuven Lifschitz
Dimensions: 11.3" x 8.75"

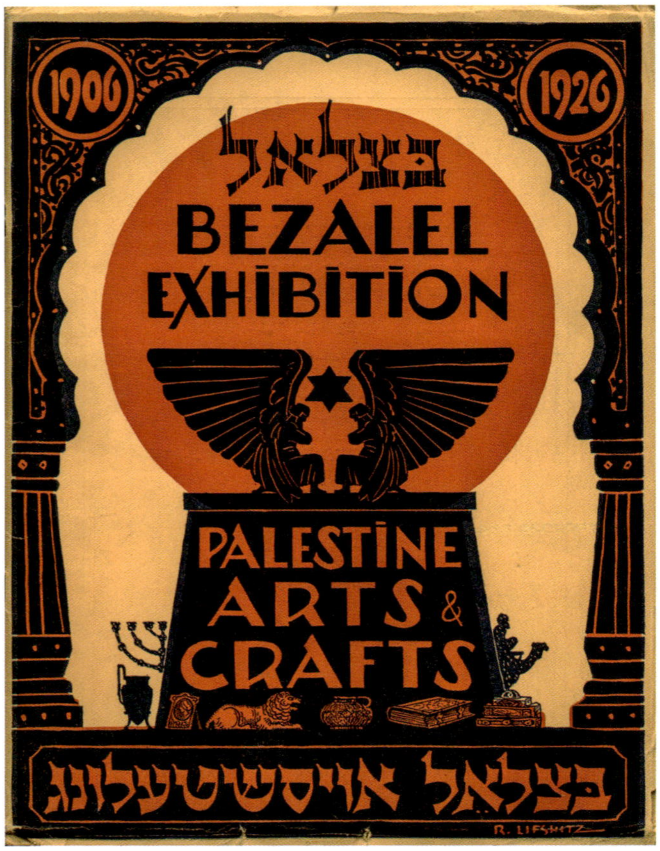

In Vienna in 1903, the court sculptor to the King of Bulgaria, Boris Schatz, met with the founder of modern political Zionism, Theodor Herzl, and presented an idea to him about establishing an academy of art in Jerusalem. Herzl gave Schatz his blessing, and in 1906 Schatz opened the Bezalel Academy of Arts and Crafts, named after the Biblical architect Betzalel ben Uri: "I have filled him with a divine spirit, with wisdom, understanding and knowledge, and with [the talent for] all types of craftsmanship," (Exodus 31:3).

Schatz's dream was to have an explicitly Jewish style of art created in Jerusalem. This vision was fulfilled at the Bezalel School in the form of functional, decorative, and ritual handicrafts that were made in a unique style that blended classicism, art nouveau, and Middle Eastern elements, in which Biblical and Zionist themes were often portrayed.

Like the Wiener Werkstatte in Vienna, or the William Morris firm in England, the Bezalel School produced art objects in a wide range of materials including silver, brass, wood, ivory, and fabric.

Schatz enjoyed moderate levels of success in selling his wares to Europe and the Americas, but due to financial difficulties, the Bezalel School shut its doors in 1929. Schatz passed away in 1932 while on a fund-raising trip in Colorado. The "New Bezalel" opened in 1935, under the leadership of Joseph Budko, Ludwig Wolpert, and David Heinz Gumbel. Wolpert and Gumbel attempted to change the romantic style of Bezalel crafts that was Schatz's vision to one that was reserved, which was in line with the teachings of the German Bauhaus school, which both Gumbel and Wolpert revered.

The largest Bezalel exhibition ever staged was in New York City, at the Grand Central Palace in 1926. Shown here is the cover of the catalog from that event.

PLAQUE

Materials: Silver, wood, brass
Origin: Israel, circa 1920
Hallmarks: "Bezalel Jerusalem" in Hebrew
Dimensions: 7.75" x 7.75"

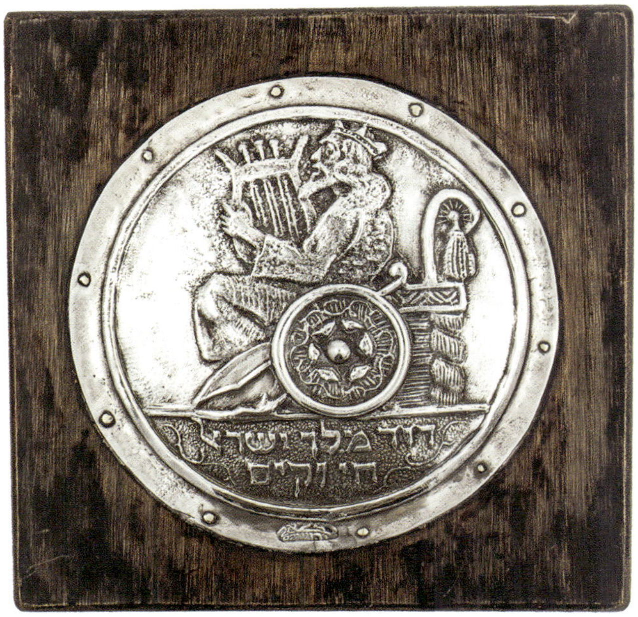

This wall hanging typifies a Bezalel piece of decorative art. It shows King David in his old age, playing a lyre on his throne. At his side is his sword and shield from the fighting days of his youth, the shield depicting the hexagram that bears his namesake. Underneath this scene, in Hebrew, it says: "David, King of Israel, lives and endures."

The exposed, handmade brass nails reveal the influence the Arts and Crafts movement had in the creation of this piece.

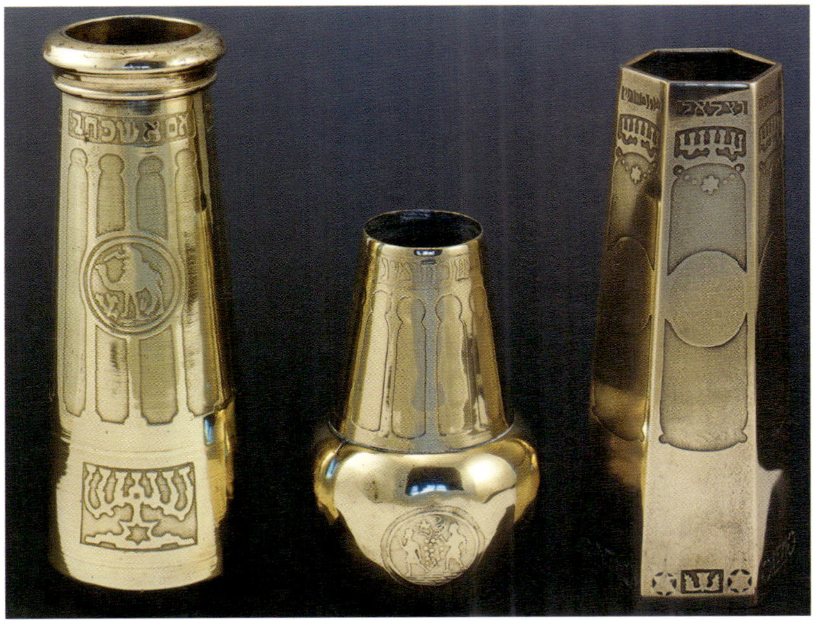

VASES

Material: Brass
Origin: Israel, circa 1913 - 1925
Hallmarks: "Bezalel Jerusalem" in Hebrew
Dimensions: 7" x 2.6" / 4.75" x 2.75" / 6.75" x 2.5"

These vases were decorated using the metalwork technique of acid-etching. All state the Hebrew verse: "If I forget thee O Jerusalem, let my right hand forget her cunning," (Psalm 137:5). The vases depict religious motifs, Zionist scenes of farming, and a Biblical scene. The sides of the vases shown here depict a menorah; a man on a camel; a scene from the Book of Numbers; the spies returning from the land of Canaan carrying a large cluster of grapes between them. The hexagonal vase is dated 1913 in Hebrew.

POCKET KNIFE / SPICE BOX / BUD VASE / BIBLE COVER / PICTURE FRAME

Material: *Silver, semi-precious stones / Silver/ Silver-plated brass / Silver / Wood*
Origin: *Israel, circa 1910 - 1925*
Hallmarks: *"Bezalel Jerusalem" in Hebrew*
Dimensions: *.6" x 3.25" / 1.75" x 1.5" / 4.25" x 1" / 5" x 3.25" / 4.5" x 3.75"*

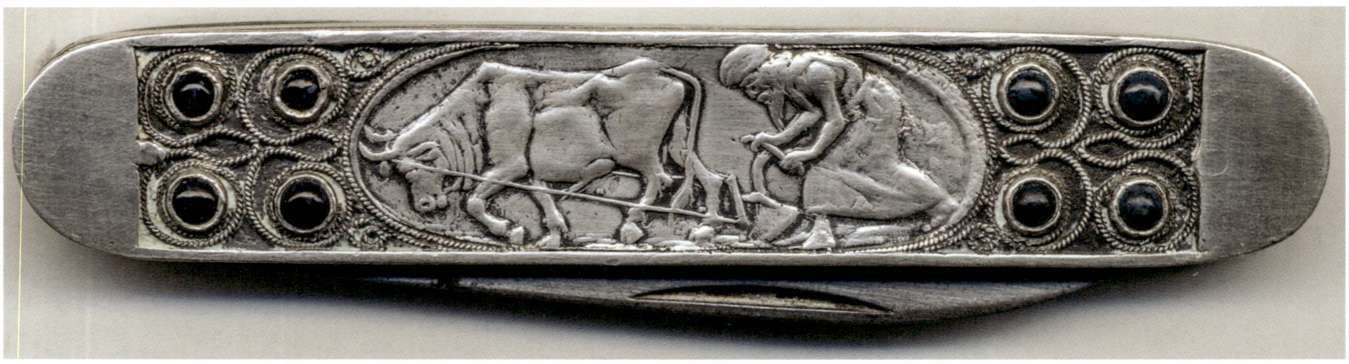

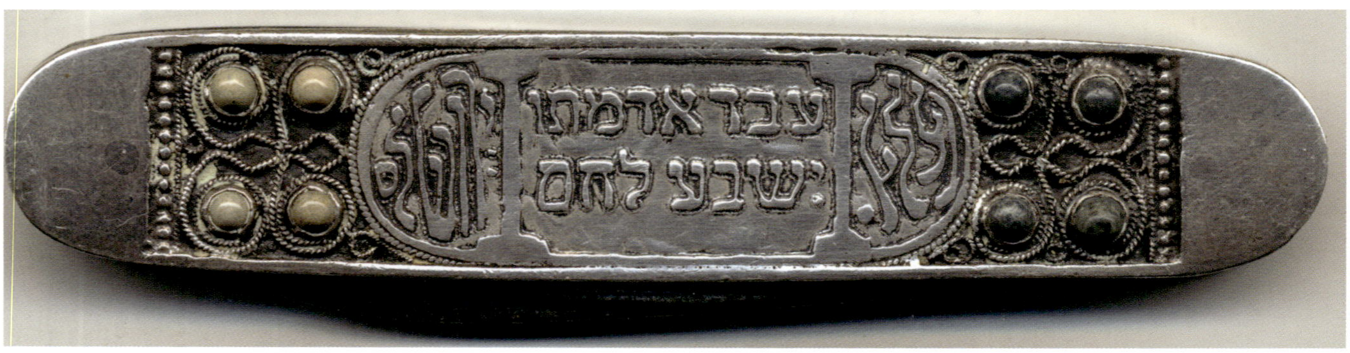

The pocket knife is of the highest quality made by Bezalel, both in its artistry and the execution of materials. One side of the knife depicts an elderly Yemenite Jew, his back bent, plowing land with an ox. The other side of the knife reads: "He that tills his land shall have plenty of bread" (Proverbs 28:19). Flanking this quote is a stylized signature of "Bezalel Jerusalem," which is only found on items made in the very first years of the Bezalel School. During this period in the twentieth century, it was commonplace for men to carry pocketknives to cut food such as fruit and bread. This is the likely reason for the verse and correlating scene presented here.

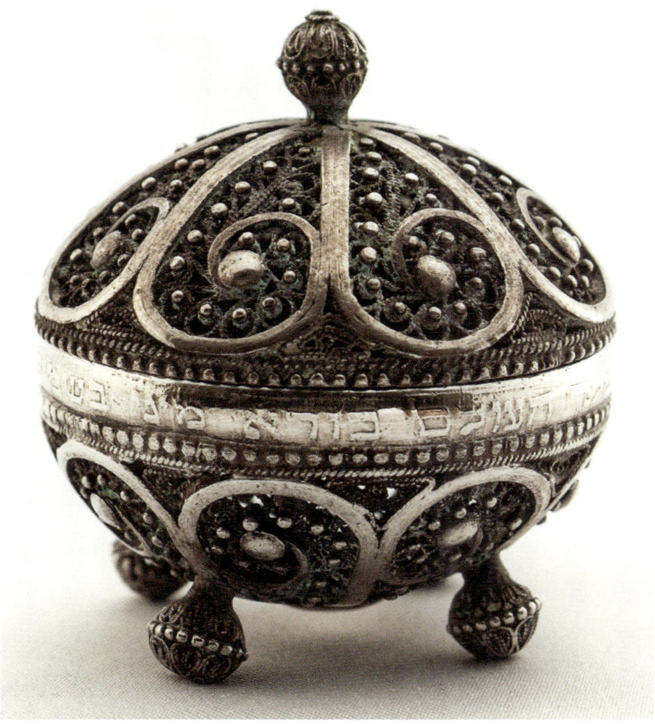

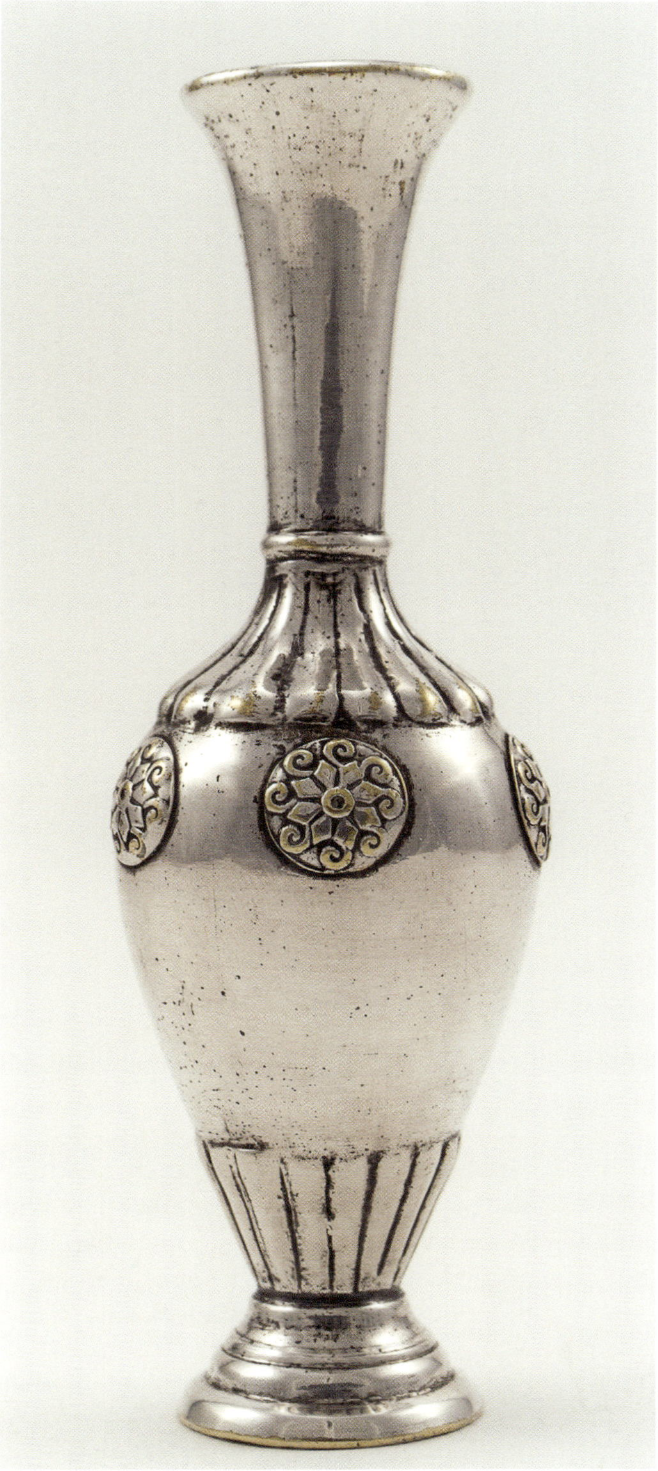

At first glance, it would appear that the diminutive round spice box would require delicate handling. However, it is quite sturdy, as there is thick strapwork interspersed with the finely spun filigree wire, which gives it substantial weight. Acid-etched on the center band of silver that connects both halves is the prayer for spices said at the conclusion of the Sabbath.

The vase is small when compared to other vases made by Bezalel. The opening only holds one flower, but the vase has great form, imitating objects made in ancient Greece.

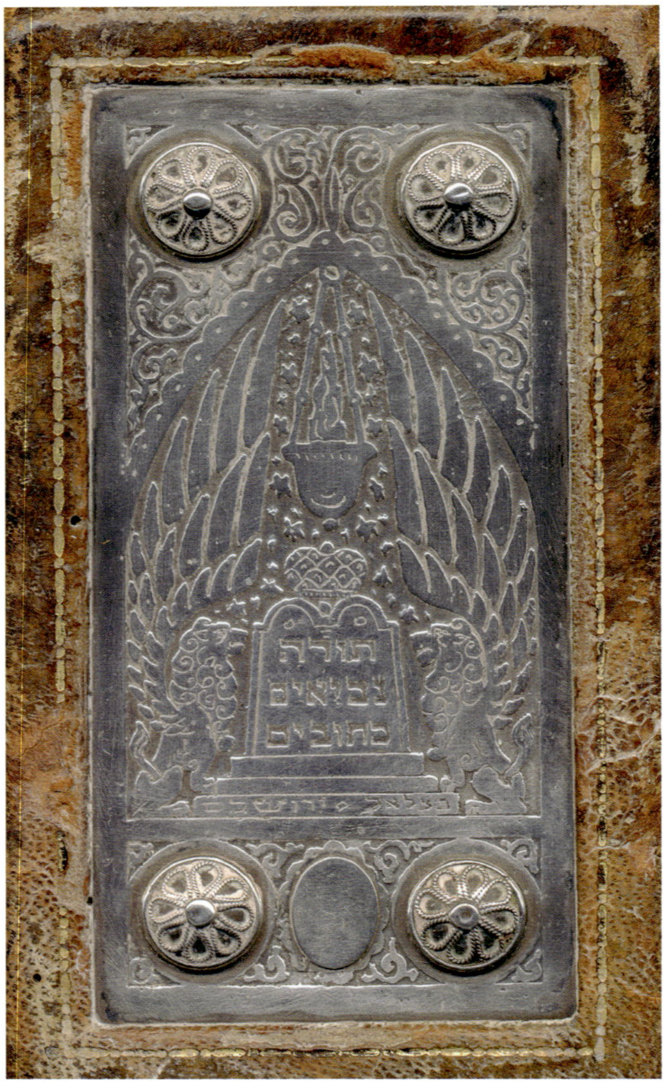

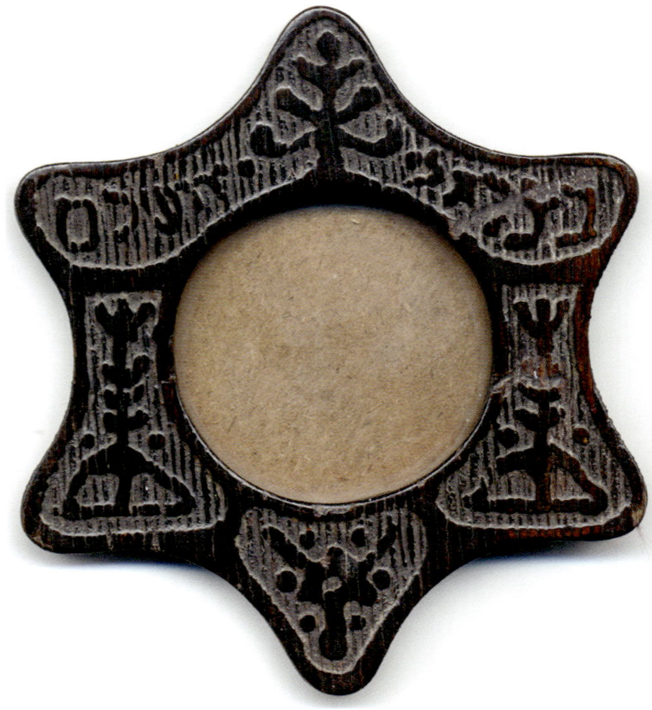

The front of the Star of David form picture frame is hand-carved and etched.

The Bible cover is comprised of leather with an inlaid silver plaque. It has four roundels of filigree set at each corner, and acid-etched onto the silver are two majestic winged lions flanking a crowned Ten Commandments that reads in Hebrew "Torah Prophets Writings," which is the entirety of the Jewish Bible, known by its Hebrew acronym *Tanach*. The designer of this Bible cover is by the Bezalel artist Ze'ev Raban.

TILE

Material: Ceramic
Origin: Israel, circa 1925
Identifying Marks: "Keramica Bezalel" in Hebrew
Dimensions: 6.1" x 6.1"

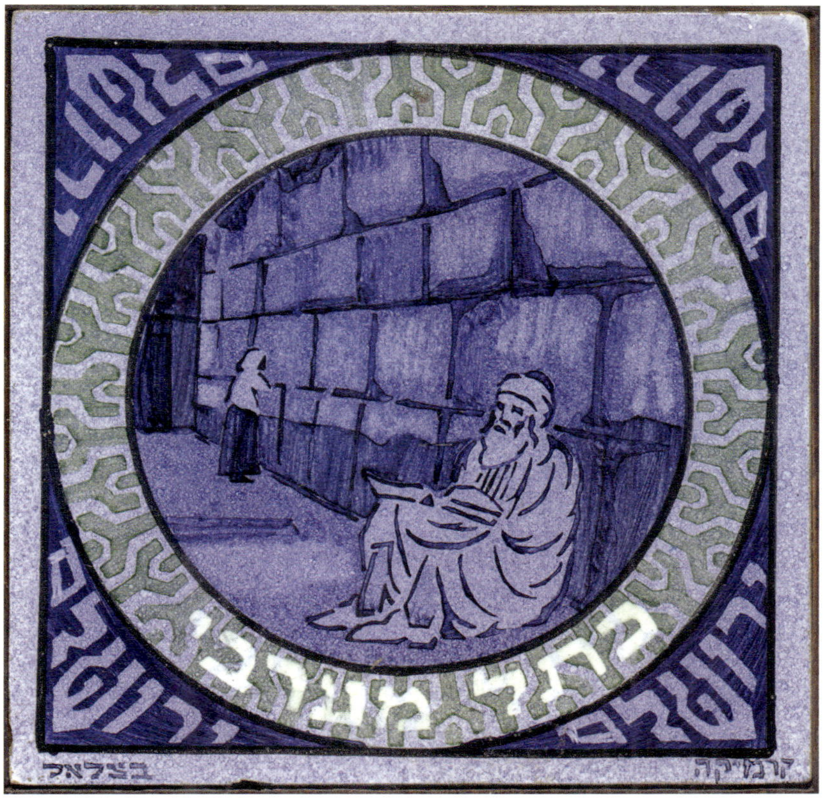

Perhaps the most prolific of the Bezalel School workshops established by Boris Schatz in the 1920s was the one producing ceramics. At this studio, most of what was made were square-shaped tiles painted in bold colors, many of which depicted Zionist or Biblical themes, as in keeping with the ideals of Schatz. Blank tiles were imported from England and Germany, which were then hand-decorated in Jerusalem.

This tile is titled "The Western Wall" in white Hebrew lettering, and it shows an elderly man leaning against the wall, an open book on his lap. A standing figure praying is in the background. The design for this scene was executed by Ze'ev Raban; it can be viewed as part of a much larger work in Raban's finely detailed watercolor painting of the Western Wall.

Surrounding this image is a repeating "Y" pattern, which is of Middle Eastern origin and is most often found as a decorative motif on brass objects inlaid with silver and copper.

At each corner of the tile, in modernistic, art deco-styled Hebrew lettering is the word "Jerusalem."

Bezalel tiles crafted in such a way in which two or more tiles are affixed to each other to depict a Zionist or Biblical scene are prized for their size, beauty, and scarcity. Even a large crack in one tile that forms part of a multi-tiled mural tends not to discourage collectors.

In addition to flat tiles, the Bezalel ceramics workshop produced vases, jugs, cups, plates, and bowls. Unlike singular tiles, these vessels can be quite difficult to locate, either because fewer of these were made or because of their inherent fragile nature. Once damaged, a bowl or jug might be discarded, its practical use no longer applicable.

DISH

Material: Brass inlaid with silver and copper
Origin: Israel, circa 1910
Dimensions: 4.5"

For hundreds of years in Damascus, Syria, workers have been performing the skilled craft of inlaying silver and copper onto brass vessels to sell as utilitarian objects. The term for these types of wares is Damascene, named after the city that made this type of handwork famous. While on a trip to Damascus, the founder of the Bezalel School, Boris Schatz, noted that although the owners of the shops that sold this merchandise were gentiles, all of the workers were Jewish. One of the first workshops Schatz set up at Bezalel was one that produced Damascene objects.

This small dish depicts a lit seven-branched menorah inside a Star of David. The dish is not hallmarked; while most pieces of early Bezalel Damascene ware have the word "Bezalel" inlaid in silver on a prominent place on the item itself, this was occasionally skipped on smaller items. This piece was likely meant to be sold with a matching cup. Examples of cups that would fit on this plate can be seen in photographs of Bezalel Damascene ware from the 1910s, and have the world "Bezalel" on them in large, interlaced letters as part of the cups' design. It would be repetitive to have the word "Bezalel" on both a cup and its saucer, so the lack of the word "Bezalel" here fits accordingly. This stylized menorah is an original Bezalel design and is registered in their archives.

Due to the increasingly high prices Bezalel objects have realized in recent years, an industry of "faking" Bezalel objects has emerged, intended to fool the naive collector and inexperienced dealer. The most pervasive area of fake Bezalel objects being produced today are those in Damascene, i.e. silver and copper decoration inlaid onto brass. Nearly one hundred percent of the purportedly authentic Bezalel Damascene objects offered today on the Internet, in antique shops, and even at some respected auction houses, are fakes. The majority of these fakes are easy to spot to one familiar with authentic Bezalel Damascene ware; however, I am reluctant to provide clues to uncovering fakes as then the forgers would correct their tell-tale mistakes.

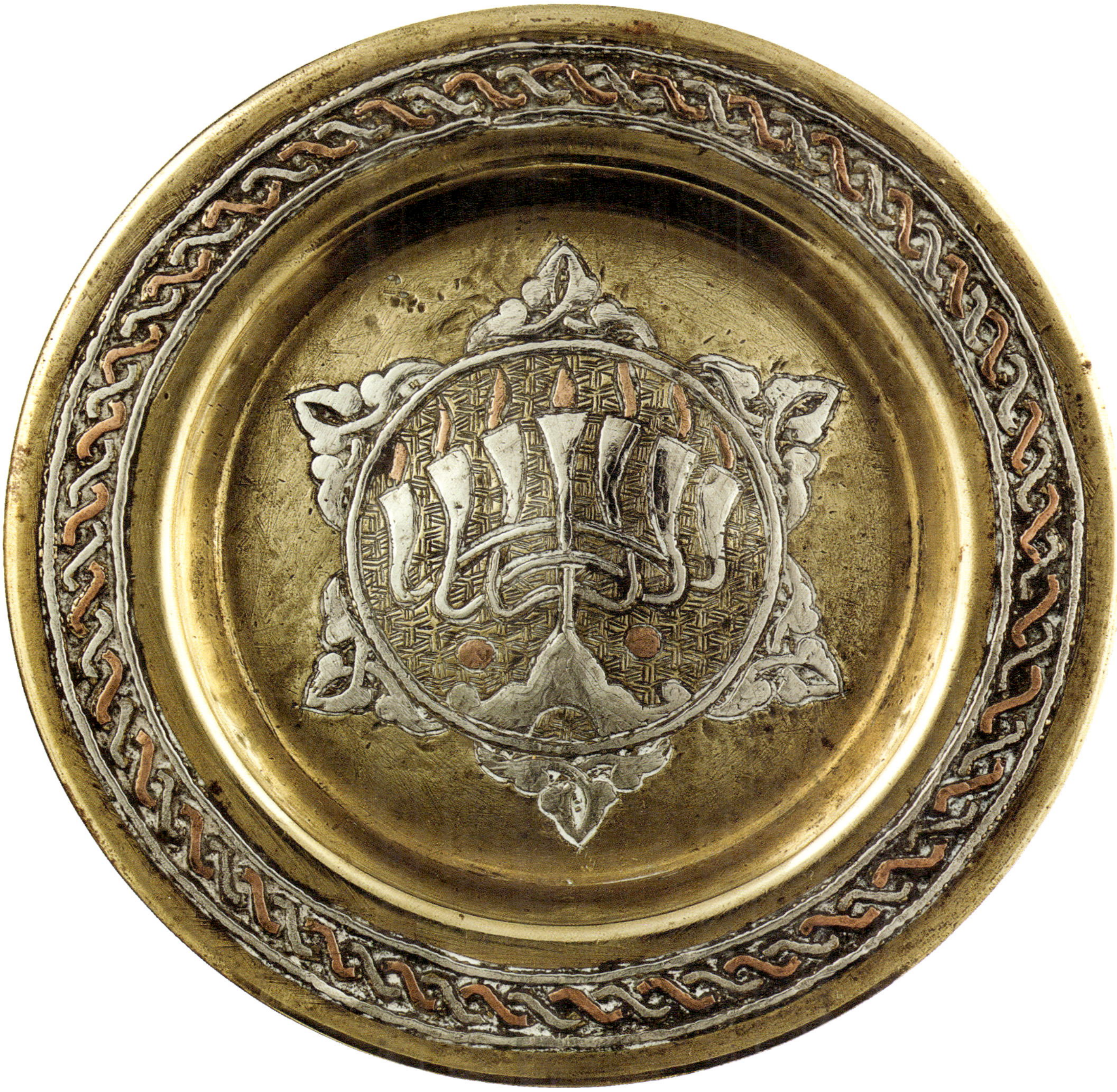

PLAYING CARDS

Material: Paper
Origin: Israel, circa 1925
Identifying Marks: "Drawn by Z. Raban Bezalel Jerusalem" on box in Hebrew and English
Total Pieces: 52 cards, lidless box
Dimensions: 3.1" x 2.25" (card), 3.1" x 5.75" (box, unfolded)

Ze'ev Raban was born in Lodz, Poland, in 1890. During 1905-1906, he studied at the *Kunstgewerbeschule* (school of applied art) in Munich, and between 1908 and 1911, he attended École des Beaux Arts and the Royal Academy of Art in Brussels. At the invitation of Boris Schatz, he moved to Jerusalem in 1912 and joined the faculty of the Bezalel School. He soon took on a central role there as a teacher of *repoussé*, painting, and sculpture. By 1914, most of the works produced in the workshops of Bezalel were of his design.

Raban is my favorite Bezalel artist, and these playing cards are the Raban design I admire most. Each suit depicts figures from the books of Esther and Kings, the heroine Judith as well as the demon Ashmodai, who is mentioned in the Talmud a few times. The classical suits found in standard playing cards have been replaced with Jewish-themed symbols; hearts and spades have been changed to pomegranates and fig leaves, two of the "seven species" mentioned in the Book of Deuteronomy. Clubs are now menorahs, and diamonds, Stars of David.

The box these cards came in is hardly that at all, as it has no lids to enclose the deck. This is because the box is actually a folded postcard; the reverse is printed with lines to write on and a spot for a stamp. A British soldier stationed in Jerusalem in the 1920s was able to purchase two items in one: a deck of cards to play with his buddies while off-duty, and a postcard to write to loved ones back home. This is the reason for the scarcity of complete decks of these cards: Due to the lack of a functional box, cards were easily damaged or lost.

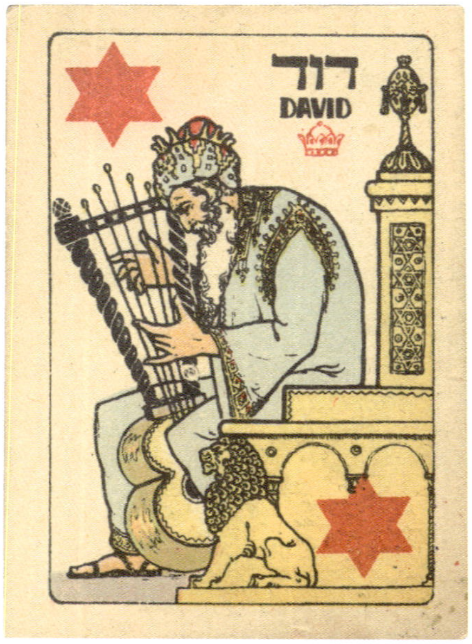

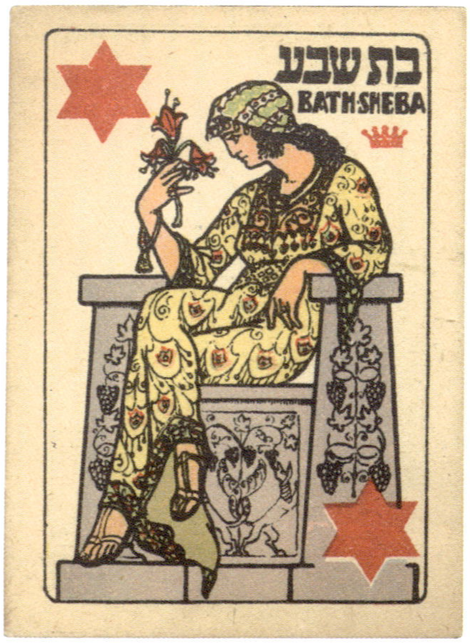

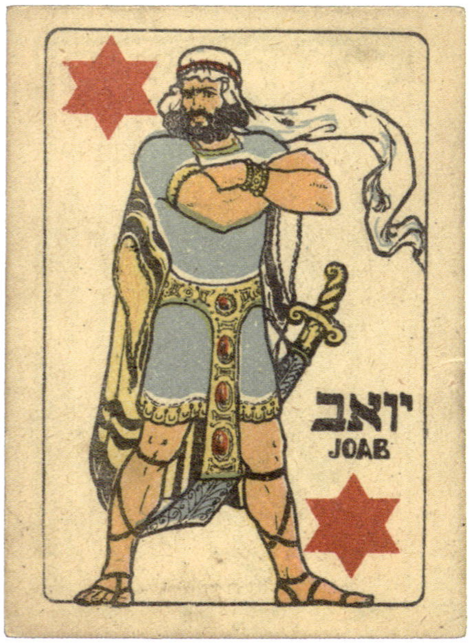

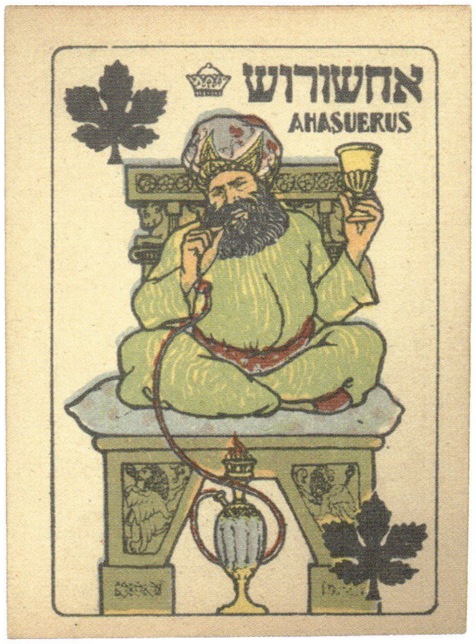
אחשורוש
AHASUERUS

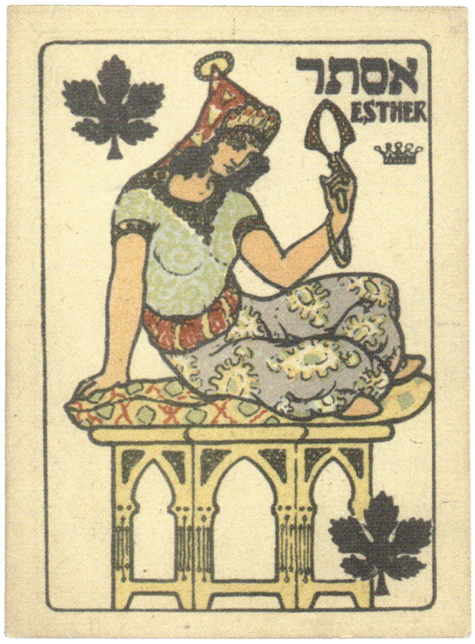
אסתר
ESTHER

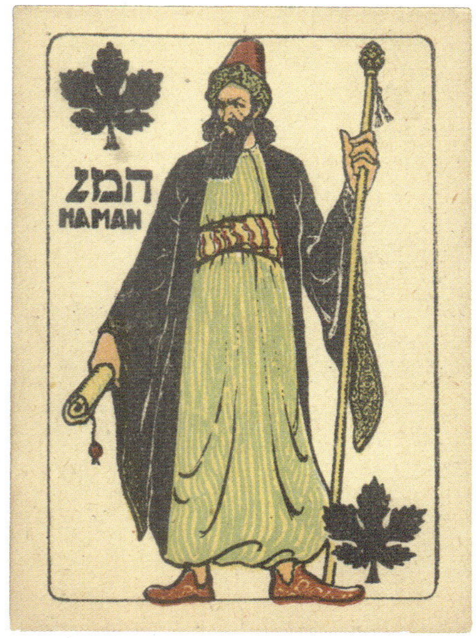
המן
HAMAN

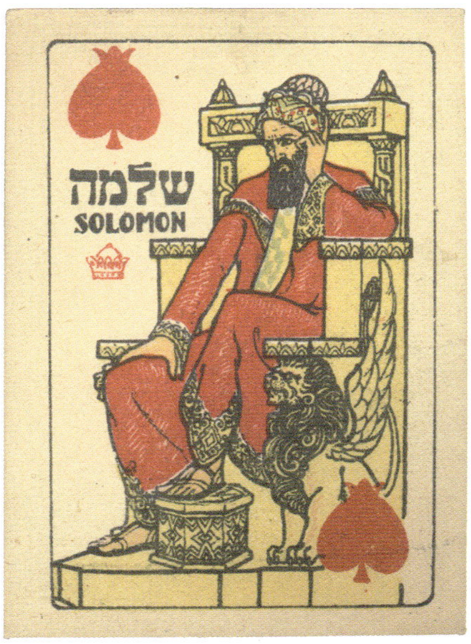
שלמה
SOLOMON

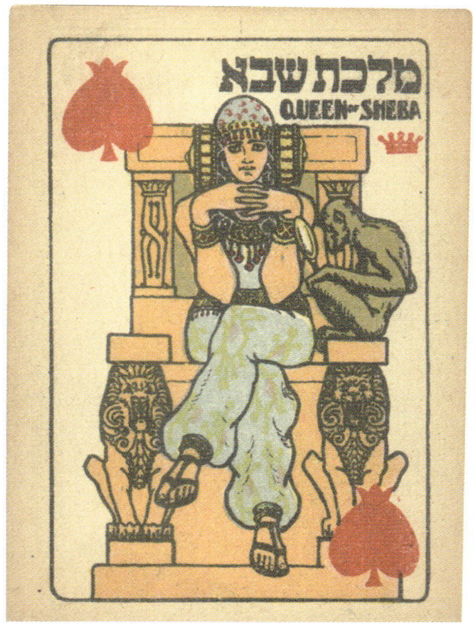
מלכת שבא
QUEEN of SHEBA

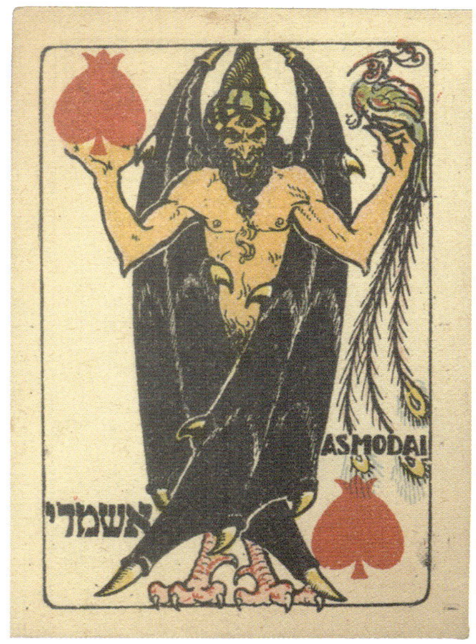
ASMODAI
אשמדי

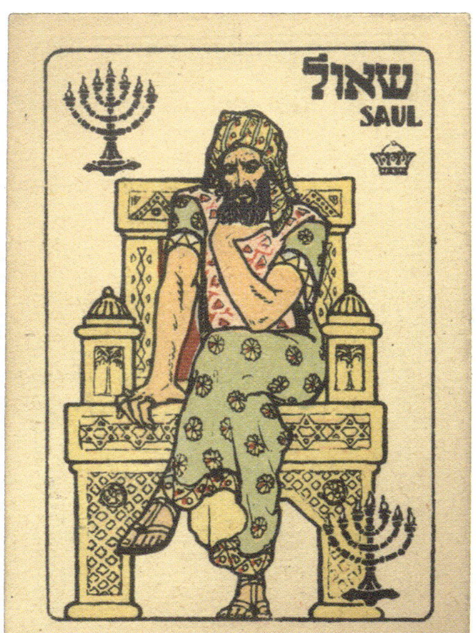
שאול
SAUL

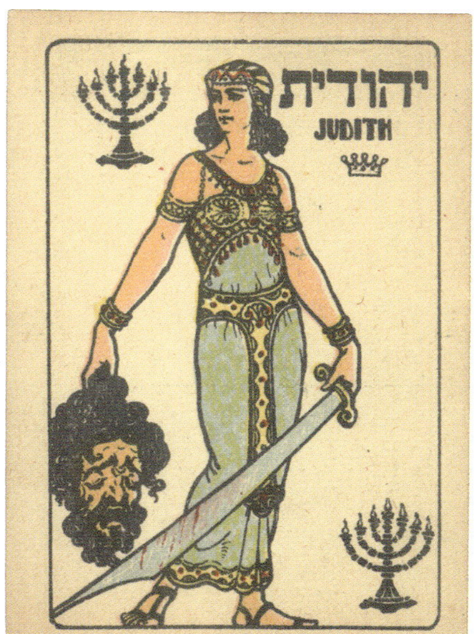
יהודית
JUDITH

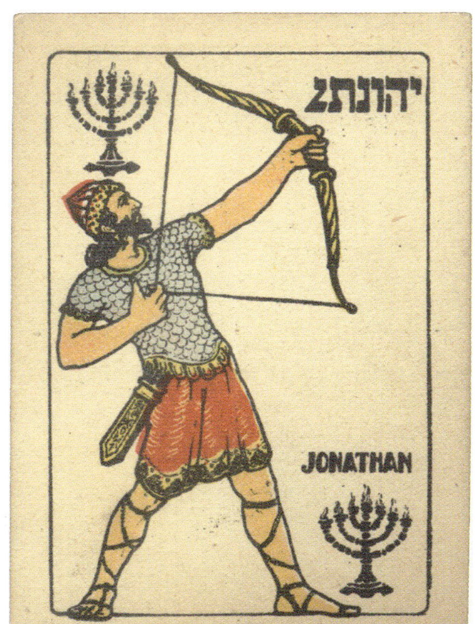
יהונתן
JONATHAN

JEWELRY

Materials: *Center brooch is a cameo in 14 karat gold frame, everything else is silver*
Origin: *Brooches are circa 1915-1925 / pendants are 1920s and '30s / bottom bracelet is 1930s / other bracelets are 1940s / all from Israel*
Hallmarks: *"Bezalel" or "Bezalel Jerusalem" in Hebrew for all pieces except the 1940s era bracelets which have "Made in Palestine St. 925 Reg. Design 313" and "Jerusalem St. 925"*
Dimensions: *.75 – 1.75" (range of brooch sizes) / .5" x 7" (bracelets)*

The carved cameo brooch (second row, second from left) is the earliest piece. Titled above her head in Hebrew is "Rachel," as this is a romanticized image of that Biblical matriarch.

Two other brooches have Stars of David with the word "Zion" or "Bezalel" in its center. One brooch has "Jerusalem" in large, interlaced Hebrew letters, another has a depiction of the Temple Menorah, and the remaining brooch has a Lion of Judah with "*Shaddai*" above it along with inlaid green glass. One pendant has three interlocking doves, while the other shows Ruth picking wheat.

The top bracelet depicts the "end of days" prophecy from the Book of Isaiah.

The middle bracelet shows the seven days of creation, and the bottom bracelet has incredibly detailed scenes from the Bible, with each scene individually described in English.

Because of original signed artist sketches that have survived, for the pendants depicting doves and Ruth, and for all of the bracelets, it is confirmed they were designed by Ze'ev Raban.

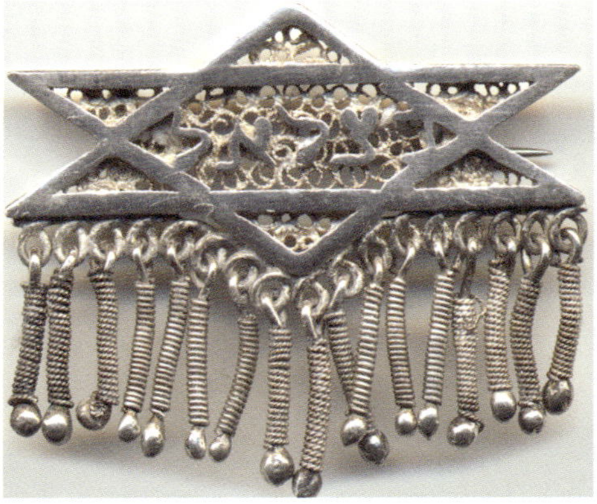

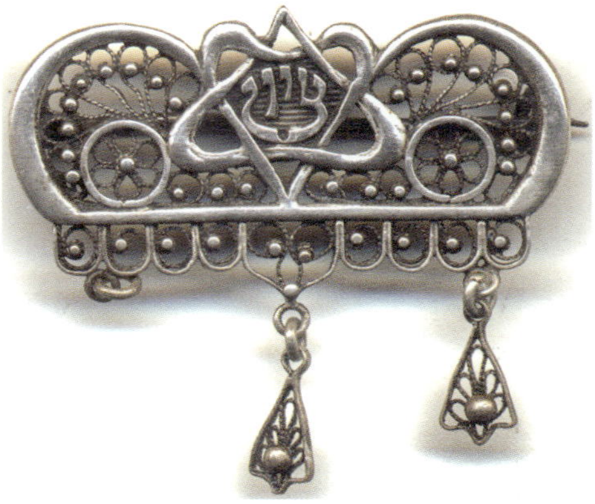

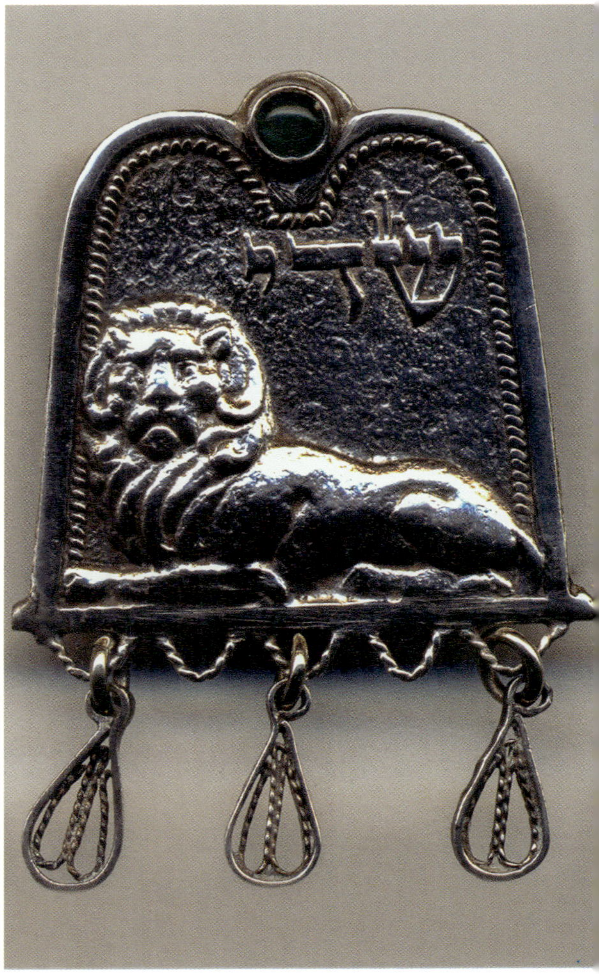

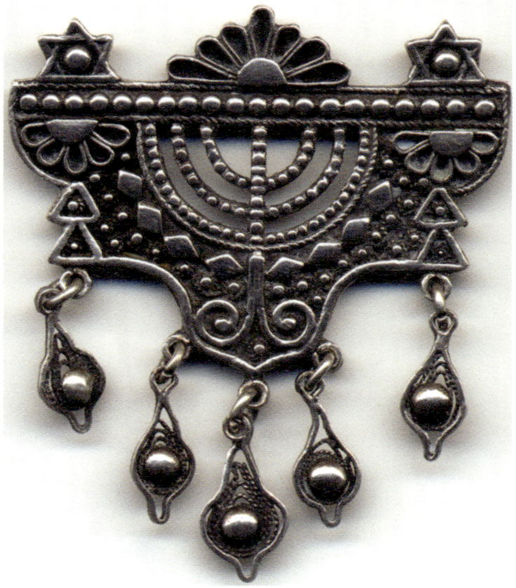

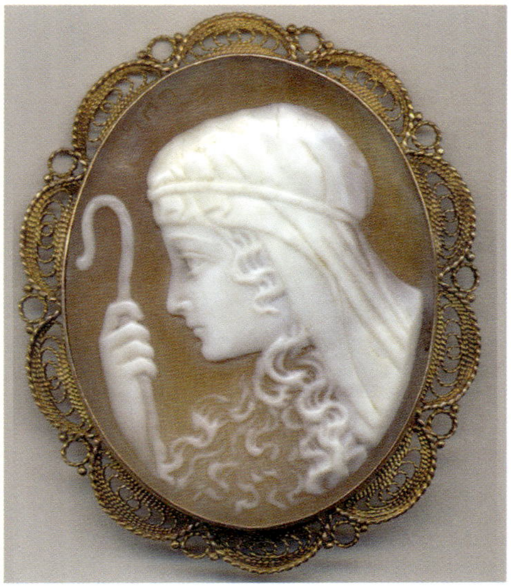

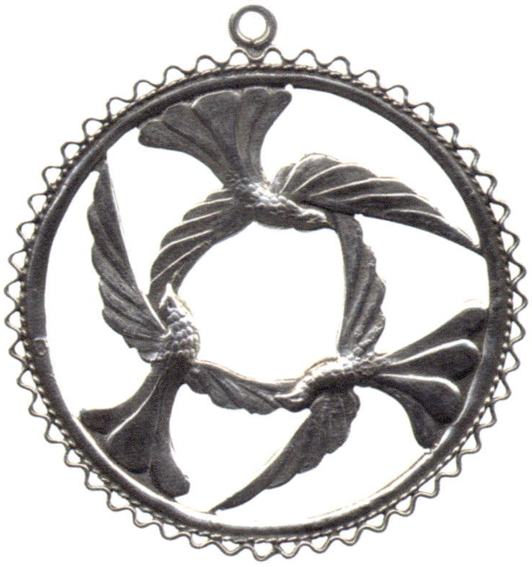

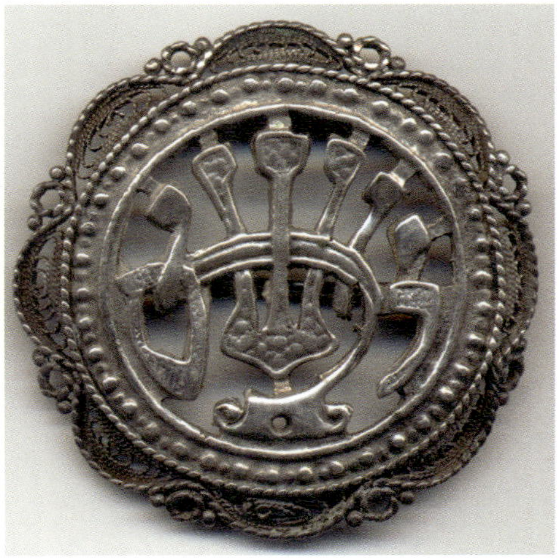

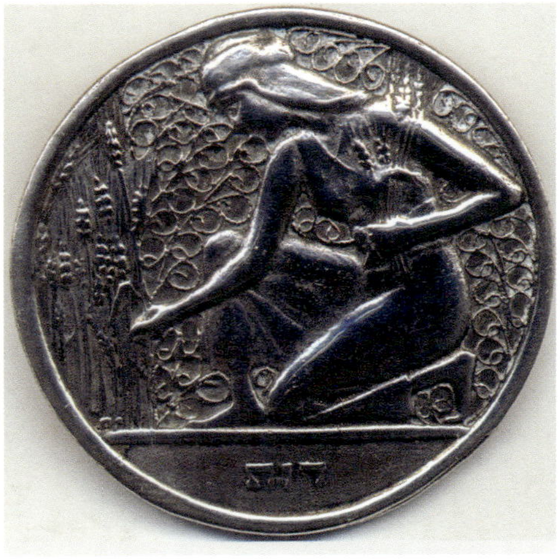

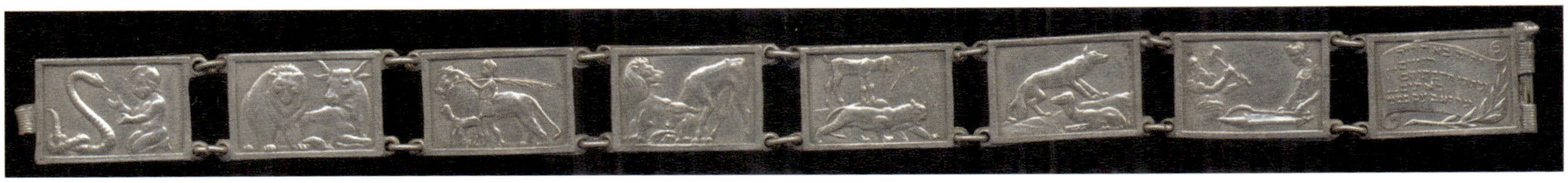

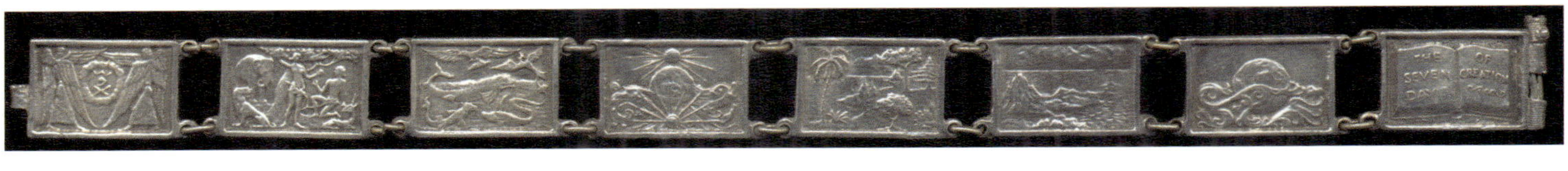

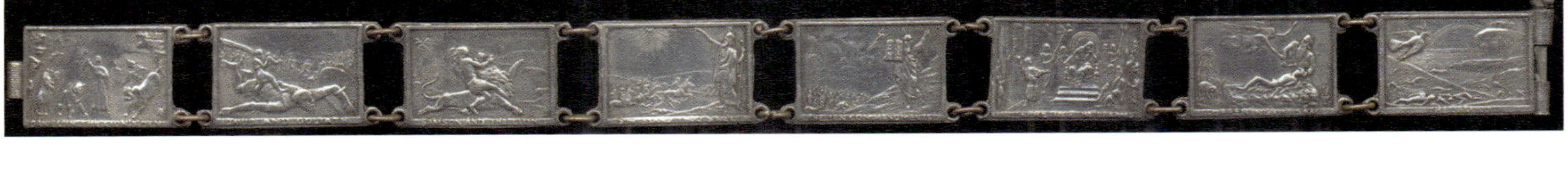

SEAL RING / LOCKET / TALLIS CLIPS

Material: Carnelian in 4 Karat Gold setting / Gold-filled silver / Silver
Origin: Germany, eighteenth century / Russia, 1878 / Germany (?), 1925
Hallmarks: "800" (tallis clips)
Dimensions: 1" x .75" / 1.25" x 1" / 3.75" x 1.2" (both clips attached)

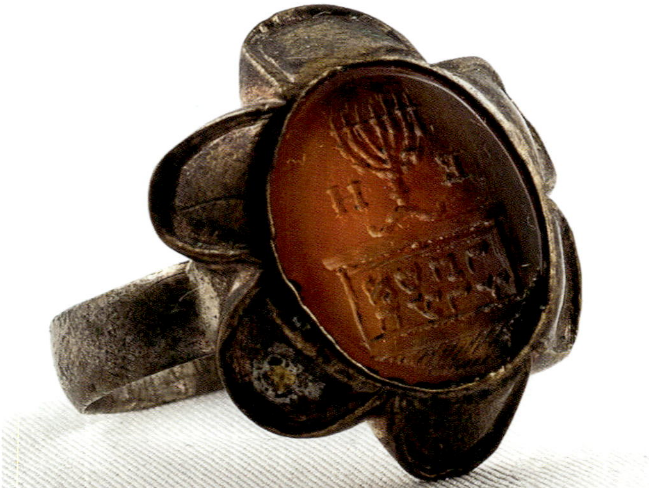

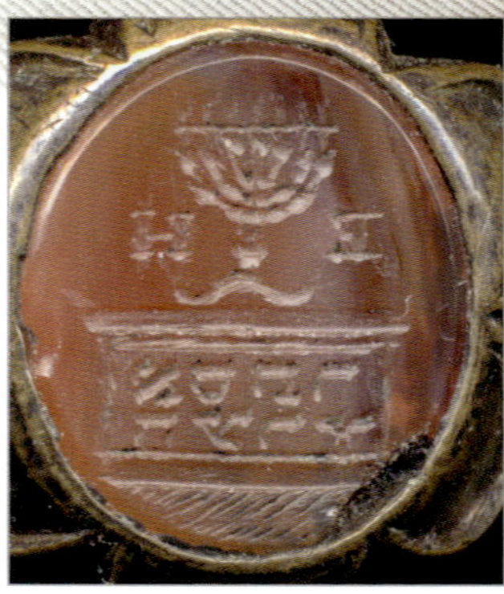

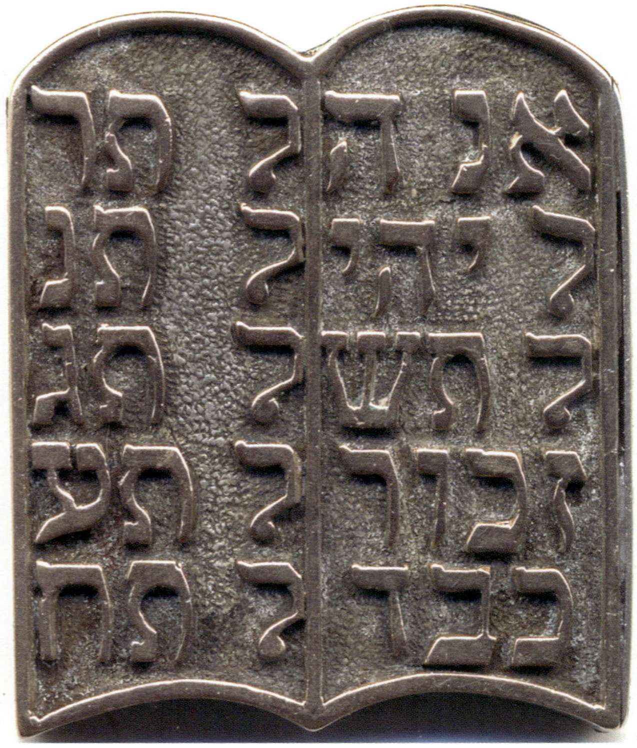

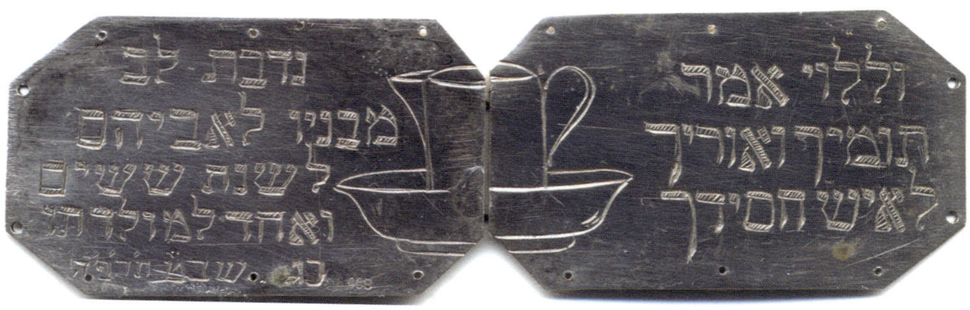

The seal ring shows a menorah, the initials "EH," and in Hebrew, "Esther Hertz." All the extant Jewish seal rings of eighteenth- and nineteenth-century Europe have the names of men or Jewish institutions engraved on them. A seal ring with the name of a woman is almost unheard of; Esther Hertz must have been someone of substantial wealth and social standing.

The locket is of the highest quality. It states The Ten Commandments in Hebrew and is in the traditionally accepted shape of the "Tablets of the Law." The Hebrew letters are beautifully executed, and the locket opens to reveal two oval spaces for photographs. The reverse has a lengthy dedication in Russian.

The clips are meant to keep the *tallis* (prayer shawl worn by men) in place when worn. The right side reads: "To Levi, he said: Your Urim and Thumim belong to Your pious one," (Deuteronomy 33:8). The left side reads: "A heartfelt gift from the sons to our father who is sixty-one years old today from the day of his birth," and a Hebrew date correlating to February 17, 1925. When both clips come together as shown here, a basin with cup appears, which is what the Levites used to wash the hands of the *Cohanim* (priests), in the Temple, a practice still done today in the synagogue on some holidays. Obviously the recipient of these clips was a Levite.

ISRAELIANA

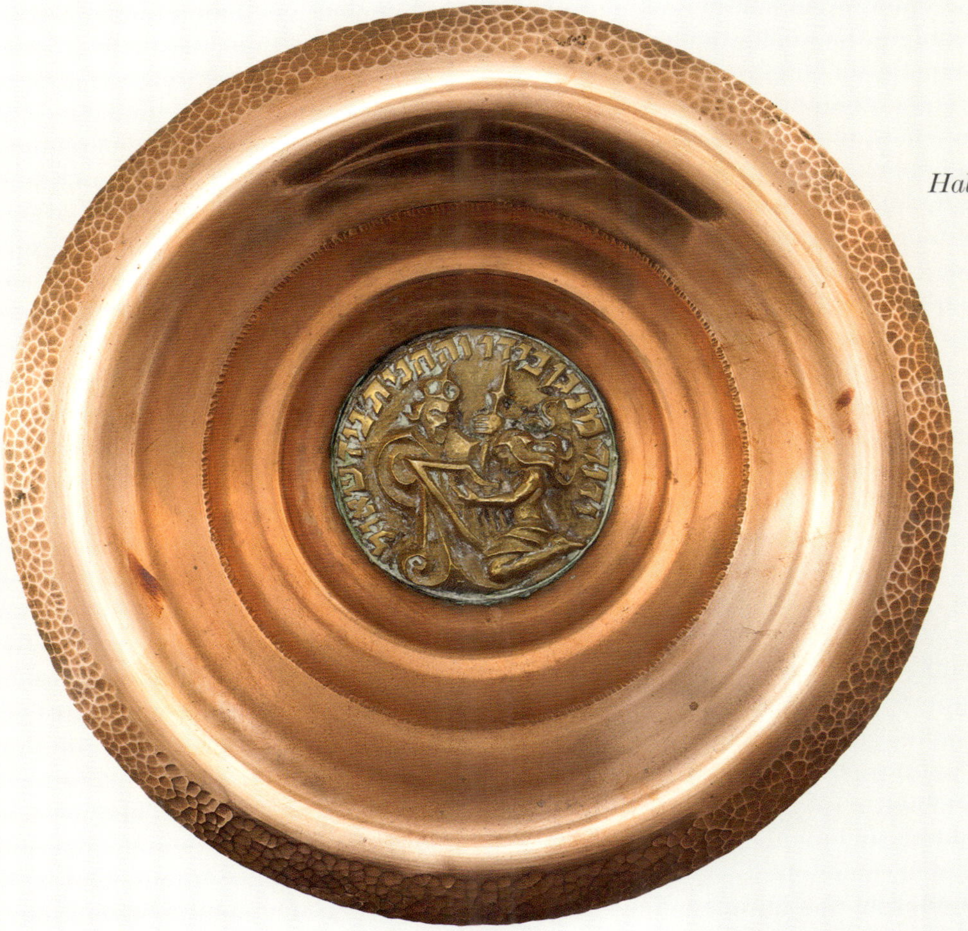

BOWL

Material: Copper and brass
Origin: Israel, early 1940s
Hallmarks: "A.N. Oppenheim" in Hebrew, "Made in Palestine"
Dimensions: 11.5"

While the Bezalel School was a very large producer of Israeli-made handicrafts, by no means was it the only one. Workshops dotted Jerusalem and Tel Aviv in the first half of the twentieth century, either selling wares directly from where they were made, or through a third party, such as a tourist shop.

The rim of this bowl is hand-hammered and the center has an applied plaque cast in thick and heavy brass. "David was playing [the harp] with his hand as [he did] every day, and the spear was in Saul's hand" (I Samuel 18:10) is displayed in Hebrew above a very young David with a lyre and King Saul with a spear.

This piece has both Arts and Crafts and art deco influences; the bowl rim has the former, while the bold Hebrew lettering and human figures show the latter.

FIGURINES

Material: Bronze
Origin: Israel, late 1930's or early 1940's
Hallmarks: "Omanut Klein Komm Hand Made Tel-Aviv Palestine," in Hebrew and English
Dimensions: 2.25" x 1.25"

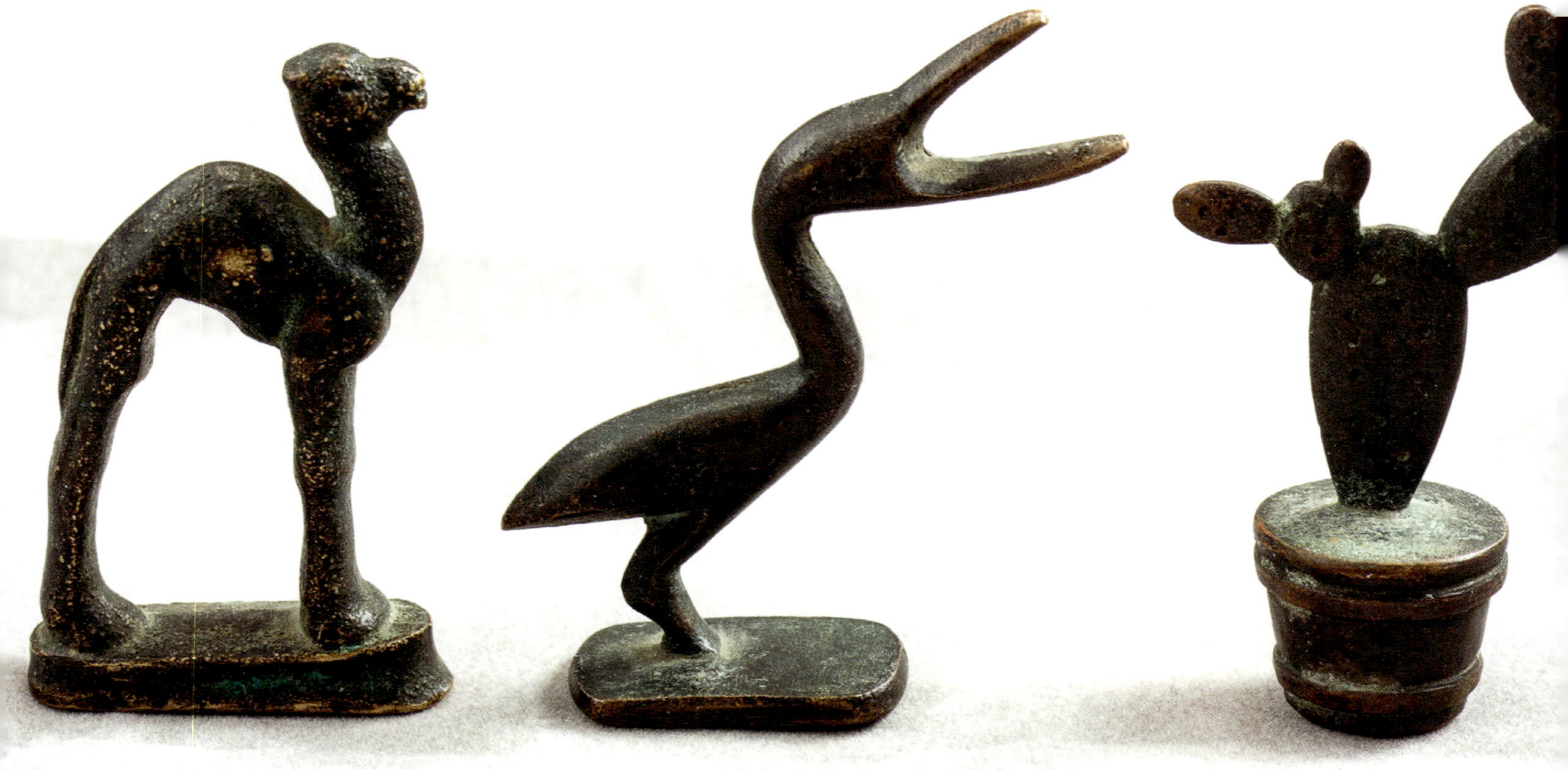

These small bronze figurines depict a camel, a seagull, and a cactus plant, all of which are indigenous to the Land of Israel. The pieces are marked "Klein Komm," as this company was started by two men, Moshe Klein, a Hungarian immigrant in Israel, and Avram Komm, his brother-in-law. Klein later changed his name to Maurice Ascalon (his surname taken after a city south of Tel Aviv) and renamed the company "Pal-Bell" (see page 29 for a Pal-Bell mezuzah case). Pal-Bell closed its doors in 1956.

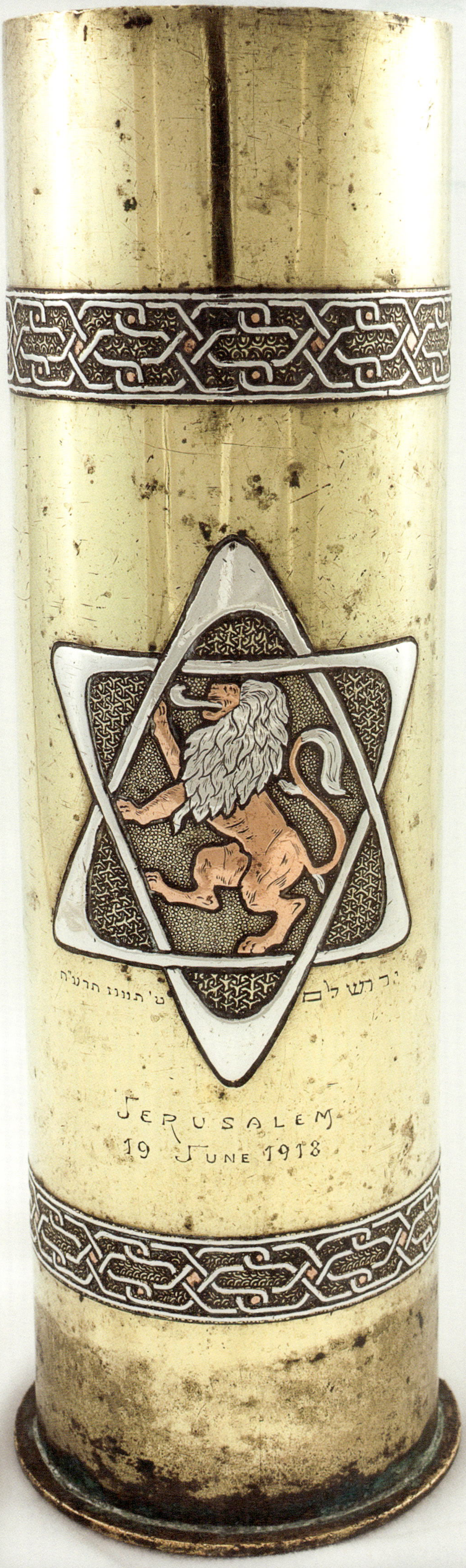

SHELL CASE VASE

Material: Brass inlaid with silver and copper
Origin: Israel, 1918
Dimensions: 11" x 3.5"

During the First World War, a trend developed among soldiers fighting on both sides, in which spent bullets and mortar shells were cut and decorated to form objects such as letter openers, ashtrays, vases, and other items. This area of collectibles is called "Trench Art."

The fields of battle in Israel between the British and Turks during World War I were also fertile ground for artisans (including those working at the Bezalel School) to gather materiel, decorate it, and sell it. In some contemporary collecting circles, the decorated shell casings made by these Jews are mistakenly included in the category of Trench Art, however that is incorrect. Trench Art is defined as being created by soldiers; shell casings with civilian ornamentation are not that at all.

This shell has German factory markings on the underside, as Germany supplied the Turks with weapons for fighting in the Middle East. At first glance, this impressive work of Damascene art would have the viewer assume it to be made by the Bezalel School, but if this was the case, it most certainly would have been hallmarked with a Bezalel stamping on the underside at the very least. It is not, which indicates it was decorated by an unknown artisan acting for one of the workshops in Israel that sold ornamented shell casings as souvenirs during and after World War I. The shell is engraved "Jerusalem June 19, 1918" in Hebrew and English, in an Arts and Crafts-styled font.

British soldiers and officers stationed in Jerusalem made up the majority of the customer base for these items. Even today, Israeli decorated shell casings from World War I routinely appear for sale at antique markets in England.

The area of collecting medals and tokens is a field unto itself, called exonumia. I collect Judaic exonumia in a very limited capacity, only buying examples that appeal to me from a historic, emotional, or aesthetic level (ideally they have all of these attributes). Some pieces shown here are quite scarce; this is the first time they have been published.

EXONUMIA

MEDAL

Material: Bronze
Artist: Samuel Friedrich Beer
Diameter: 63 mm

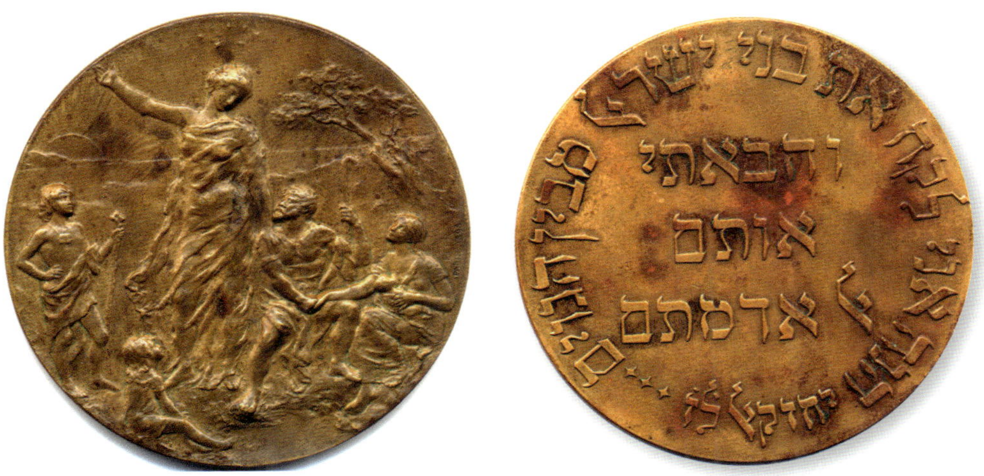

This medal commemorates the Second Zionist Congress, held in Basel, Switzerland, in 1898. The obverse shows a female figure representing Zionism, pointing toward the new dawn of the Jewish people. The reverse has in Hebrew: "Behold I will take the people of Israel from the nations…and bring them to their own land" (Ezekiel 37:21)

**Beware of old re-strikes and modern cast copies of this medal*

MEDAL

Material: Gilded bronze
Artist: Carniol Fiul
Diameter: 63 mm

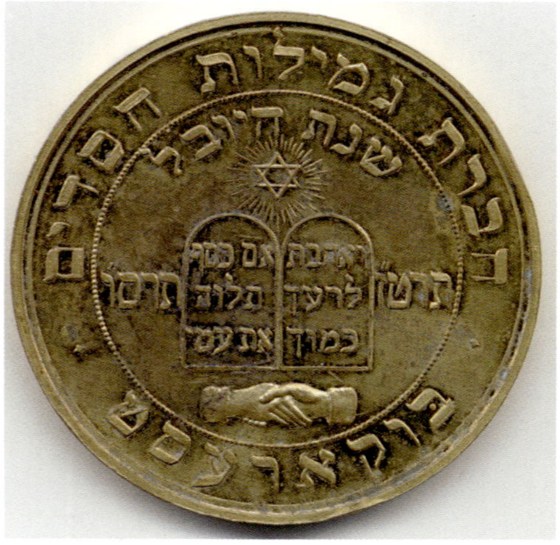

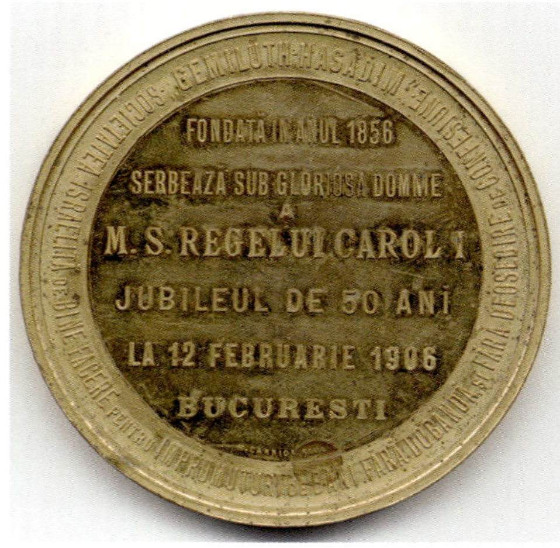

This medal commemorates the fiftieth anniversary of the Jewish charity organization of Bucharest, Romania, in 1906. The obverse states this in Hebrew, along with clasped hands and two tablets that read: "You shall love your friend like yourself," "If you loan money to my people." The reverse pays homage to the ruler of Romania, King Carol I, who in 1906 celebrated forty years on the throne. This medal was also issued in silver.

MEDAL

Material: Brass alloy
Diameter: 60 mm

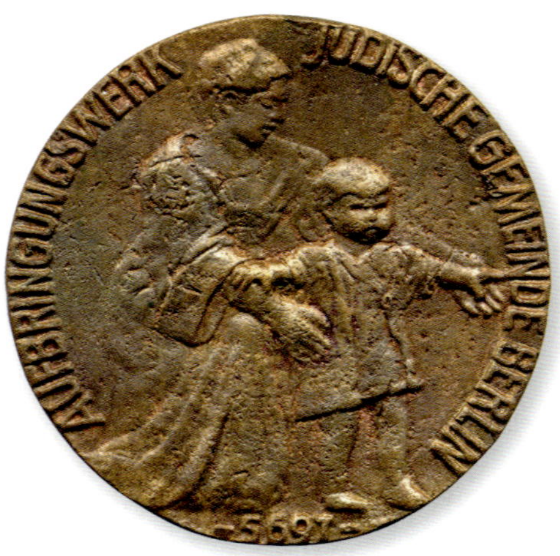

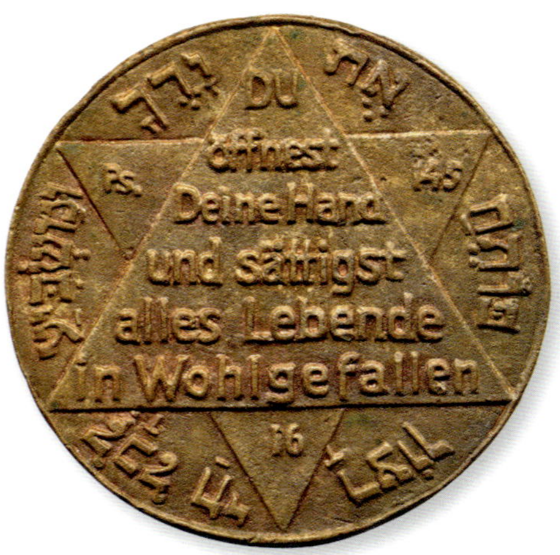

This medal is from Nazi-era Germany. The obverse has the Hebrew year of 5697 (September 1936–September 1937), a woman helping a young child walk, and, in German, "Work Creation Jewish Community Berlin." The reverse has in Hebrew and German: "You open Your hand, and satisfy the desire of every living thing," (Psalm 145:16). This was given in appreciation to someone who donated to this charity. The director of this charity was Rabbi Martin Salomonski, an Iron Cross award recipient for his service as a German Army field Rabbi in World War I. With this charity, Rabbi Salomonski tried to raise money to preserve the financial stability of Jewish institutions in Berlin (quite the undertaking in 1936-1937 Germany). Rabbi Salomonski died in Auschwitz in 1944.

MEDAL

Material: Brass
Diameter: 97 mm

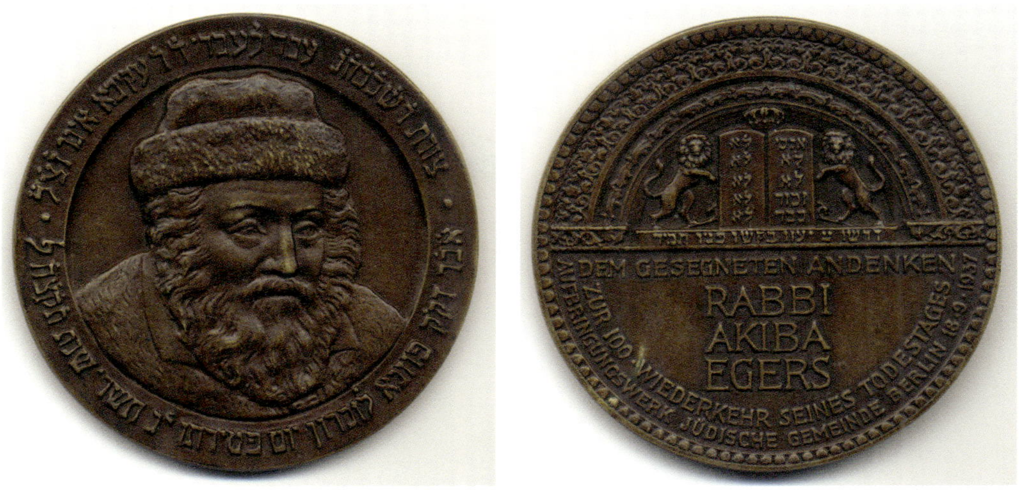

This was issued by the Jewish community of Berlin in commemoration of the one hundredth anniversary of the death of Rabbi Akiva Eger, which was September 18, 1937. The obverse shows his portrait; the reverse has the Ten Commandments flanked by Lions of Judah. One example struck in gold is known.

This remarkable medal was created in Germany four years after Hitler took power, a year before *Kristallnacht* and the beginning of the destruction of the German-Jewish community.

**Beware of modern copies of this medal*

MEDAL

Material: Bronze
Diameter: 43 mm

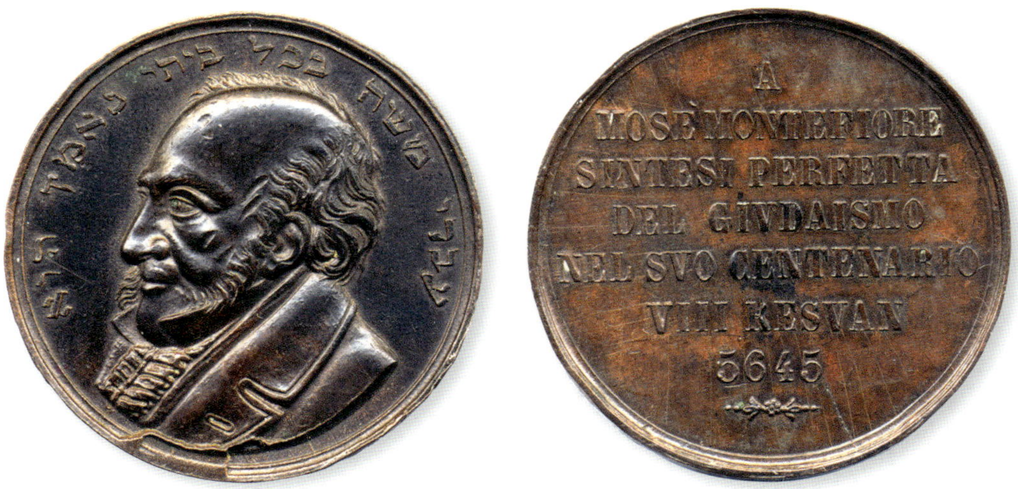

This medal celebrates the one hundredth birthday of Moses Montefiore, the legendary English philanthropist. Issued in Italy, the country of his birth, the obverse has his portrait and, in Hebrew: "My servant Moses, who is like a trusted servant throughout My house," (Numbers 12:7). The reverse is in Italian, and gives the Hebrew date of this occasion, which correlates to October 24, 1884.

MEDALETS

Material: Brass, bronze
Diameters: 31 mm & 27 mm
Artist: Israel Rouchomovsky
(first example only)

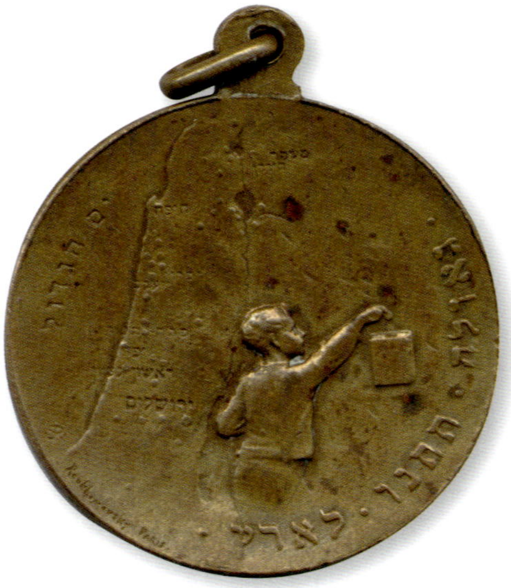

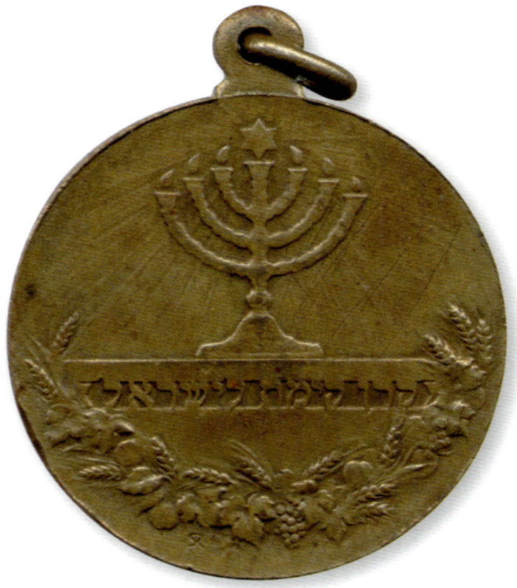

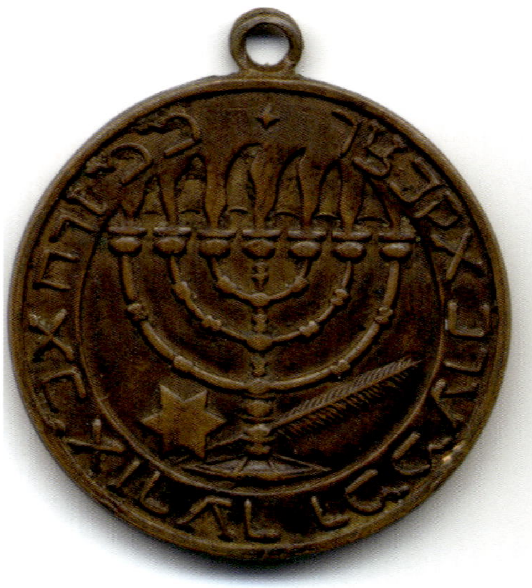

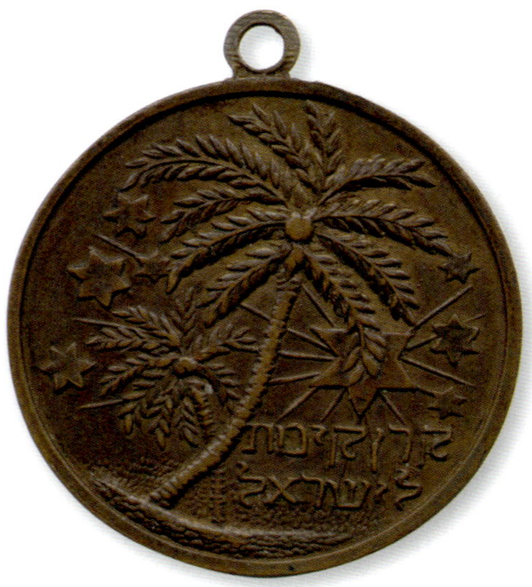

These medalets date to about 1915. The obverse of the Rouchomovsky-designed piece shows a young boy putting money into a charity box against a backdrop of a map of Israel, along with the Hebrew legend "We have redeemed the land." The obverse of the other medalet depicts a lit menorah and around it "I will bring your offspring from the east, and gather you from the west," (Isaiah 43:5). The reverse of both pieces have "Jewish National Fund" in Hebrew.

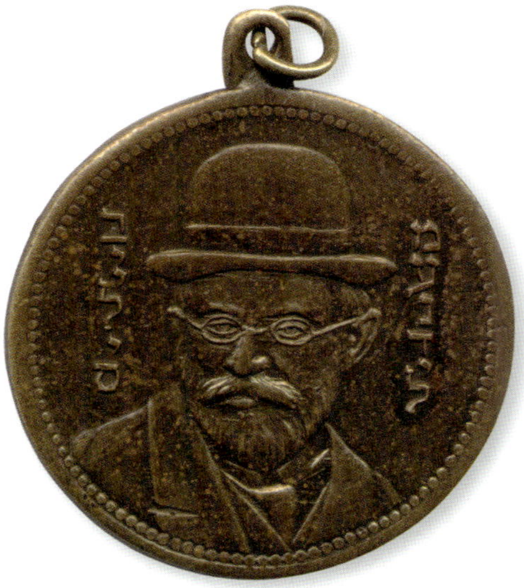

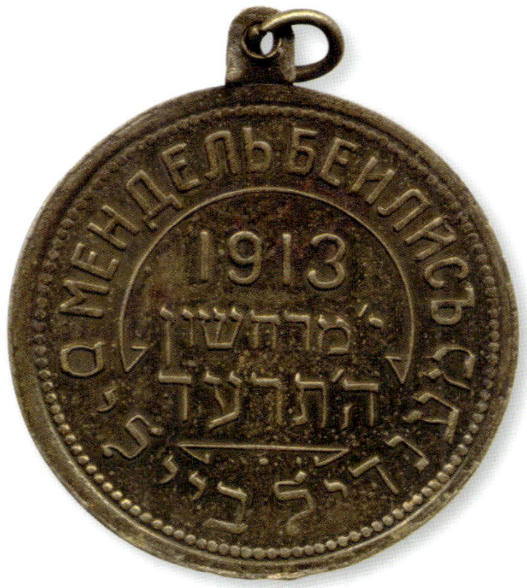

MEDALET

Material: Brass
Diameter: 23 mm

This medalet celebrates the acquittal of Mendel Beiliss, a secular Ukrainian Jew accused in the kidnapping and murder of a thirteen-year-old Christian boy, Andrei Yushchinsky, in order to use his blood for Jewish ritual purposes (of which there are none, as the consumption of even one drop of blood, be it animal or human, is expressly forbidden in the Torah; even chicken eggs, when cracked open and found to have a blood spot, are immediately discarded). Arrested on July 21, 1911, Beiliss sat in prison for two years before his case came to trial in September of 1913 and ended with his being set free in October by an all-Christian jury.

The obverse shows a portrait of Beiliss along with his name in Hebrew, while the reverse has his name in both Hebrew and Cyrillic, the date 1913, and, in Hebrew: "The month of Cheshvan 5674", which correlates to October 1913. While it is not known exactly who and where this medalet was made, it is assumed it was done shortly after the trial's end, as a memento showing justice had prevailed.

The millennia-old canard of Jews kidnapping and murdering a gentile child in order to use its blood in the baking of Passover matzahs, unfortunately, has been revived today in some circles, notably in Europe and the Middle East. This is known as a blood libel.

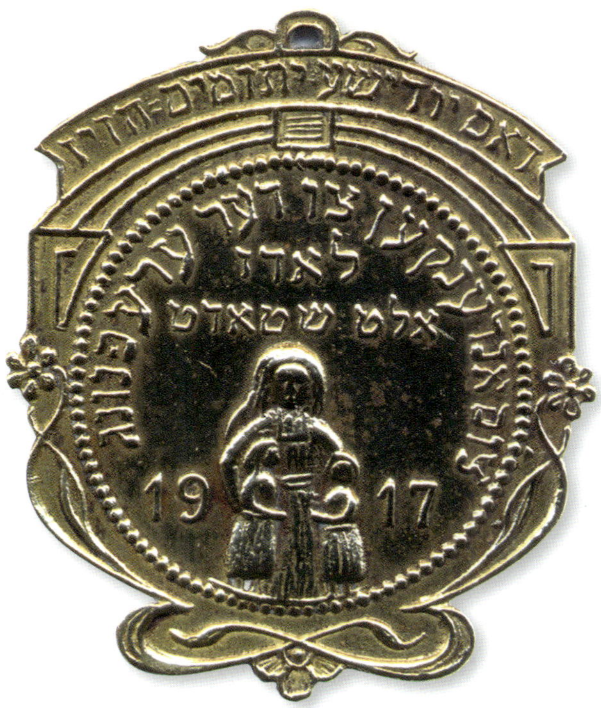

MEDALET

Material: Brass
Diameter: 1.25" x 1"

This one-sided piece shows a sad-faced woman holding two young children in between the year 1917. In Yiddish it reads: "The Jewish Orphanage Home: As a memory for its opening in the old city of Lodz".

TOKEN

Material: Brass
Diameter: 26 mm

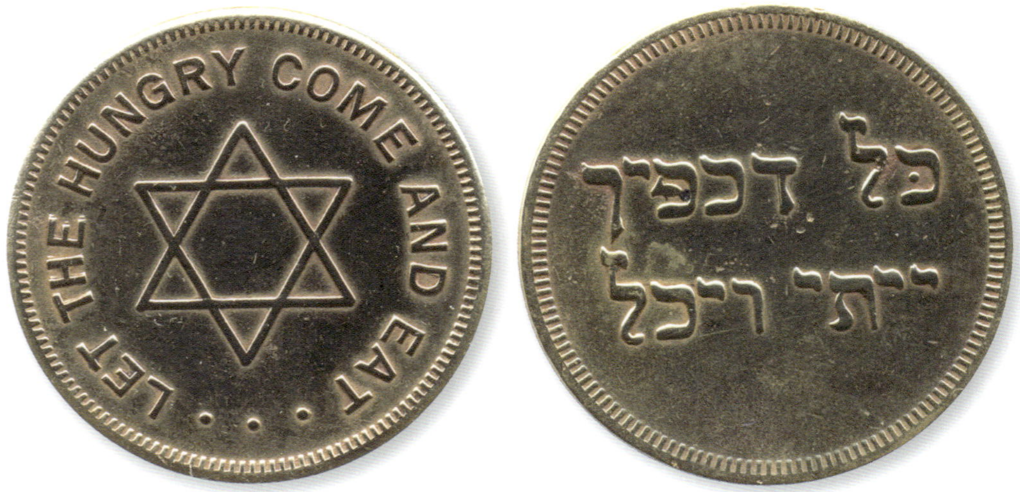

During the holiday of Passover, there is an established custom of *Maos Chitim* (literally "money for wheat"), which ensures that the poor of every Jewish community are supplied with their Passover needs. Paper tickets are sometimes issued, which the redeemer can present at his or her local Jewish grocery store and take matzahs and the like, gratis.

"Let the hungry come and eat" is from the *Haggadah*, and is on both sides of this token, in Hebrew and English. Nothing is known about this piece, so I am not sure if it was used as currency for a poor person who wanted to buy Passover goods, or this was given as a gift of appreciation to an individual who donated money for a *Maos Chitim* fund. This dates to around 1920, from New York most likely.

TOKEN

Material: Brass
Diameter: 25 mm

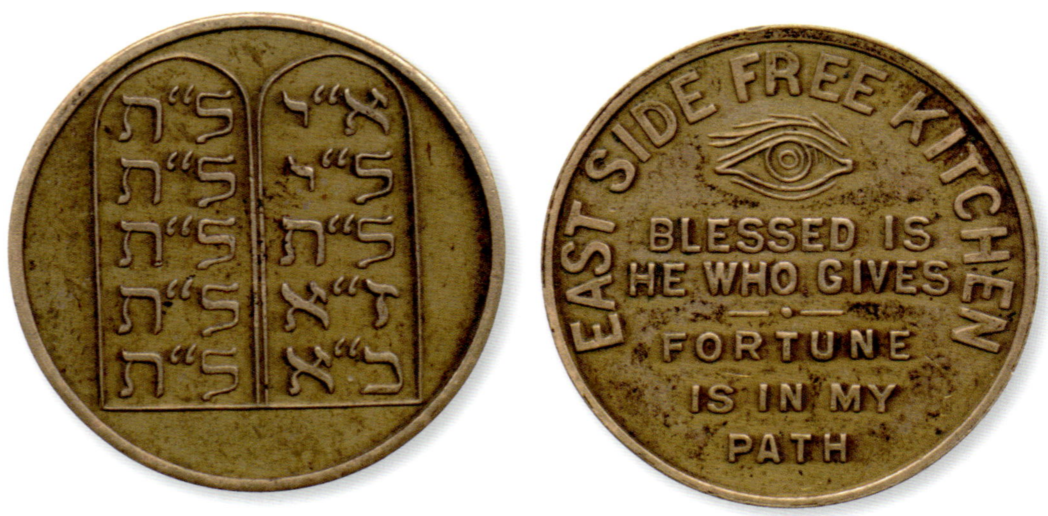

One side shows the Ten Commandments, while the other states "East Side Free Kitchen," along with an icon for the "All seeing eye of G-d" (which while not Jewish per se, could have been used for a Jewish charity during that era). New York, circa 1920.

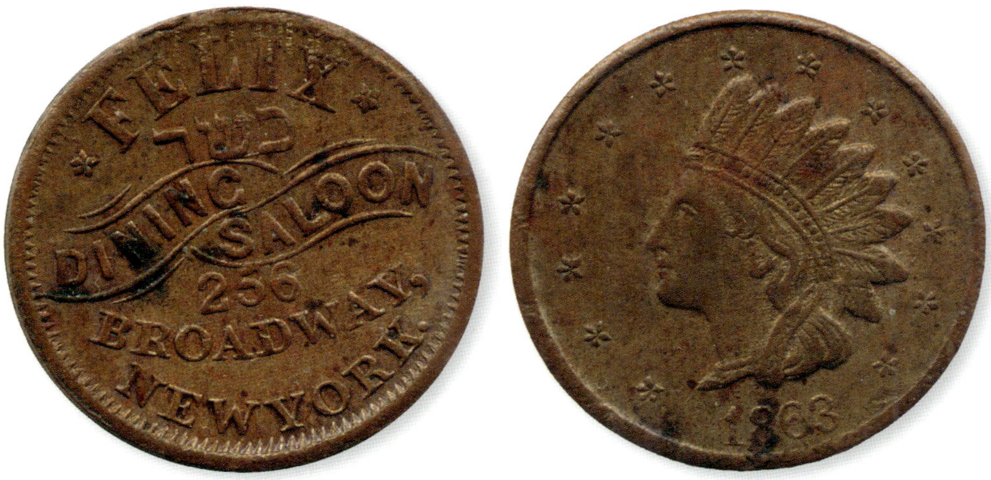

TOKEN

Material: Copper
Diameter: 20 mm

This is one of thousands of different types of tokens issued during the American Civil War by private individuals. The obverse states it is for the Felix Dining Saloon in New York City. This is the only Civil War token that has Hebrew, as the word "Kosher" is in between "Felix" and "Dining," The reverse imitates the obverse of an 1863 penny.

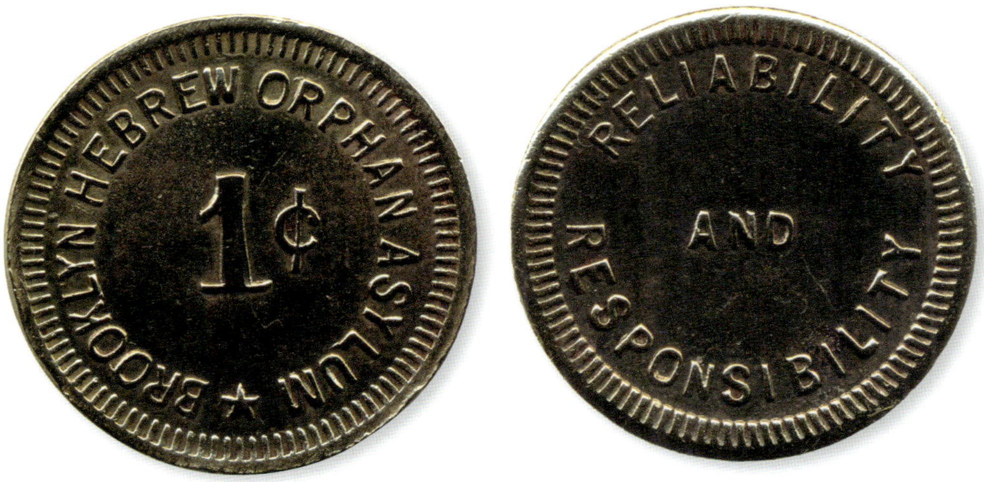

TOKEN

Material: Brass
Diameter: 20 mm

This was issued for children living at the Brooklyn Hebrew Orphans Asylum. The value was for one penny's worth of goods (candy!) at the orphanage's canteen. Notice the maxim "Reliability and Responsibility." This dates to about 1920.

MEDALETS

Material: Copper
Diameter: 28 mm & 35 mm

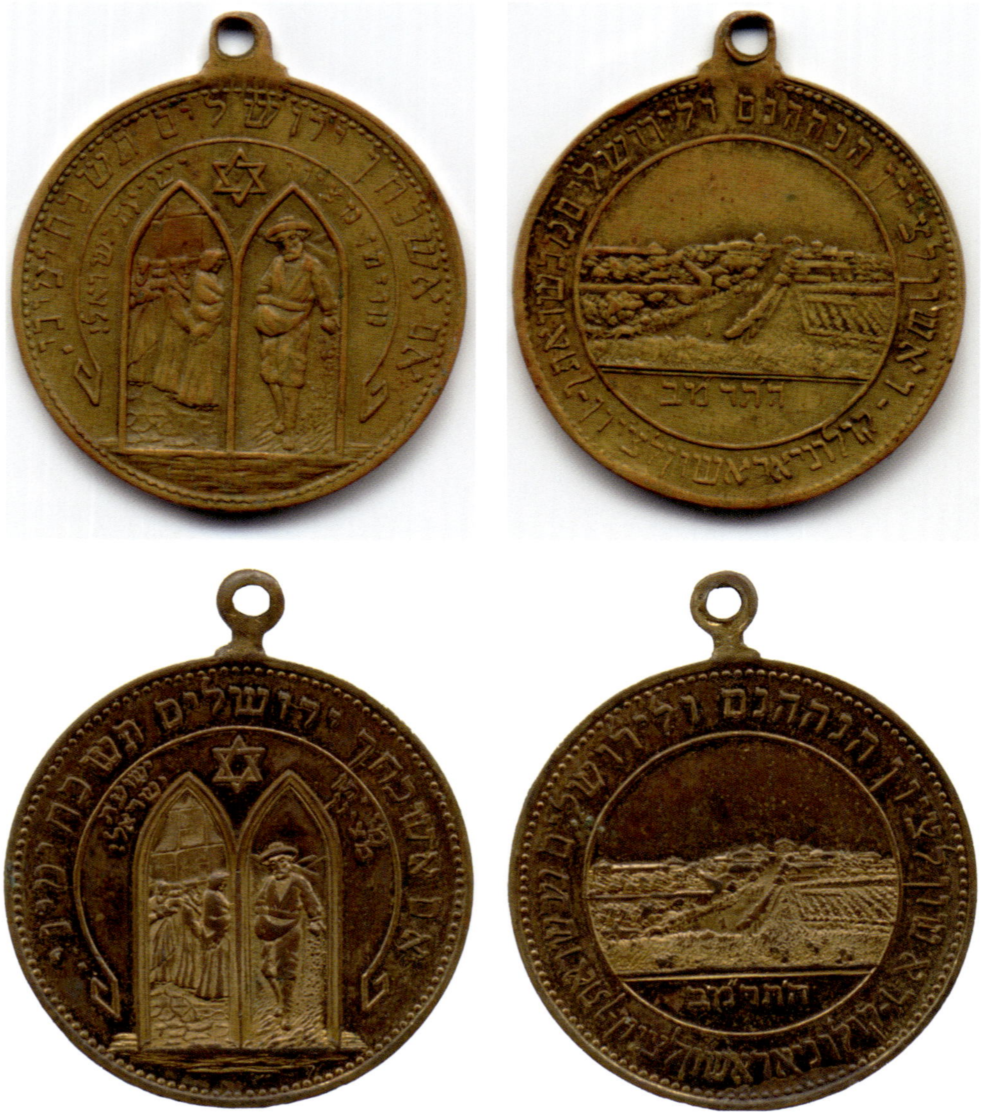

These medalets are thought to have been made in 1892, in Russia, to celebrate the tenth anniversary of the founding of the second Jewish farm colony established in Israel, that of Rishon Le'Tzion (the first was Petach Tikva, in 1878). The obverse depicts people at prayer at the Western Wall, a farmer sowing seeds, and in Hebrew, the verse "Would that from Zion salvation will come to Israel" (Psalms 14:7) and the verse "If I forget thee O Jerusalem let my right hand forget its cunning," (Psalms 137:5). The reverse has "1882 Rishon Le'Tzion: Here is the miracle," a panoramic view of the colony, and "The first shall say to Zion, Behold, behold them: and I will give to Jerusalem one that brings good tidings," (Isaiah 41:27).

MEDALET

Material: Silver
Artist: Israel Rouchomovsky
Diameter: 16 mm

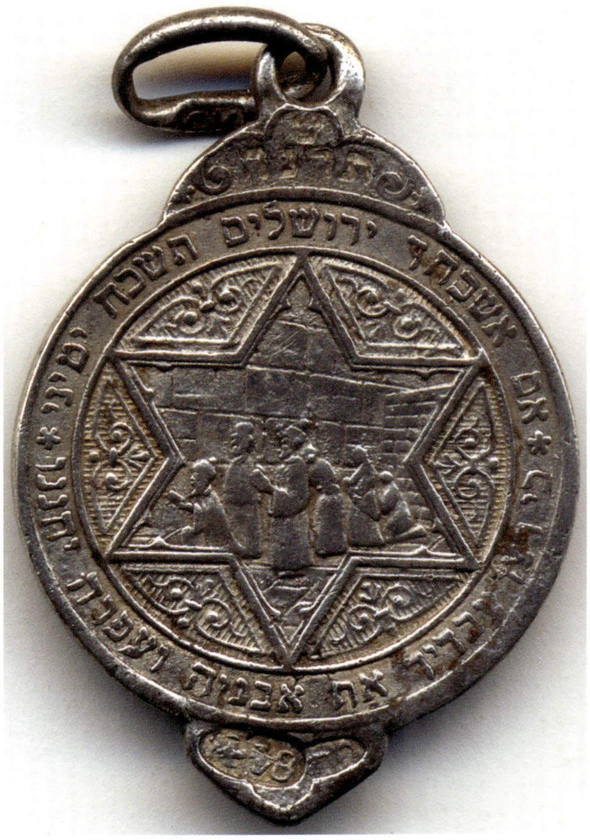

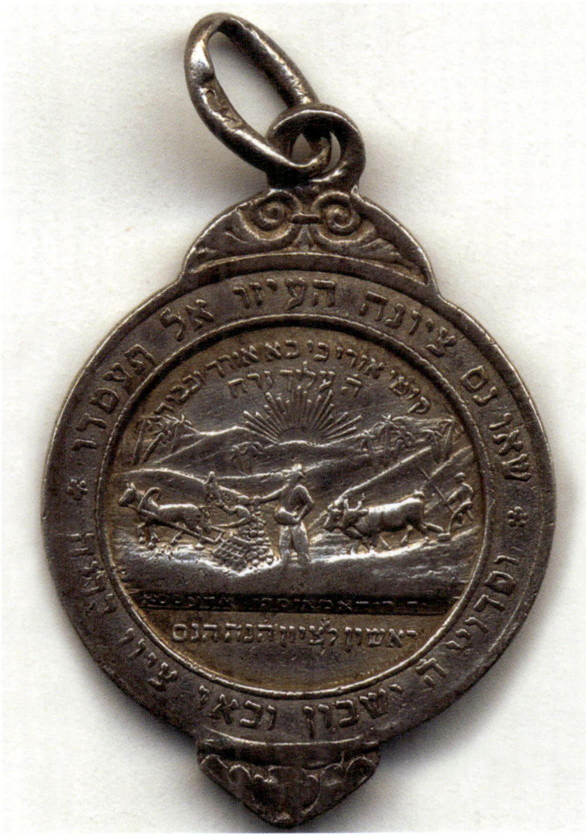

The amount of detail on this piece is simply amazing, as this medalet is a bit smaller than a dime. It has the Hebrew year that correlates to the period between September 1895 and September 1896, has a scene of Jews praying at the Western Wall on the obverse, and a farmer plowing land on the reverse. There are a total of six different Biblical verses that appear; two on the obverse (Psalm 137:5, Psalm 102:150) and four on the reverse (Jeremiah 4:6, Isaiah 60:1, 25:10, 41:27). All of these verses are statements about how Jews will settle and inherit the land of Israel. Beneath the panoramic view it reads: "Rishon Le'Tzion: Here is the miracle." This medalet is from Odessa, as it is signed as such, next to the artist's name.

MEDAL

Material: Gilded brass
Diameter: 81.5 mm

This one-sided piece has a hole in the center of the reverse, indicating this was made to be mounted. It reads in Hebrew "Youth Committee / Beograd" along with the Hebrew year that correlates to the period between September 1922 and September 1923. In highly stylized art deco fashion, a man is seen lifting a rock, the sun beating upon him. Like so many Jewish youth movements in Europe from the early 20th century, this group from Belgrade, Serbia, was Zionist in nature. Presumably the scene depicted is of a pioneer in the Land of Israel.

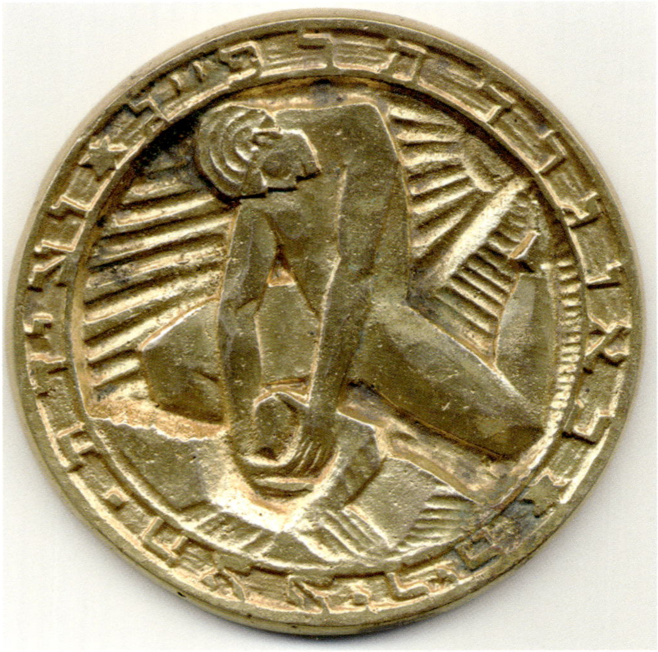

MEDAL

Material: Bronze
Artist: C.J. van der Hoef
Diameter: 93 mm

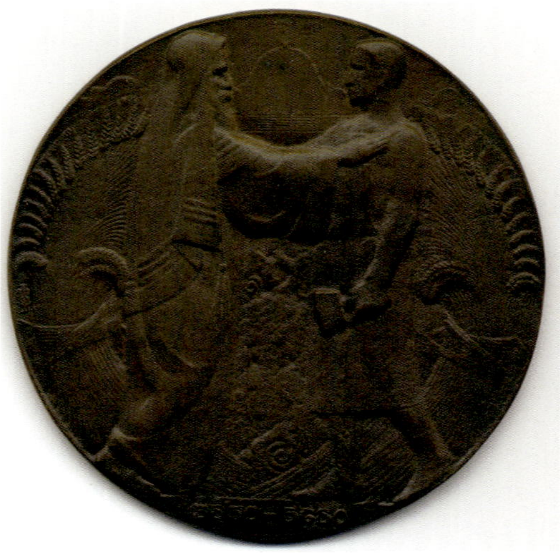

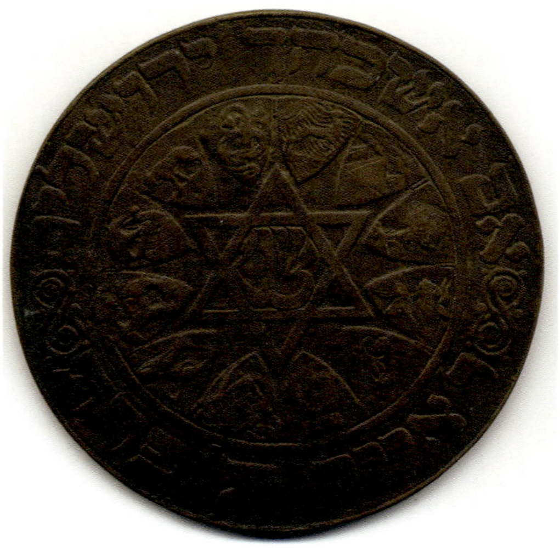

This medal was issued by the Dutch Zionist Organization in celebration of the San Remo Conference of 1920. The obverse has a Patriarchal figure, dressed in attire from the times of antiquity, giving his blessing to a young pioneer holding a stone mason's chisel in his hand. Underneath them are the Hebrew years 3830–5680, which correlate to the secular years 70–1920. The year of the destruction of the Second Temple was 70 CE.

The reverse has "Zion" in Hebrew inside a Star of David, the emblems of the Twelve Tribes of Israel, "If I forget thee O Jerusalem" at top (Psalm 137:5), and "10 Iyar 5680" at bottom, which is April 28, 1920.

Material: Silver
Origin: Germany, 1816-1838
Artist: Aaron Kohn
Diameter: 21 mm / 33mm / 41mm

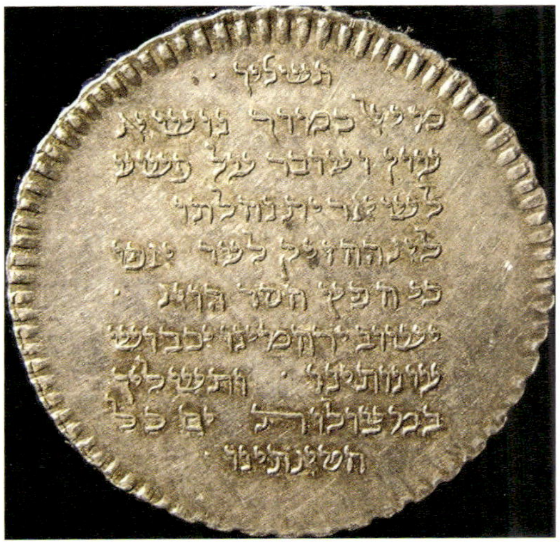

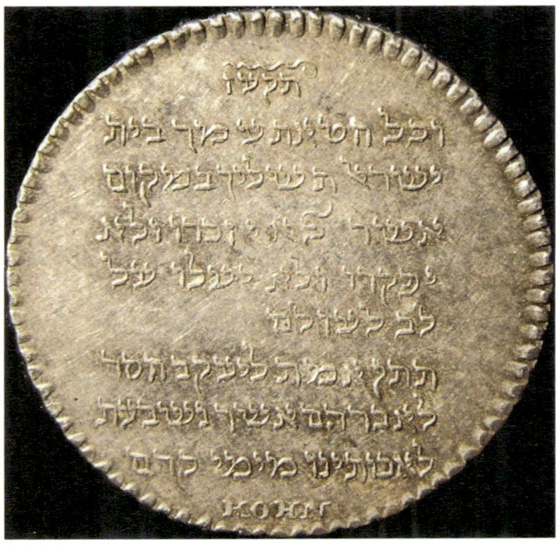

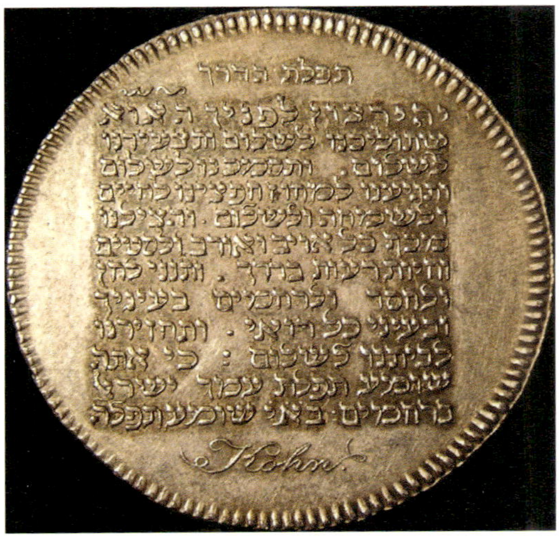

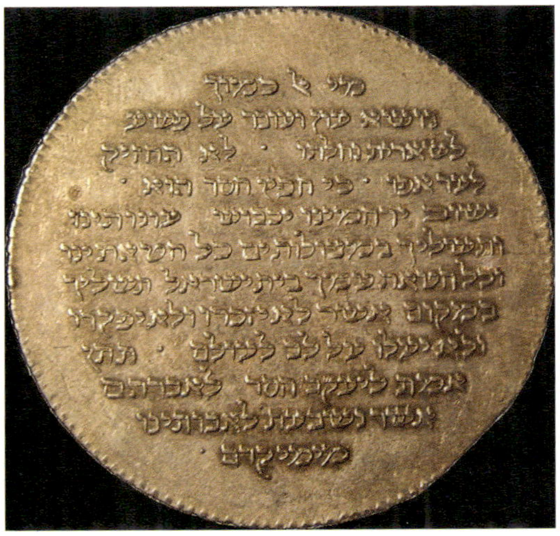

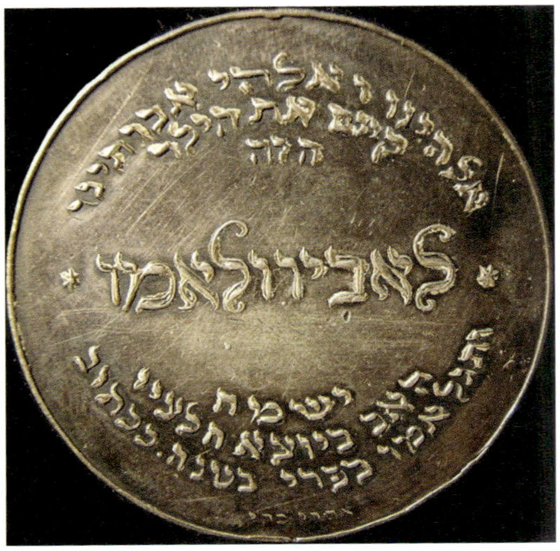

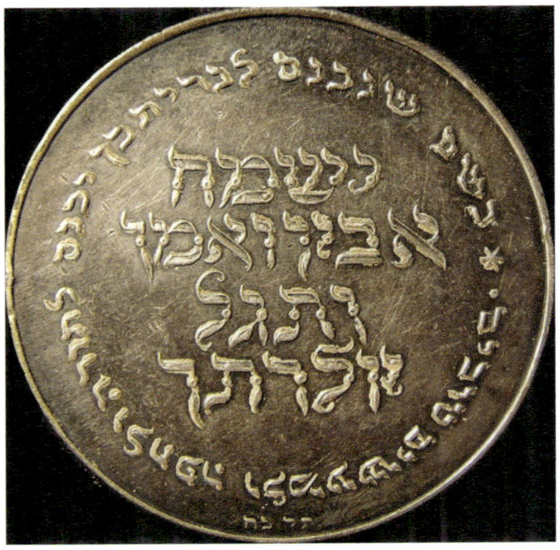

Aaron Kohn was one of four Jewish medalists working in nineteenth-century Germany. The uniqueness of Kohn's work lies in his exclusive focus on Jewish themes using Hebrew text.

The first medal has the Rosh Hashanah prayer of *Tashlich* on it, along with a Hebrew date of 1816/1817.

The second medal has *Tefilat HaDerech* (blessing for a person who travels) on one side, and the Tashlich prayer on the other side.

The third medal has the prayers of the circumcision ceremony on both sides, along with a Hebrew date of 1837/1838.

These medals were also issued in bronze.

AMERICANA

STENCIL

Material: Copper
Origin: United States, 1876 (?)
Dimensions: 6.25″x6.5″

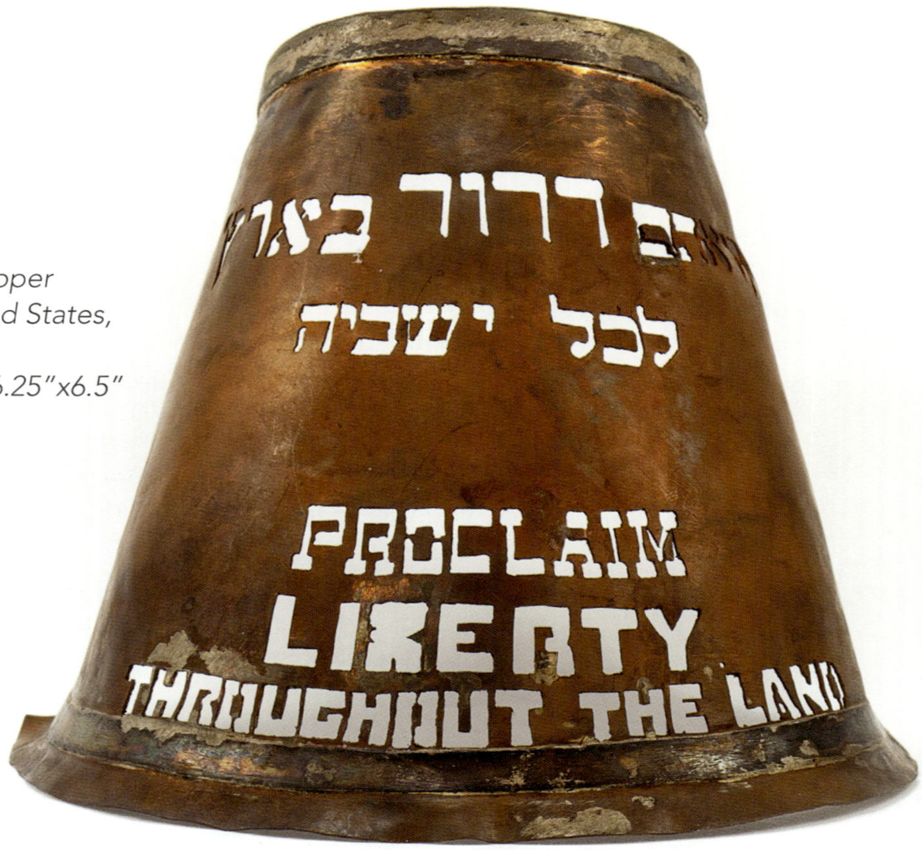

The use of stencils in decorating and identifying items has a tradition in the United States that dates back to the eighteenth century. During the Civil War, for example, many soldiers would own a stencil, usually made of tin, with cut-out letters making up their name, so they could label personal gear such as their water canteens.

This stencil has the verse from Leviticus 25:10 cut out on it in both Hebrew and English; this verse is on the Liberty Bell in Philadelphia (in English only), which was cast in 1751.

Of the thousands of eighteenth- and nineteenth-century American stencils held in both private and public collections, this is the only stencil known that has Hebrew wording. The typeface of the English characters, specifically the word "Proclaim," matches a font popular during the 1870s and '80s. It best known for being on "Wanted" posters of criminals in the American Old West.

The shape of the stencil combined with the patriotic motto that is cut out leads me to believe this was used to paint paper hats worn by celebrants in an Independence Day parade. This stencil might have been commissioned by a contingent of Jewish-Americans (a chapter of B'nai B'rith for instance) who wished to participate in the fervent celebrations that were held in towns and cities across this country on a particularly jubilant Independence Day, that of the centennial, July 4, 1876.

VETERAN'S MEDAL

Materials: Bronze, enamel, silk
Origin: USA, 1899
Hallmarks: "Dieges & Clust John St. N.Y."
Dimensions: 4" x 1.75"

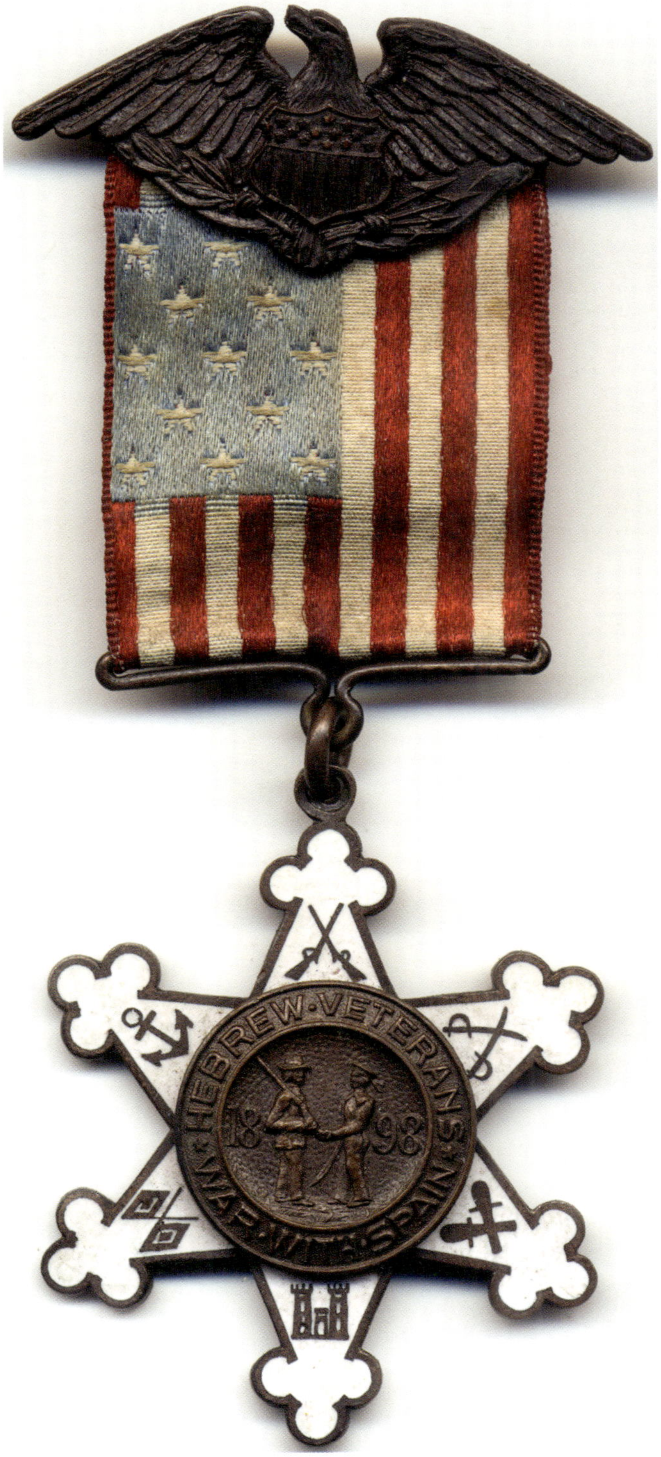

Jews have had a long and distinguished history of fighting for the United States of America, even before there was a U.S.A. In New Amsterdam, in 1655, Jacob Barsimson and Asser Levy fought for the right to stand guard by the entrance of the settlement. During the French and Indian Wars, New York resident Isaac Meyers was appointed captain and led a company of men across the Allegheny Mountains. Most Jews living in the colonies took up the cause of the Revolutionary War. During the war that was costliest in terms of American lives lost, the Civil War, Jews fought on both sides. Roughly 8,500 out of a total Jewish population of about 100,000 served, including eight Generals and twenty-one Colonels.

Due to accusations that Jews had not served their country during the Civil War, the Hebrew Union Veterans Association was founded by Jewish veterans of the Union Army in 1896. In 1898, the United States was at war again, this time with Spain. Because the veterans of this war were of a younger generation than those who fought in the Civil War, on December 11, 1899, the Hebrew Veterans of the War with Spain was founded. Five thousand Jews served in this war, including 400 who were killed.

This medal has the standard flag ribbon with American eagle and shield, however, the badge itself is in the shape of a Star of David. Each point of the star has a different branch of the Armed Forces represented: Infantry, Cavalry, Field Artillery, Corps of Engineers, Signal Corps, and Navy.

Eventually the Hebrew Union Veterans Association merged with the Hebrew Veterans of the War with Spain to form the Hebrew Veterans of the Wars of the Republic. In 1924, this organization changed its name to the Jewish Veterans of the Wars of the Republic, and then in 1929, changed its name to Jewish War Veterans of the United States of America.

The Jewish War Veterans continues to operate today, providing services to both Jews and gentiles serving our country in the current conflicts of Afghanistan and Iraq.

ALPHABET CHART

Material: Paper
Origin: United States, circa 1900
Identifying Marks: "For Sale at J. Katzenelenbogen 35 Ludlow Street, New York" in English and Yiddish
Dimensions: 9" x 14"

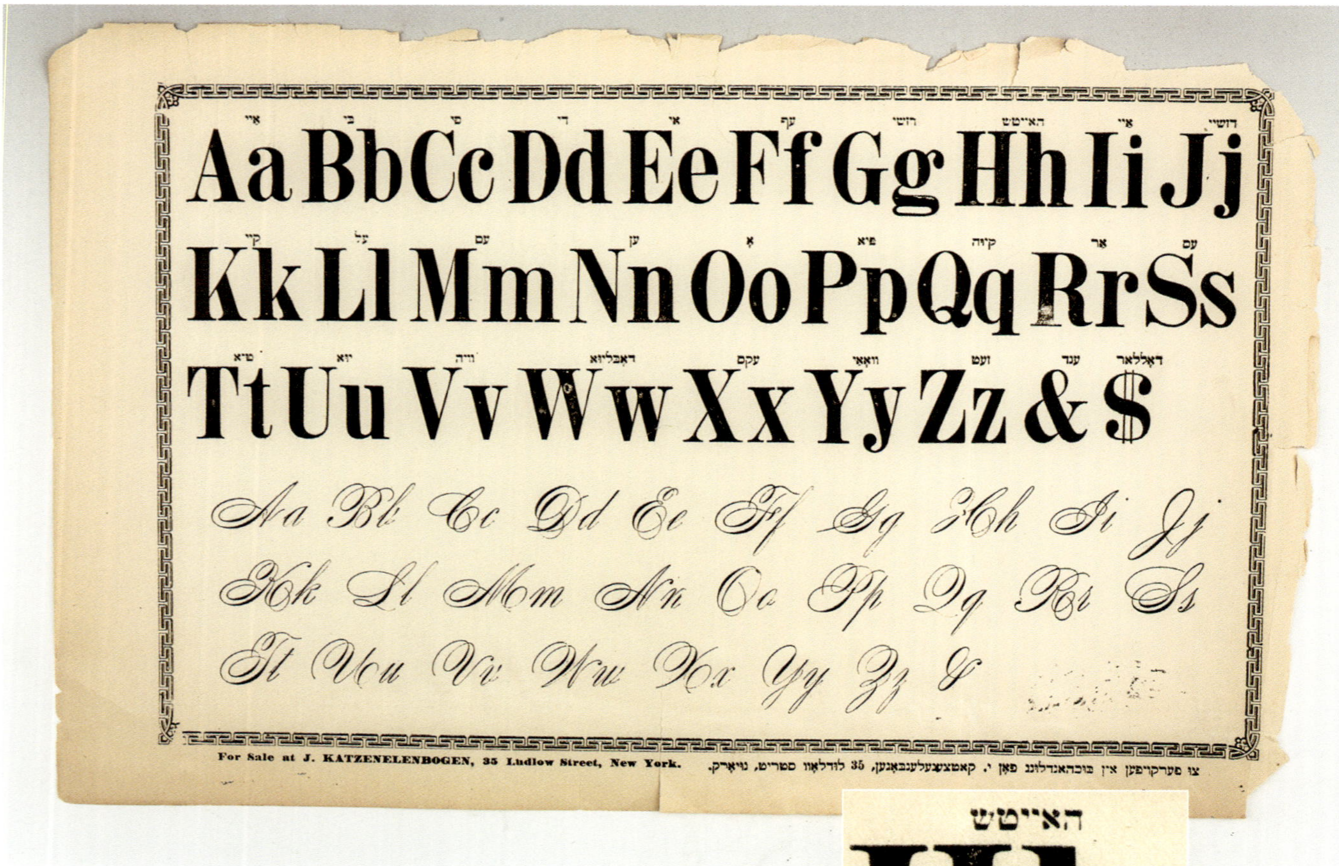

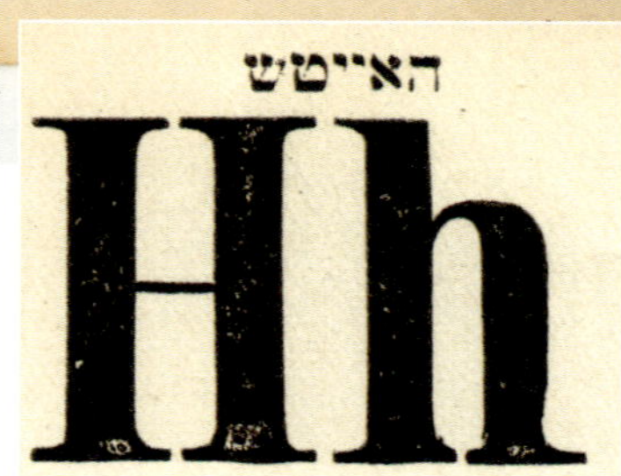

Between 1880 and 1914, two million Jews from Russia immigrated to the United States, the largest Jewish immigrant wave to ever enter this country. These people were eager to leave their homeland so they could escape the oppression they faced there, which included not being able to own property, quotas denying 95% of them entry to universities, restrictions that prohibited them from practicing most professions, and *pogroms*, where thousands of men, women and children were killed by unruly mobs, all simply because they were Jews.

This chart was published on New York's Lower East Side, home to the largest Jewish immigrant population in the United States. It was designed to help recent arrivals learn a completely new alphabet because for the Jews of Russia, most only knew Cyrillic or Hebrew. Here, above each English letter, is the transliteration of that letter in Yiddish, so the pronunciation and recognition of the letter could be taught. For example, above the letter "W" it says in Yiddish "Dublyoo." Included is the transliteration for the dollar sign, indicating that mastering the English language was an indispensable step towards financial success.

This is the first Yiddish/English alphabet chart printed in the United States.

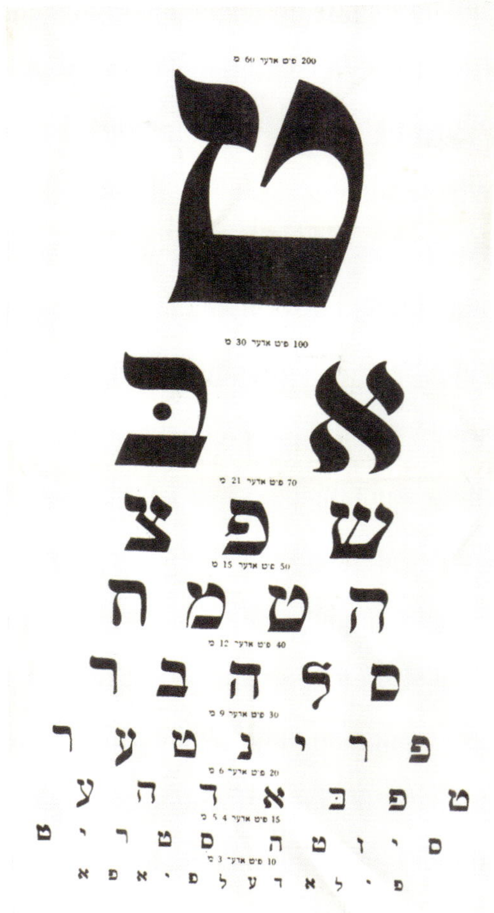

EYE CHART

Material: Linen
Origin: USA circa 1920
Dimensions: 34" x 19"

This eye chart is a promotional item showcasing the printing ability of Sol Haber from Philadelphia. There are nine lines of Hebrew letters in total, of which the final five lines of letters form Yiddish words that read" "Sol Haber / Printer / Type-Bi(n)der / South Street / Philadelphia / PA."

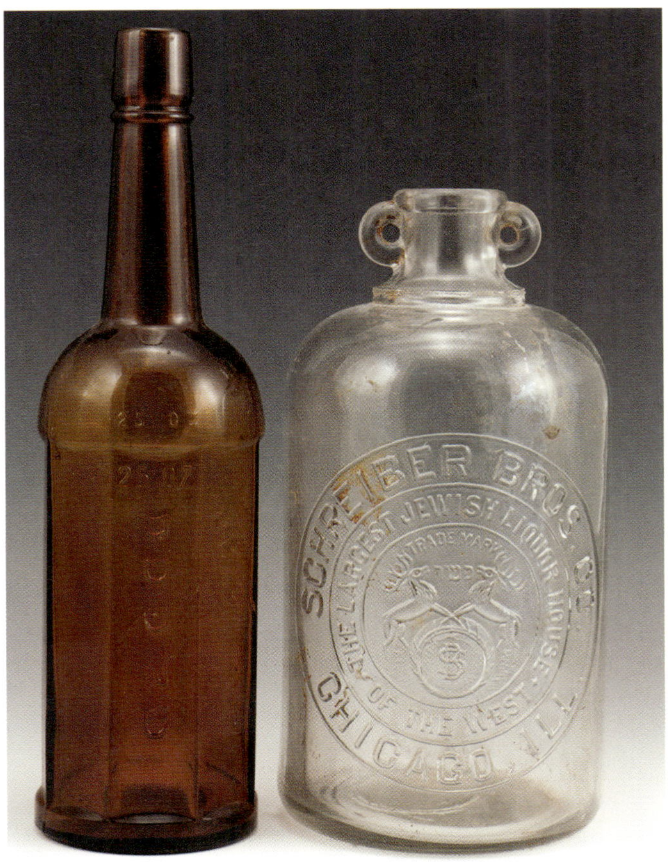

ALCOHOL BOTTLES

Material: Glass
Origin: United States, circa 1895, 1915
Dimensions: 10" - 12" high

The brown bottle has the form of standard American whiskey bottles. What is unusual is the inclusion of "For Passover" in Hebrew letters going down the length of the middle section.

The clear bottle is from Chicago. Notice the amusing slogan, "The Largest Jewish Liquor House of the West". Two stags flank the Hebrew word "Kosher."

SCRAPS

Material: Paper
Origin: United States, 1909
Marks: "Copyright By Heb. Pub. Co. 1909"
Dimensions: 3.9" x 3.4" / 4.1" x 3.25"

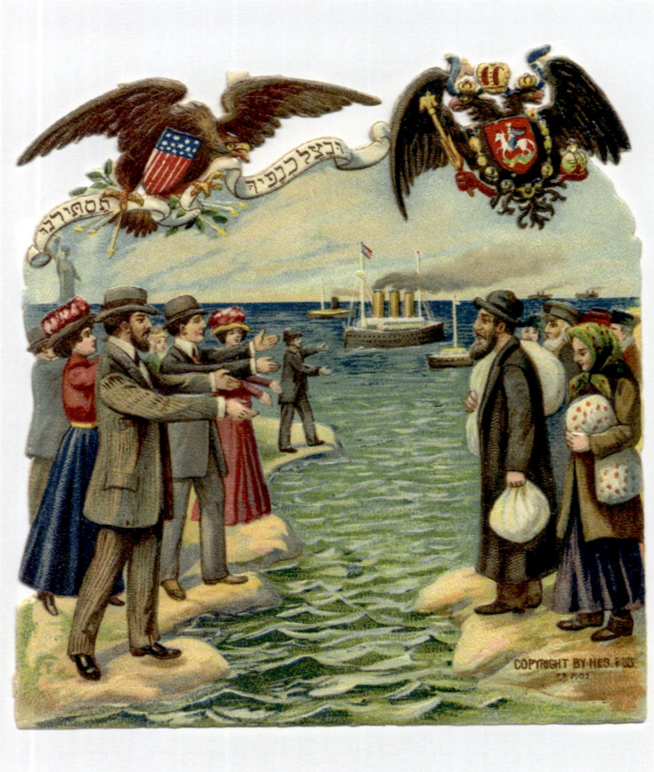

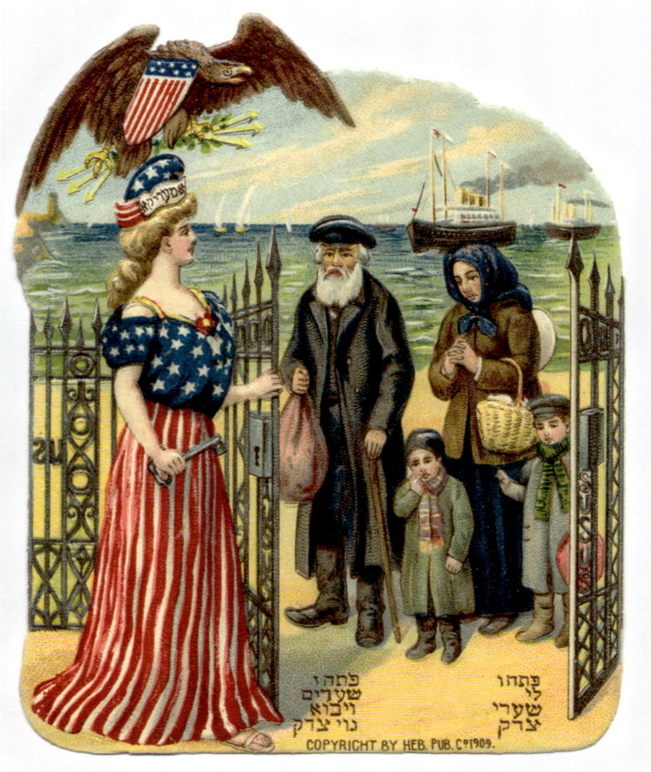

During the nineteenth century a fashionable craze emerged across Europe and the United States: People started collecting postcards of all types and purchasing albums to hold the cards. These collections included "scraps," one-sided chromolithographed pieces of paper that are cut out. Publishers of scraps depicted every topic imaginable, from every corner of the world, including many religious subjects. The term "scrapbook" derives from this practice of assembling scraps into an album.

While the scrap-collecting phase lasted through the 1880s and 1890s, the Hebrew Publishing Company in New York decided to reintroduce scraps to the ever-increasing Jewish population of early twentieth-century America. These scraps, while made for American audiences, were actually produced in Germany, as at that time, Germany had the best equipment in the world for implementing the chromolithograph process on paper.

One scrap shows forlorn Jews underneath the Imperial Russian coat of arms. They are ready to leave their country for a new one that does not target them in humiliating and violent ways. Waiting for them under an American eagle with a banner saying, "Shelter me in the shadow of your wings" (Psalm 17:8) in Hebrew are their Americanized relatives.

The other scrap has a tall, buxom female wearing the American flag. She represents the United States itself, as "America" is emblazoned on her hat in Yiddish. She has unlocked the gates of her country, allowing oppressed Jewish immigrants entry. In Hebrew, it says: "Open for me the gates of righteousness" (Psalm 118:19), and "Open the gates so a righteous nation may enter," (Isaiah 26:2).

CHARITY BOX

Material: Copper
Origin: United States, circa 1920
Dimensions: 6.25" x 7" (including handle)

The concept of *tzedakah* (charity) can be found in this Biblical verse: "For destitute people will not cease to exist within the Land; therefore I command you, saying, 'You shall surely open your hand to your brother, to your poor, and to your destitute in your Land,' " (Deuteronomy 15:11)

This charity container (see page 144) likely hails from one of the dozens of modest-sized synagogues that once made up part of the Lower East Side of New York City. Applied to the bottom half of the can are two Lions of Judah flanking the Hebrew word *tzedakah*. This simply made container speaks of the obligation that charity has in Judaism, even for the humble audience of this charity box, who were mainly immigrants, most of them struggling to survive on a daily basis.

If this type of container suddenly appeared for sale at an antique shop today, I would be hesitant to purchase it. Even though it does exhibit honest signs of wear, it would not be terribly difficult for a skilled artisan to construct a similar piece and attempt to "age it" through various nefarious methods. Fortunately, this object has an excellent provenance, as it was once part of the collection of Daniel M. Friedenberg.

Besides being the curator of coins and medals at The Jewish Museum of New York for 35 years, Mr. Friedenberg had a keen eye for collecting antique Judaica. When he acquired this container decades ago, the collector market for this type of Judaica was nonexistent, therefore there would have been no point to "faking" such a piece at that time. Affixed to the underside of the can are notes and an inventory number in Mr. Friedenberg's hand. Mr. Friedenberg sold off most of his collection between 2002 and 2005 at public auction. As of this writing, Daniel M. Friedenberg is 89 years of age.

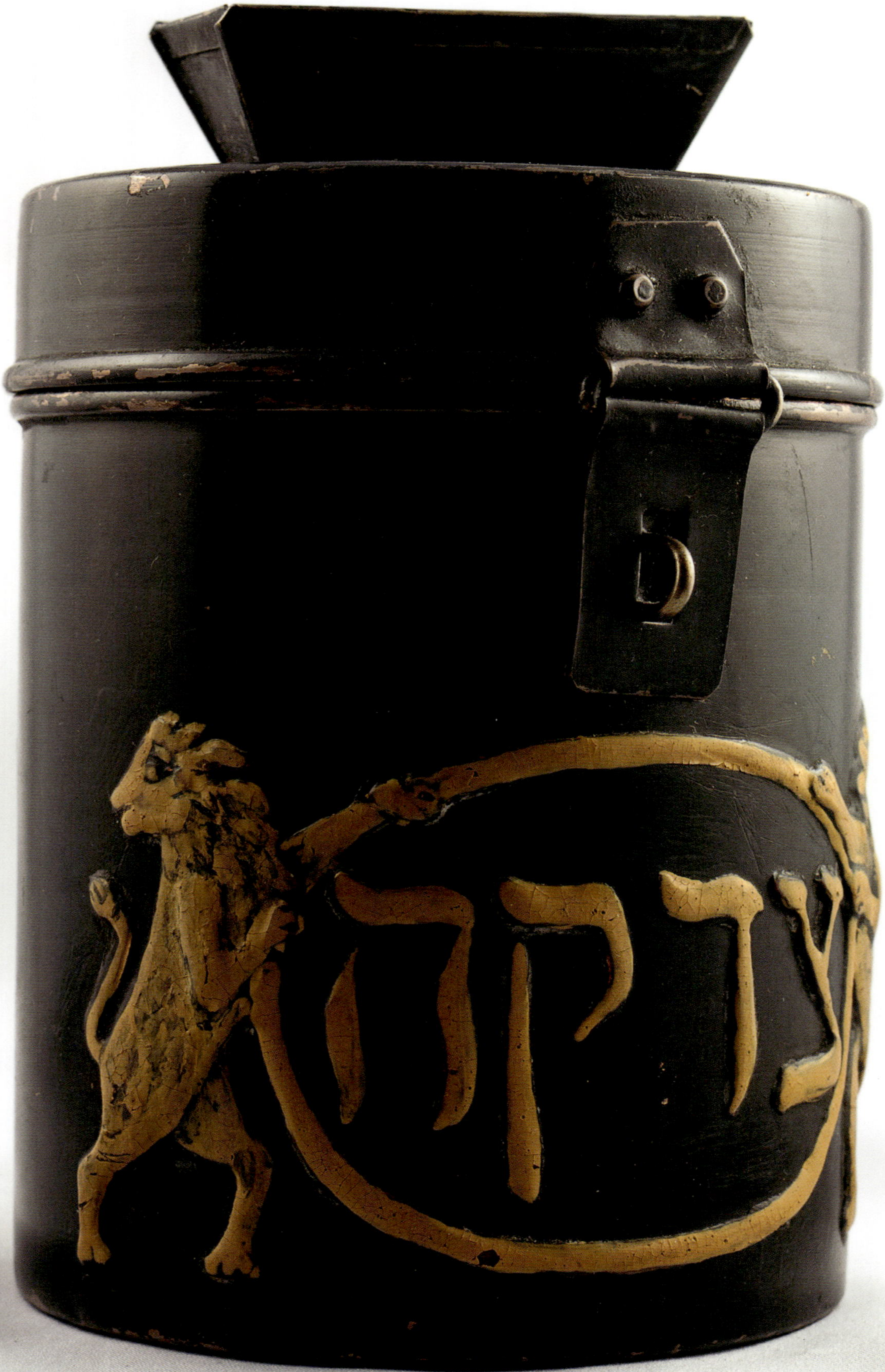
צדקה

FAN

Material: Cardboard
Origin: United States, circa 1918
Dimensions: 8.5" x 9"

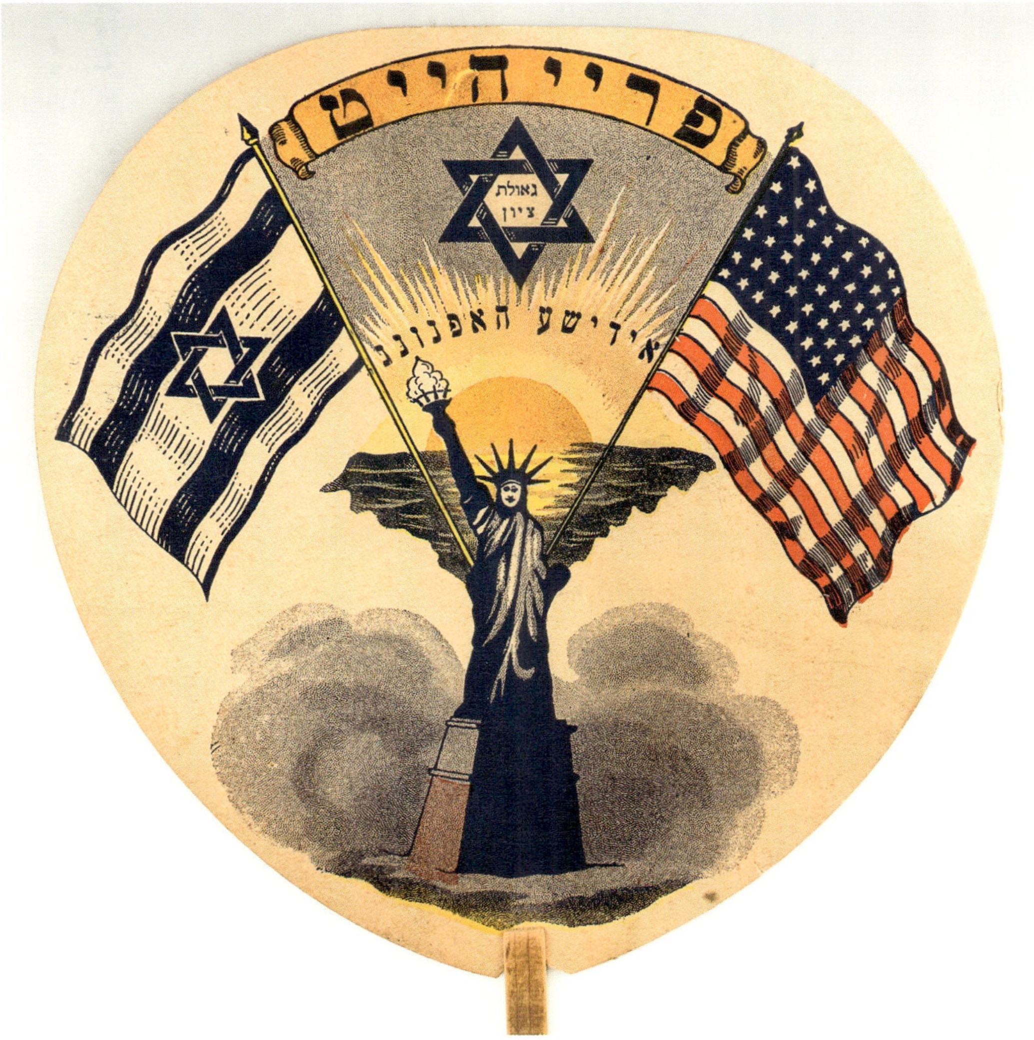

During the era of World War I, the display of patriotism by citizens of the United States reached a fever pitch. Many wanted to show their support in one form or another, displaying American flags of all sizes at every available opportunity.

This paper fan is one in a series that had graphics of the Statue of Liberty and two flags. One of the flags was American, and the other was from another country, usually European. These fans were marketed specifically toward the immigrant population, so they could remember their ethnic roots as well as show love for their new home. The fans were sold in the weeks leading up to July 4 so people could cool themselves during a hot summer day filled with parades and fireworks.

The significance of the fan that was marketed toward Jewish immigrants is that the graphics did not show a flag from the land of their European birth but instead showed a Zionist flag, which calls out for a safe homeland for Jewish people worldwide. This fan shows a proto-Israeli flag, along with the word "Freedom" in Yiddish in a banner across the top. "Redemption of Zion" is written in Hebrew in the center of a Star of David, and "Jewish Hope" is in Yiddish underneath the star.

This fan is made of thin, fragile cardboard and was intended to be discarded after the Fourth of July. I am not aware of another example of this fan, either in a private or public collection.

DISHES

Material: Porcelain
Origin: United States, 1924-5
Hallmarks: "Gimbel Bros. New York Jackson China"
Dimensions: 4.5" x 9.75" / 6.75" x 9.5"

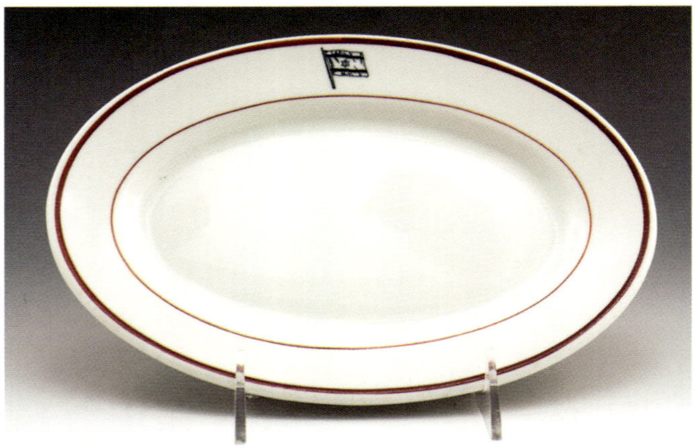

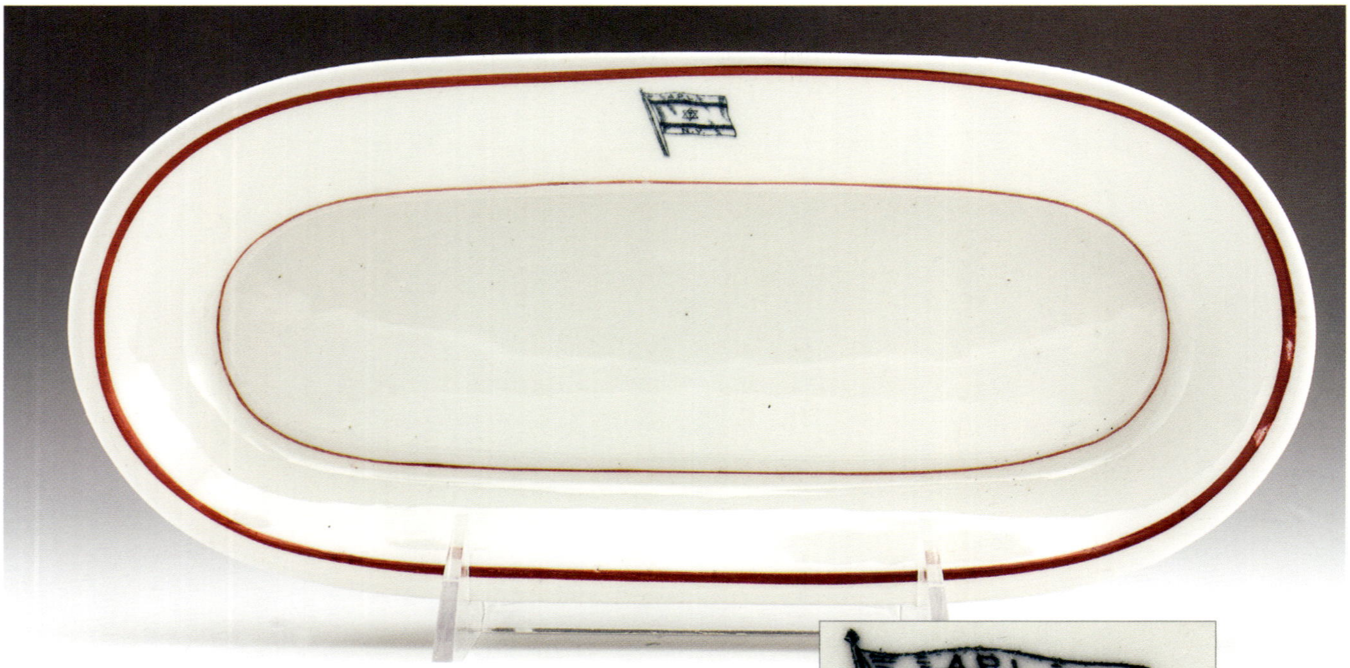

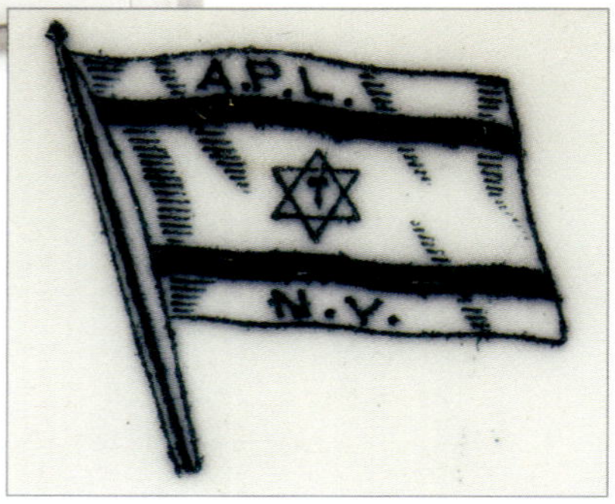

These dishes feature modified proto-Israeli flags on their rims; they include the initials A.P.L. and N.Y., along with the Hebrew letter "*daled*" inside the Star of David. This is the house flag of the American Palestine Line, a shipping line based in New York under Jewish ownership, which was active for about a year, from November of 1924 until late 1925.

These china dishes were part of the dining room service for passengers of the American Palestine Line; the company provided trips to Israel from New York. At the first ship's departure from New York harbor, a crowd of five thousand attended. There was a Zionist-themed ceremony with flags and anthems. Jacob Strahl, the president of the company, said at the ship's launch, "This event marks the advent of the first time in more than 2,000 years of the flag of Judea on the high seas" (this statement is a bit Barnum-esque, as any kind of Zionist flag is a modern creation).

The American Palestine Line had only one ship, which it purchased from the United States government, the steamship *President Arthur*. APL failed after about a year, as apparently there were some financial problems within the company and even reports of some sort of mutiny!

SELTZER BOTTLES

Material: Glass
Origin: United States, 1920s-1930s
Hallmarks: "Made in Austria" or "Made in Czechoslovakia"
Dimensions: 11" x 3.5" (clear) / 12.75" x 4" (colored)

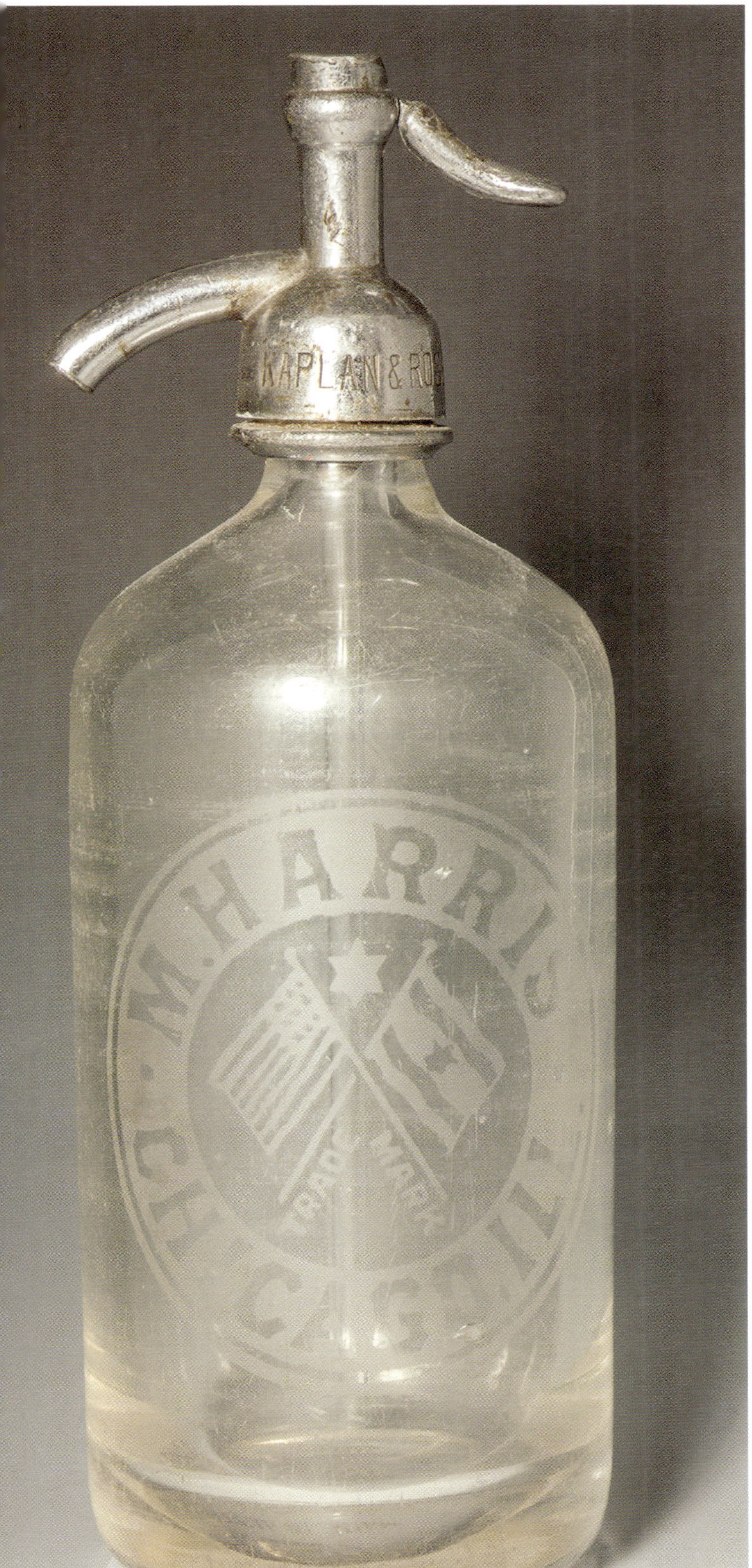

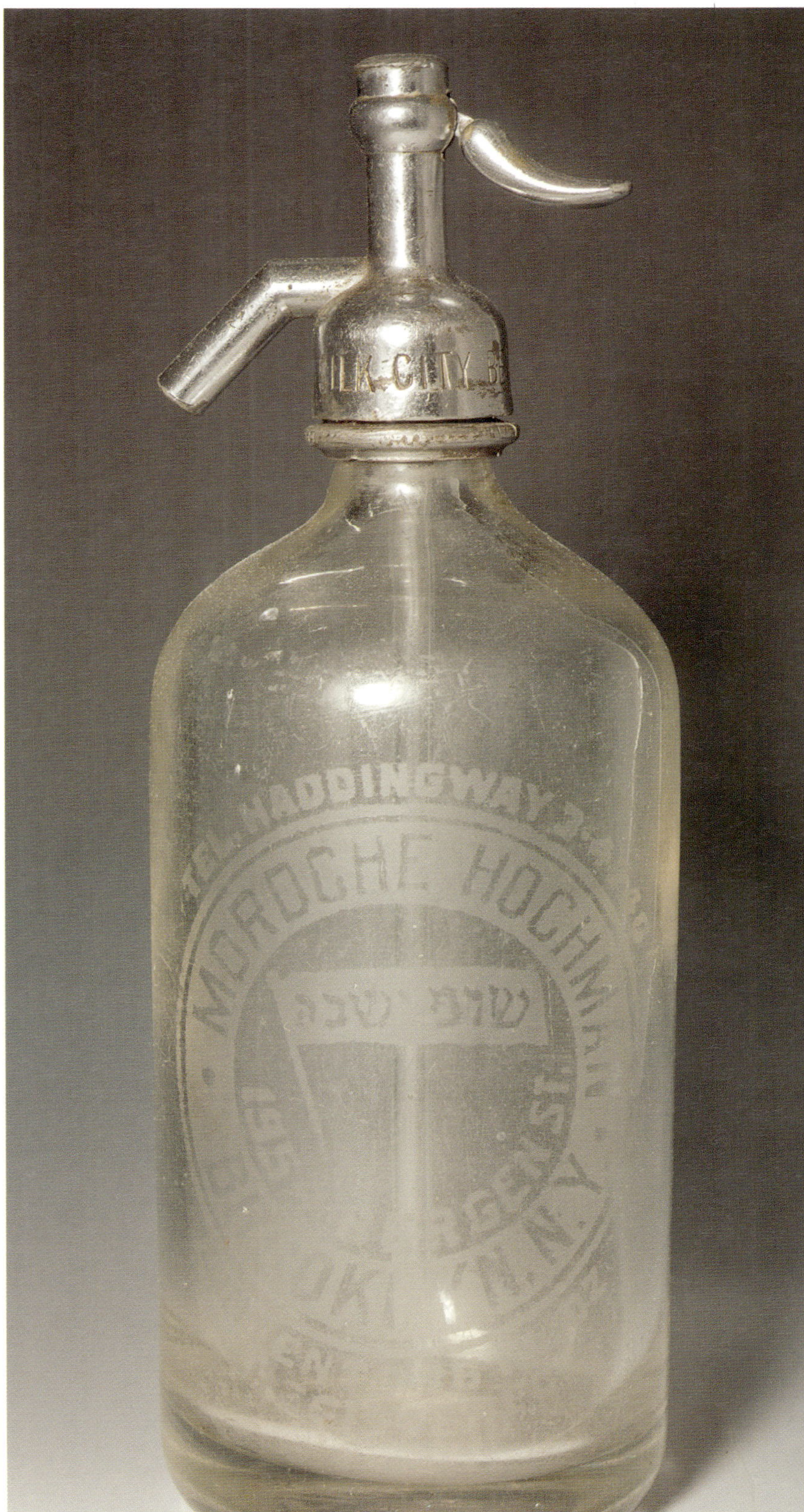

During the early twentieth century in New York, soda water became known as seltzer. What had previously been called a "soda syphon bottle" was now a seltzer bottle. The word seltzer comes from the German words *selterser wasser,* meaning mineral water from Nieder Selters, a village in Germany. Immigrants from Europe used the word seltzer when referring to soda water, and it quickly became part of the American vernacular.

A possible reason for the enormous following seltzer had with Jews is that it went well with the meat-heavy and starch-laden foods typically found in the Ashkenazic Jewish diet of the early twentieth century. Drinking seltzer aided digestion. Even today, the ever-dwindling numbers of elderly Jews who grew up in New York neighborhoods such as the Lower East Side can still remember when seltzer was called *grepsvasser* or *belchvasser* (Yiddish terms meaning "belch water") by their parents and grandparents.

There has always been a connection between seltzer and Jews in America. The vast majority of seltzer delivery men (*shleppers*), were Jewish, however their customers were not exclusively Jews; other clientele included Poles, Italians, and the Irish.

Thick and heavy glass bottles from Austria and Czechoslovakia were imported to hold what was lovingly called "Jewish champagne." Many Jewish vendors of seltzer had their bottles etched with their name and location, and some of them, proud of their heritage, would have a Star of David included in the etching.

Drinking seltzer from seltzer bottles was widespread in 1920s and '30s New York, but because of the rise of sealed bottled carbonated beverages and the destruction in Europe during World War II of many of the plants where the seltzer bottles had been manufactured, there was a sharp decline in the popularity of seltzer during the postwar era.

The clear bottles shown here (see page 147) are scarce examples of Jewish-themed seltzer bottles.

The first bottle depicted is from a "M. Harris" of Chicago, who not only had a Star of David etched on his bottles but also included two crossed flags: one American and one proto-Israeli. The message Mr. Harris sent to his seltzer clientele is clear: He was proud of being a Jew, proud of being a Zionist, and proud of being an American.

The second bottle is from a "Mordche Hochman" of Brooklyn. In the center of the bottle, he displayed not the Star of David but what was most important to him: On a banner is etched: "*Shomer Shabbos*" (Sabbath Observant).

Typically, the Jewish immigrants who became seltzer vendors in America, while proud of their heritage, would be eager to "fit in" as well, perhaps changing their first name from Yitzchak to Isidore, or from Mordechai to Max. In order to scrape together a living, many would also drop a cornerstone of their religious upbringing and work on Saturday as well.

Mr. Hochman was not typical. He not only kept his name "Mordche" (the Yiddish-ized version of "Mordechai"), but through his seltzer bottles he effectively declared: "Order my seltzer instead of my competitors'. I won't make seltzer on Saturday because I don't work on the Sabbath. I therefore earn less money, but isn't our religion more important than money?"

These Jews made a living in the land where "the streets are paved with gold." Their "gold" was seltzer.

Also shown are more commonly found seltzer bottles in colored glass, all with Stars of David.

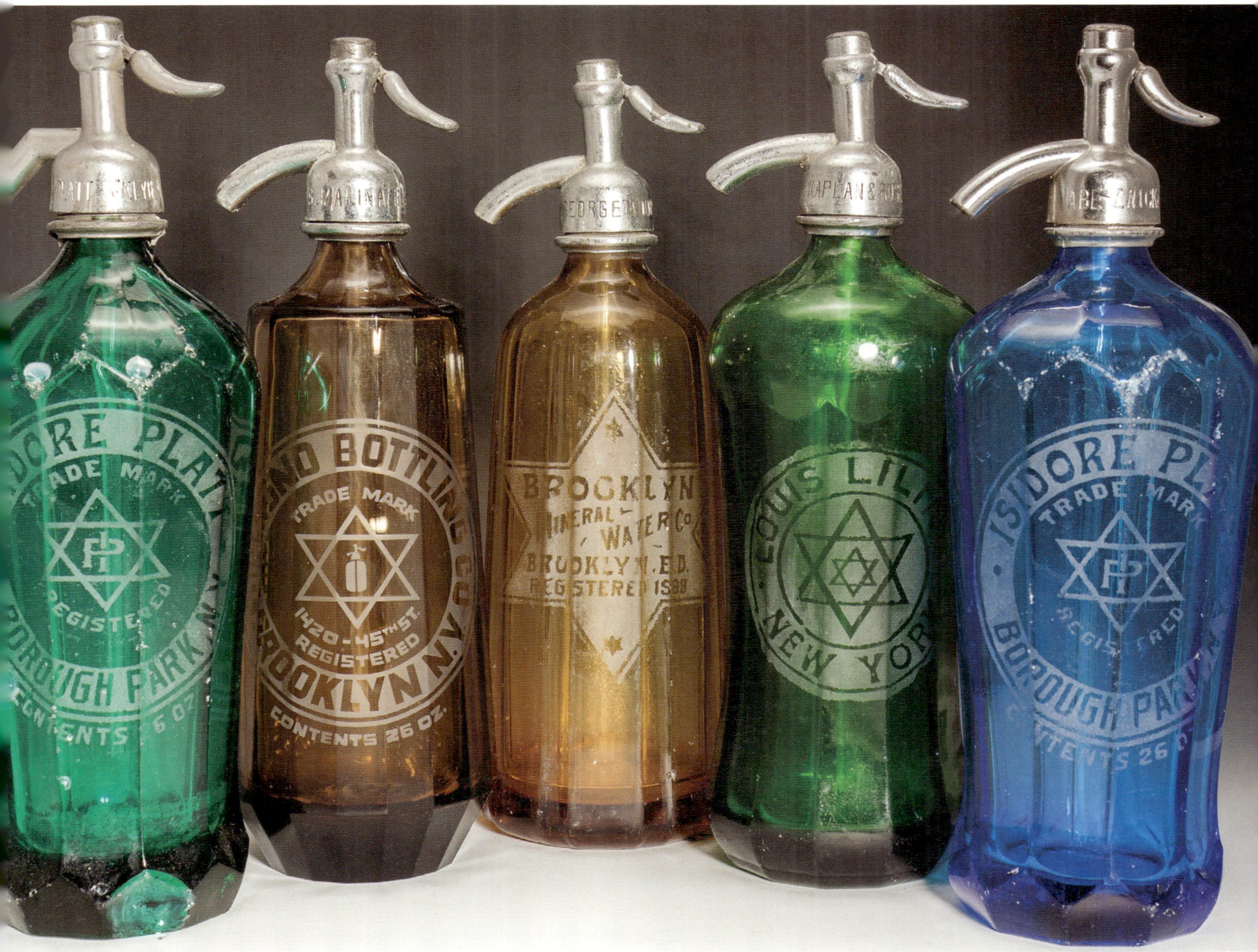
TRADE MARK
REGISTERED
1420-45TH ST.
REGISTERED
CONTENTS 26 OZ.
BROOKLYN
BROOKLYN E.D.
TRADE MARK

WORLD WAR I

Materials: Silver, celluloid, paper, bronze / Tin-plated copper, paper
Origin: Israel, Great Britain, United States / Austro-Hungarian Empire, Germany
Hallmarks: "Bezalel Jerusalem," "Whitehead & Hoag Co." (celluloid pins)

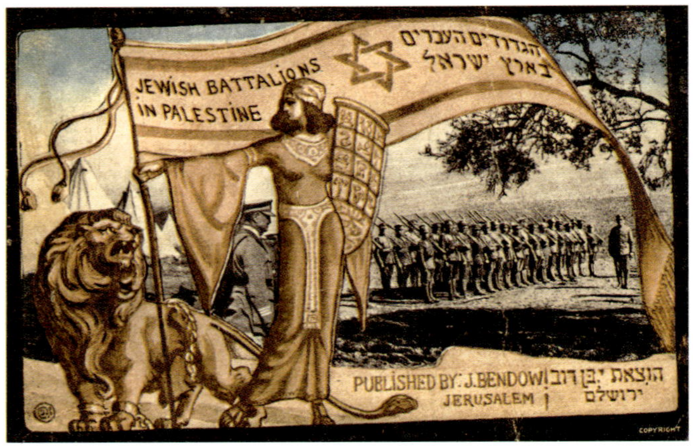

At the outbreak of World War I in 1914, Jews, eager to demonstrate their loyalty to their respective countries, rallied to the war effort. About 500,000 Jews donned Russian uniforms, while on the opposite side, almost 100,000 Jews served in the German Army. By war's end, 12,000 Jews died fighting for Germany. Thousands of Jews enlisted in the armed forces of Great Britain, including more than 1,500 from Egypt and Israel who served in all-Jewish squadrons of the Royal Fusiliers, collectively known as the Jewish Legion. When the United States entered the war in 1917, more than 250,000 Jews enlisted; more than 3,500 were killed, 12,000 wounded, and more than 1,100 decorations for bravery were awarded. Because there were Jews fighting on both sides of this war, in all likelihood there were cases in which Jews killed other Jews during battle.

For the Allied Powers, shown are two veterans badges of the Jewish Legion, with "Jewish Units in the Land of Israel, For Our People, For Our Land" written along with the dates of 1917/1918 and 1918/1919, all in Hebrew.

Next is the cap badge of the Jewish Legion, a menorah with the Hebrew word "forward."

The cover to a booklet of twenty photographic postcards of the Jewish Legion, issued in Israel, shows an illustration by the Bezalel school artist Ze'ev Raban.

Here is a pin to raise funds for Jewish refugees of Europe. It depicts a drowning man being thrown a life buoy, and it says, in Yiddish, "New York Volunteer Women for War Victims."

Here is a stamp of the Jewish Welfare Board, as well as a medal issued by Jewish-American war veterans shortly after the conclusion of WWI.

For the Central Powers, shown is a badge given out to Jewish soldiers in the Austro-Hungarian armed forces, for attending the army-held Yom Kippur service. Next is a charity stamp issued in Berlin to help support children of Jewish soldiers of Germany. Last is the title page to a prayer book for Jewish soldiers in the field issued by the German army.

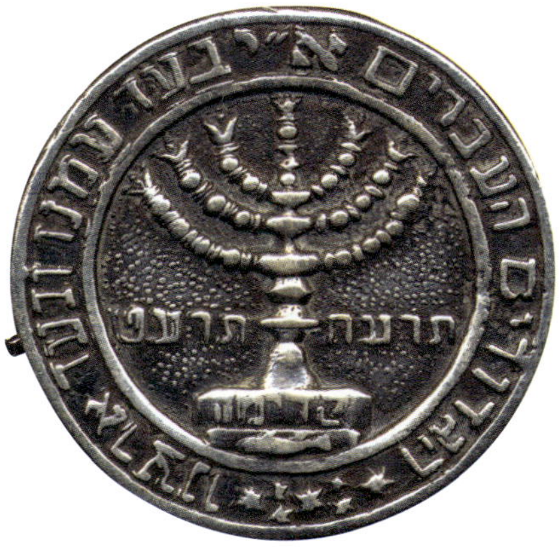

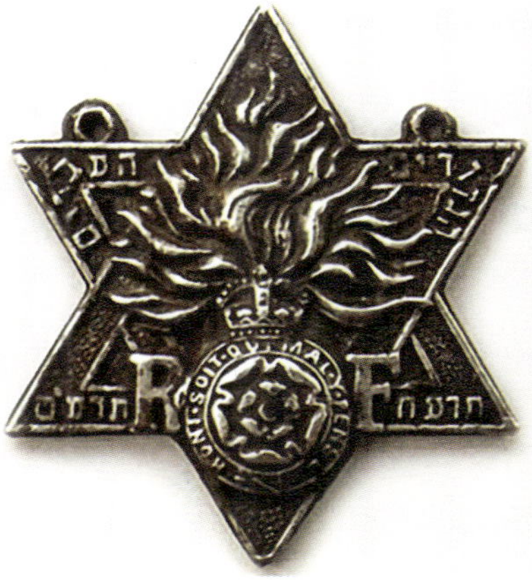

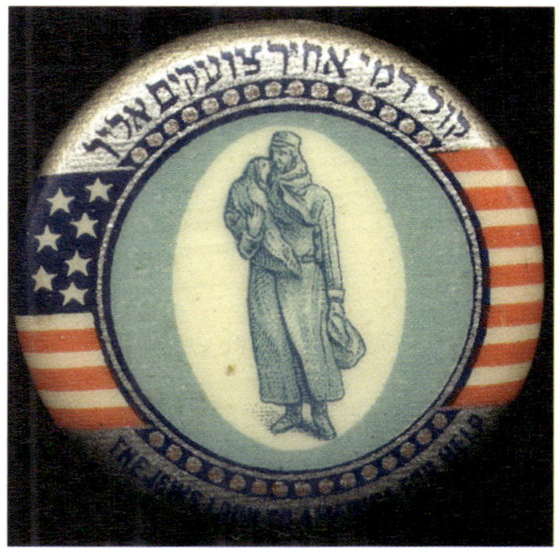

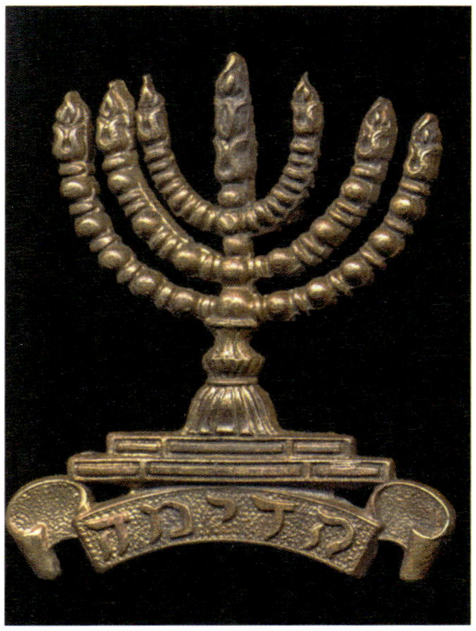

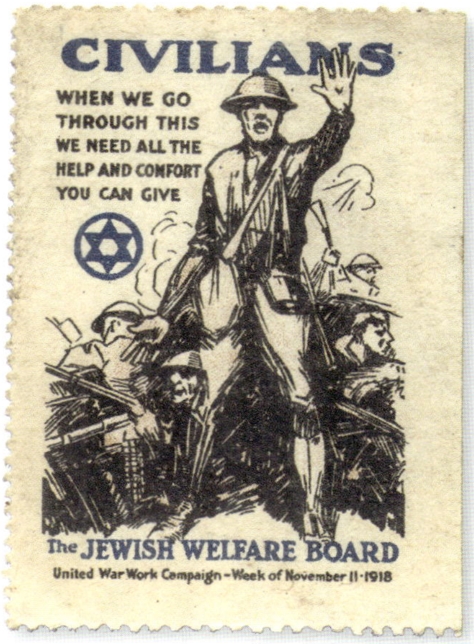
CIVILIANS
WHEN WE GO THROUGH THIS WE NEED ALL THE HELP AND COMFORT YOU CAN GIVE
The JEWISH WELFARE BOARD
United War Work Campaign – Week of November 11-1918

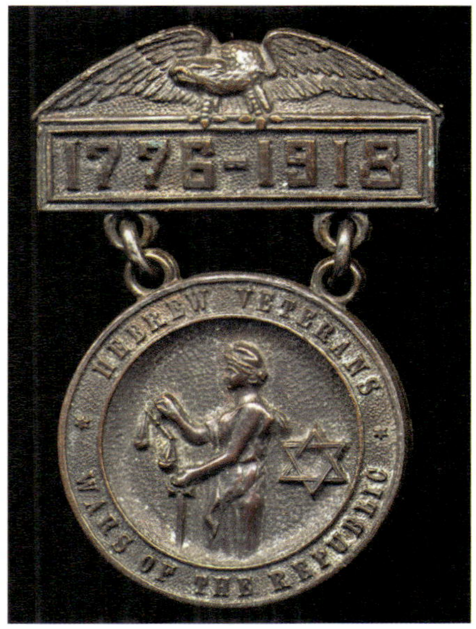
1776-1918
HEBREW VETERANS
WARS OF THE REPUBLIC

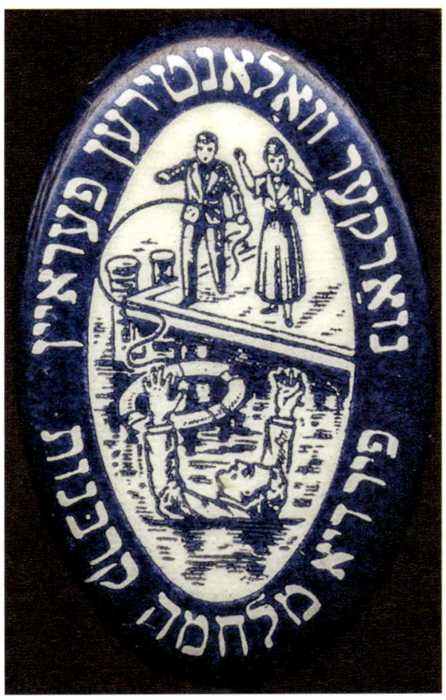

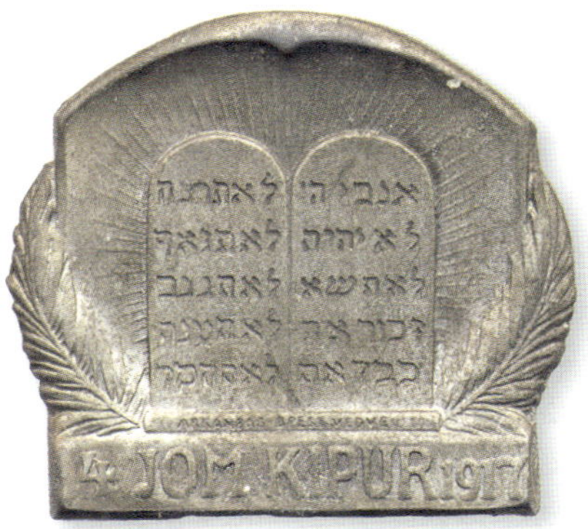
4. JOM KIPUR 1917

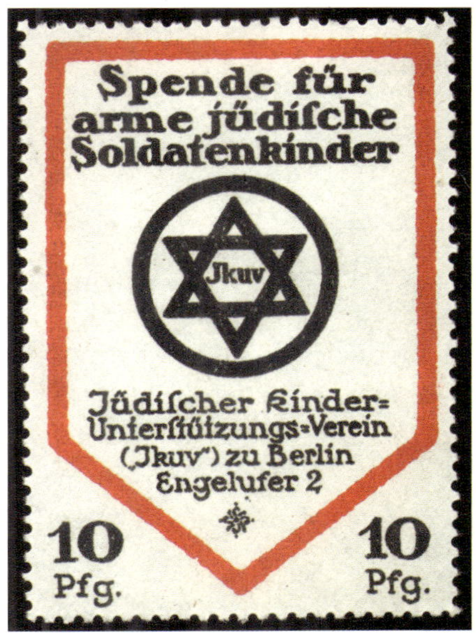
Spende für arme jüdische Soldatenkinder
Jkuv
Jüdischer Kinder-Unterstützungs-Verein („Jkuv") zu Berlin Engelufer 2
10 Pfg.
10 Pfg.

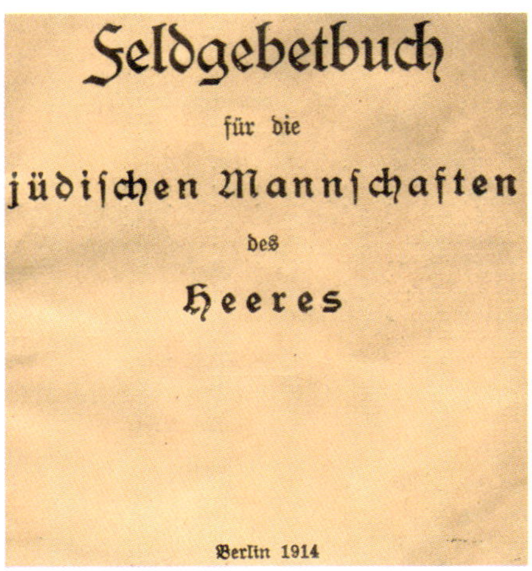
Feldgebetbuch
für die
jüdischen Mannschaften
des
Heeres
Berlin 1914

ATHLETICS

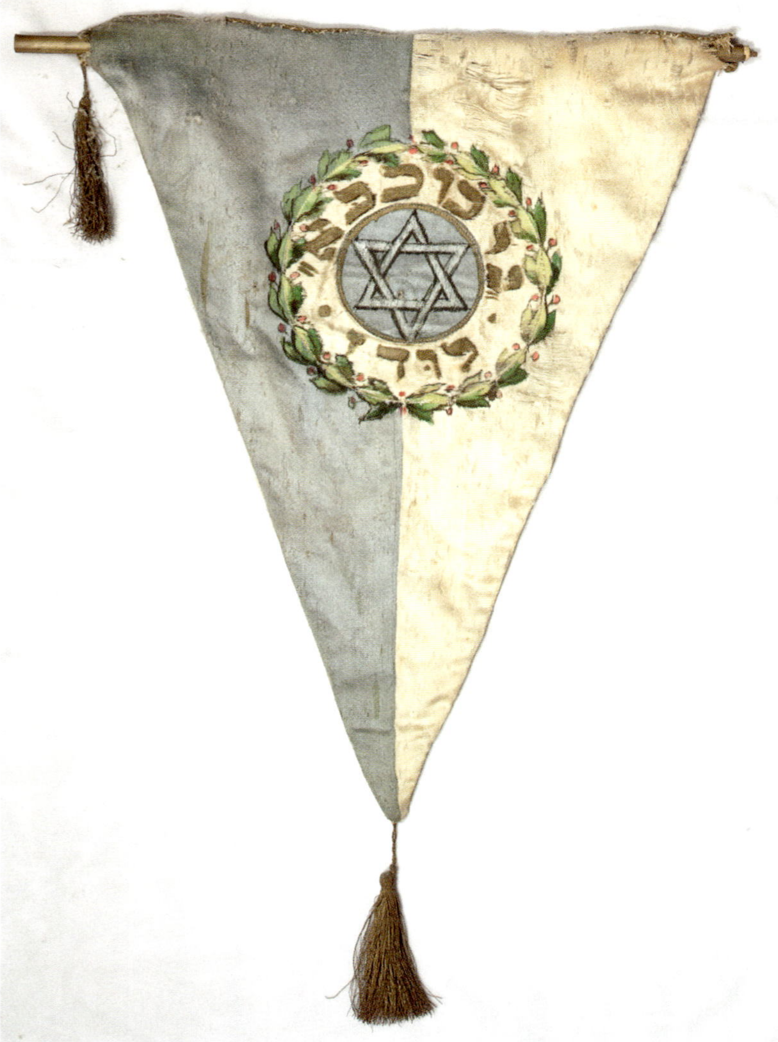

PENNANT AND MEDALS

Material: Painted silk / Gilt bronze / White metal / Bronze, enamel
Origin: Lodz, Poland, circa 1930 / Czechoslovakia, 1936 / Austria, 1922
Dimensions: 17" x 14" / 65.5 mm / 32.75 mm / 1.75" x 3.25"

At the turn of the twentieth century, in large cities across Europe, Jewish sports organizations sprang up, as many young Jews were tired of being denied entry to public sports fraternities because of blatant anti-Semitism. The sports organizations, however, served another purpose, too: to revive Jewish pride. They reached their peak in the years between the first and second world wars. Some clubs were named after ancient Jewish military heroes, like the Maccabees from the holiday of Chanukah, and Bar Kochba, the tough guerrilla fighter who led the last revolt against Roman rule in 132 CE.

Shown here is a gymnasium pennant for the Bar Kochba club, a medal for the Maccabi club for skiing, a medal from the Hakoah (strength) club, and a stunningly designed swimming plaque for the Hagibor (the hero) club.

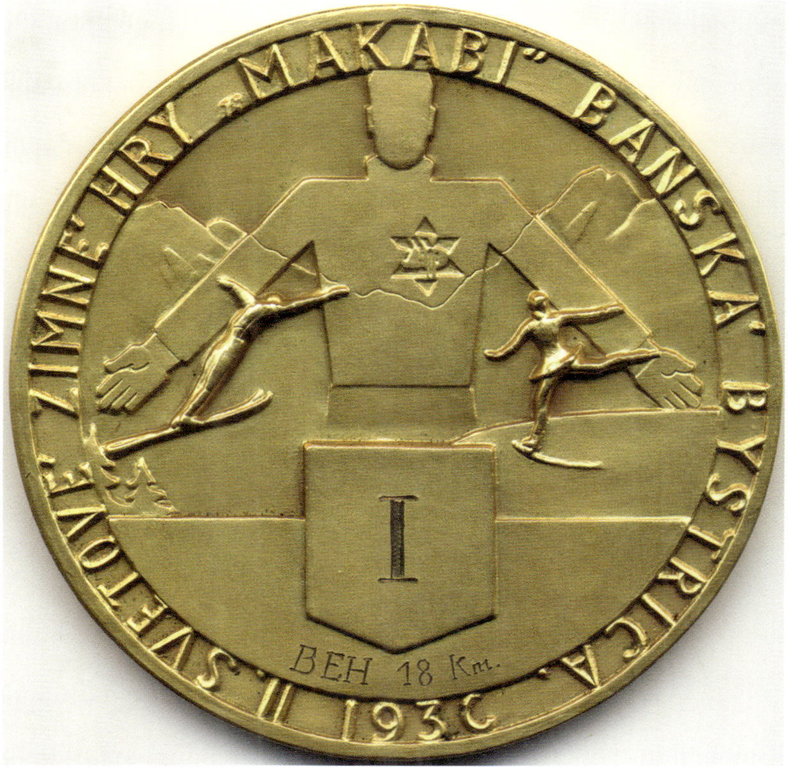
II. SVETOVÉ ZIMNÉ HRY „MAKABI" BANSKÁ BYSTRICA
I
BEH 18 Km.

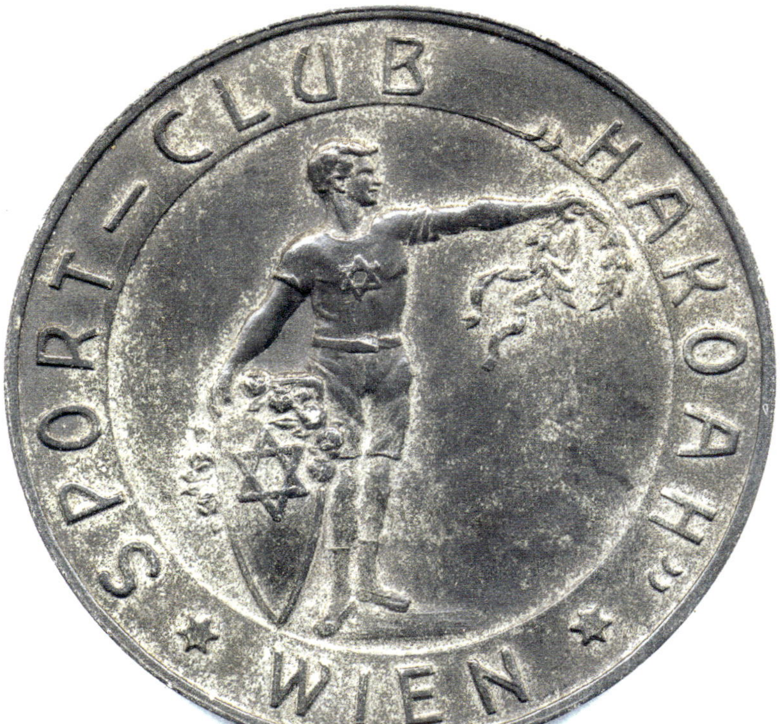
SPORT-CLUB „HAKOAH"
WIEN

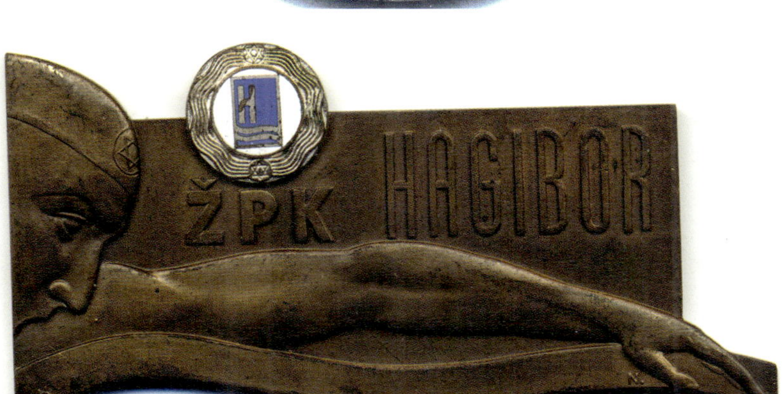
ŽPK
HAGIBOR

WORLD WAR II

CHILDREN'S CARD GAME

Material: Paper
Origin: Charlottenburg, Germany, 1925-1935
Dimensions: 4" x 3"
Artist: Adele Sandler
Total Pieces: 48 cards, checklist, instructions, box

The definition of modern Zionism, which was established in the late nineteenth century, is to have a continuous settlement of Jews in the land of Israel, in conjunction with the support of philanthropic and political efforts. The 1880s marked the first period in which Jews en masse began leaving the countries of their birth to settle in the land of Israel, beginning with Russia, where Odessa became a center in that region for the Zionist movement.

With the appointment of Adolf Hitler as chancellor of Germany in 1933, an ominous tone was set for the comfortable lifestyle most of the Jews in Germany enjoyed. Many refused to believe that anything of serious consequence would befall them, but others realized that danger lurked around the corner, and they left their "Fatherland."

This card game for children was issued in Germany parallel to the rise of Hitler to power. The theme revolves around the land of Israel, and while it is essentially a game, it is also an educational tool, teaching young people all about this patch of land in the Middle East: the names of its cities and towns, rivers and mountains, agriculture, inhabitants, and historical sites. This is a Zionist game intended to familiarize Jewish children with their Biblical birthright, and it also perhaps carried a subliminal message for the parents who procured this game for their young: "GET OUT OF GERMANY BEFORE IT'S TOO LATE."

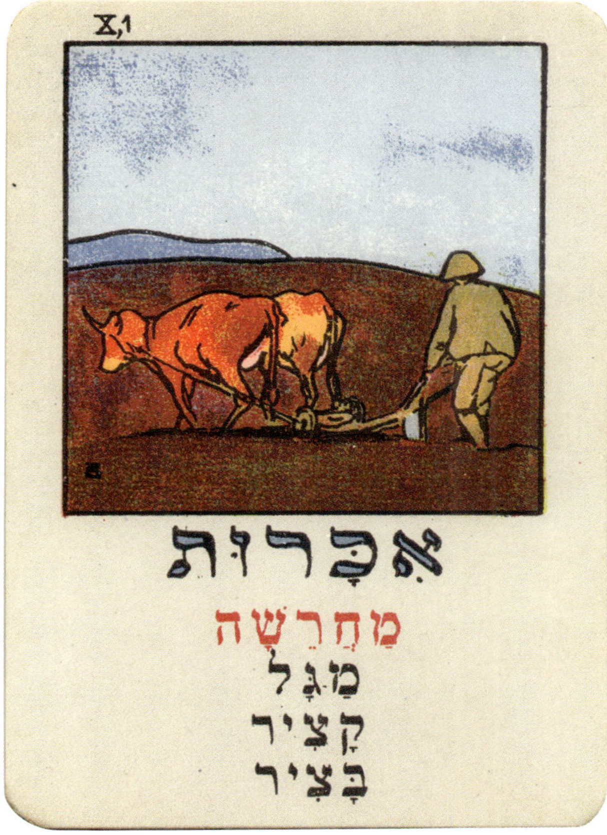
X,1
אכרות
מחרשה
מגל
קציר
בציר

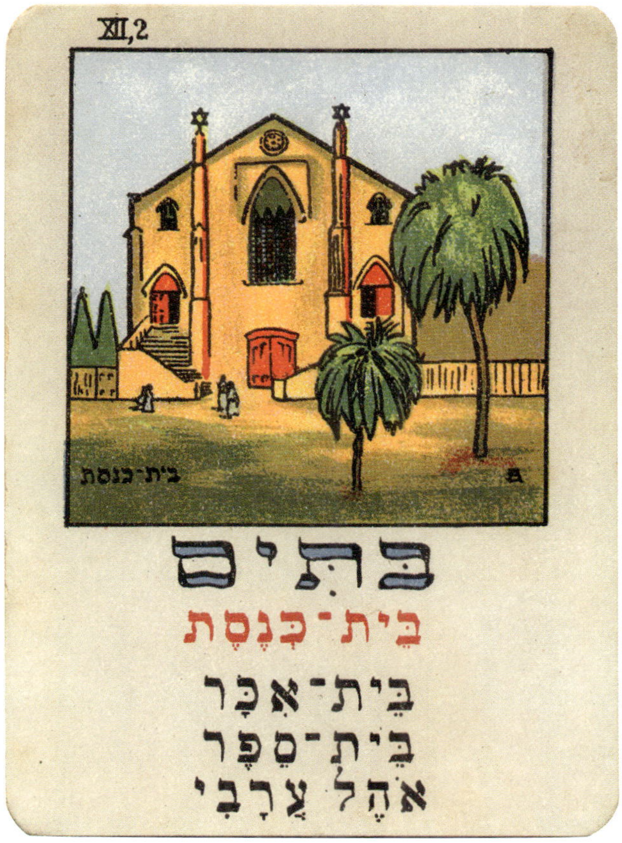
XII,2
בית-כנסת
בתים
בית-כנסת
בית-אכר
בית-ספר
אהל ערבי

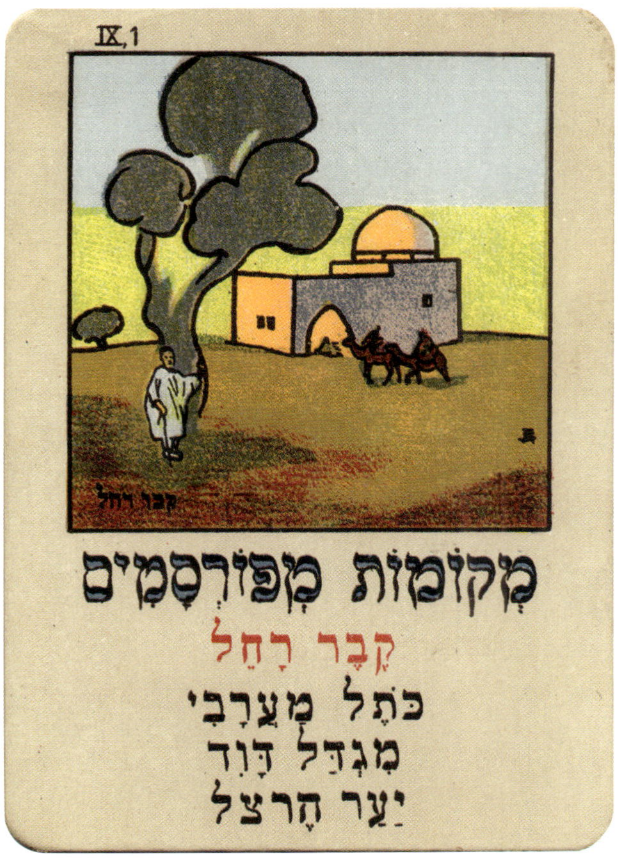
IX,1
קבר רחל
מקומות מפורסמים
קבר רחל
כתל מערבי
מגדל דוד
יער הרצל

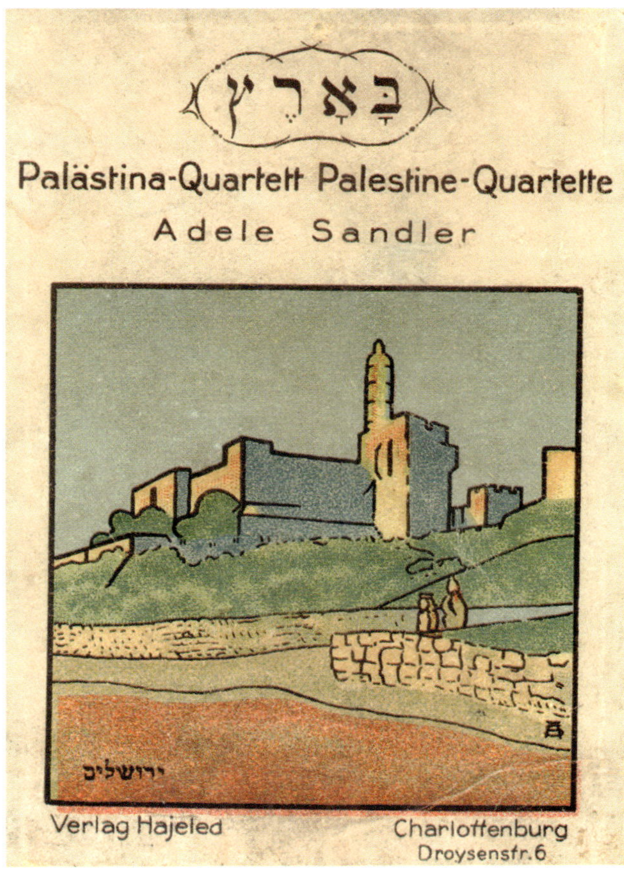
בארץ
Palästina-Quartett Palestine-Quartette
Adele Sandler
ירושלים
Verlag Hajeled
Charlottenburg
Droysenstr. 6

SYNAGOGUE TABLETS

Material: Lead
Origin: Szekelykeresztur, Hungary (Romania), nineteenth century
Dimensions: 30" x 13" (each tablet)

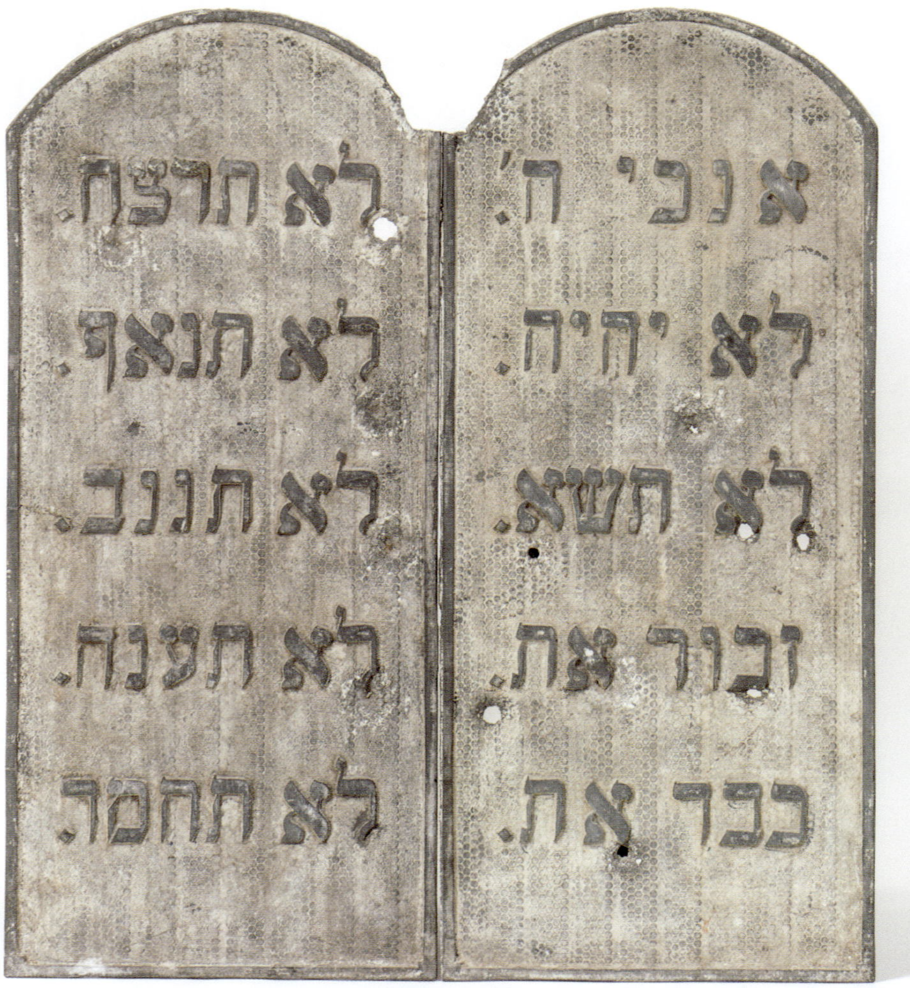

In 1941, Hungary officially became part of the Axis powers when it joined Germany in declaring war on the Soviet Union. During the German occupation of Hungary in the spring of 1944, Hungarian police and the militantly anti-Semitic, pro-Nazi Hungarian Arrow Cross Party deported nearly 440,000 Jews, mostly to Auschwitz. During this era, the Arrow Cross Party ran wild with power, killing many Jews who had not been deported through other means, including daily mass executions—often in the street in broad daylight, in front of the eyes of ordinary bystanders.

These tablets, representing the Ten Commandments G-d gave to Moses at Mount Sinai, were once part of the architectural facade of a synagogue in the town of Szekelykeresztur, which during the war was part of Hungary. On occasion, Arrow Cross Party members used the structure of the synagogue for target practice. Hence the bullet holes.

LODZ GHETTO ARTIFACT

Material: Nickel
Origin: Poland, 1943
Dimensions: 1.75" x 1.25"

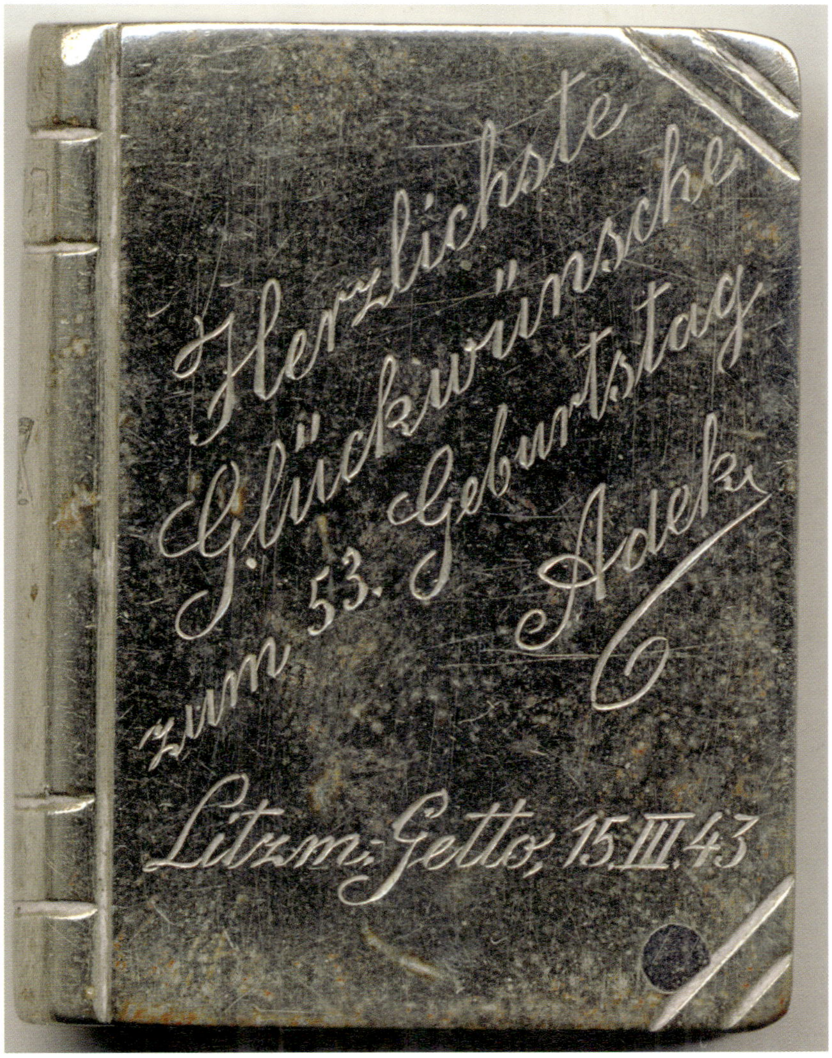

When German forces occupied Lodz in September 1939, the city had a population of 672,000. More than one-third of the people (233,000) were Jews. Lodz was immediately annexed as part of the "Reich" and renamed "Litzmannstadt" to honor General Karl Litzmann, who had led German forces in the area in 1914. On February 8, 1940, Jewish residence was limited to specific streets in the Old City of Lodz and the adjacent Baluty Quarter, areas that would formally become the ghetto on May 1, 1940.

The Lodz ghetto was transformed into an enormous industrial complex, where by 1943, in harsh working conditions, 95% of the adult population manufactured garments, metalwork, and electrical equipment for the German military. It was because of this productivity that the Lodz ghetto managed to survive long after all the other ghettos in occupied Poland were liquidated. Since Germany needed this cheap source of labor, food was distributed by German authorities to keep 117 workshops functioning. Still, about 43,500 people died in the ghetto of disease and starvation.

This cigarette lighter is a rare relic of the Lodz ghetto, giving us a glimpse into the personal life of one of its inhabitants. The lighter is inscribed in German: "Most cordial congratulations on your fifty-third birthday" and signed "Adek," "Litzm. Getto

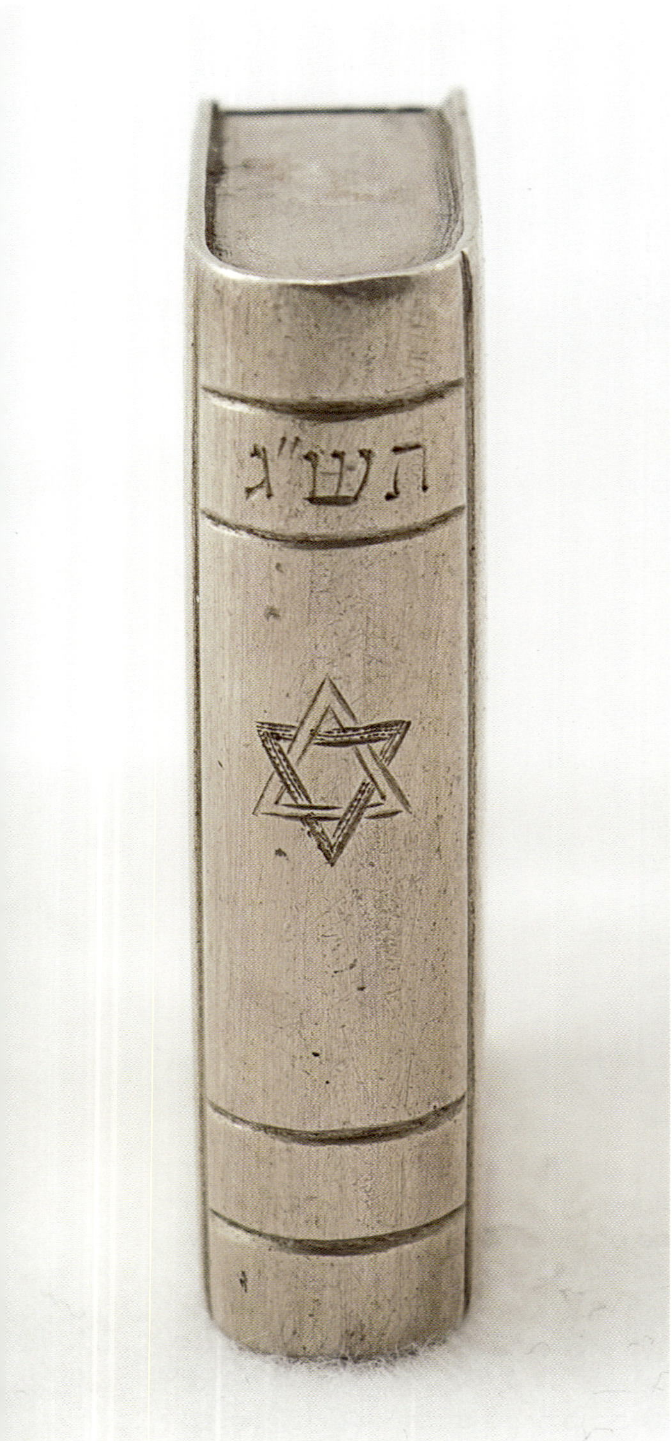

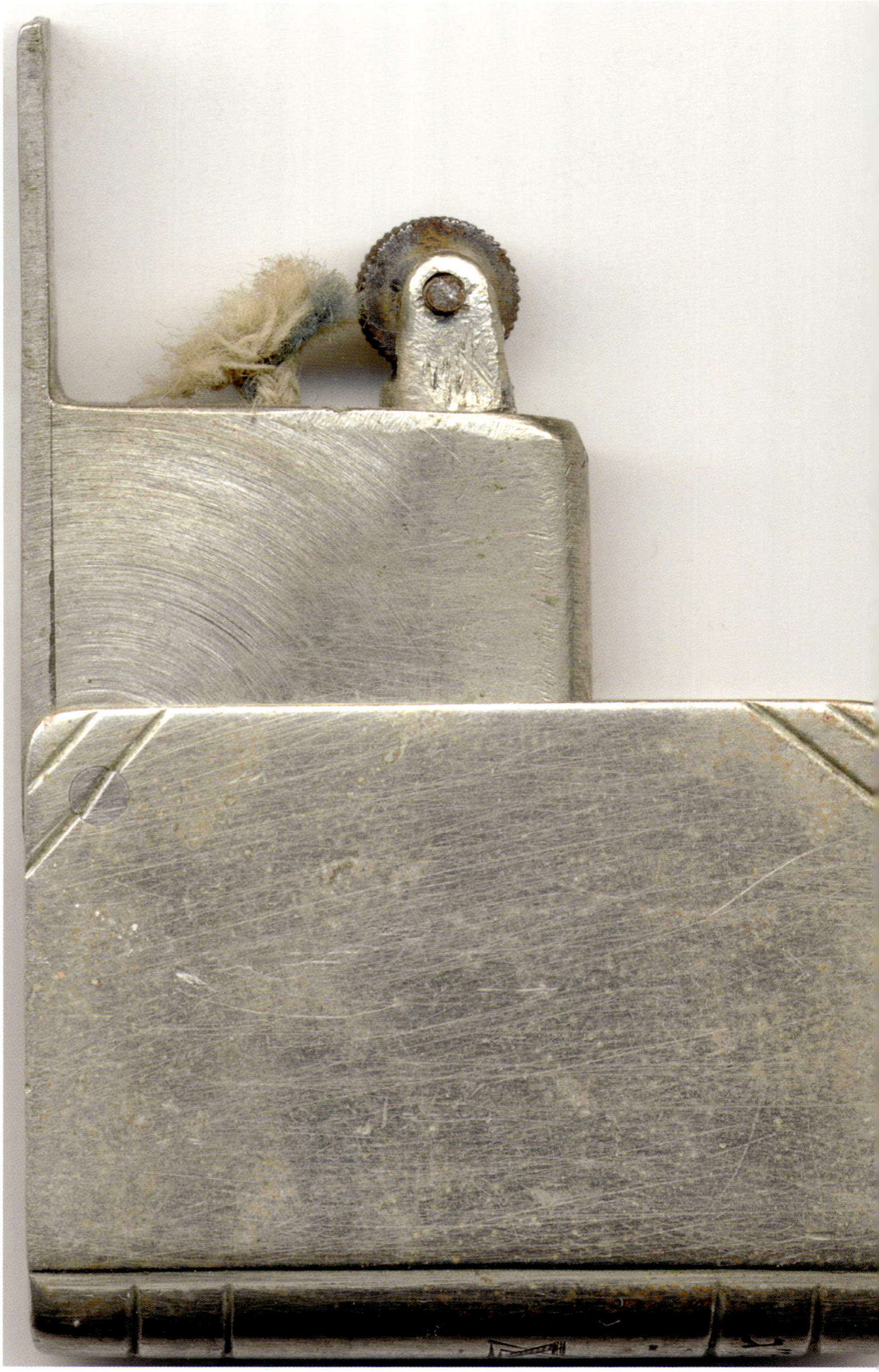

15.III.43." The edge of the lighter is engraved with the Hebrew year 1943 and a Star of David.

Who was this Adek? What is the identity of the friend or relative he gave this to? We'll probably never know, as Adek and/or the receiver of the gift likely perished at a death camp during one of the numerous deportations the ghetto underwent between 1941 and 1944. Only 10,000 of the 204,000 Jews who passed through the Lodz ghetto survived the war.

POSTER

Material: Paper
Origin: United States, 1943
Identifying Marks: "U.S. Government Printing Office 1943"
Dimensions: 28" x 22"

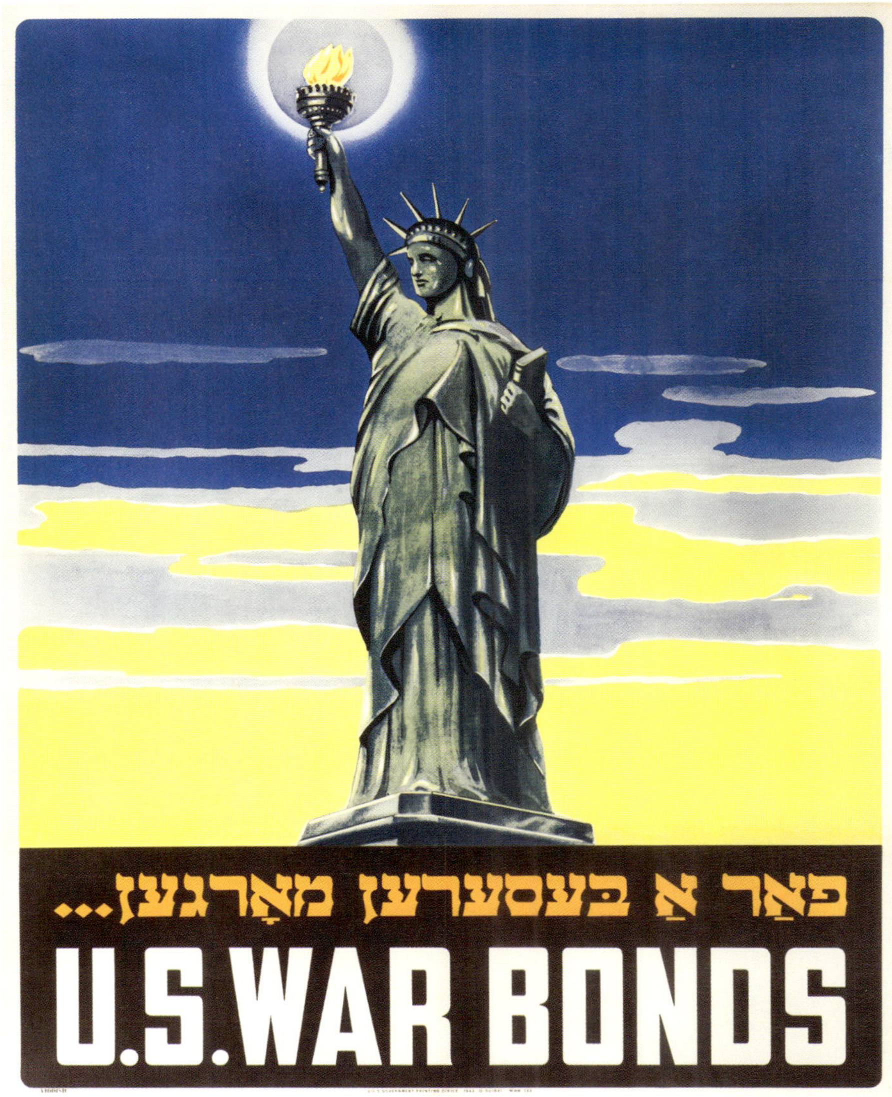

By 1943, the tide of war began to turn against the Axis powers. In the Pacific, the United States had a decisive victory against the Japanese fleet in June of 1942 in the Battle of Midway. In Europe, Hitler's armies, formerly unstoppable in their conquest of territory, were beaten back by Soviet soldiers in the bloodiest conflict in the history of warfare (combined casualties estimated near two million) during the Battle of Stalingrad, which took place between July 1942 and February 1943. Americans were becoming optimistic in their hopes of an Axis defeat.

Coupled with these morale-boosting victories, however, came increasingly frequent reports of atrocities occurring against Jews in countries under Nazi rule. In October of 1941, *The New York Times* reported on the massacres of thousands of Jews in Galicia. In November of 1942, the first reports of Jews being methodically murdered at Auschwitz reached the free world. On December 19, 1942, The United Nations Information Office in New York released a report authenticating the accounts of the Holocaust.

This poster, issued by the American government in 1943 to be plastered across Jewish neighborhoods, drives a simple point home, urging Jews to buy war bonds with the Yiddish phrase "For A Better Tomorrow," along with a powerful, if not altogether moving, image of the Statue of Liberty, its yellow torch high in the sky.

Although this poster was issued in other languages such as Spanish, Polish, and Hungarian, to be placed in areas that housed large concentrations of those respective ethnic groups, there is little doubt that when a member of the American-Jewish community viewed this poster, its message was unique to him or her in that it was of the utmost urgency. Buying war bonds that would lead to victory would end the bloodshed not only of American soldiers (including 550,000 Jews serving in the American armed forces) but also of their Jewish brethren being systematically exterminated in Europe. "For A Better Tomorrow," indeed.

UNIFORM SLEEVE PATCHES

Materials: Cotton, wool
Origin: Israel, 1944–1946
Dimensions: 1" x 4.25"/ 1"x 4"/ 3.25" x 2.25" / 2.25" x 2.25"

With the onset of another world war becoming apparent in the late 1930s, Jews residing in Israel in 1938 petitioned for an all-Jewish military unit to be established in the British Army, as had been done before, in World War I. Neville Chamberlain, prime minister of Great Britain from 1937 to 1940, disapproved of an all-Jewish brigade, fearing it would give legitimacy to the idea of national independence for the Jews of Israel. Chamberlain's successor, Winston Churchill, was much more receptive to the idea of a Jewish unit, but it took years of negotiations until the British government finally agreed to the establishment of a Jewish Brigade in September of 1944.

The Jewish Brigade Group was comprised of approximately 5,000 Jewish soldiers from Israel and took part in the final battles of the war on the Italian front against the German army. After the war, members of the Jewish Brigade secretly formed assassination squads in order to execute former SS and Wehrmacht officers who had participated in atrocities against the Jews of Europe. The soldiers of the Jewish Brigade also encountered survivors of the Holocaust in Displaced Persons Camps; the Brigade was instrumental in bringing many of these survivors out of Europe en route to Israel, although most were caught at the entry of Israel and temporarily held in detention camps in Cyprus by the British, as the British government sealed the borders to Israel, barring immigration.

In total, 30,000 Jewish volunteers from Israel served in the British Army during World War II, including the 5,000 of the Jewish Brigade, which the British government disbanded in 1946. The wartime combat experience accumulated by the men of this group proved invaluable just two years later, as many of these soldiers became commanders in Israel's War of Independence.

As with all areas of antiques and collectibles where demand far outweighs supply, one should be aware that the current market is flooded with reproductions of these patches, with fakes being sold as originals.

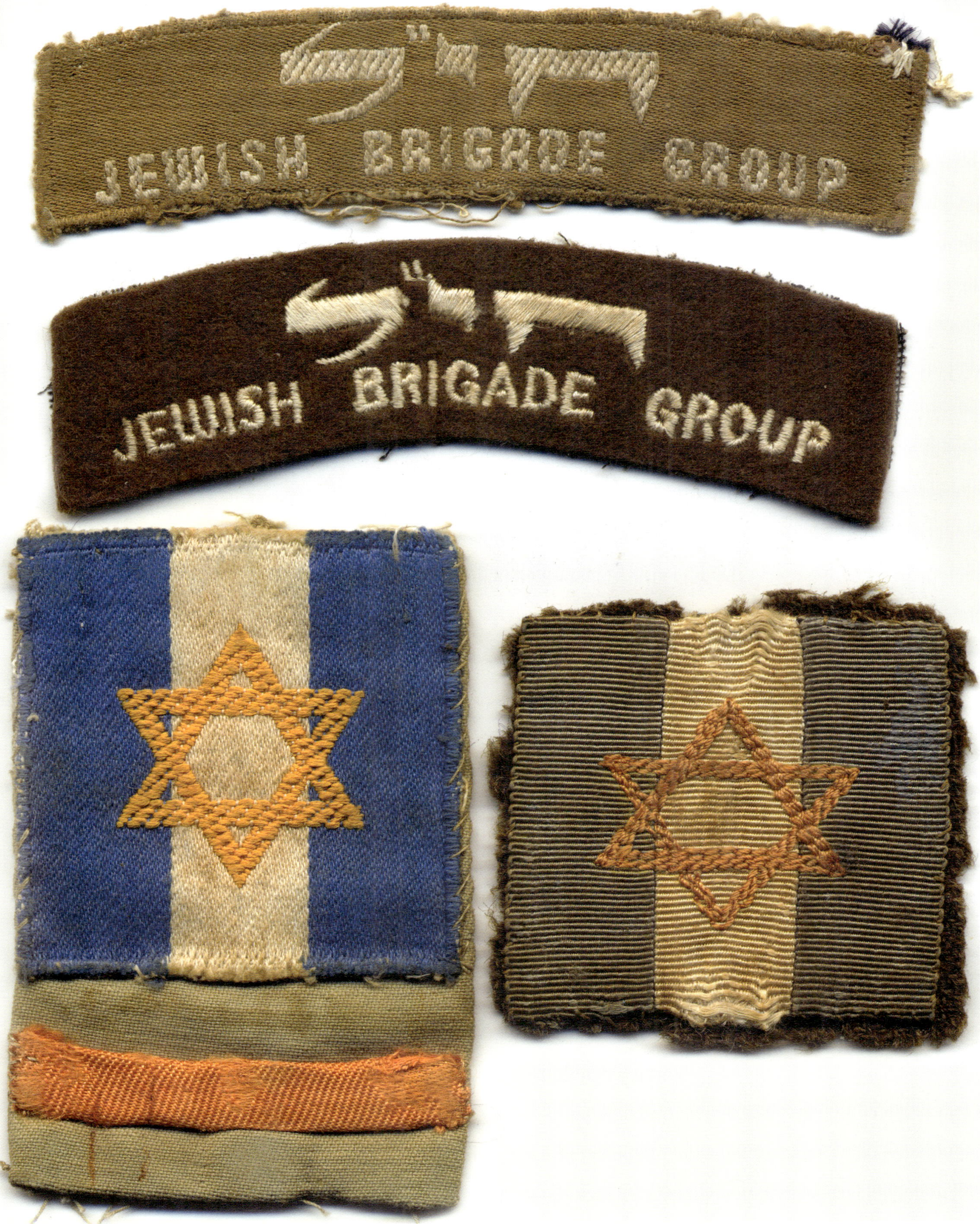
חי"ל
JEWISH BRIGADE GROUP
חי"ל
JEWISH BRIGADE GROUP

WEDDING CANOPY

Material: Cotton
Origin: Germany, 1946-1948
Identifying Marks: "Joint" and "Made in the Land of Israel" in Hebrew, "A.J.D.C"
Dimensions: 57" x 56"

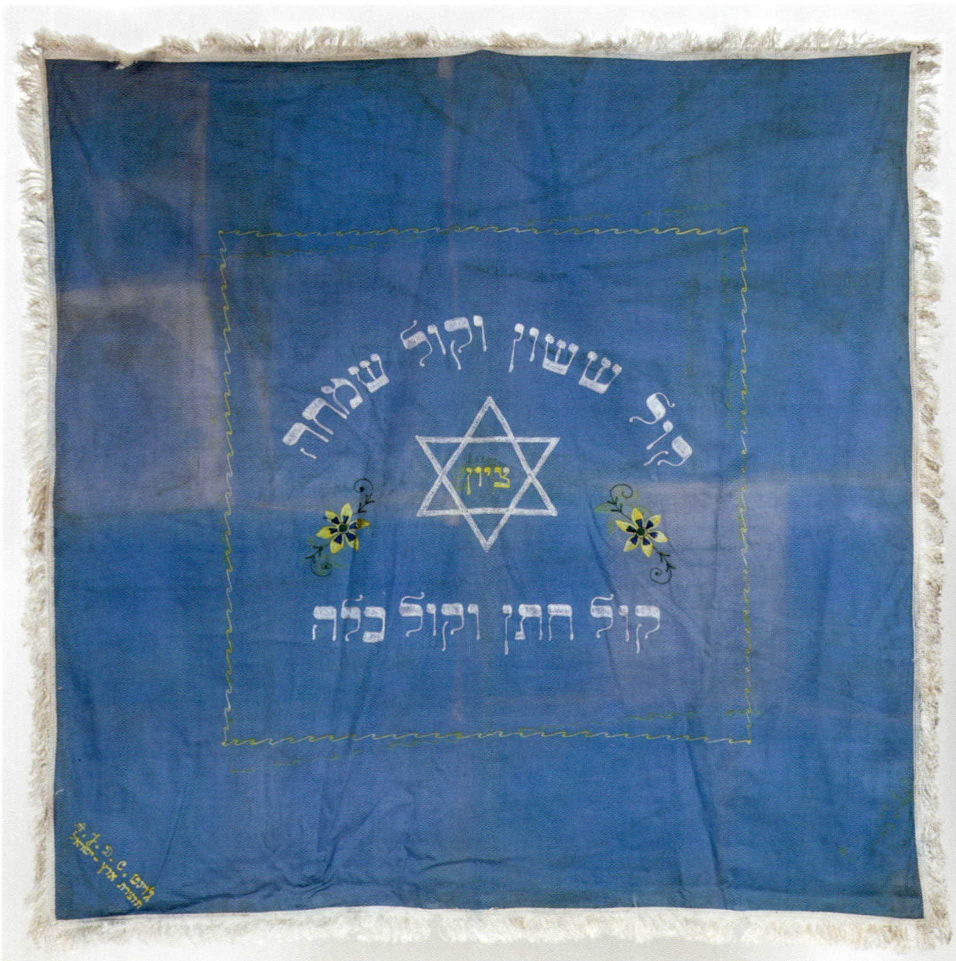

With the surrender of Germany to the Allies on May 7, 1945, the war was over for the Jews of Europe. After liberation from the concentration camps, however, survivors often found they had no home to return to, so they were placed in shelters set up by the American military called Displaced Persons Camps.

The American-Jewish Joint Distribution Committee was originally founded in 1914 to assist Jews in Israel caught up in the throes of World War I. At the end of 1944, the AJDC entered Europe's liberated areas and organized a massive relief effort. By the end of 1947, some 700,000 Jews received aid this way, including more than 250,000 who lived in DP camps. The retraining programs of the AJDC helped people in the DP camps learn trades that would enable them to earn a living, while the cultural and religious activities that were provided helped reestablish Jewish life.

This *chupah*, or wedding canopy, was made in Israel for the AJDC to distribute in the DP camps. In Hebrew it says, "The sound of joy and the sound of gladness, the sound of the groom and the sound of the bride" (Jeremiah 7:34), as well as "Zion" inside a Star of David.

My maternal grandparents met in the Leipheim DP camp, and after a few months of dating, married in the camp, likely using a *chupah* identical to this one.

SEDER TRAY

Material: Ceramic
Origin: Germany, 1946-1948
Hallmarks: "Employment Board," and in Hebrew "Production of the remnants of the refugees in the diaspora of Germany"
Dimensions: 10"

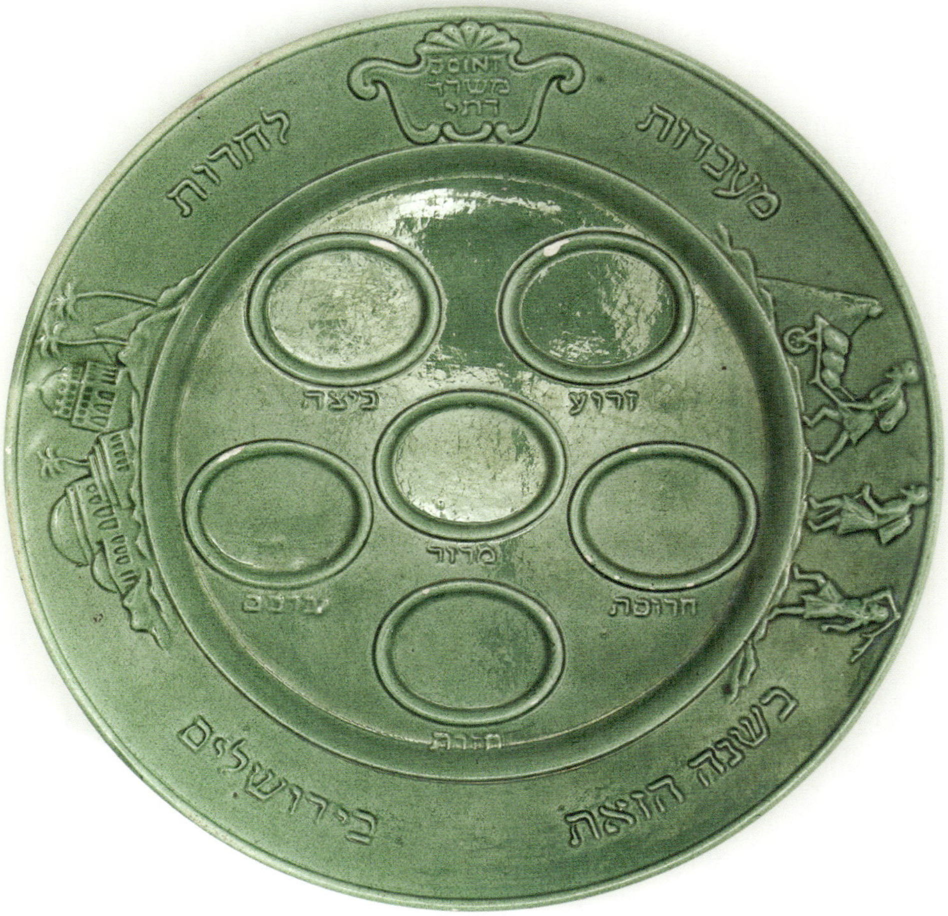

This plate was made by survivors residing in the Displaced Persons Camps, and as such, it merged both of the objectives of the AJDC: teaching those in the camps a skill and enhancing Jewish life.

At first glance, this Passover Seder tray appears quite generic in its design. However, upon close inspection a dramatic difference can be seen between this example and all other Seder trays that had been made for hundreds of years beforehand.

In the center are six spaces for the ritual foods, titled appropriately in Hebrew. On the rim it reads "Joint" and "Bureau of Religion," along with "From slavery to freedom," which is accompanied by a scene of slaves whipped by a taskmaster and pyramids of Egypt.

At the conclusion of the Seder service, the very last words of the *Haggadah*, "Next year in Jerusalem," are recited with loud conviction. On the bottom of this Seder plate, that famous phrase has been altered to "*This* year in Jerusalem." The message to the viewer of the plate is clear: Leave Europe (now essentially one large Jewish graveyard) and go to Israel to help establish a new country, a homeland for a secure, continuous survival of the Jewish nation.

CHANUKAH MENORAH

Material: Ceramic
Origin: Munich, Germany, 1947
Hallmarks: "Employment Board," and in Hebrew "Production of the remnants of the refugees in the diaspora of Germany"
Dimensions: 4.25" x 9.75"

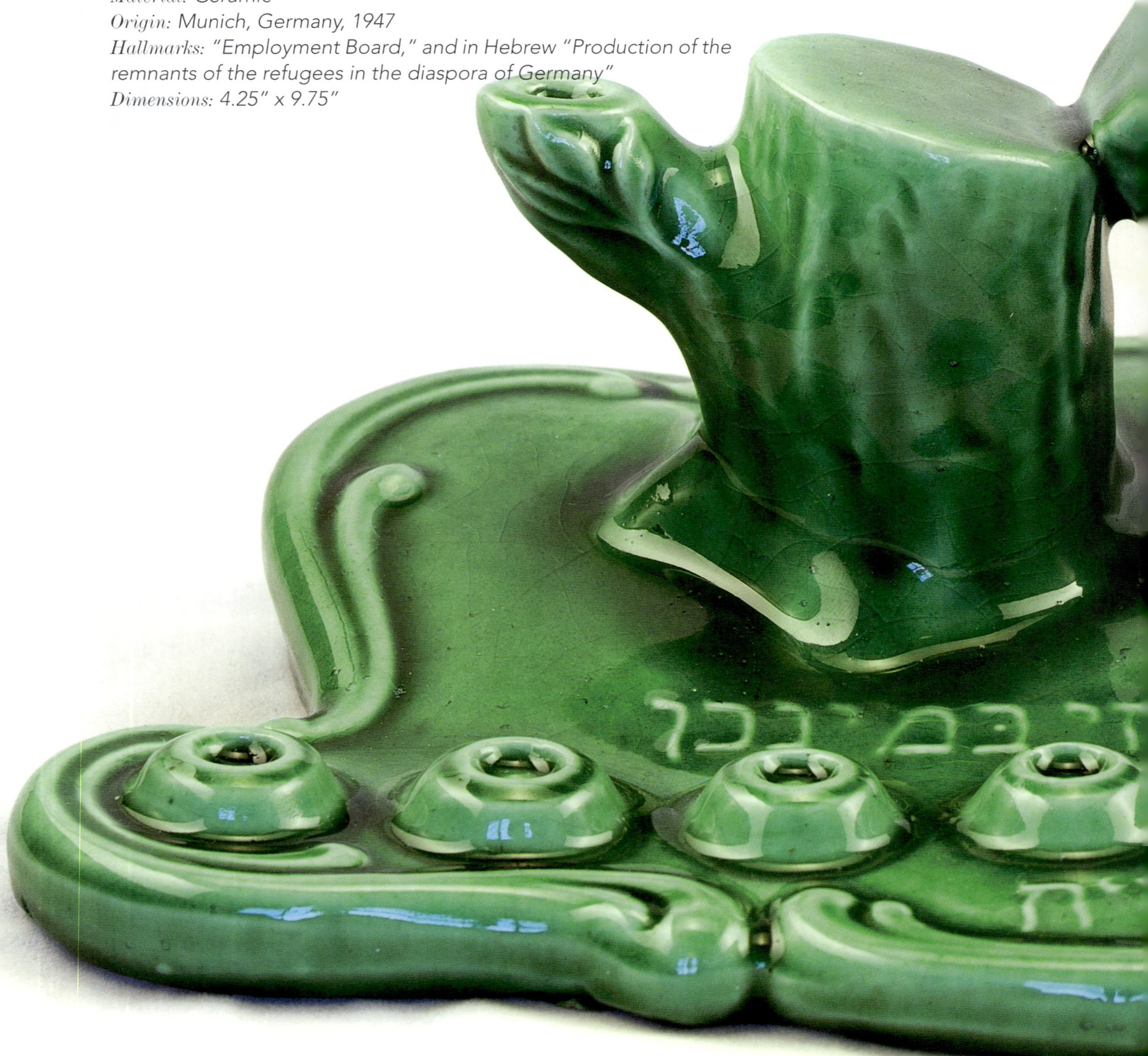

This menorah presents a tree cut down almost to a stump, yet the tree is not dead, as a branch has grown out from its side and leaves are apparent, denoting life. The branch is the *shamash*, the servant light of the menorah.

"But a shoot shall grow out of the stump of Jesse, and a twig shall grow forth out of his roots." (Isaiah 11:1). This passage references the Davidic dynasty, as Jesse was the father of King David. The designer of this menorah used this Biblical verse to illustrate a powerful analogy of hope. In spite of two-thirds of European Jewry being erased from existence, a nation "cut down to a stump," all is not lost, all Jews are not dead. On the contrary, remnants survive and the Jewish people will thrive again.

The celebration of the Chanukah holiday is an analogy that the previous analogy is wrapped in, as overwhelming odds of targeted destruction

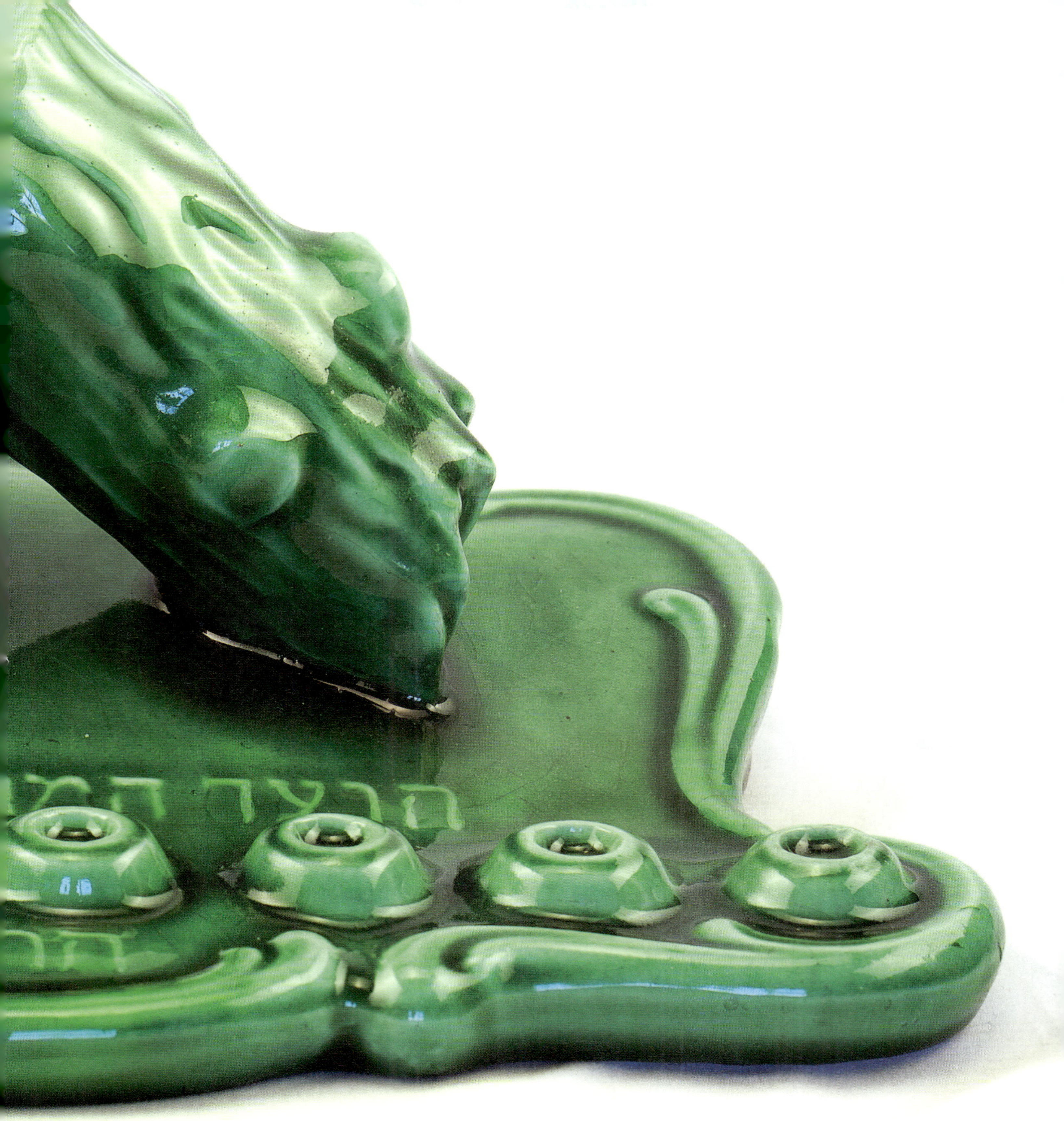

were beaten back during those ancient days, and at the conclusion of the Second World War, that has been achieved as well, albeit at an incomprehensible price.

This Displaced Persons Camp-made item is quite rare, as I am aware of only three other examples, two housed in Jewish museums in California, and one in a museum in Jerusalem. The California examples simply have the word "Joint" in English by the candle holders (shorthand for "American-Jewish Joint Distribution Committee"), while the menorah in the Israeli Holocaust museum Yad Vashem (like the menorah shown here) has in Hebrew "Central Committee Munich 5708" by the candle holders. The Jewish year 5708 is the period between September 1947 and September 1948, so this was made for the Chanukah of 1947.

NOTE from the author

I started buying Judaica when I was 22 years old, and a small hobby quickly turned into a life-changing one, as the more I learned about this area of collecting, the more I wanted to know. I chose to show what I consider to be the highlights of my collection in this book. Since my first purchase sixteen years ago, I have made as my credo an adage from the antiques trade that goes: "If the buyer is pleased, and the seller is pleased, only that is a truly successful transaction."

In hoping that you, the buyer of my book is pleased, I am including a little something extra—it is unusual, it is Jewish, and it is edible!

The immediate access to any type of ready-made Jewish cuisine in New York City is delightful and can even be overwhelming; from German and Romanian deli meats in Manhattan, to Hungarian dishes of Williamsburg, to Syrian foods in Flatbush, and more.

There is, however, one specific concoction that is rarely available, and if found, the taste is nothing short of abominable; it's called *charoset*. This is the sweet paste served during the Passover Seder meant to recall the mortar with which the Israelites bonded bricks when they were enslaved in Egypt. *Charoset* should be made up of nuts, apples, cinnamon, and sweet wine; however, many of these ingredients are mixed improperly or left out altogether when buying ready-made *charoset*.

This amazing recipe for *charoset* comes from my Aunt Hava. Be careful however, as when you taste this dish, you may be compelled to make it on a regular basis, not just once a year at Passover!

Charoset

1.5 cups Medjool dates, pits removed

1 cup dark raisins

5 red apples, cored and peeled (gala or fuji are recommended)

20 ounces chopped walnuts

6 ounces finely ground walnuts

1 banana

2 teaspoons cinnamon (flat, not heaping)

2/3 cup honey (drizzle it in all over)

1.5 cups Kedem Malaga wine

Put the dates and raisins into a food processor and whip into a paste. Put the apples into a food processor until they're chopped into small bits. In a large bowl, add one ingredient at a time, mixing with your hands and tweaking to your own liking. For example, I prefer cutting the banana portion in half and adding more wine.